Do you know the difference between *historic* and *historical? Thoroughbred* and *purebred?* Among *jolly, jocular* and *jovial?* If you're not sure, this remarkable and informative reference guide can help you find the correct definitions and show you how to use the words properly. *DICTIONARY OF PROBLEM WORDS AND EXPRESSIONS* describes, discusses and illustrates the precise meanings of such words as *transitory* and *transient, figure* and *number,* and gives you clues for remembering correct usage. Discover how to eliminate redundancy and fillers in speaking and writing—to clearly construct what you want to say.

THIS COULD BE ONE OF THE MOST IMPORTANT BOOKS YOU WILL EVER OWN!

HARRY SHAW, well known as an editor, writer, lecturer and teacher, is a contributor to many popular and scholarly national magazines. He is the author or co-author of many books on English composition and literature, including *Spell It Right!*, *Errors in English* and *Dictionary of Literary Terms*. He has been managing editor and editorial director of *Look* magazine, editor of Harper & Brothers, senior editor and vice-president of E.P. Dutton & Co., and editor-in-chief of Henry Holt & Co.

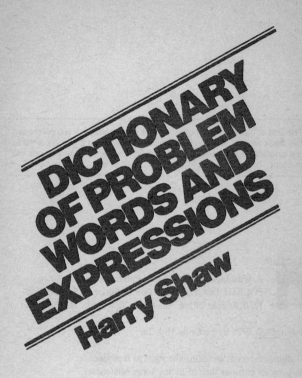

DICTIONARY OF PROBLEM WORDS AND EXPRESSIONS

Harry Shaw

WSP

WASHINGTON SQUARE PRESS
PUBLISHED BY POCKET BOOKS
New York London Toronto Sydney Tokyo Singapore

WSP

A Washington Square Press Publication of
POCKET BOOKS, a division of Simon & Schuster Inc.
1230 Avenue of the Americas, New York, NY 10020

ISBN: 0-671-54558-2

First Washington Square Press printing September 1985

10 9 8 7 6 5

Printed in the U.S.A.

CONTENTS

To the Reader	vii
You and the Way You Talk and Write	xiii
Wordiness	xv
Triteness	xix
Troublesome Verbs	xxv
Idiomatic Usage	xxx
Euphemisms	xxxiv
Slang	xxxvii
Dictionary of Problem Words and Expressions: A–Z	1

To the Reader

This book is designed to alert you to faulty speech and writing habits you may have acquired and to confirm and strengthen you in good ones. To these ends, *Dictionary of Problem Words and Expressions* singles out, defines, explains, and illustrates some 1,500 of the most common mistakes in word use made by speakers and writers of our language. Also, it suggests that every speaker and writer can use his language with increasing ease, flexibility, assurance, and accuracy if he will rid himself of outmoded notions about "grammar" and "correctness."

The author of a book with these aims owes some explanation of the convictions that led to its writing.

First, I believe with Thomas Mann that "Speech is civilization itself." Many changes are going on in American society that tend to make the life of each of us more and more impersonal. Computers and other machines now perform work that once was done by people. From birth to death, we are assigned numbers that try to transform us into cogs in a machine. Throughout the country, television and radio use the same programs and commercial messages. People tend to dress alike, eat alike, often even think alike. But in one activity, at least, people differ: they rarely *speak* alike.

Millions of other people may share our ideas, but the words we use and the way we say them differ in many ways. The speech and writing habits of everyone have been formed by individual influences: family, locale, friends, acquaintances, schooling, travel, housing, and occupation. Each of us has his own dialect: the choice, use, and pronunciation of words called an *idiolect*. Individuality has been preserved in speech more than in any other activity of our lives solely because speech is a more integral and more individual aspect of our outward personalities than any other.

Many scholars have argued that speech is the characteristic of man that most clearly and powerfully distinguishes him from other animals. Other scholars feel that not speech alone but language in general (which includes writing) should bear this distinction. Still others have insisted that the ability to communicate, rather than solely language or speech, is man's most distinguishing characteristic.

A good case can be made for speech, however, as man's clearest distinction among hominids and all mammals. Actually, both people and animals can and do communicate in nonverbal ways. Apparently, animals issue and receive messages: bees send instructions for locating nectar; dogs bark differently at friends and strangers; birds emit warnings when a cat or other marauder appears. With people, gestures and facial expressions communicate ideas and states of mind even when no words are spoken. Music can also communicate feelings and emotions without words. Even smoke signals convey thoughts.

Almost everyone would agree, however, that nonverbal methods of communication are inadequate makeshifts in comparison with language itself.

Second, I believe that the way you talk tells more about you than any other activity of your life. What you say and how you say it are more revealing of your intelligence, personality, and character than the ways you dress, eat, walk, read, or make your living. Knowing how to read and write is a significant accomplishment for everyone, but neither reading nor writing is an *essential* part of anyone's actual existence. Communicating with others through some sort of speech signals *is* essential.

Everyone perusing this book obviously can read and certainly can communicate with others. Most people spend many school years learning to read, but few of us have ever paid real attention to learning how to speak and write. In infancy we learned to speak, have talked ever since, and now assume that talking is as simple and as natural as breathing. It isn't.

More time, opportunities, money, and friendships are lost through careless, slovenly, inaccurate speech (and writing) than through any other activity in people's lives. Because no one can speak perfectly (any more than he can read perfectly), this condition will persist. And yet everyone can learn to speak and write with greater confidence, fewer errors, and more genuine communication if he will only study his habits and give the problem of communication with others the attention it fully deserves.

Third, in every speaking situation, one's aim should be to use only words and phrases that are appropriate, fit, suitable, and proper. The appropriateness of language is determined by the subject being discussed, the place where talk is taking place, and the identity and relationship of speaker and listener. Each of us employs a different level of usage depending upon whether we are speaking or writing, upon our audience or readers, and upon the kind of occasion involved.

The words we use in talking with the person working at the desk next to us may not be appropriate when we are conversing with a member of our family, with a company official, or with a minister, rabbi, or priest. A word or phrase in correct or suitable usage a decade ago may now be outmoded. An expression appropriate in one section of the country may be unclear and therefore ineffective in another locality. Technical expressions used before a specialized group of listeners may be inappropriate in general conversation.

The best course to follow is to try to choose and use words and expressions that are normally employed by reputable speakers in all sections of the country at the present time. That is, diction is effective and appropriate when it is in *national, present,* and *reputable* use. Any word or expression is correct if it meets these three standards; it may also be effective (appropriate although not "correct") if it does not meet these standards but is used for a particular purpose in a particular situation.

Among *cultural* levels of speech may be included illiteracies, narrowly local dialects, ungrammatical speech, slovenly vocabulary and construction, and an excessive resort to slang, shoptalk, and even profanity and obscenity. On a higher level is the language spoken by cultured people over wide areas; such speech is clear, relatively concise, and grammatically correct. In general, these two levels may be referred to as *substandard* and *standard,* with the latter category divided into *informal standard* and *formal standard.*

Functional varieties of speech may loosely be grouped in two classes, *familiar* and *formal.* Included in functional varieties of speech independent of cultural levels are colloquialisms. Such expressions exist in varying degrees of formality: familiar conversation, private correspondence, formal conversation, public worship, platform speech, and so forth.

For every occasion when one needs to speak formally, a hundred or a thousand situations involve informal talk. Here the aim should be to speak naturally and easily, with as much interest and animation as one can summon up. No matter how important what one has to say is, and no matter how interested one is in saying that something, he should try to choose words to fit the occasion. In doing so, he should strive to avoid such roadblocks to effective communication as illiteracies, improprieties, grammatical errors, excessive slang, unidiomatic expressions, wordiness, and triteness.

Fourth, the belief that "anything goes" in the use of language can be embarrassing and costly. Speech and writing that communicate are one thing; speech and writing that do so clearly, interestingly, and effectively are something else. Literacy and competency are different matters. Naturalness and ease in speaking and writing are worthwhile goals, but casualness, ignorance, and lack of concern are destructive attitudes in reaching for them. Certain language standards are important. The credo of the author is that expressed by Theodore M. Bernstein of *The New York Times* in *Watch Your Language:*

> To be sure, the English language is a changing and growing thing. All its users have, of course, a perceptible effect upon it. But in changing and growing it needs no contrived help from chitchat columnists or advertising writers or comic-strip artists or television speakers. It will evolve nicely by itself. If anything, it requires protection from influences that try to push it too fast. There is need, not for those who would halt its progress altogether, but for those who can keep a gentle foot on the brake and a guiding hand on the steering wheel. . . .

During the long years of study and preparation that this book required I have been helped by many persons. Oblique but nonetheless hearty thanks should go to hundreds of students at New York University and Columbia University whose talk and papers revealed the need for a book such as this. Colleagues in the editorial offices of six magazine and book publishers have suggested, sometimes inadvertently, scores of items that are included.

Without aid from many scholars, teachers, linguists, and lexicographers this book would be far less accurate and thorough than hopefully it is. I am especially indebted to H. W. Fowler's *A Dictionary of Modern English Usage,* to *The Oxford English Dictionary,* and to the unabridged edition of *The Random House Dictionary of the English Language.*

Individuals to whom I am particularly indebted include the late Professors Paul Roberts of California and Havilah Babcock of South Carolina. In years past, the conversation and writings of these gifted teachers have helped me immeasurably in my approach to language. I also express gratitude to a longtime friend and colleague, Professor George S. Wykoff of Purdue University. Hesitantly, I mention the name of Theodore M. Bernstein once again. His lively, fact-packed, and solid work (especially *Watch Your Language, The Careful Writer,* and *Miss Thistlebottom's Hobgoblins*) has played a prominent part in my thinking about speech and writing. I have never met Mr. Bernstein, but his work suggests that he is eminently worth knowing.

Finally, I acknowledge the encouragement and support of McGraw-Hill officials and editors, especially Leonard Josephson, who suggested this book, Mrs. Tobia Worth, who has made many wise editorial suggestions, and Daniel N. Fischel, their chief and, I claim with pride, my one-time prize student.

H.S.

You and the Way You Talk and Write

Two basic problems underlie and precede everything this book tries to offer about the use and abuse of words and expressions. This *Dictionary* cannot solve either, but it can bring them to your attention.

First, little value resides in studying words unless one has something worthwhile to say and some interest and purpose in saying that something, whatever it is. Oliver Wendell Holmes once remarked "A word is the skin of a living thought." If one's thought is nonexistent or valueless, so will be the word itself.

Reading, listening, seeing, experiencing, and, above all, thinking are the methods by which one insures having something to say. The book in your hands provides thousands of suggestions, none of which deals directly with this fundamental problem. But it can, and does, suggest at the outset that with rare exceptions, people tend to talk more and say less than they should. After all, speech is only the faculty or power of speaking. The ability to talk and write is one thing; thoughts and emotions are another. Spinoza once wrote that mankind would be happier if the power in men to be silent were the same as that to speak; that "men govern nothing with more difficulty than their tongues." John Ruskin wrote: "The greatest thing a human soul ever does in this world is to see something and tell what it saw in a plain way. Hundreds can talk for one who can think." It was a wise person who remarked at a meeting that it was better for him to remain silent and be thought a fool than to speak and remove all possible doubt. Think first, talk second.

Next, it is important to form a suitable attitude toward writing and speaking. Despite the comments that appear throughout the *Dictionary,* one should not think of these processes as a complicated series of do's and don'ts, a long list of prohibitions, taboos, and thou-shalt-not's. The American language is a flexible medium. One should consider it the most important method he has for communicating clearly and interestingly with and to others. What possible activity could be more meaningful?

The author whose work you most enjoy is possibly not the greatest stylist of all time. He may repeatedly violate many of the recommendations set forth in following pages. Not by the niceties of his style but by his drive, imagination, and animation he gets, and holds, your fascinated attention. Similarly, the person with whom you most enjoy talking may make many so-called mistakes in grammar and may frequently confuse one word with another. But he uses his tongue interestingly and forcefully, however many "errors" he may make while doing so.

In short, using words and expressions effectively depends not on "correctness" alone but on having something of value to communicate and doing so with ease and assurance.

It is true, however, that in our society few people fail to realize the importance of using good English. The late Will Rogers was never more humorous than when he remarked, "A lot of people who don't say *ain't,* ain't eatin'." Most of us, however, are properly concerned when others react unfavorably to mistakes we make in expressing ourselves. We understand that our use of language represents a significant form of behavior.

By learning basic good usage one can concentrate on what he wishes to communicate and stop worrying about detailed methods of doing so. Freed from restraint and anxiety, he can reveal his thoughts to others in the natural easy way he should speak and write our language but all too often does not.

This book will help you to improve your use of language by

emphasis upon those common errors, and only those, which hinder communication and impede thought. As you study the entries that follow, keep these four "commandments" in mind:

Be concise. Most statements of any kind are wordy. All of us repeat an idea in identical or similar words and then say it again. Talk should not be cryptic and mysteriously abrupt, but it should be economical. Make it snappy!

Be original. It's impossible for anyone to conceive of a wholly new idea or to express an old one in fresh, original diction. And yet the greatest single error in speaking and writing is the use of trite, worn-out expressions that have lost their first vigor, picturesqueness, and appeal. Avoid clichés. Don't be a rubber stamp.

Be specific. Much of our speech is indefinite, not clearly expressed, uncertain in meaning. Even when we have a fairly good idea of what we wish to say, we don't seek out those exact and concrete words that would convey what we have in mind. Try to use words that have precise meaning. Don't be vague.

Vary the approach. The sole requirement of effective speech and writing is that they should communicate. The choice and use of words should vary from situation to situation, from person to person. At times, one's speech and writing should be racy and pungent; at other times, deliberate and formal. Communication should be appropriate. Shift gears.

Put another way, a major fault in writing and speaking is using too many words, many of which are not so much "wrong" as stale and worn-out from overuse. These major faults of wordiness and triteness (along with allied problems that largely contribute to them) are briefly mentioned in the pages that follow.

Wordiness

Nearly everyone uses more words than he needs. In rapid-fire talk, in the give-and-take of conversation, each of us is likely to repeat himself and to use words that are meaningless or unnecessary. (When writing, we have a chance to go over our work and remove the verbiage.) Truly effective speech is economical, but using enough words to cover the subject and not too many is a standard of perfection unattainable by ordinary mortals. But if one can grasp and keep in mind a few suggestions, his speech and writing will become more concise and consequently more interesting and appealing.

In Shakespeare's *Hamlet*, Polonius says:

> Therefore, since brevity is the soul of wit,
> And tediousness the limbs and outward flourishes,
> I will be brief.

In this context, *wit* means "understanding" or "wisdom." Actually, Polonius was a garrulous, tiresome bore, but what he said is that being brief and to the point is the best way to convey real thought. Conciseness alone does not guarantee good writing and speaking, but it is difficult for someone to speak or write forcefully and entertainingly when he is using four words where one would be sufficient.

The golden rule contains 11 words. The Ten Commandments are expressed in 75 words. Lincoln's Gettysburg Address consists of 267 words.

Three suggestions may be helpful:

First, never use two or more words where one will serve. It is better to refer to "the chance of war" than to say "in the regrettable eventuality of a failure of the deterrence policy." A speaker was once asked whether certain rules should be observed. Instead of replying yes, he remarked, "The implementation of sanctions will inevitably eventuate in repercussions." A foreman suggested that an assistant give instructions to workers "very precisely and carefully." He might better have said, "Give precise instructions." A recent governmental pamphlet contained this sentence: "Endemic insect populations cause little-realized amounts of damage to forage and timber." The meaning? "Native insects harm trees and grass more than we realize."

Eliminating Wordiness

REDUCE THESE	TO THESE
a certain length of time	a certain time
advance planning	planning
after the conclusion of	after
am (is, are) going to	shall, will
are (am) of the opinion	believe
as a result of	because
at the present time	now
before long	soon
both alike	alike
by means of	by
by the time	when
come in contact with	meet
destroyed by fire	burned
due to the fact that	due to, since
during the time that	while
for the amount of	for
in accordance with	by
inasmuch as	since
in case	if
in connection with	with
in lieu of	instead
in order to	to
in regard to	about
insofar as	because, since, as
in the event that	if
in the month of May	in May
in this day and age	today
in view of the fact that	since
it has come to our attention that	(begin with the word following *that*)
it is interesting to note that	(begin with the word following *that*)
I would appreciate it if	please
long in size	long
of an indefinite nature	indefinite
of great importance	important

REDUCE THESE	TO THESE
on a timely basis	fast
on condition that	if
one of the purposes (reasons)	one purpose (reason)
prior to	before
provided that	if
the length of 5 yards	5 yards (or 5 yards long)
the necessary funds	money
under date of July 5	of July 5
with the exception of	except

Second, avoid overusing *there is, there are,* etc. Usually, *there* beginnings are superfluous words, adding nothing. The words *there are* can be removed from the following sentence with no loss in meaning or force: "In this building *there are* five elevators awaiting inspection." Better: "In this building five elevators await inspection."

Third, avoid adding words to an idea already expressed. When meaning is expressed or implied in a particular word or phrase, repeating the idea in additional words adds nothing but verbiage. Common examples of this fault are using *again* with verbs beginning with *re-;* using *more* or *most* with adjectives and adverbs ending in *-er* and *-est;* and using *more* or *most* with such absolute-meaning adjectives as *unique, round, square,* and *equal.*

A list of sixty representative wordy expressions follows:

absolutely essential
around about that time
audible to the ear
back up
bisect in two
call up on the phone
choose up
Christmas Eve evening
combine together
completely unanimous
complete monopoly
connect up with
consensus of opinion
cooperate together
cover over
descend down
each and every one
endorse on the back
entirely eliminated
extreme prime importance
few (many) in number
final end (outcome)
first beginnings
four-cornered square
from whence
important essentials

individual person
join together
long length
loquacious talker
many in number
meet up with
more angrier
more better
more older
more paramount
more perfect
more perpendicular
most unique
most unkindest
necessary essential
necessary need
old adage
personal friend
recur again
reduce down
repeat again
resume again
return back
revert back to
rise up
separate out
(a) short half-hour
small in size
sunset in the west
round in form
talented genius
this afternoon at 4 P.M.
this morning at 8 A.M.
visible to the eye

Brevity is more than "the soul of wit": it is well-nigh impossible. Even so, care and thought will eliminate many useless, time-wasting, space-consuming words and expressions that constitute one of the major problems in communicating with others.

Triteness

Triteness, sometimes referred to as the use of hackneyed language or clichés, applies to words and expressions that are worn out from overuse.

The words *triteness, hackneyed language,* and *cliché* have origins that illuminate their meaning: *triteness* comes from the Latin word *tritus,* the past participle of a verb meaning "to rub," "to wear out." *Hackneyed* is derived from the idea of a horse, or carriage (*hackney* coach), let out for hire, devoted to common use, and consequently exhausted in service. *Cliché* comes from the French word *clicher,* meaning "to stereotype," "to cast from a mold."

Trite expressions resemble slang in that both are stereotyped manners of thoughts and expression. Clichés may be stampings from common speech, outworn phrases, or overworked quotations. Usually they express sound ideas (or ideas considered sound) and are always couched in memorable phrasing. (If they were not sensible and stylistically appealing, they would never have been used so much as to become stale.) The problem with clichés is not that they are inexpressive but that they have been overused and misused to the point of weariness and ineffectiveness.

People with whom we often talk may bore us precisely because we know in advance the words and phrases they are going to use. What they say and how they say that something have become "molds" of thought and expression, constantly repeated. It should be kept in mind, too, that expressions which seem fresh and original to us may be clichés to those who have read and listened more than we have.

In daily speech, in letters, and in all kinds of writing except that which is most formal and carefully written and rewritten, everyone is certain to use clichés. This is understandable: trite expressions are familiar, often apt, and always expressive. For instance, if one wishes to describe a recent bout with insomnia and his inability to get needed rest, he might mention his longing to "sleep the sleep of the just." The phrase is colorful and even appropriate, but it is jaded from overuse. Charles Dickens may have thought so when, in *Night Walks,* he needed to convey this same idea. He discarded the cliché and came up with the memorable phrase "As restless as an evil conscience in a tumbled bed." An anonymous writer used no hackneyed expression in describing the tumult of thoughts that kept him awake; he referred to the emotions coursing through his mind as being "restless as willows in a windstorm."

Trite expressions cannot be eliminated from our speech and writing, but their quantity can be reduced and, who knows, perhaps occasionally something substituted effective enough eventually to become a cliché itself.

The following list of more than 300 trite expressions will remind everyone of the problem and possibly cause some readers to resolve to strive even harder for freshness and originality in speaking and writing.

absence makes the heart grow fonder
acid test
add insult to injury
age before beauty
all in a lifetime
all in all
all is not gold that glitters
all sorts and conditions . . .
all things being equal
all wool and a yard wide
all work and no play
apple of one's eye
apple-pie order
arms of Morpheus
as luck would have it
at one fell swoop
bark up the wrong tree
bated breath
bathed in tears
battle of life
beard the lion in his den
beat a hasty retreat
beggars description
best foot forward
best-laid plans of mice and men
better late than never
better to have loved and lost
beyond the pale
bitter end
blood is thicker than water
blow off steam
blow one's horn
blushing bride
blush of shame
bolt from the blue
born with a silver spoon
bosom of the family
brave as a lion
brawny arms
breathe a sigh of relief
bright and early
bright future
bright young countenance
bring home the bacon
briny deep
brown as a berry
budding genius
busy as a bee (beaver)
butterflies in (my) stomach
caught red-handed
checkered career
cheer to the echo
cherchez la femme
chip off the old block
clear as mud
coals to Newcastle
cock-and-bull story
cold as ice
cold feet
cold sweat
cool as a cucumber
common, or garden, variety
conspicuous by his (her) absence
consummation devoutly to be wished
cradle of the deep
crow to pick
cut a long story short
cynosure of all eyes
daily repast
dead as a doornail
dead giveaway
deaf as a post
depths of despair
die is cast
distance lends enchantment
dog days

doomed to disappointment
down my alley
downy couch
draw the line
dreamy expression
drown one's sorrows
drunk as a skunk
duck (fish) out of water
dull thud
each and every
ear to the ground
eat, drink, and be merry
eat one's hat
epoch-making
et tu, Brute
exception proves the rule
eyes like stars
eyes of the world
face the music
fair sex
far cry
fast and loose
fat as a pig
fat's in the fire
favor with a selection
fearfully and wonderfully made
feathered choir
feather in his (her) cap
feel one's oats
festive board
few and far between
few well-chosen words
fight like a tiger
fill the bill
filthy lucre
fine and dandy
first and foremost
flash in the pan
flat as a pancake
flesh and blood
fly off the handle
fond farewell
(a) fool and his money
fools rush in . . .
free as the air
fresh as a daisy
garden (common) variety
gentle as a lamb
get one's number
get the sack
get the upper hand
get up on the wrong side . . .
get what I mean?
gild the lily
give hostages to fortune
glass of fashion
God's country
golden mean
(a) good time was had by all
goose hangs high
grain of salt
grand and glorious
graphic account (description)
greatness thrust upon . . .
green as grass
green with envy
Grim Reaper
grin like a Cheshire cat
hail-fellow well met
hale and hearty
hand-to-mouth
hapless victim
happy as a lark
happy pair
hard row to hoe
haughty stare

haul over the coals
head over heels
heartless wretch
heart of gold
hew to the line
high on the hog
hornet's nest (stir up a)
hot as a pistol
hungry as a bear
if the truth be told
inspiring sight
interesting to note
intestinal fortitude
in the last (final) analysis
in the long run
irons in the fire
irony of fate
it goes without saying
it stands to reason
jig is up
land-office business
last but not least
last straw
law unto himself (herself)
lead to the altar
lean and hungry look
lean over backward
leave in the lurch
left-handed compliment
let one's hair down
let the cat out of the bag
lick into shape
like a newborn babe
limp as a rag
little did I think
lock, stock, and barrel
mad as a wet hen
mad dash
make a clean breast of
make ends meet
make hay while the sun shines
make night hideous
make no bones
make things hum
mantle of snow
meets the eye
method in his madness
mind your *p*'s and *q*'s
missing the boat
monarch of all he (she) surveys
moot question
more easilly said than done
Mother Nature
motley crew (crowd)
naked truth
neat as a bandbox
necessary evil
needs no introduction
never a dull moment
nipped in the bud
not to be sneezed at
not worth a continental
number is up
of a high order
Old Sol
on the ball (stick)
open-and-shut
opportunity knocks but . . .
out of sight, out of mind
over a barrel
ox in the ditch
parental rooftree
pay the piper (fiddler)
penny for your thoughts
pillar of society
pillar to post
play fast and loose
play second fiddle

play up to
point with pride
poor but honest
pretty as a picture
pretty kettle of fish
pretty penny
psychological moment
pull one's leg
pull the wool over . . .
pull up stakes
pure as the driven snow
put a bug (flea) in one's ear
put on the dog
rack one's brain
raining cats and dogs
read the riot act
reckon without one's host
red as a beet
rendered a selection
ring true
rub the wrong way
sadder but wiser
sad to relate
sail under false colors
save for a rainy day
seal one's fate
seething mass
self-made man
sell like hot cakes
set one's cap for
set up shop
seventh heaven
show the white feather
shuffle off this mortal coil
sick and tired
sight to behold
sing like a bird
sleep the sleep of the just
snare and a delusion
sow wild oats
start the ball rolling
steal one's thunder
stick in the craw
strong as an ox
stubborn as a mule
stuffed shirt
take it easy
teach the young idea
tell it to the Marines
tenterhooks (be on)
terra firma
that is to say
throw in the sponge
throw the book at
time hangs heavy
tired as a dog
tit for tat
too funny for words
too many irons in the fire
truth to tell
turn over a new leaf
view with alarm
wee small hours
wet to the skin
where ignorance is bliss
wide-open spaces
without further ado
wolf in sheep's clothing
you can say that again
your guess is as good as mine

Troublesome Verbs

Insufficient knowledge of the principal parts of verbs causes many problems in speaking and writing. An English verb has three principal parts: *present tense* (or *present infinitive*), *past tense*, and *past participle*. A good way to recall the principal parts of a verb is to substitute those of any verb for the following:

I *run* today. (present tense)
I *ran* yesterday. (past tense)
I *have run* every day this week. (past participle)

The past tense and past participle of many verbs are formed by adding *-d* or *-ed* or *-t* to the present tense:

save, saved, saved
dream, dreamt (or dreamed), dreamt (or dreamed)

Such verbs are called *regular*, or *weak*, verbs.

Other verbs do not follow this pattern. Called *irregular*, or *strong*, verbs, they form the past tense and past participle in several ways. One group has a vowel change in the past tense, and in some instances in the past participle as well:

cling, clung, clung; fight, fought, fought

Some verbs in this group, in addition to the vowel change, add *-n* for the past participle:

wear, wore, worn; swear, swore, sworn

Another group changes in form completely in the past tense and past participle:

bind, bound, bound; stink, stank, stunk

A few verbs change the last consonant, but not the vowel:

have, had, had

Several verbs have the same form for all three principal parts:

quit, quit, quit; spread, spread, spread

Following is a list of 150 troublesome verbs that illustrate each of the methods of formation just mentioned.

PRESENT TENSE	PAST TENSE	PAST PARTICIPLE
arise	arose	arisen
ask	asked	asked
attack	attacked	attacked

Troublesome Verbs

PRESENT TENSE	PAST TENSE	PAST PARTICIPLE
bar	barred	barred
bare	bared	bared
be	was	been
bear	bore	borne (passive: born, given birth to)
bear (a burden)	bore	borne
beat	beat	beaten
become	became	become
begin	began	begun
bend	bent	bent
bet	bet	bet
bid (at an auction)	bid	bid
bid ("command")	bade, bid	bidden, bid
bite	bit	bitten
bleed	bled	bled
blow	blew	blown
break	broke	broken
breed	bred	bred
bring	brought	brought
broadcast	broadcast, broadcasted	broadcast, broadcasted
build	built	built
burn	burned, burnt	burned, burnt
burst	burst	burst
buy	bought	bought
cast	cast	cast
catch	caught	caught
choose	chose	chosen
climb	climbed	climbed
come	came	come
creep	crept	crept
cut	cut	cut
deal	dealt	dealt
dig	dug	dug
dive	dived, dove	dived
do	did	done
drag	dragged	dragged
draw	drew	drawn

PRESENT TENSE	PAST TENSE	PAST PARTICIPLE
dress	dressed, drest	dressed, drest
drink	drank	drunk, drunken (rare, except as adjective)
drive	drove	driven
drown	drowned	drowned
dwell	dwelt, dwelled	dwelt, dwelled
eat	ate	eaten
fall	fell	fallen
feed	fed	fed
feel	felt	felt
find	found	found
fit	fitted, fit	fitted, fit
flee	fled	fled
fling	flung	flung
flow	flowed	flowed
fly	flew	flown
fly (in baseball)	flied	flied
forbid	forbade	forbidden
forecast	forecast, forecasted	forecast, forecasted
forget	forgot	forgotten, forgot
forsake	forsook	forsaken
freeze	froze	frozen
get	got	got, gotten
give	gave	given
go	went	gone
grow	grew	grown
hang (for an object)	hung	hung
hang (for a person)	hanged	hanged
happen	happened	happened
hear	heard	heard
help	helped	helped
hide	hid	hidden
hit	hit	hit
hurt	hurt	hurt
keep	kept	kept
kneel	knelt, kneeled	knelt, kneeled
know	knew	known
lay	laid	laid

Troublesome Verbs

PRESENT TENSE	PAST TENSE	PAST PARTICIPLE
lead	led	led
learn	learned, learnt	learned, learnt
leave	left	left
lend	lent	lent
let	let	let
lie ("recline")	lay	lain
lie ("tell a falsehood")	lied	lied
light	lighted, lit	lighted, lit
loan	loaned	loaned
loose	loosed	loosed
lose	lost	lost
make	made	made
mean	meant	meant
meet	met	met
pass	passed	passed, past
prejudice	prejudiced	prejudiced
prove	proved	proved, proven
put	put	put
raise	raised	raised
read	read	read
rid	rid	rid
ride	rode	ridden
ring	rang	rung
rise	rose	risen
run	ran	run
say	said	said
see	saw	seen
sell	sold	sold
send	sent	sent
set	set	set
shake	shook	shaken
shine	shone	shone
shoot	shot	shot
show	showed	shown, showed
shrink	shrank, shrunk	shrunk
shut	shut	shut
sing	sang	sung

PRESENT TENSE	PAST TENSE	PAST PARTICIPLE
sink	sank	sunk
sit	sat	sat
sleep	slept	slept
slide	slid	slid
sling	slung	slung
smell	smelled, smelt	smelled, smelt
speak	spoke	spoken
spell	spelled, spelt	spelled, spelt
spend	spent	spent
spin	spun	spun
split	split	split
spoil	spoiled, spoilt	spoiled, spoilt
spring	sprang, sprung	sprung
stand	stood	stood
steal	stole	stolen
stick	stuck	stuck
sting	stung	stung
strike	struck	struck, stricken
strive	strove, strived	striven, strived
suppose	supposed	supposed
swim	swam	swum
take	took	taken
teach	taught	taught
tear	tore	torn
tell	told	told
think	thought	thought
throw	threw	thrown
thrust	thrust	thrust
tread	trod	trodden
use	used	used
wake	waked, woke	waked, woken
weave	wove	woven
win	won	won
wind	wound	wound
work	worked, wrought	worked, wrought
wring	wrung	wrung
write	wrote	written

Idiomatic Usage

For one who is a native-born speaker of American English, idiomatic usage is likely to cause little trouble. Most of the idiomatic expressions one uses and hears are familiar, deep-rooted, widely employed, and readily understandable.

The words *idiom* and *idiomatic* come from Greek terms the key meaning of which is "peculiar" or "individual." Idiomatic expressions conform to no basic principles in their formation and are indeed laws unto themselves. Every language has its peculiarities. For example, Spanish people say (in translation), "Here one speaks Spanish"; the English equivalent is "Spanish is spoken here." The French say, "We have come from eating," but our equivalent would be "We have just eaten."

As speakers of American English, we might tell foreigners not to say "many boy is," "a pupils," and "10 foot." We would utterly confuse them with such acceptable idiomatic usage as "many *a* boy is," "a *few* pupils," and "a 10-foot *pole*." Much correct idiomatic usage is indeed illogical or a violation of grammatical principles.

One generalized statement about English idioms is that several words combined often lose their literal (exact) meaning and express something only remotely suggested by any one word: "bed of roses," "birds of a feather," "black list," "dark horse," "get even with," "open house," "read between the lines," "toe the line."

Another comment is that parts of the human body have suggested hundreds of idiomatic expressions: "burn one's fingers," "all thumbs," "rub elbows with," "step on someone's toes," "take to heart," "catch one's eye," "put one's foot in one's mouth," "bend one's ear," "with half an eye," "pay through the nose," "down in the mouth," and "have a leg to stand on."

A third generalization is that hundreds of idiomatic phrases are formed by various parts of speech in combination with others in a haphazard way. For example, the same word can combine with others to form phrases that are quite different in meaning: "make away with," "make believe," "make bold," "make do," "make fast," "make for," "make good," "make merry," "make out," "make over," "make ready," and "make up." An even more complex idiomatic situation involves *look*:

look alive ("be wide-awake")
look after ("minister to")
look back ("review the past")
look daggers ("stare angrily")
look down on ("regard with scorn")
look for ("seek," "search")
look forward to ("anticipate")
look in on ("visit")
look on ("observe")
look oneself ("appear normal")
look out ("be on guard")
look over ("examine")
look sharp ("be alert")
look to ("give attention")
look up ("refer to")
look up to ("respect")

Still other examples are these:

accompanied	*by* others *with* grief
affinity	*of* persons or things *between* two persons or things *with* another person or thing
agree	*on* a plan *with* a person
analogous	*in* a quality *to* or *with* others
contend	*for* a principle *with* an individual *against* an obstacle
differ	*with* a person *from* something else *on*, *over*, or *about* a question
impatient	*at* someone's conduct *with* someone else *for* something desired *of* restraint
rewarded	*with* a gift *by* a person *for* something done

One's speech should conform to the idiomatic word combinations generally acceptable. Reliable dictionaries contain some explanations of idiomatic usage following words that require such detail, but the information provided is not always complete or clear.

Twenty idiomatic and unidiomatic expressions follow. They are representative of several hundred idioms that can cause genuine problems:

IDIOMATIC	UNIDIOMATIC
according to	according with
accord with	accord to
acquaint with	acquaint to
adverse to	adverse against
aim to prove	aim at proving
among themselves	among one another
angry with (a person)	angry at (a person)
as regards	as regards to
authority on	authority about
cannot help talking	cannot help but talk
comply with	comply to
conform to, with	conform in
correspond to (a thing)	correspond with (a thing)
desirous of	desirous to
identical with	identical to
in accordance with	in accordance to
prefer (one) to (another)	prefer (one) over (another)
prior to	prior than
superior to	superior than
unequal to	unequal for

The following 150 idiomatic expressions involving prepositions will serve as a check list, containing as it does many of the most commonly used idioms in the language:

abstain from
accede to
acquiesce in
acquit of
addicted to
adept in
adhere to
adjacent to
advantage of, over
agreeable to
alien from, to
amused at, by, with

apart from
append to
approve of
arrive at, in
assent to
associate with
assure of
averse to
basis of, for
blanket with
blasé about
blend with
boast of, about
bordon on, upon
capable of
careful of, with, about
caution against
characterstic of
coincide with
compare to (as an illustration)
compare with ("examine")
compatible with
concur in, with
conducive to
confide in
confident of
consent to
consistent with
contemptuous of
convict of
cured of
deficient in
deprive of
derive from
desire for
desist from
detract from
different from
disagree with
disapprove of
disdain for
dissatisfied with
dissent from
distinguish between, from
emigrate from
empty of
endowed with
envious of
essential to
estimated at
exclusive of
expert in
fascination for
fondness for
fond of
foreign to
fugitive from
grateful to, for
guard against
hint at
hope for, of
impeach for, of
implicit in
inconsistent with
independent of
inter from
inferior to
infested with
initiate into
inseparable from
instruct in
intercede with, for
isolate from
jealous of
jeer at
laugh at, over
made from, out of, of
monopoloy of
negligent of, in
obiedient to

oblivious of
observant of
occupied by, with
opportunity for, of
originate in, with
parallel to, with
part from, with
partial to
participate in
peculiar to
preserve in
pertinent to
pleased at, by, with
plunged in (despair)
plunged into (liquid)
preclude from
pregnant by, with
preparatory to
prerequisite of (noun)
prerequisite to
  (adjective)
proficient in
profit by
prohibit from
protest against
provide with, for, against
punishable by
purge of, from
pursuit of
qualify for, as
question about, concerning
  on, of
range between, along, with
reason for (noun)
reason with (verb)
regret for, at
repugnant to
responsibility for
revel in
rich in
rid of
scared at, by
sensitive to
separate from
similar to
solution of, to
subsitute for
suitable to, for, with
sympathize with
tamper with
tax with, for
thrill at, to, with
treat of (a topic)
treat with (an opponent)
unfavorable to, toward, for
unmindful of
vie with
worthy of
yearn for, after, toward
zealous in

Euphemisms

A *euphemism* is a softened, bland, inoffensive word or phrase used for one that may suggest something unpleasant, offensive, coarse, or blunt. The word *euphemism* comes from a Greek phrase meaning "the use of words of good repute." For example, a writer might think that the words *jail* and *prison* would be offensive to some readers or hearers and thus substitute the phrase "correctional institution," a euphemism for the more direct term. In avoiding the use of such nonstandard expressions as "croak," "take the last count," and "kick the bucket," one might be tempted to say "pass away," or "depart this life."

In recent years, effective writers have condemned euphemisms as oblique ways of expressing supposedly uncouth or vulgar ideas. If they mean *die*, they say or write *die*. If they mean *belly*, they do not resort to *abdomen*. If they mean *chicken*, they do not write *villatic fowl*. Such practice is recommended, but with a caution: religious dictates may prevent the use of direct words on all occasions; moral scruples should not be ignored; considerations of taste are important. Some topics are better left unmentioned; if brought up, they should be treated according to one's own sense of what is fitting and appropriate.

Conversely, some outspoken writers delight in using words and phrases that appear deliberately offensive. This device (or practice) is known as parrhesia: instead of using *dying*, a writer might use the colorful but tasteless "turning one's toes up to the daisies." Instead of writing *food* he might use *grub*, *outhouse* instead of *privy*, and *whore* instead of *prostitute*.

Unless religious dictates or personal taste prevent, one should use direct, forthright words to express meaning. If a topic can be treated at all (and some subjects are in debatable taste), it should be handled frankly. Euphemisms are nearly always wordy and usually somewhat vague.

Sixty examples of euphemisms, with their actual meanings, follow:

amenity center	village green, public toilet
archivist	museum or library clerk
cardiovascular accident	stroke
casket	coffin
collection correspondent	bill collector
combustible fieldman	garbageman
comfort station	public toilets
confrontation	heated argument, fight

creative conflict	civil rights demonstration
crowd engineers	police dogs
custodial engineer	janitor
delicious repast	a good meal
devouring element	fire
emerging (developing)	backward
exceptional child	retarded child
expecting	pregnant
expectorate	spit
experienced tires	recaps, retreads
extrapolation	educated guess
facial dew	perspiration, sweat
finalize	end
food preparation center	kitchen
glow	sweat, perspire
indisposed	sick, ill, nauseated
interment	burial
intoxicated	drunk
in trouble	pregnant
love child	illegitimate (bastard) child
lowing herd	cattle
lung affliction	tuberculosis
memorial park	cemetery
mistress	kept woman
moisture	sweat
mortician	undertaker
mortical surgeon	undertaker
motion discomfort	nausea
obsequies	funeral
odor	smell, stink
opportunity school	school for the retarded or handicapped
park under construction	town dump
paying guest	boarder
perspire	sweat
plant food	manure
powder room	toilet
prevaricate	lie
previously owned car	secondhand car
problem skin	acne

rotund	fat
sanitary engineer	garbage collector
scent	smell
senior citizen	old person
separate from school	expel
separate from the payroll	fire
slow learner	unintelligent person
social disease	syphilis, gonorrhea
succulent viands	appetizing food
tissue	toilet paper
trial marriage	free love
underprivileged	destitute, poor
unmentionables	underwear

Slang

Slang is a label for a particular kind of word usage that ranges from illiteracies to colloquialisms (informal standard English). Slang terms usually involve exaggerated or forced humor, fantastic or flippant novelty, and clipped or shortened forms of words. Much slang is colorful, fresh, and pungent and provides effective shortcuts in expression. Some slang appeals to such widespread popular fancy that it survives and is eventually labeled in dictionaries as informal or colloquial speech.

It is useless to suggest that no one should use slang. Slang is understandably a part of everyone's informal talk and is so inbred in one's consciousness that giving it up entirely would leave a gap in communication. Also, slang, or at least some of it, is so readily and widely understood that it assists face-to-face, person-to-person contact, which is fundamental in human relations. Despite the color, force, and occasional charm of slang, however, three good reasons exist for using it carefully and sparingly:

1. Using slang expressions prevents a speaker from searching for the exact words needed to convey meaning. Many slang expressions are only rubber stamps. To call someone a *swell guy* or a *square* hardly expresses exactly or fully any real critical judgment or intelligent description. Instead, such

words are more likely to suggest the speaker's own laziness, careless thinking, and poverty of vocabulary. Slang may be colorful and humorous, but few slang expressions by themselves convey a clear and accurate message from speaker to listener.

2. Slang has its place in conversation and in informal writing, but occasionally it is not in keeping with the context —what precedes and follows. For example, a sensible and serious talk with a public official about current affairs might be thrown off if suddenly a slang term such as *mod* or *cool* were injected.

3. Most slang words and expressions last for a brief time only and then pass out of use, becoming unintelligible to hearers and readers.

Slang appears in numerous forms.

Many neologisms (newly coined words) are slang:

beatnik	payola
grandiferous	pizzaz
hornswoggle	scram
ixnay	scrumptious
mooch	sockdologer
nix	teenybopper
oops	wacky

Some slang words and expressions are formed from other words by abbreviation or by adding new endings to change the part of speech:

chintzy	nervy
C-note	phony
groovy	psych out
legit	snafu
mod	VIP

Sometimes words in acceptable use are given extended meanings:

acid	chicken
bean	corny
blow	dish
buck	fuzzy
cat	grease

grind	snow
guts	square
lousy	swell
mainline	tough
sack	trip

Some slang is formed by compounding or bringing together two or more words:

egghead	hepcat
flyboy	stash (store and cache)
go-go girl	whodunit

Slang often consists of one or more coined words combined with one or more standard terms:

blow one's top	jam session
bum steer	live it up
cool it	off one's rocker
get in orbit	shoot the bull (breeze)
have a ball	shoot the works

Illustrating the various methods by which slang is concocted is the following list of 150 expressions. If the reader does not recognize every item (or all of the terms mentioned above), his inability to do so provides two reasons why slang should not be overused: it is not always understandable; it often has a short life.

all-fired	blow your stack	dimwit
attaboy (attagirl)	bolix (or bollicks)	double dome
babe	booboo	elbow grease
back number	brass hat	eyewash
baloney	bread	fishy
bamboozle	bushed	flack
barf	buzz off	flatfoot
barge in	chump	flivver
bats	clip joint	floozy
beanery	conk (conk out)	flossy
beef	cornball	fork over
big shot	crackpot	fourflusher
bigwig	cut the mustard	gate-crasher
blind date	dame	geezer
bloke	deadbeat	get lost

Slang

get one's goat
get with it
girlie
go-getter
goldbrick
gold digger
goner
goo
gooey
goof (and goof off)
goofy
gook
goon
grub
gung ho
gunk
guy
gyp
half-baked
half-cocked
hick
high-hat
hightail
hogwash
hooey
hunky-dory
jeez
jerk
jinx
jughead
kibosh
kick around
kickback
kick in
kick the bucket
kid
lemon
long green
lulu
lummox
meathead
moniker
mooch
moola
moxie
natch
nix
nut
nuts
nutty
on the ball
on the beam
on the level
on the loose
on the make
on the wagon
oodles
pad
pantywaist
party pooper
peach
phiz
piker
poop
pork barrel
pusher
ratfink
rat race
raunch
razz
razzberry
razzle-dazzle
razzmatazz
rhubarb
ritzy
sad sack
sawbuck
scads
screw
screwball
screw loose
screw out of
screwy
shakes
shebang
shenanigans
shiv
shyster
simoleon
slaphappy
sound off
stool pigeon
sucker
swing
tizzy
turn off
turn on
weirdie
weirdo
wheeler-dealer
wise guy
wisenheimer
wise up
yak (yack, yuk)
yap

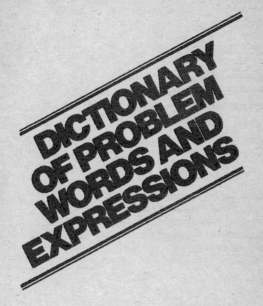

DICTIONARY OF PROBLEM WORDS AND EXPRESSIONS

A

a, an. Correct choice of *a* and *an* depends on the initial sound, not on the initial letter, of the word that follows. *A* should be used before all words beginning with a consonant sound except silent *h* (an *honor*) and before words beginning with vowels that represent combined consonant and vowel sounds *(university, unit)*. *An* should be used before all vowel sounds.

a boy	an entry
a European	an *f*
a *g*	an hour
a picture	an orange
a store	an unbeliever

With the words *history* and *historian,* a preceding *a* is more often used today than *an.* In *history,* the *h* is always pronounced; the *h* in words such as *historian* and *historical* was formerly not pronounced, but it frequently is in contemporary usage. Always say "*a* history book," but refer to "*an* (or *a*) historian" and "*an* (or *a*) historical novel" as you please. Both are standard usage.

Neither *a* nor *an* is needed in such expressions as "no such *(a)* thing," "no greater *(an)* honor."

a, per. Both *a* and *per* are commonly used with meanings of "each" and "for every." Thus one may write "once *a* minute" or "once *per* minute." Because *per* comes from Latin, old-time grammarians insisted that it should not appear before nouns in English, but this restriction no longer applies. The appearance of *per* is widespread and acceptable in all commercial, economic, and statistical writing. Using *a* (or *an*) for *per* in a sentence such as "The yield per acre per year is 200 bushels" is not incorrect but does sound repetitious and overly refined. In most instances, *a* is an acceptable substitute for overused *per* and is preferable in such expressions as "once *a* week," "50 cents *a* gallon," and "Admission is $1 *a* person."

abdomen. This term, from Latin and pronounced with the accent on the first or second syllable, refers to that part of any mammal's body that lies between the pelvis and the rib cage. Some speakers consider it an evasion, a euphemism (inoffensive word) for *belly,* a perfectly proper term descended from Old English. (Possibly *belly* will be restored to common use on all levels, just as *leg* is now generally used instead of *limb.*) *Abdomen* is an anatomical term, as is *stomach* (which really applies to one organ within the *abdomen,* or *belly*). Trite or childish expressions with differing meanings include *potbelly, corporation, stummick, bay window, paunch, guts,* and *tummy.* In everyday usage, say *belly;* in formal or fastidious situations, use *abdomen.*

ability, capacity. *Ability* means the physical, mental, financial, or legal power to do something (*ability* to walk, to read, to pay a bill, to assess property). *Capacity* is the ability to hold, absorb, or contain (a bucket with a *capacity* of 1 gallon, a motel filled to *capacity*). *Ability* takes varied prepositions (ability *in* physics, ability *with* languages, ability *at* riding horses). *Ability* is often followed by an infinitive (ability *to think* clearly, not *of thinking* clearly). *Capacity* is followed by the preposition *for* (capacity *for* hard work) or *of* (capacity *of* 10 quarts).

Ability is a more positive quality or attainment than is

capacity. A person may or may not have the *capacity* to learn singing; after study and practice he may or may not have the *ability* to sing. Approximate synonyms for *ability* are *competence, skill, aptitude, faculty,* and *talent*.

abjure, adjure. These "look-alikes" are often confused but can be kept straight by concentrating on their prefixes. *Ab-*, a formal element occurring in loan words from Latin, means "away from." *Abjure* suggests putting aside, renouncing, repudiating, giving up. *Ad-* means "toward"; *adjure* means "to direct a charge or command to or toward someone." "'The man without a country,' Philip Nolan, *abjured* allegiance to the United States." "The minister *adjured* us to stop stealing and swearing."

able to. This is a wordy and unidiomatic expression for *can* or *could*. "This work *could* not be finished in a month" is preferable to "This work was not *able to* be finished in a month." Confine use of *able* to persons or objects that possess ability: "He was *able* in science."

about, around, round. *About* is a commonly used word with several meanings and shades of meaning, most of which develop the idea of circling, on every side, or here and there (walk *about*, look *about*). It has also the meanings of "nearly" or "approximately" (*about* 100 books). *About* is informally used in the sense of "almost" (*about* ready to go). The phrase "at *about*" (at *about* midnight) is wordy; the *at* can be omitted unless you intend *about* to mean "approximately."

Around has many of the basic meanings of *about* ("on all sides," "here and there"), as in "walk *around*" and "look *around*." But in such senses *around* is more informal than *about*. "Wait *around*," "to travel *around*," "to have been *around*," and "*around* noon" are fully permissible in colloquial (spoken) usage.

Around is usually preferred to *round* in such expressions as "*around* the world" and "*around* the Horn." "Meet me *round* noon" is more informal than "Meet me *around* noon"; preferably, say or write "Meet me *about* noon."

about to. The word *about* has a meaning of readiness or willingness; the phrase "not *about* to" conveys an idea of unwillingness, unreadiness, or opposition of some sort: "He was not *about to* pay the bill." The expression is trite and informal and should be avoided. Write "He *was not ready to* (or *was unwilling to* or *refused to*) pay the bill."

above. Some grammarians object to the use of *above* in the meaning of "preceding" or "previously mentioned or written" (the examples given *above,* the *above* examples). However, *above* can be an adjective as well as an adverb, so that no grammatical error is involved. The objection to using *above* in this sense is that the word may refer vaguely or even loosely and incorrectly to preceding material; overuse of it may make you sound legalistic or stilted.

As a preposition, *above* presents no usage problems (*above* the earth). As a noun, *above* is both vague and informal. Instead of "The *above* states my position fairly," it is preferable to say "This is my position" or "The preceding statements present my position fairly."

abridged. *See* UNABRIDGED.

absolute. This word means "complete," "unlimited," "unconditional." Logically, *absolute* admits neither comparison nor shading; to refer to one's *"very absolute* effort" or *"too absolute* approval" is illogical. However, if a qualifying word such as *nearly* is used, this objection is removed: "one's very *nearly absolute* approval."

absolutely. This word means "positively" or "definitely." All three words are overused to mean "quite," or "very," or even "yes": "She was *absolutely* lovely; he was *positively* godlike; it was *definitely* the wedding of the year; did you attend it?" can be gushily answered,

"Absolutely!" Suggestion: omit the italicized words in the question and supply the simple answer "Yes."

academic. This term relating to the characteristics and qualities of a school (academy) provides an example of how words acquire associated and extended meanings. Because *academic* refers to formal education and scholarship, it has come to mean "conventional" and "traditional." In fact, an *academic* person is sometimes considered as being so unaware of the outside world that he lives in an ivory tower. Thus the word also means "speculative" or "theoretical," not "actual" or "realistic": "I took only an *academic* interest in the progress of the campaign."

accept, except. These words have different pronunciations and different meanings. *Accept* means "to receive," "to agree with," "to say yes to." As a verb, *except* means "to omit," "to exempt," "to exclude"; as a preposition, it means "other than." *Except* should not be used as a conjunction: "He won't go *except* I tell him to" is substandard. Some correct sentences follow: "He did not *accept* the proposal." "Tod was *excepted* from the list of those invited." "Everyone *except* me knew the right answer."

accident, mishap. An *accident* is an event that occurs without apparent plan. Such a chance, undesigned occurrence may be fortunate (a lucky *accident* that we saw each other), unfortunate (a fatal *accident*), or neutral (the *accident* of birth). A *mishap* is an unfortunate *accident*. Breaking a shoelace when in a hurry is a *mishap*. There is no such thing as a fortunate or neutral *mishap*. A disaster, catastrophe, or calamity cannot be called a *mishap*, a word reserved for a misadventure, mischance, or misfortune. A *mishap* might be referred to as a minor *accident*.

accidentally, accidently. Meaning "by chance," "without design," or "unexpectedly," *accidentally* is often mispronounced and misspelled. The word has five syllables (ac·ci·den·tal·ly); omit *al* in neither spelling nor pronunciation. There is no such word as *accidently*.

accredit. *See* CREDIT.

accusation. *See* RECRIMINATION.

accused. *See* ALLEGED.

acknowledge, admit. One may *acknowledge* or *admit* an error. One may *acknowledge* or *admit* being in error. Thus, these words have approximately the same meaning, "to concede, grant, or declare something to be true." *Acknowledge,* however, is preferable when referring to a statement made reluctantly, especially one previously denied: "The bank teller *acknowledged* his error." *Admit* suggests the presence of force, duress, or pressure: "The culprit *admitted* the crime."

acme, climax. *Acme* means "summit," "highest point." *Climax* implies a scale of increasing, ascending values and is applied to the highest point in interest, force, or intensity. "His performance was the *acme* of professional skill." "The *climax* of the indoor games was the mile run."

act, action. An *act* is a deed, a thing done. *Action* is related in meaning but more precisely suggests the doing of something, of being in operation or motion. "That was an *act* of kindness." "Your *action* was unselfish."

activate, actuate. These words have a common meaning, "to set or put in motion": "The foreman *activated* (or *actuated*) the mechanism." They are confused, however, when used to refer to persons and the impulses that govern their deeds. Some outside agent or influence can *activate* a person or thing as a stimulus, but only a principle, desire, or motive can *actuate* an individual and determine his actions: "His desire for fame *actuated* his constant efforts." "*Actuated* by good will, he *activated* a group of generous persons."

actor, actress. The suffix *-ess* is used to form distinctively feminine nouns such as *hostess, lioness, duchess,* and *heiress.* Even before the Women's Lib movement, its use was considered offensive in such words as *Jewess, Negress,* and *poetess,* because emphasis on sex seemed irrelevant and possibly prejudicial. With an *actress,* however, femininity is essential to her art, so that the term is appropriate and useful. An *actor,* of course, is a male performer.

actual, real, virtual. *Actual* and *real* are related in meaning ("existing in fact," "not imaginary"), but they may be distinguished. *Actual* places emphasis upon coming into a sphere of fact or action and applies to facts as they now are or have become. *Real* expresses objective existence and applies especially to facts rooted in nature. *Virtual* means "having the effect but not the form of what is specified." "Is this an *actual* assignment or only something to keep me busy?" "Is this *real* money or counterfeit?" "After the president resigned, the vice president was the *virtual* head of the firm."

actuate. *See* ACTIVATE.

ad. This is a clipped form of *advertisement.* It is informal (colloquial) and should appear rarely, if at all, in formal writing, but the use of *ad* in everyday speech is widespread and justified. Also, one could hardly score tennis without using *ad,* here an abbreviation for *advantage.*

adage. *See* AXIOM.

adapt, adept, adopt. To *adapt* is "to adjust," "to make suitable." Note the second syllable *(dapt),* which resembles *apt,* meaning "fit" or suited to the purpose." *Adept* has something of the meaning of *apt* ("skilled," "proficient"): one can say "Bob was *apt* in science" or "Bob was *adept* in science." *Adopt* means "to accept" or "to take as one's own." "You must *adapt* yourself to this situation." "He is *adept* in dancing the latest steps." "I shall *adopt* your proposal." "This dress designer is *adept* in *adapting* styles from abroad and finds that women here *adopt* them eagerly."

addendum, addenda. An *addendum* is an addition, something added or to be added. The term is specifically applied to an appendix of or supplement to a book or other printed material. It should be used with a singular verb only: "This *addendum* is an important part of the report." The standard plural form is *addenda,* although *addendums* is being used more and more frequently by educated speakers and writers and most authorities no longer consider it incorrect. *See also* AGENDUM.

addicted, devoted. *Addicted* has an unfavorable or undesirable sense of "given to a practice or habit." *Devoted* also suggests attachment but only to that which the speaker or writer considers good, beneficial, or favorable. "He was *addicted* to narcotics (or lying or thievery or alcohol)." "Jim was *devoted* to his mother (or his country or good literature)." If you approve of mystery stories, for example, you may say that a friend of yours is *devoted* to such reading; if you dislike mysteries, you may say that he is *addicted* to them.

adduce, deduce. The first of these words means "to cite as evidence that is conclusive or persuasive," "to present as an argument." *Adduce* is sometimes confused with *deduce,* which means "to infer," "to derive as a conclusion from something assumed or known." "The speaker *adduced* three reasons for his actions." "The jury *deduced* that the accused was not guilty."

adept. *See* ADAPT.

adhere, cohere. These words have related meanings, as is suggested by their common Latin root *(here,* from *haerere),* which implies sticking or clinging together. One object *adheres* to another through the use of glue; a person *adheres* to a belief, a cause, a religion, or a political party. *Cohere* suggests the sticking together of items already present (The particles *cohered* to form a sticky mass) and the logical or natural connection of ideas and objects (Each part of his presentation seemed to *cohere* with established facts).

ad hoc. This phrase, straight from Latin and pronounced "ad hock," literally means "toward this." In English it is used to mean "with respect to this" or "for this purpose only" and is applied to a group created to deal with a particular situation, case, cause, or purpose: "The chairman appointed an *ad hoc* committee to supervise the voting."

adjacent, contiguous. In exact usage, *adjacent* means "lying near," "close at hand," "neighboring," and *contiguous* means "touching," "in actual contact." Beads strung loosely are *adjacent;* if strung tightly, they are *contiguous*. In general usage, however, the words are interchangeable. *Adjacent,* much the more commonly used word, has these approximate synonyms: *adjoining, abutting, bordering, connecting,* and *juxtaposed*.

adjudge. *See* JUDGE.

adjure. *See* ABJURE.

ad-lib. This verb, meaning "to improvise," "to deliver spontaneously," is derived from Latin *ad libitum,* meaning "at pleasure." It can correctly be used to mean "freely" but is often overused. *Ad-lib* is a trite expression when used to mean adding words or gestures hastily improvised, or concocted, that are not in the script or are not intended to be expressed by word or action.

admission, admittance. *Admission* means "allowing to enter" or "permitted entrance" and applies to acceptance that carries certain rights and privileges. *Admittance* means "physical entry" without reference to rights or membership privileges. "He sought *admission* to the party." "*Admittance* is by invitation only." "It was easy to secure *admission* to the public library, but she soon found several doors marked '*Admittance* to staff members only.'"

admit, allow. These words have a shared meaning: "to acknowledge," "to concede," "to make a disclosure." One may *admit* a mistake or *allow* that he had made one. *Admit* also suggests the influence of pressure. In general usage, however, *admit* and *allow* are interchangeable in this meaning. The preposition *to* is unnecessary in such statements as "I *admit (to)* the mistake" and "I *admit (to)* having made an error." *See also* ACKNOWLEDGE.

admit, confess. *See* CONFESS.

admittance. *See* ADMISSION.

adopt. *See* ADAPT.

adopted, adoptive. An *adopted* child is one taken by others in a formal, legal act. The foster parent or parents who have undergone such a legal maneuver are called *adoptive:* "The *adopted* infant grew fond of her *adoptive* parents."

advance, advanced. As a verb, *advance* means "to move or bring forward." As an adjective, it emphasizes position (*advance* guard) or time (*advance* notice). As a noun, *advance* refers to the act or process of moving forward. *Advanced,* as an adjective, has several meanings: "at a late stage," "far on in life," "ahead of contemporary progress or thought," "at a high level": "You may wish to *advance* the time that you start studying for an *advanced* degree." The phrase "*advance* planning" is a classic example of the tendency to use more words than necessary. *Planning* itself involves the idea of looking ahead, of devising a program for future action. The word *advance* is here a useless addition.

advantage. *See* AD.

adversary, antagonist. Each of these words refers to persons or animals engaged in struggles or contests. Related words are *opponent, competitor,* and *rival.* An *adversary* is an opponent toward whom one does not necessarily feel animosity or hatred. An *antagonist* is a definitely hostile opponent. "Counsel for the defense faced an experienced *adversary* in District Attorney Smythe." "A flyweight boxer is not a suitable *antagonist* for a middleweight."

adverse, averse. *Adverse* means "opposed," "contrary," "hostile." *Averse* means "reluctant" and "unwilling" and implies a holding back because of distaste or dislike. "The employees had an *adverse* opinion of the company plan." "The company treasurer is *averse* to lending money to anyone."

advert, avert. These "look-alikes" have a common root in Latin (*vertere*, "to turn") but quite different meanings in English. *Advert* means "to refer," "to turn attention to," "to comment about": "He *adverted* to a topic mentioned earlier by another speaker." *Avert* means "to turn away or turn aside," "to prevent," "to ward off": "She *averted* her eyes from the injured man." "The driver braked hard to *avert* an accident."

advise, advice. With a basic meaning of "to counsel," "to give advice to," *advise* can also mean "to tell" or "to inform." It is overused in business letters and other forms of commercial communication. Say "I wish to *tell* (not *advise*) you that your order has been received." *Advise* is always and only a verb; *advice*, a noun spelled and pronounced differently, means "an opinion" or "a recommendation": "I *advise* you to take no *advice* from Tom." A noun formed from *advise* is spelled *adviser* or *advisor*. *See also* BEG TO ADVISE.

advisedly, intentionally. An action or step taken *advisedly* is one that is deliberate, one taken with careful consideration. An action or step taken *intentionally* suggests purpose, design, and intent. One might *intentionally* talk back to a traffic policeman, but he is not likely to do so *advisedly*.

affect, effect. These words have slightly different pronunciations and quite different meanings. *Affect* is always a verb (except for one use as a noun in psychology) and means "to influence," "to cause a response": "This article will *affect* my thinking." *Affect* also means "to assume," "to be given to," or "to pretend": "She *affected* a silly manner of speaking." As a noun, *effect* means "result," "accomplishment": "What was the *effect* of this appeal for money?" As a verb, *effect* means "to cause," "to bring about": "The new manager will *effect* major changes in our sales methods." In plural form, *effects* can mean "goods," "property": "The deceased man's *effects* were willed to charity."

affective, effective. The primary meaning of *affective* is "emotional," "caused by or expressing feeling and sentiment": "Many scenes in Dickens's novels are *affective.*" *Effective* has several meanings, the primary one being "producing the intended or expected results": "The supervisor suggested *effective* steps to handle the work load." The contrast in meaning can be illustrated thus: "The *affective* death scene of Little Nell Trent in Dickens's *The Old Curiosity Shop* is dramatically *effective.*"

affinity. This word, from a Latin term meaning "connection by marriage," refers to a natural liking for, or attraction to, another person. An *affinity* is a bond or tie of sympathy, feeling, or kinship and refers only to relations between people, not to people themselves. Also, *affinity* should not be confused with *aptitude, knack, ability,* or *capacity*. One does not have an *affinity* for sports or music but rather a *knack* or *talent* of some sort. In fact, *for* should not be used as a preposition following *affinity;* use *between, with,* or *to:* "The *affinity between* Sue and Ralph is based upon musical interests." "Sue has an *affinity to* Ralph because of their common musical interests."

afflict. *See* INFLICT.

affluent. *See* RICH.

afraid. This word, meaning "filled with fear, apprehension, concern, or regret," is overused in everyday conversation with the verb *to be* as a loose, inaccurate synonym for "to think," "to feel," "to believe." Avoid such statements as "I'm *afraid* you're wrong" and "I'm *afraid* not," unless your concern, regret, or worry is strong and intense. In speaking and writing, do not use *afraid* unless you could equally well employ *scared, apprehensive, fearful, frightened, alarmed,* or *terrified*. In casual and informal conversation, *afraid* is often used either apologetically or in an attempt to soften or lessen an unpleasant statement: "I'm *afraid* I have bad news for you."

aftermath. The *math* in *aftermath* comes from an Old English word meaning "mowing." Originally, *aftermath* meant a second mowing of a field of grain or grass. Now it is used figuratively to mean "results" or "consequences." *Aftermath* loosely refers to anything that follows, but it should be applied only to results (second harvests) that are unpleasant, harmful, or tragic: "Destruction is an *aftermath* of war." Blowing automobile horns after a wedding ceremony is not an *aftermath* but a custom or practice.

afternoons, evenings, mornings. Some purists object to the use of these plural forms in the senses of "during the afternoon" and "every afternoon." Idiomatically, however, it is permissible and correct to say or write "Sue works only *afternoons*" when what is meant is "Sue works *every afternoon*" or "Sue works only *in* (or *during*) the *afternoon*."

In various parts of the country, *afternoon, evening,* and *morning* have different meanings and applications. *Afternoon* means the time from noon until evening, but when does *evening* come? In certain sections of the West and South, one hears "Good *evening*" as a greeting anytime from noon until midnight. To some, *evening* may mean the period between noon and nightfall. But what is *night?* Is it the time between sunset and sunrise? Does *morning* apply to the time between midnight and noon or that between sunrise and noon? The only sensible plan is to use these terms as your friends and neighbors do, recognizing that such usage may be misunderstood in other sections of the country.

afterward, afterwards. Each of these words, meaning "subsequently" or "at a later time," is acceptable. *Afterward* is preferable because it is shorter and is generally used throughout the United States. *Afterwards* is in common use in Great Britain.

agendum, agenda. These terms (from a Latin word meaning "to act," "to do") refer to something to be done. The former is singular; the latter, plural. *Agendum* is rarely used but occasionally is employed to refer to one item in a list or a program of action, to a single act or topic for discussion. *Agenda* applies to a list of items, such as a program for a meeting or discussion group. Although plural in form, *agenda* is a collective noun and is commonly used with a singular verb: "The *agenda* for this meeting *has* been set." A less-used form, *agendums,* requires a plural verb: "The agendums *are* lengthy and involved." Preferably use *agenda* (with a singular verb) or *agendum* if you wish to single out a particular item. *See also* ADDENDUM.

aggravate, annoy, irritate. *Aggravate* means "to intensify," "to increase something unpleasant," "to make worse," "to make more grave or serious." Used informally and loosely, *aggravate* means "to irritate," "to annoy." *Annoy* means "to harass," "to pester," "to disturb," "to irritate by bothering." *Irritate,* meaning "to excite to impatience," is a virtual synonym for *annoy* but refers to a milder disturbance or lesser upset. *Aggravate* is the strongest of the three terms. "Sneezing *aggravated* Jack's open wound." "The buzzing mosquito *annoyed* me." "Rude remarks about his ability *irritated* the foreman."

agnostic, atheist. An *agnostic* disclaims any knowledge of God; an *atheist* denies the existence of God. That is, an *agnostic* says "I don't know whether there is a God"; the *atheist* says "There is no God." An *agnostic* does not deny the existence of a deity but claims that he does not know and that no one else can either. An *atheist* believes that God does not now exist and that He never has existed. Related terms are *disbeliever, doubter, freethinker, unbeliever.*

ago, since. These words refer to past time, but they should not be used together. Do not write "It was five years *ago since* I last saw Ben." Follow *ago* with *that* or omit *ago:* "It was five years *ago that* I last saw Ben." "It is five years *since* I last saw Ben." The construction *ago since* is both wordy and illogical. *Ago* carries thought from present to past time; *since* conveys thought from past to present Our minds are shaky already; they are not helped by meeting themselves coming back.

aid. *See* HELP.

aim, intend. When *aim* is used in the sense of positioning, it is always followed by *at:* "Don't *aim* the gun *at* me." When used in the sense of "to intend" or "to try," it may be followed by *at* (I *aim at* your happiness) or by an infinitive (I *aim to make* you happy). *Aim* should not be followed by both *at* and a gerund. Avoid saying or writing "I *aim at* proving you wrong." *Intend,* meaning "to design" or "to have in mind," is considered a more suitable and refined word than *aim. Intend* may be followed by an infinitive (I *intend to ride* with you), by a gerund (I *intend riding* with you), or by a clause (I *intend that you follow me promptly*).

ain't. This contraction of *am not* has been extended to mean also "is not," "has not," "are not," and "have not." *Ain't* is considered illiterate, colloquial, or dialectal and is cautioned against in so-called standard speech and writing. It is occasionally used informally by educated persons, but it has not been accepted as have been *isn't* (is not), *hasn't* (has not), *haven't* (have not), *aren't* (are not), and *weren't* (were not).

à la. This phrase from French is a shortened form of *à la mode de* ("in the style of"). In English, *à la* is used, frequently overused, to mean "in the manner of," "like," "according to." Its appearance in a sentence such as "She dressed *à la* a Hollywood star" is correct but also pretentious and forced. Restrict use of *à la* to such standard expressions as "*à la* carte" and "*à la* mode," for which there are no acceptable substitutes in English.

alibi. Precise and careful speakers and writers limit the use of *alibi* to its meaning in law; "a plea or fact of having been elsewhere when an offense was committed": "The defendant's *alibi* was that he was out of town when the crime took place." *Alibi* is overused in the informal sense of "excuse" or "any kind of defense." Instead of saying "The players offered no *alibi* for their defeat," say

"They offered no *excuse.*" Instead of saying "Honest men never *alibi,*" use some form of *plea, justification,* or *acknowledgment*.

alien, alienist, alienate. An *alien* is a foreigner, someone born in or belonging to another country: "He was an *alien* for ten years and then became a naturalized citizen." The term is also applied to one who is excluded in some way (that is, is an outsider) and to matters that are strange or unfamiliar: "He was forced to adjust to an *alien* culture." "In his ragged clothing, he felt an *alien* in such plush surroundings." An *alienist* is a medically trained person who gives testimony (legal evidence) on questions of sanity and insanity: "Opposing *alienists* will testify at this murder trial." *Alienate* means "to turn away," "to affect by causing an atmosphere of unfriendliness," "to make indifferent": "His constant rudeness *alienated* most of his friends." *Alien, alienist,* and *alienate* imply or suggest either difference or opposition.

all, all of. When preceding a pronoun, *all* must be followed by *of* (*all of* them, not *all* them or *all* us). When *all* is followed by a noun, *of* may be omitted and often is by speakers and writers who wish to avoid using an unnecessary word: "*All* (or *all of*) the workers went on strike."

all-around. *See* ALL-ROUND.

all but one. *See* MORE THAN ONE.

alleged, accused, suspected. Each of these words is used to refer to persons involved in legal problems. To *allege* means "to state positively," "to assert without proof," or "to urge as an excuse or reason." To *accuse* is "to charge someone with an error or crime." To *suspect* means "to imagine," "to think guilty without proof of guilt." Newspapers and broadcast news programs often publish stories about an *alleged* swindler, an *accused* burglar, or a *suspected* arsonist. These terms are used as a possible hedge against being sued for libel, but their use in such instances is both debatable and doubtful. One cannot *allege* a swindler but rather a condition or a crime. An *accused* burglar is not a burglar who has been accused but a person who has been accused as a burglar. Even so, individuals need the protection such words attempt to provide as a defense against the charge of slander, just as newspapers and radio and television stations do against suits for libel. For this purpose, *alleged* is preferable to either *accused* or *suspected*.

allegedly, reportedly, reputedly. Each of these words means "according to a statement or affirmation," but the two have slightly different connotations. "The driver was *allegedly* ill" means that someone asserted, claimed, or openly stated an opinion of the driver's condition. "The driver was *reportedly* ill" means that the driver's condition was actually reported in writing or through rumor, gossip, or common talk. "The driver was *reputedly* ill" indicates that he was estimated to be or considered ill, a condition not necessarily made public or openly declared. *Reputedly* also has a slight connection with *reputation*, a shade of meaning not present in *allegedly* or *reportedly*.

allergic. This word means "unusually sensitive to a condition or substance" (an *allergic* reaction to nylon) and is also loosely overused to suggest dislike or disregard (*allergic* to the plays of Shakespeare). *Allergic* is often misused as in this sentence: "Tom is *allergic* to hay fever." Tom's condition results from an *allergy* (a state of hypersensitivity); he is *allergic* not to hay fever but to the pollens of goldenrod or ragweed or whatever.

all of. *See* ALL.

allow, permit. *Allow* means "to grant," "to let have," and implies that no direct prevention or obstruction is involved: "Does your supervisor *allow* you to dress as you please?" *Permit*, a more formal word than *allow*, specifically involves the idea of permission: "Does your ticket *permit* you to enter at that gate?" An everyday synonym for *allow* and *permit* is *let*. *See also* ADMIT, ALLOW.

all ready. *See* ALREADY.

all right. *See* ALRIGHT.

all-round, all-around. In such phrases as "*all-round* man" and "*all-round* athlete," this hypenated adjective is preferable to its twin, *all-around*. In this sense, *round* provides the idea of completeness or fullness, whereas *around* suggests position with relationship to a center. By this reasoning, one should say "The dog walked *around* the chair" rather than "*round* the chair." Neither *all-round* nor *all-around* (both adjectives) should be confused with *all round* and *all around* (two adverbs): "Jack walked *all around* the waterfront."

all the farther. This expression is colloquial or dialectal and should not be used in speaking or writing. Do not say "This is *all the farther* I intend to go." Say "This is *as far as* I intend to go." Similarly, do not say "Is this *all the faster* your car will go?" but "Is this *as fast as* your car will go?"

all together. *See* ALTOGETHER.

allude, elude. *Allude* means "to refer indirectly or casually" and is followed by *to:* "He *alluded to* his former occupation." "This memo *alludes to* a misplaced letter." *Elude* is sometimes confused with *allude* because of similarity in pronunciation and spelling but has an entirely different meaning ("to avoid," "to escape," "to slip away from," "to dodge"): "He *eluded* the pursuing policemen."

allusion, delusion, elusion, illusion. These words, somewhat alike in sound and spelling, have different meanings and uses. An *allusion* is an indirect reference or mention: "He made an *allusion* to a character in a TV melodrama." *Delusion* means "a false belief," one usually held as a result of self-deception. It is commonly used to refer to a person suffering from a mental disorder: "Bob suffers from *delusions* of grandeur." "Alice is under the *delusion* that she is Joan of Arc." *Elusion,* a rarely used word, means "an escape," "an evasion": "Not attending the meeting is an *elusion* of your obligation to vote." *Illusion* is related in meaning to *delusion;* it refers to a false mental image or idea, to something that is imagined and that may or may not be based on fact: "A mirage is an *illusion.*" "At times, Charlie is under the *illusion* that he is a star football player." A *delusion* is more likely to be harmful or serious than is an *illusion.*

all ways. *See* ALWAYS.

almighty. This word, meaning "having unlimited power" or "overpowering," is informally overused in the senses of "extreme" and "terrible." A Supreme Being is *almighty,* but it is doubtful that one can or should be "in an *almighty* bit of trouble" or "*almighty* tired." Even the *almighty* dollar has lost much of its worth and worldwide standing.

almost, most. As an adverb, *almost* is preferable to the colloquial *most* in the senses of "all but," "very nearly." Say "*almost* every person there," rather than "*most* every person there." As a pronoun or adjective, *most* means "the greater part or number": "*Most* of us agreed with the speaker." "This is the *most* money he ever earned in one day." As an adverb, *most* is used in the comparison of adjectives and adverbs: wisely, more wisely, *most* wisely. *See also* NEARLY.

alone, only. *Alone* has several meanings ("separate," "apart," "isolated," "unique"), as in such expressions as "all *alone*" and "Man shall not live by bread *alone.*"

Only means "without others," "solely," "exclusively." *Alone* and *only* can be synonymous. One may say "She worked *alone*" (No one was with her) and "*Only* she worked" (No one else worked). But one can also correctly say "She *alone* worked" (No one else worked).

along this line. This expression meaning "in this manner," "similarly," or "according to this pattern" is not incorrect, but it is vague and trite. In most instances, it is a mere filler and can be omitted without real loss.

aloud, out loud. Each of these expressions means "audibly," "in a loud tone." Both are correct, but *aloud* is considered less colloquial and is also preferable because it is shorter.

already, all ready. *Already* is an adverb expressing time and means "earlier," "previously": "When she arrived, her friend had *already* left." "We discovered that the tickets were *already* sold." *All ready* is used as an adjective to mean "completely ready": "They will start for the office when they are *all ready.*"

alright, all right. *Alright* is a common misspelling of *all right,* an expression with numerous meanings: "satisfactory," "correct," "very well," "yes," "safe," "acceptable." There is no such word as *alright.*

also, and also. *Also* is an adverb meaning "besides," "in addition,": "He *also* likes music" implies that he likes something other than or in addition to music. In writing, *also* should not be used as a conjunction to join words or to introduce a sentence; avoid such statements as "I like steak, *also* bacon." Preferably write "I like steak *and* bacon" or "I like steak *and also* bacon." In talking, one might carelessly say "We played bridge during the party. *Also* we danced." In writing, *also* should not be forced to do the job of *and, and also, likewise, moreover,* and *in addition.*

alter. *See* CHANGE.

alternate, alternately, alternative, alternatively. As a verb, *alternate* means "to change back and forth," "to occur in successive turns." It is pronounced with primary accent on the first syllable and is usually followed by *with:* "Sunny and rainy days *alternate with* each other at this season." As an adjective, *alternate* is also pronounced with accent on the first syllable but is not followed by *with:* "He introduced an *alternate* proposal." *Alternately,* an adverb, carries the same general meaning as *alternate:* "The hiker *alternately* walked and jogged." *Alternative* refers to a situation involving a choice: "You have the *alternative* of speaking or of keeping quiet." As both noun and adjective, *alternative* is pronounced with primary accent on the second syllable. The distinction between *alternately* and *alternatively* is that the former suggests a meaning of "one after the other" and the latter carries a meaning of "one or the other." Neither *alternative* nor *alternatively* is restricted to a choice between only two: "The *alternatives* are stagnation, cold war, peace, or compromise." To keep these distinctions in mind, remember that *alternate* and *alternately* have a basic meaning of "by turns" and *alternative* and *alternatively* pertain to some kind of choice.

although, though. These words meaning "even though," "regardless," "in spite of the fact that" may be used interchangeably in most instances: "*Although* I was nervous, I got to my feet." "*Though* I was nervous, I got to my feet." However, *although* is more commonly used at the beginning of a sentence. *Though* is the more commonly used word in linking words and phrases (sadder *though* wiser man) and is preferred over *although* at the end of a statement (He looked healthy to me, *though*).

altogether, all together. The first of these, "look-alikes" means "wholly," "completely": "He was not *altogether* pleased with his new car." *Altogether* also has the specialized meaning of "in all" or "all told": "Six men *altogether* volunteered for the mission." "In the *altogether*" is an informal, artificial phrase meaning "nude." *All together* means "all in company" or "everybody in one place": "The family was *all together* for the holidays."

alumnus, alumna, alumni. An *alumnus* is a male graduate of some institution, usually a college or university. An *alumna* is a woman graduate. Respective plurals are *alumni* and *alumnae*. The term *alumni* is now often used to refer to men and women graduates of coeducational institutions. To refer to graduates as *alum* or *alums* is nonstandard. "Beth is an *alumna* of Smith College." "Jack is an *alumnus* of Duke University." "Joy, Jill, and Tom are *alumni* of Dartmouth College."

always, all ways. *Always* is an adverb meaning "forever," "ceaselessly," "on every occasion": "He was *always* on time for appointments." "Joe said he would love Becky for *always.*" *All ways* is a phrase meaning "every way," "all possible ways": "The teachers tried in *all ways* to interest Joe in studying."

amateur, novice, neophyte, tyro. *Amateur,* much the most widely used of these four terms, is applied to someone who follows or pursues any art, study, or other activity simply from love of doing so. In certain activities, especially sports, an amateur is one who, regardless of excellence, receives no payment for his performance: "Stan played as an *amateur* for five years before becoming a professional." A *novice* is a beginner, a person new to any field or activity: "Some young brides are *novices* at housekeeping." *Tyro* is closely related in meaning to *novice;* it refers to someone who is inexperienced: "Bill was a *tyro* during his first weeks at training camp." *Neophyte* also refers to a beginner *(novice, tyro),* but the term is usually applied to a recent convert, especially to a *novice* in a religious order and to a recently ordained priest. An *amateur* may be skilled and even experienced, but *novices, tyros,* and *neophytes* never are. A *tyro,* *novice,* or *neophyte* may be a professional, but an *amateur* never is.

amatory, amorous. These terms refer to lovers or love-making. Each has a sexual connotation and may be considered less chaste than *loving* when used as an adjective. An *amatory* or *amorous* look is stronger (more sexual) than a *loving* glance. There is little distinction in meaning and usage between *amatory* and *amorous,* although the latter is more often applied to persons than is the former (an *amatory* letter; an *amorous* relationship between Hal and Judy).

amaze, astonish, surprise. *Amaze* means "to bewilder," "to perplex," "to astound," "to stun." Its meaning can be recalled by thinking that to be *amazed* is to be "lost in a maze": "I thought you were dead; your reappearance *amazes* me." *Astonish* means "to strike with sudden fear or wonder." To be *astonished* is to be dazed or silenced, to be "turned to stone." *Surprise* means "to take unawares." We are *amazed* at what seems extremely difficult, impossible, or improbable; we are *astonished* when our *surprise* is so great as to silence or daze us. Paralyzing (numbing) shock is implied by *astound* and its colloquial equivalent, *flabbergast.* A story is told of Dr. Samuel Johnson (1709–1784), English author and lexicographer. His wife unexpectedly came upon him kissing a household maid and said, "I am surprised." Dr. Johnson reportedly replied, "No, Madam; *I* am *surprised; you* are *astonished.*"

ambiguous, equivocal, unequivocal. *Ambiguous* means "having several possible meanings," "open to differing interpretations": "I don't understand your answer; it's *ambiguous.*" *Equivocal* is closely related in meaning to *ambiguous,* but it is more often used to signify "not determined," "of doubtful nature," "open to a double interpretation": "The judge found the loyalty of this citizen to be *equivocal.*" *Ambiguous* is applied only to written or spoken statements; *equivocal* can apply to speech, writing, actions, and ideas. *Unequivocal,* directly opposite in meaning to *equivocal,* means "clear," "having only one possible meaning or interpretation": "His refusal to pay the bill is *unequivocal.*"

amend, emend. *Amend* means "to put right," "to change for the better." We *amend* by adding or altering, as the noun *amendment* suggests. *Emend,* once merely another spelling of *amend,* has a similar meaning but is properly used only to refer to corrections or changes made in a literary or scholarly work; the corresponding noun is *emendation.* Both *amend* and *emend* are verbs; *amend* in plural form *(amends)* becomes a noun meaning "recompense" or "compensation": "He made *amends* for his careless driving."

amiable, amicable. These words are closely related in meaning; they are derived from the same Latin word meaning "friendly." *Amiable* implies sweetness of temper, kindheartedness, or good-natured obligingness. *Amicable* has somewhat similar meanings but stresses the idea of being at peace, not disposed to quarrel. "Mr. Jacks is a kindly and *amiable* employer." "All of my fellow employees are *amicable.*"

amn't. This is a contraction for *am I not?* It has not been so fully accepted or so widely used as have been *hasn't* (has not), *weren't* (were not), and other similar shortened forms. One reason for its lack of acceptance is its sound. At present, *amn't* is considered silly or pretentious.

among, between. Standard usage requires that *among* be employed to show the relationship of more than two objects or persons and that *between* be employed to refer to only two objects or, occasionally, to more than two when each object is considered in relation to others. This distinction probably traces from the fact that the *tween* in *between* comes from the Old English word for *two.* The majority of careful speakers observe this distinction, but remember that *between* can correctly refer to more than two objects in certain instances. We speak of "a trade agreement *between* Great Britain, France, and the United States" because each country has an individual obligation to each of the others. And we do not say that a triangle is the space *among* three points or that the water-level route runs *among* New York, Albany, Cleveland, and Chicago. Keep these examples in mind: "We distributed the toys *among* Heather, Greg, and Gray." "We distributed the toys *between* Jill and Gray." "Understanding *between* nations is desirable."

amoral, immoral, unmoral. *Amoral* means "not concerned with moral standards," "not to be judged by the criteria or standards of morality." Animals and morons may be considered *amoral*. *Immoral* means "wicked," "depraved," "contrary to accepted principles of right and wrong." The acts of thieves, rapists, and murderers are *immoral*. *Unmoral* means "having no morality," "unable to distinguish right from wrong." Thus, an infant or a mentally retarded person may be considered *unmoral*. *Amoral*, *unmoral*, and the less-used *nonmoral* are virtual synonyms.

amorous. *See* AMATORY.

amount, number. *Amount* is used of things involving a unified mass—bulk, weight, or sums. In accounting, it has the same meaning as *total;* generally, it is safe to use *amount* to refer to anything which can be measured. *Number* is correctly used to refer to items which can be counted in individual units. "What is the *amount* of the bill?" "He has left only a small *amount* of food." "Joe has a *number* of old suits for sale."

ample, enough. *Ample* means "more than enough," "more than adequate in size, capacity, or scope." *Enough* means "sufficient," "in or to a degree or quantity that satisfies." Since *ample* means what it does, it is silly to attempt to qualify it; "barely *ample*" and "scarcely *ample*" are illogical. Adequate synonyms: *abundance* for *ample, sufficient* or *adequate* for *enough*. "The cabin was stocked with an *ample* supply of food, *enough* to last us longer than our two-week stay." *See also* ENOUGH.

an. *See* A, AN.

analysis, synthesis. Meaning "separation of a whole into its parts," *analysis* is the antonym (opposite) of *synthesis* ("putting together"): "This is an *analysis* of the campaign for mayor." "The *synthesis* of cadmium acetate is accomplished by the interaction of acetic acid and cadmium oxide." Both *analysis* and *synthesis* are overused for the words *study, examination,* and *consideration*. Few persons other than laboratory scientists normally engage in either *analysis* or *synthesis*. Corresponding verbs, *analyze* and *synthesize,* are also often used inexactly. Noun plurals are *analyses* and *syntheses,* with the last *e* in each having the sound of *ea* in *easy*.

and all. This is what is known as a filler, a word or expression that adds little or nothing to meaning but consumes time in saying and space in writing: "You know what I mean *and all.*" This useless phrase, as well as other fillers, is likely to appear only in informal talk, hardly ever in writing.

and also. *See* ALSO.

and etc. This is a redundant expression from which *and* should be dropped. *Etc.* is an abbreviation of the Latin *et cetera* and means "and so forth." It looks out of place in formal writing. Furthermore, it cannot be pronounced in speech without sounding individual letters or giving the entire phrase. Sometimes we use *etc.* at the end of a list to suggest that much more could be added. But do we really have anything in mind?

and/or. This expression, formerly used exclusively in legal documents and business communication, has become acceptable English primarily because it is a convenient saver of time and words. *And/or* means about the same as *each and every* and is often equivalent to the simple word *or*. You can say "boots *and/or* shoes." You can also say "boots *or* shoes *or both.*" Purists object to *and/or* as being awkward and unsightly, but it is permissible in all save fastidious usage.

and so forth. This English form of *etc.* (*see* AND ETC.) is standard but is sometimes used unnecessarily at the end of a statement to suggest that something could be added. Probably all that needs to be said has been said, and anything else would be waste or wordiness.

and which, and who. Correct sentence structure provides that these phrases should appear in clauses only if preceded by clauses also containing *which* and *who*. This rule, which also applies to *but which* and *but who* clauses, is a matter of parallel construction. Do not say "He is a man of intelligence, *and who* is an industrious worker." You can omit *and* or add a *who* clause: "He is a man *who* is intelligent *and who* is an industrious worker." Better still, eliminate the verbiage and say "The man is intelligent and industrious." The best way to improve "He showed much energy at first, *but which* soon vanished" is to omit *but*.

angry, mad. *Angry* means "indignant," "wrathful," "inflamed." In idiomatic English, you may be *angry about* a situation or event, *angry at* an animal or an inanimate object, and *angry with* (not *at*) a person. In precise English, *mad* has a suggestion of abnormality, of being "disordered in intellect," "insane." A *mad* person is insane; a *mad* dog has rabies; *mad* haste is frenzied; a *mad* idea is senseless or unwise. The formal word for *wrathful* is *angry*. Colloquially (that is, informally), *mad* is often used to mean "angry," but *mad* is employed by careful speakers and writers to convey only a sense of disorder or abnormality.

annoy. *See* AGGRAVATE.

antagonist, protagonist. An *antagonist* is someone who contends with, or opposes, another in a fight, struggle, or battle of wills: "Once close friends, they became *antagonists* in the courtroom." In literature, an *antagonist* is the principal opponent of the main character involved in a play or novel, a person known as the *protagonist*. In Greek, *protagonist* meant "first combatant," the principal or central character. In Shakespeare's *Hamlet,* the *protagonist* is Hamlet; among the *antagonists* are King Claudius and Laertes. *See also* ADVERSARY.

ante-, anti-. The first of these common prefixes means "before" or "prior"; the second means "against" or "opposite": "Wait in the *anteroom* for me." "Do you have an *antidote* for this poison?"

anxious, eager. In careful use, *anxious* implies anxiety, worry, or uneasiness: "The physician was *anxious* about the pulse rate of his patient." *Eager* means "keenly desirous," "wanting to": "Bob was *eager* to see his old friend." *Eager* is rarely used where *anxious* is meant, but *anxious* is often incorrectly substituted for *eager:* "The small boy was *eager* (not *anxious*) to go fishing." One is *anxious* about something of which he is fearful. He is *eager* concerning something looked forward to.

any, any and all. *Any* is a useful word with several meanings, "one," "a," "an," "some," "no matter which," "every." "Do you have *any* money?" *Any* is considered informal (colloquial) when it is used as an adverb to mean "at all": "He did not work *any* last month." You can substitute *at all* for *any* in such a sentence. Or you can, if you wish, consider that *any* in the sentence quoted is a pronoun rather than an adverb. *Any and all* is a wordy, trite expression.

anybody. *See* ANYONE.

anyhow. This adverb means "in any manner whatever," "in any event." It is a standard word but one which is overused, vague, and imprecise. Omit *anyhow* from a sentence such as "I didn't want to go *anyhow.*"

anymore. This term, preferably spelled as one word rather than two, means "now," "at present," "from now on." It is a standard word, but when it is placed at the beginning or end of a sentence, it often is meaningless or ineffective: "*Anymore* they are coming to see us." "They are picking apples *anymore.*" Yet when used with a negative, *anymore* is standard: "Susie doesn't stay there *anymore.*" Suggestion: use *anymore* only when it is accompanied by a negative such as *not, doesn't,* or *won't.*

anyone, anybody. These pronouns are singular forms and take singular verbs: "*Is anyone* going with me?" "*Anybody is* welcome to come." They may be used interchangeably in the sense of "any person," but formal speakers and writers prefer *anyone* to *anybody,* possibly because of sound or appearance. *Anyone* should be spelled as one word except when it singles out a particular or definite person or item: "He saw three plays that week and did not enjoy *any one* of them." *Anybody* should also be spelled as one word unless you are referring to an actual body: "A homicide was thought to have been committed, but the police could not discover *any body.*"

anyplace, noplace, someplace. Preferably spelled as one word, *anyplace* is an adverb, a colloquial and informal synonym for *anywhere.* It should be avoided in careful speech and writing. As a noun, *anyplace* (or *any place*) is standard: "You may go to *anyplace* (or *any place*) you want to." The same restrictions apply to *noplace* and *someplace* when they are used adverbially, although both expressions are standard as nouns.

anyway, anyways. *Anyway* should be spelled as one word when it is used to mean "in any event," "no matter what": "Whether or not the storm is bad, we plan to leave at noon *anyway.*" In all other possible meanings, write the expression as two words: "You cannot in *any way* be blamed for the accident." *Anyways* is a nonstandard form of *anyway*, used only by illiterate or uneducated persons. As two words, the expression may be used correctly: "I can't think of *any ways* in which we could have acted differently."

anywheres. *Anywheres* is an expression characteristic of uneducated speakers. So are *nowheres* and *somewheres.* Omit the final *s* in each word; say *anywhere, nowhere, somewhere.*

apology, excuse, pardon. An *apology* is an admission of discourtesy or error together with an expression of regret. An *excuse* is a statement made or reason given for being released from blame. An *apology* accepts guilt and seeks to make amends; an *excuse* seeks to shift blame, deny guilt, and avoid censure: "Please accept my *apology* for neglecting to send you an invitation." "His *excuse* for being late is that his alarm clock failed to go off." Does one correctly say "*Excuse* me" or "*Pardon* me"? The former is a weaker expression than the latter, which implies guilt and a request for forgiveness. "*Excuse* me" is the correct term to use when asking someone to be allowed to pass or to overlook a minor matter. "*Excuse* me," should be used many times more often than "*Pardon* me," which is usually an expression of mistaken gentility and affectation.

apparent, evident. These words are closely related in meaning, but *apparent* often suggests the use of reasoning: "It is *apparent* that Jackson will win the election." *Evident* implies the existence of external signs, facts of some sort: "His sorrow was *evident.*" *Apparent* has another meaning, that of "seeming," "not necessarily real or actual": "The *apparent* unconcern of the patient did not fool Nurse Brown."

appraise, apprise, apprize. *Appraise* means "to judge," "to estimate": "The auctioneer *appraised* the furniture." *Apprise* means "to inform," "to notify": "A newspaper account *apprised* me of the tragedy." *Apprize* is another, less-used spelling of *apprise*.

apprehend, comprehend. *Apprehend* means "to seize," "to capture": "The sheriff will *apprehend* the forger." *Comprehend* means "to understand": "I did not *comprehend* the lecturer's remarks."

apprise, apprize. *See* APPRAISE.

a priori. This Latin phrase meaning "from the one before" is used in English to refer to matters not based on examination or prior study: "The lawyer made an *a priori* judgment of his client's case." Like most foreign expressions brought intact into our language, it should be used sparingly. Even so, it is an expression for which there is no satisfactory English equivalent.

apt, liable, likely. Distinctions in the meanings of these words have broken down somewhat, but careful speakers continue to observe them. *Apt* suggests fitness or tendency: "Jake is *apt* in physics." *Liable* implies exposure to something unwanted, disadvantageous, or burdensome: "The driver is *liable* for damages." *Likely* means "expected," "probable": "It is *likely* to rain today." *Likely* is the most commonly used of the three words; *apt* and *likely* are near-synonyms; use *liable* only in the sense of "responsible," "answerable."

arbitrate, mediate. Although similar in meaning, these words have different applications. *Arbitrate* means "to decide between contending or opposing parties or sides." An arbitrator actually hears evidence, arrives at a decision, and then makes an award. *Mediate* means "to act as an intermediary in a dispute," "to be a go-between." Arbitrators have no authority to *mediate,* just as mediators have no right to make ultimate decisions and issue awards. A mediator offers suggestions that may or may not be acceptable to contending parties; an arbitrator arrives at a solution intended to be binding upon both sides in a dispute: "The Family Court judge asked a marriage counselor to *mediate* the couple's disagreements." "An impartial expert was appointed to *arbitrate* the issue of fringe benefits."

aren't I? *Aren't I* is ungrammatical and not entirely logical (no one would say "I are not"). The phrase, which seems pompous or affected to most users of American English, is often employed by educated Englishmen and, occasionally, by speakers in the Northeastern part of the United States.

arise. *See* GET UP.

around. *See* ABOUT.

artless. *See* UNSOPHISTICATED.

as. One of the most useful and most overworked words in the language, *as* is a proper conjunction and adverb essential to good idiomatic English. As a conjunction, however, *as* is usually weaker (less effective) than *since, because,* and *when,* each of which is more exact: "*Since* (preferably not *as*) it was snowing, we stayed indoors." *As* is often used for a more specific *that* or *whether:* "I don't say *that* (not *as*) he was right." "I doubt *whether* (not *as*) he was correct." *As* is incorrectly used for *who* in a sentence such as "Those *as* have no tickets are out of luck" and for *whom* or *that* in "The car hit the man *as* I had just spoken to."

as . . . as, so . . . as. In negative comparisons, unusually careful writers and speakers prefer *so . . . as* to *as . . . as:* "Tom is not *so* talkative *as* his sister." But *as . . . as* is in reputable use, although the term is not considered quite *so* correct *as "so . . . as."*

as a whole, on the whole. These two phrases are trite through overuse and should usually be avoided. If you do use them, note that *as a whole* applies to a group but not necessarily to individuals; *on the whole* means "for the most part," "in general." "*As a whole,* our salesmen get much credit and attention, but some salesmen are low in prestige and income." "*On the whole,* the storm did little damage."

as follows. *See* FOLLOWS.

as good as. This expression indicates comparison: "This suit is *as good as* that one." But it is a wordy substitute for *practically* in sentences such as "He *as good as* promised to go" and "This suit is *as good as* new." *See also* PRACTICALLY.

ashamed of, ashamed for. Ordinarily, use *ashamed of:* "I am *ashamed of* myself (*of* them, *of* their deed)." Use *ashamed for* only when referring to someone who should be, but isn't, *ashamed of* himself: "I am *ashamed for* the team's action."

aside from. This is a wordy expression more economically expressed by *besides:* "*Besides* (or *aside from*) his cruelty, he was also arrogant."

as if, as though, like. Each of these expressions is permissible. *As if* is used more often in speech and in informal writing than is *as though,* which is preferred by careful writers. Both expressions are followed by a verb in the subjunctive mood: "He left the room *as though (as if)* he were angry." In informal or substandard use, *like* sometimes substitutes for *as if* and *as though* but is never followed by the subjunctive mood. *See also* LIKE.

ask a question. The verb *ask* means "to inquire about," "to put a question to." In nearly every conceivable situation and meaning, *a question* should be omitted from *ask a question; ask* implies a question and should stand alone: "A member of the audience *asked* (not *asked a question*) about inflation."

as per, as regards. *As per* is an overworked business expression for *in accordance with* or *according to.* Often the expression itself, as well as its less-tired equivalents, is not needed at all. *As regards* is a wordy and overworked expression for *concerning* or *about.* It is an example of jargon and should be avoided. *See also* REGARD.

assay, essay. *Assay* means "a test" or "to test": "The chemist started to *assay* the mineral." *Essay* means "to attempt," "an attempt," or "a literary effort": "Will you *essay* this difficult task?" "This is a delightfully written *essay.*"

assist. *See* HELP.

assume, presume. These words have related but distinguishable meanings. To *assume* is "to take for granted," "to infer without proof": "Mrs. Black *assumed* that her husband had paid the bill." To *presume* is "to believe something to be a fact," "to infer as true without actual proof to the contrary." When Stanley came upon another explorer in the jungle, he did not say "Dr. Livingstone, I *assume*" but "Dr. Livingstone, I *presume?*" because circumstances clearly indicated that the man he was meeting could be no one else. In ordinary conversation, however, the words may be used interchangeably.

assure, ensure, insure. *Assure* means "to convince," "to guarantee": "I *assure* you of my good intentions." *Ensure* and *insure* mean "to make certain," "to guard against loss": "Please *insure* this package." *Insure,* the preferred spelling, is applied to both people and property, but *assure* usually refers only to persons.

as though. *See* AS IF.

as to. Are these words necessary? Usually, a more precise single word will serve better. "Eleanor was in doubt *as to* his meaning" is better expressed "Eleanor was in doubt *about* his meaning." *As to whether* is even more useless and wordy. Instead of saying "Sandy expressed concern *as to whether* it would snow," say "Sandy expressed concern *that* it would snow." *As to where* can usually be shortened to *where*.

astonish. *See* AMAZE.

at, at about, at all. *At* is a preposition and requires an object. One should not ask "Where are you staying *at?*" but "What motel are you staying *at?*" or, better, "*At* what motel are you staying?" *At* is unnecessary in expressions such as *at about* and *at around* (*see* ABOUT). *At all,* meaning "to the slightest degree," is nonstandard when used in a statement such as "They were thoughtless *at all.*" When used to mean "wholly" or "completely," *at all* should be replaced by *of all:* "Sue is the finest girl *of all.*"

at, in. These two prepositions are among the most used words in the language; "look *at* her," "*at* the door," "*at* night," "*at* the party," "*at* noon," "*at* the controls," "*at* peace"; "*in* the rain," "*in* a moment," "struck *in* the leg," "*in* cash," "*in* control," "*in* fear," "*in* haste." But can these two words be used interchangeably? If you are a native speaker of English, your sense of idiom will not fail you: you will say "I am all *at* sea" but "Whales live *in* the sea." And yet, do you arrive *in* a city or *at* a city? An airplane arrives *at* its destination, but does it arrive *in* or *at* a city? Is there a distinction between reaching a place and arriving at a place and then entering it? No clear rules can be stated for the use of these words. Let your ear and your sense of idiom be your guides.

at about, at all. *See* AT, AT ABOUT, AT ALL.

atheist. *See* AGNOSTIC.

attend to, tend to. *Tend to* is more often used than *attend to:* "Please *tend* to the store while I'm away." However, *attend to* is idiomatically more acceptable in the sense of "to wait upon" or "to care for": "Will you *attend to* that customer?" "Kindly *attend to* this matter at once." *Tend to* has the more exact meaning of "to lean toward": "Sam *tends to* be cautious about new ideas." In many constructions, *to* can be omitted from either phrase.

au. This is a term from French meaning "to the," "at the," "with the." It is considered an affectation to use foreign words unnecessarily, but there is no suitable English equivalent for *au* in such phrases as *au beurre* ("with butter"), *au contraire* ("on the opposite side," "to the contrary"), *au fait* ("expert" or "experienced"), *au gratin* ("with cheese"), and *au naturel* ("in the natural state"). Unlike *à la*, it is always used with another French word. *See also* À LA.

audience. Because *audience* is derived from a Latin word meaning "to hear," some experts insist that the word can properly apply only to a group of persons engaged in listening. Such purists feel that where looking (seeing) is the primary activity involved, persons comprising an *audience* should be called *spectators*. *Audience* is now widely and acceptably applied to listeners and viewers collectively—to persons attending a theater or concert as well as those reached by radio or television broadcasts, by books, newspapers, and magazines, and by public speakers: "The studio *audience* was convulsed with laughter." "Many works of art have a wide and devoted *audience*."

audio. *See* VIDEO.

aught, ought, naught. *Aught* means "any little part," "in any respect": "You are right for *aught* I know." *Ought* indicates duty, obligation: "Everyone *ought* to attend the meeting." *Naught* means "nothing," "zero": "Our work availed *naught.*"

aural. *See* ORAL.

authentic, genuine. These words may be used interchangeably to mean "trustworthy," "reliable." *Authentic* has an added meaning of "not fictitious," "not false or copied": "This is an *authentic* seventeenth-century antique." *Genuine* has an additional meaning of "sincere," "free from pretense": "My friend Sally is a *genuine* person."

author. An *author* is a person who writes, one who practices writing as his profession or vocation. The use of the word as a transitive verb (to *author* a book) is widespread but is not considered standard. Instead of "to *author*" say "to *write*" or "to *compose*" or "to *create.*"

autograph. *See* SIGNATURE.

avenge, revenge. *Avenge* is used in the sense of achieving justice: "Jim *avenged* his mother's injury." *Revenge* stresses retaliation and usually has for its subject the person wronged: "He *revenged* himself" or "He *revenged* the injury done to him."

average, median, mean. *Average* applies to what is midway between extremes on a scale of evaluation. With a series of numbers, you would find the *average* by adding them and dividing by their number. You would find the *median* by discovering the middle number in an arithmetically arranged series. You would find the *mean* by adding the two extreme numbers and dividing by 2. Thus, with the numbers 4, 6, 8, 12, and 15, the *average* would be 9, the *median* would be 8, and the *mean* would be 9½.

averse. *See* ADVERSE.

avert, divert. These words are both based upon a Latin term meaning "to turn," but they have different meanings and applications in English. *Avert* means "to turn away," "to ward off": "He quickly *averted* his eyes." "Drive carefully and try to *avert* an accident." *Divert* means "to turn aside," "to distract," "to entertain": "Listen carefully; don't let anything *divert* your attention." "After the conference, the diplomats *diverted* their minds by attending a musical comedy." *See also* ADVERT.

avocation, vocation, calling. *Avocation* suggests a hobby, something one does apart from regular work. One's *vocation* is one's calling, one's principal endeavor or source of livelihood. "My *vocation* is teaching school, but my *avocation* is gardening." *Calling* is synonymous with *vocation* but is usually applied to work that has been entered as a result of a call, summons, or strong impulse: "He began the study of theology as a result of an inner *calling.*" "He felt a *calling* to become a minister."

awake, awaken. *See* WAKE.

award, reward. *Award* implies a decision or something given as a prize. *Reward* usually refers to something given in recompense for a good deed or for merit. "Jack received an *award* for his flower display." "The fireman received a *reward* for saving the child's life."

aware, conscious. *Aware* implies knowing something either by perception or through information: "The lecturer was *aware* that he had lost his audience." *Conscious* has much the same meaning but is more often applied to a physical situation: "The injured player was *conscious* but could not stand." In informal use, the words are employed interchangeably.

away. This frequently used adverb has many meanings, all acceptable in standard English: "hence," "far," "aside." As an adjective, *away* means "absent," "gone," "distant." *Away* is colloquial when used to mean "without delay," "immediately," as in "All right, sing *away*" and "Let's leave right *away*."

awhile, a while. These words cause trouble with spelling, but their meanings are easily distinguished. *While* is a noun meaning "a period of time" and with *a* is correctly spelled and pronounced as two words in a sentence such as "Ellie had to wait *a while* for the bus." The meaning of *awhile* is "*for* a period or interval of time." The *for* is definitely part of the meaning, so that it is wordy to write "I then rested for *awhile*." The distinction between *awhile* (an adverb) and *while* (a noun) is shown in this sentence: "He asked me to stay *awhile*, just a little *while* longer."

axiom, adage, proverb. An *axiom* is a universally accepted rule or principle or a self-evident truth: "There can be only one straight line between two points." "It is an *axiom* of economics that supply and demand are closely related." An *adage* is a statement given credit by long usage and general acceptance: "It never rains but it pours." "It is always darkest before the dawn." A *proverb* is a short saying, usually of unknown origin, that expresses a useful thought or commonplace truth: "A rolling stone gathers no moss." "A stitch in time saves nine." The general word *saying* embraces the meanings of these terms and also those of *aphorism*, *maxim*, *apothegm*, *epigram*, and *motto*.

B

back of, in back of, behind. Use of *back of* and *in back of* to mean "behind" is widespread, but opinions differ as to their respectability. Each should be considered standard, but both are wordy and can safely be omitted in favor of *behind:* "The wheelbarrow is *behind (back of* or *in back of)* the barn." No one questions the reputability of *in front of,* although *before* is shorter and normally will serve as well.

backward, backwards. The first of these terms is generally preferred to mean "toward the back or rear," "in the reverse," "retrogressive," or "bashful." It can always be used in these meanings, whereas *backwards* is improper in a sentence such as "Jack was a *backwards* youth." One can move *forward* or *backward* or *backwards,* but why not use the shorter form in every instance?

bacteria. *See* GERM.

bad, badly. *Bad* is an adjective, *badly* an adverb. Despite this clear grammatical distinction, people tend to say "I feel *badly*" about as often as the more correct "I feel *bad.*" In time, distinction between the forms may break down further, but as of now "I feel *bad*" is preferable. When the verb is to be modified, that is, when one is referring to a sense of touch, or feel, only *badly* is accurate: the student learning braille might say, "I feel *badly* this morning."

balance. The use of *balance* in an extended sense of "rest" or "remainder" is debatable and should be avoided except in informal speaking situations. The central meanings of *balance* deal with weighing and bookkeeping. Say "The *remainder* (not *balance*) of the day was wasted." Also, "on *balance*" has become a tiresome phrase through overuse.

baleful, baneful. These "look-alikes" mean "harmful," "pernicious," "menacing." In ordinary use, the words are interchangeable, although *baneful* also means "poisonous" and is normally applied to substances, causes, and influences that result in death. "The gathering clouds promised a *baleful* storm." "Some poisons are merely injurious, but others are *baneful.*" You are not likely to be arrested if you give a rival a *baleful* glance, but watch out if you give him a *baneful* dose of arsenic.

bank on. This trite expression is overused to mean "to depend on," "to count on": "You can *bank on* his giving you bad advice." In this sense the phrase departs from its original meaning of making bank in gambling games. The literal meaning of *bank on* is not "to rely on" but "to be absolutely certain of": "You can *bank on* this, a gamble that you cannot lose."

barbaric, barbarous. These words are closely related to each other and to such terms as *barbarian, barbarism,* and *barbarity*. Both *barbaric* and *barbarous* are adjectives meaning "uncivilized," "primitive," "without civilizing influences." *Barbaric* is occasionally used in a favorable sense to refer to those elements in a culture, such as vigor, ardor, and love of splendor, that the speaker or writer finds praiseworthy (a splendidly *barbaric* people). *Barbarous* is more often used to refer to the cruel and vicious customs and practices of uncivilized groups (the inhuman deeds of *barbarous* Huns).

barely. *See* HARDLY.

basal. *See* BASIC.

based on. This phrase is not an absolute participle such as are *considering* and *given*. As a result, a sentence such as "*Based on* your record, you are clearly qualified for the job" is ungrammatical because *based on* is a dangling modifier with nothing to attach to. Instead of using *based on* in such a statement, try *given* or *considering* or *on the basis of*.

basic, basal. Each of these words means "fundamental." *Basal* is rarely used except in such phrases as "*basal* metabolism," but *basic* is overused in the senses of "fundamental" and "bottom." Instead of referring to "Jim's *basic* problem in learning," why not say *fundamental?* Instead of writing "the *basic* salary for this position" why not refer to the *bottom* or *starting* salary?

bear, borne, born. *Bear* has numerous meanings, one of which has to do with procreation: carrying and giving birth to something or someone. In this sense, the past participle *borne* is the correct form for all active constructions and for passive constructions followed by *by:* "Ten children have been *borne* by Mrs. James." "Mrs. James has *borne* ten children." *Born,* also a past participle, is the correct form for all other passive constructions dealing with birth: "One of Mrs. James's children was *born* in Singapore."

because. This conjunction is definite and specific in its meaning of "since" or "for the reason that." It is used solely to express cause or reason: "He left the party early *because* he was tired." As a subordinating conjunction, *because* should not be used to mean "that" (a relative pronoun); say "The reason is *that,*" not "The reason is *because.*" We do not say "The cause is *because*"; logically, we should state not the cause for the reason but the reason itself. "The reason for my absence was illness" is more concise and more logical than "The reason for my absence was *because* of illness" or ". . . *because* I was ill." Also, note that "*because* of the fact that" is an excessively wordy expression.

begin, commence. These words are alike in meaning—"to start," "to originate," "to cause to come into being": "Come on, let's *begin* the meeting." "When will the fireworks display *commence?*" *Commence* is stronger in its suggestion of initiative, of action originated by some person or force; it is also a more formal word than *begin:* "The prosecuting attorney will *commence* proceedings in the trial." In normal speech and writing, prefer the shorter, less formal *begin.*

beg to advise. This expression is overworked, particularly in business correspondence. "I *beg to advise* you that your valued order has been received" can more simply and economically be expressed by omitting all words before *your:* "Your valued order. . . ."

behind. *See* BACK OF.

being as, being as how, being that. Each of these phrases borders on illiteracy; all are vague, wordy, and illogical. Say "*Because* (not *being as, being as how,* or *being that*) I am already here, I'll help."

believe, feel. Precisely, *believe* suggests "to have convictions about," "to judge," "to think"; *feel* indicates emotion rather than reason. In daily use, the words are interchangeable: "I *feel* (or I *believe*) that we should go." Careful distinction is shown in such a sentence as "I *feel* cheerful when I hear from you, because I *believe* you still like me."

belittle, disparage. These words are related in meaning: "to speak of as unimportant," "to regard something as less important or impressive than it apparently is." *Disparage* is a stronger word than *belittle* in that it tends to bring reproach or discredit upon the topic being considered, whereas *belittle* means simply "to make less," "to minimize": "Don't *belittle* my efforts; I'm trying hard." "The prosecuting attorney *disparaged* the testimony of the witness."

belly. *See* ABDOMEN.

beside, besides. In reputable usage, *beside* is usually a preposition meaning "by the side of." *Besides,* also a preposition, meaning "except," is more commonly used as an adverb in the sense of "moreover" and "in addition to." "I am resting *beside* (not *besides*) the stream." "I have more work to do; *besides* (not *beside*) I am not in the mood to go."

be sure and. Each of these three words is inoffensive, but the idea which their combination expresses should be conveyed by "be sure *to.*" In such a construction, what follows *be sure* is always an infinitive, not a group of words connected by *and: "Be sure to* (not *and*) let me hear from you."

bet. *See* GAMBLE.

better had. This is a substandard (illiterate) expression used to mean "should," "must," or "ought to." When one is told to do something, a nonreputable reply would be "I guess I *better had."* These two words reversed (*had better,* meaning that something would be safe or wise or to one's advantage) are also often substituted for *ought* or *should,* but inversion does not remove the inexactness. Also illiterate are some other forms of these expressions: *would better* and *'d better* (you'd better). *See also* HAD BETTER.

between. *See* AMONG.

between you and me. This is a standard phrase, grammatically and idiomatically acceptable. It is overused, however, in situations in which a speaker or writer attempts to create an atmosphere of familiarity or shared secrets: "Don't tell anyone, but just *between you and me. . . .*" *Between* is a preposition in this construction and requires a following pronoun (or noun) in the objective case: *me, him, her*. Avoid the mistake of saying *"between* you and *I"* or *"between* you and *she."*

bewilder. *See* PUZZLE, PERPLEX, BEWILDER.

biannual, biennial. A distinction exists between *biannual* ("twice a year," "semiannual") and *biennial* ("once in two years" or "lasting two years"). Fix in mind that *bimonthly* means "every two months" and that its use as "twice a month," or "semimonthly," is nonstandard. *Biweekly* means "once in two weeks." If you remain in doubt, it's always safe to say, somewhat wordily, "twice a month" and "twice a week." *See also* BIMONTHLY.

big, large. Each of these words refers to quantity and size and in most speaking and writing situations can be used interchangeably (a *big* building, a *large* building). *Large,* however, carries a meaning of immensity or importance not conveyed by *big* (a man of *large* vision rather than a man of *big* vision). *Big* carries additional meanings of generosity or kindness, as in the phrases "a *big* heart" and "a *big* man in every way." Although distinctions in meaning have broken down somewhat and although *big* is more often used than *large*, your language sense will tell you to use *big* when you mean either size or importance and *large* when there is an added suggestion of scope or range: "a *big* liar," not "a *large* liar," and "a man of *large* outlook" rather than "a man of *big* outlook." But remember that *big* is an overworked term and that it appears in numerous trite, slangy expressions that should be avoided in all but informal conversation: *"big* on" ("enthusiastic about"); "talk *big"* ("to speak boastfully"); "go over *big"* ("to be successful"); *"big* cheese," *"big* shot" ("important person"); *"big* eye" ("invitation," "summons"); *"big* idea" ("unsolicited or objectionable proposal or plan"); *"big* mouth" ("loud person"); *"big* talk" ("exaggeration"); "*big* time" ("enjoyable time," "high level"); *"big* wheel," *"big* wig" ("influential person"); *"big* head" ("conceit," "egotism"); *"big* house" ("penitentiary"). It's possible that you use *big* in even more expressions than those listed here. Be *big* and avoid them all.

bilateral. *See* UNILATERAL.

bimonthly. *See* BIANNUAL. Because *bi-* (a learned borrowing from Latin) can correctly mean both "two" and "twice," our language would be more exact if we employed *semi-* ("half") more often. A good rule to follow is this: use *bi-* to mean "two" and *semi-* to mean "half."

bipartisan, partisan, bipartite. *Bipartisan* is made up of the prefix *bi-*, meaning "two," and *partisan*, meaning "an adherent or supporter." Thus we refer to "a strongly *partisan* member of the Democratic party" and to "a *bipartisan* foreign policy supported by Democrats and Republicans." Soldiers fighting against an invader of their country may be called *partisans;* members of a United Nations force attempting to keep peace in a country may be referred to as *bipartisan. Bipartite* means "joint," "shared by two," "in two parts": "Germany and Italy signed a *bipartite* pact prior to World War II. After World War II, Germany had a *bipartite* government of occupying forces and its own leaders."

bisect. This word can mean only "to cut or divide into two parts": "This is where the road *bisects* the railroad tracks." *Bisect* and *dissect* should not be confused. One *bisects* a laboratory animal when he divides it into two equal or nearly equal parts; he *dissects* it when he cuts it into numerous segments.

biweekly. *See* BIANNUAL.

black. *See* NEGRO.

blame it on me, blame me for it. When a preposition is needed with the verb *blame,* standard idiomatic usage requires *for:* "She *blamed* me *for* the accident," not "She *blamed* the accident *on* me." The construction *"blame* on" (*Blame* this situation *on* your employee) is becoming acceptable, although formal usage would stipulate "*Blame* your employee *for* . . ." or "Place the *blame on*. . . ."

blatant, flagrant. *Blatant* means "offensively noisy" and "brazenly obvious" (a *blatant* orchestra, a *blatant* lie). *Flagrant* means "shocking" and "disgraceful" (a *flagrant* criminal act, a *flagrant* oversight). *Blatant* stresses offensiveness and noisiness; *flagrant* emphasizes evil and wrongdoing. One who eats peas with his knife commits a *blatant* error. One who drives a car on the highway while drunk performs a *flagrant* act.

bloc, block. A *bloc* is a group or coalition such as "a *bloc* of voters" or "a *bloc* of legislators opposed to the bill." In political campaigns, reference is made to the farm *bloc* and the labor *bloc*. *Block* has numerous meanings, the most common of which refers to a part of a town or city enclosed by four neighboring streets: "This *block* contains four large stores."

bloom, blossom. Each of these words refers to the flower of a plant. One may correctly say "The cherry tree is in *bloom*" or "It is in *blossom.*" One may also say "The cherry tree *bloomed*" or "It *blossomed.*" When used figuratively, that is, in a nonliteral sense, these words have slightly different applications. One would refer to the *bloom* (not the *blossom*) of youth. One would more suitably write "The slight youth *blossomed* into a sturdy athlete" than "He *bloomed* into one." Why not use *flower* and avoid worrying about the minor distinctions involved?

boat, ship. A *boat* is a small vessel, one propelled by oars, sails, or an outboard motor: "We rowed our *boat* to a nearby island." A *ship* is a large or seagoing craft, powered by engines or sails: "The *ship* required five days to cross the Atlantic." This distinction breaks down, however, in such terms as *ferryboat* and *PT boat*. Strictly speaking, one would go to Europe by *ship*, not by *boat;* yet this usage is often ignored by even educated speakers and writers. If in doubt, say *vessel* or even *craft* and avoid any possible confusion. It may also help to remember that an airplane is sometimes referred to as a *ship*, not a *boat*.

borne, born. *See* BEAR.

bourgeois, proletariat. *Bourgeois* refers to a member of the so-called middle class, sometimes defined as persons engaged in shopkeeping, merchandising, and similar pursuits. As an adjective, *bourgeois* means "conventional," "characterized by materialistic concerns or activities." The general meaning of *bourgeois* may be inferred from its origin: a *burgess* is, or was, a citizen who was neither of the nobility nor a serf. *Proletariat* refers to persons who depend for support upon employment rather than property. The word is derived from a Latin phrase referring to individuals who contributed to the state only through their offspring. In brief, *bourgeois* means "middle-class," and *proletarian* means "working-class." Most Americans do not think of themselves as being either *bourgeois* or *proletarian*.

brand-new. This expression, meaning "entirely new," "fresh," "unused," may also be spelled *bran-new*. *Brand-new* is preferred.

breadth. *See* BREATH.

breakdown. This word has two primary meanings: "a wearing out, collapse" and "analysis, decomposition": "Millie suffered a *breakdown* following the accident." "The factory was closed because of a *breakdown* in machinery." "The treasurer made a careful *breakdown* of income and expenses." In the second of its meanings, *breakdown* is overused and loosely used. Instead of using this word vaguely, occasionally say *analysis, classification, examination,* or *itemization. See also* ANALYSIS.

breath, breathe. A *breath* is an exhalation of air. To *breathe* is "to take in (or exhale) air. "His *breath* was frozen in the cold air." "*Breathe* deeply and you will feel better." Neither *breath* nor *breathe* should be confused with *breadth,* meaning "distance" or "width": "The stream was 50 feet in *breadth.*"

bridegroom. *See* GROOM.

brief, short. *Brief* applies especially to duration of time (a *brief* stay in a hospital). *Brief* also means "concise," "curt," and "succinct": "The chairman made a *brief* talk of only five minutes." *Short* applies to both time and space: "That was a *short* meeting." "Joe is a *short* man." It is informal to refer to "a *brief* distance" or "a *brief* skirt." That is, *short* can be used in almost any situation, but *brief* should be applied only in circumstances involving time.

bring, take. *Bring* indicates movement toward a place identified with the speaker; it suggests "to come here with." *Take* suggests movement away from such a place and indicates "to go there with." One *takes* money to a supermarket and *brings* home groceries (and no money). In ordinary usage, these words are often interchanged, but the distinction just noted persists to a degree. You can *take* or *bring* someone to a party, *take* or *bring* someone to have lunch, but the word selected has some bearing upon the relationship to the speaker of the place involved in the action.

Both *bring* and *take* combine with many prepositions to form phrases with distinct meanings: "*bring* about," "*bring* around," "*bring* down," "*bring* forward," "*bring* in," "*bring* off," "*bring* on," "*bring* out," "*bring* over," "*bring* to," "*bring* up"; "*take* aback," "*take* after," "*take* apart," "*take* back," "*take* for," "*take* on," "*take* over," "*take* to," "*take* up." Each word also appears in many trite expressions, normally to be avoided. "*Take* it lying down," "*take* it on the chin," "*take* a back seat," and "*take* five" are examples. So, too, are "*bring* to an end," a wordy expression since *end* conveys the full idea, as it does in "put an *end* to" and "come to an *end.*" The cliché "*bring* to a head" is really an unpleasant expression, as well as being trite and wordy: it means "to cause pus to form." Why not say, instead, *precipitate* or *crystallize?* "*Bring* to a boil" and "*bring* to a climax" are less unpleasant but equally trite expressions.

bring up. In the sense of "to rear," "to care for during childhood," this term is acceptable but is considered less refined and somewhat more informal than *rear* (*see* RAISE). Use *bring up* in ordinary conversation if it is a term widely used in your locality; use *rear* in writing and in all formal speaking situations. *Bringing-up* is acceptable in the sense of "upbringing" and "childhood training" but is less preferred than *rearing* and *upbringing*. As a verb meaning "to introduce" (Why *bring up* that subject?), the term is tiresomely overused. Possible substitutes for *bring up* in this meaning are *introduce, inject, advance,* and *suggest*.

brittle. *See* FRAGILE.

broad, wide. Each of these adjectives is used to indicate horizontal extent. *Broad* is preferable when the word it modifies is a surface or expanse viewed as such (*broad* stream, *broad* field, *broad* shoulders). *Wide* is preferably used when the sense of space is stressed (the table is 4 feet *wide*) or when the distance across a surface is mentioned indefinitely (The lake is *wide* at that point). These words are often interchangeable, but idiomatic usage normally prevails: "*wide* mouth," "*broad* grin."

broadcast, broadcasted. The past tense and past participle of *broadcast* ("to transmit—to cast abroad—programs from a television or radio station") are either *broadcast* or *broadcasted:* "The program was *broadcast* (or *broadcasted*) at noon." "The senator *broadcast* (or *broadcasted*) his appeal yesterday." Because the principal parts of *cast* are *cast, cast, cast, broadcast* may sound better to your ear, but widespread usage has made *broadcasted* an also-acceptable form.

brochure, leaflet, pamphlet. A *brochure* (derived from a French word meaning "to stitch") is a paper-covered booklet, usually not longer than 24 pages. A *leaflet* is a small flat or folded sheet of printed matter, usually not exceeding 4 pages in length. A *pamphlet* is a complete unbound publication of less than 100 pages, stitched or stapled together. These terms are often used interchangeably, understandably so, since neither the printing trades nor dictionary makers have agreed on their precise meanings. If the printed item is quite small, call it a *leaflet;* if larger, a *brochure;* if almost the length of a small book, a *pamphlet*.

bulk. This word refers to mass, volume, and size: "The steamship was of great *bulk.*" It is also used to refer to the greater part of something (the *bulk* of mankind). The alternative to *bulk* in this second meaning is *majority,* a term which indicates or suggests counted numbers. It is permissible to refer to the *bulk* of the armed forces (mass, size, volume) but preferable to say "the *majority* of those present" rather than "the *bulk* of those present."

bunch. A *bunch* is a group of similar items (a *bunch* of flowers, a *bunch* of sticks). It is informal when applied to a crowd, group of people, or set of acquaintances; "our *group* (or *crowd* or *set* or *coterie*)" is preferable to "our *bunch.*"

burglar. *See* ROBBER.

burlesque, parody. *Burlesque* is an imitation intended to ridicule by exaggeration; it consists of an attitude, style, or idea handled by distortion in such a way that an important or significant subject is treated trivially. Discrepancy between subject matter and style is the essence of *burlesque*. *Parody* is a humorous, satirical imitation of a person or event. It is designed to make fun of or to criticize by clever duplication. A striptease act is a *burlesque* of legitimate dancing, singing, and acting. A comedian delivering his version of the Gettysburg Address is engaged in *parody*. Related terms are *caricature, lampoon, travesty,* and *satire*.

burned, burnt. Each of these forms is correctly considered a principal part of the verb *to burn: burn, burned* or *burnt* (past tense), *burned* or *burnt* (past participle). Don't worry about which form to use; use the one you prefer. However, it would be well to avoid both when you mean "disillusioned" or "cheated"; also, "to *burn* oneself out" is an exceptionally trite phrase, as is "*burned* up" ("angry").

burst. *See* BUST.

business. This term is overworked as an approximate synonym for *commerce, traffic, trade, industry, calling, vocation, company, firm, duty,* or *employment*. Expressions such as "to mean *business,*" "get down to *business,*" "mind one's own *business,*" and "have no *business*" are as trite as they are inexact. "To give one the *business* (or the *works)*" is slang at its best—or worst.

bust, burst. The principal parts of *burst* are *burst, burst, burst*. As verb forms, *bust* and *busted* are illiteracies. "To get *busted*" ("to be arrested"), "to go *bust*" ("to become bankrupt"), "to *bust* up" ("to disagree," "to break up"), and "a *bust*" ("failure") are slang expressions.

but also. *See* NOT ONLY . . . BUT ALSO.

but what. This phrase is informally used for *but that:* "I don't know *but what* (better, *but that*) I had better go with you." Use *but that* instead of *but what* in all statements such as "Scarcely an hour goes by *but that* I think of you with love."

but which, but who. *See* AND WHICH.

by. This word has many reputable uses as a preposition, adjective, and noun. Such phrases as "*by* the same token," "*by* and *by*," "*by* the *by*," "*by* the boards," and "*by* and large" are tiresomely overused; the last-named not only is hackneyed but is usually a meaningless conversational filler. "*Bye* now" and "*bye-bye*" are baby talk for *good-by*.

by about. This is a wordy phrase from which *by* can usually be omitted. Drop it from a sentence such as "I can be ready *by about* midnight." *See also* ABOUT.

C

cache, hide, stash. As a noun *cache* means a hiding place, and as a verb it means "to conceal": "The Joneses placed their silverware in a *cache* upstairs." "You had better *cache* that money somewhere so that it won't be discovered." *Hide,* the most commonly used of these three related words, means "to put or keep out of sight": "*Hide* that letter in the file." *Stash* is an informal word of unknown origin that means precisely what *cache* does. Differences in use are slight: *cache* involves concealment in a place unknown to others and suggests storage with a view to later use; *hide* refers to putting physical items out of sight and also to disguising or withholding one's thoughts and feelings. Substitutes for these three words include *secrete, bury, conceal, screen,* and *cloak.*

calculate, reckon, guess. These words are localisms for *think, suppose,* and *expect.* Each has standard and reputable meanings (for example, one can *calculate* a mathematical problem), but each should be avoided as narrowly dialectal and somewhat old-fashioned terms for forming a mental concept.

calling. *See* AVOCATION.

can, may, might. *Can* suggests mental or physical ability: "Jane *can* sing beautifully when she tries." *May* implies permission or sanction: "Babs *may* borrow my suitcase if she wishes." This distinction between *can* and *may* is illustrated thus: "Jim *can* swim, but his mother says that he *may* not." *May* also expresses possibility and wish (desire): "It *may* snow tonight (possibility)." "*May* you have a good rest this weekend (desire)." *Might* is used after a governing verb in the past tense, *may* after such a verb in the present tense: "She says that we *may* go." "She said that we *might* go."

cancel out. *Cancel* means "to cross out," "to offset," "to delete." Therefore *out* is not needed and should be "canceled" from this tiresomely overused and wordy expression: "This order will *cancel* (not *cancel out*) our plans."

candid, frank. These terms mean "open," "sincere," "without reservation," "straightforward." Thus we may speak of a "*frank* statement" or "a *candid* reply," meaning something that is without disguise, pretense, or reserve. *Candid,* derived from a Latin term meaning "to glow," is less blunt in meaning than *frank;* a *candid* remark is less outspoken and perhaps more tactful than a *frank* one, but the meanings of these terms are normally interchangeable. Approximate synonyms include *open, unrestrained, uninhibited,* and *outspoken.*

cannot. This term should be spelled as one word *(cannot)* unless you wish to emphasize *not.* Such usage is rare, but it is permissible in a statement such as "I can hear you, but I *can not* understand you." Use of *can't* for *cannot* is sanctioned by widespread usage and is preferable except in very formal writing and speaking situations.

cannot (can't) help but. In this expression, *but* should be omitted because its use results in a double negative *(cannot,* or *can't,* and *but).* Instead of saying "I *can't help but* think you are mistaken," say "I *can't help* thinking you are mistaken," a more concise statement with no double negative involved. *See also* DOUBLE NEGATIVE.

can't hardly. Omit the *not* in the contraction so as to avoid a double negative. Prefer *can hardly* to *can't hardly* (and *can't scarcely*). *See also* DOUBLE NEGATIVE.

can't seem to. Is *seem to* ever needed in this expression? Doesn't *can't* express the idea by itself? What does *seem to* really add?

canvas, canvass. *Canvas* is a kind of cloth. To *canvass* is "to request," "to solicit." "The *canvas* of the tent was covered with pine needles." "Jim was asked to *canvass* the block for donations to the United Chest."

capable. This word means "having adequate capacity to do, make, or receive an action": "Larry is a *capable* player." "This problem is *capable* of solution." A common error arises from using *able* for *capable* in one of these senses: "This law is *capable* (not *able*) of being enacted." One should say "I am *able to solve* this problem" and "I am *capable of solving* this problem."

capacity. *See* ABILITY.

capital, capitol. The first of these words may be employed in all meanings except that of a building. A *capitol* is an edifice, a building. "He raised new *capital* for the company." "The sightseeing bus in the *capital* passed the state *capitol.*"

carat, caret, carrot, karat. *Carat* refers to weight: "The diamond weighed 1 *carat.*" A *caret* is a mark: "Use a *caret* to show the missing letter." A *carrot* is a vegetable beloved by rabbits and some people: "A *carrot* may be edible if it is scraped." *Karat* is a variant spelling of *carat.*

care to. In such expressions as "Do you *care to* play?" this substitute for *prefer to* or *want to* is an overworked phrase.

carrot. *See* CARAT.

carton, cartoon. A *carton* is a box, especially one made of corrugated paper; a *cartoon* is a drawing. The two words also differ in spelling and pronunciation: carton (KART·un), cartoon (kar·TOON).

case. In origin, *case* really is two different words, one derived from a form meaning "receptacle" or "container," the other meaning "instance" or "example." In both senses, the word has been abused and overused. *Case* is slang in such expressions as "*case* the joint" ("to examine the place or premises") and "Jack's a *case*" ("Jack is an eccentric or peculiar person"). The phrase "the *case* of" is nearly always verbiage and adds nothing to any statement: omit it in both speaking and writing.

casual, causal. This pair of words is often mispronounced and misspelled. *Casual,* meaning "relaxed," "unconcerned," "not planned," is pronounced "KAZH·oo·uhl" or "KAZH·yoo·uhl"; *causal* means "involving a cause" or "expressing a cause" and is pronounced "KO·zel," with the *o* sounded like *aw* in *paw*. The difference in meaning between these words is illustrated in this sentence: "The *causal* element in his failure was his *casual* approach to work."

catchup. *See* CATSUP.

category, class. Although *category* has come to be used in the sense of any division, classification, or even *class,* it is correctly employed to refer only to a scheme of classification, a specific division of some topic or item usually in the fields of science or philosophy. A *class* is a number of items or persons considered as forming a group. "This *class* of students is working exceptionally well." "A spider belongs in the *category* of arachnids that spin webs."

catholic, Roman Catholic. When spelled with a small *c*, *catholic* means "universal," "widespread," "of interest or appeal to many." When we say of someone that she has *catholic* tastes or interests, we mean that she is broad-minded and far-ranging in her attitudes and concerns. When spelled with a capital *C*, the word usually refers to the Roman Catholic Church or to an adherent of that faith. The word *Catholic* is normally used to distinguish a person or a religious faith from *Protestant* or *Jewish;* the word *catholic* does not necessarily have any religious meaning at all.

catsup. This word is interchangeable with *ketchup* and may also be spelled *catchup*. *Ketchup* is preferred by precise speakers, largely because this term for any of various sauces for meat and fish is derived from a Chinese word, *ke-tsiap,* meaning "pickled-fish brine."

causal. *See* CASUAL.

cause, cause of. *Cause* and *reason* are often confused in meaning. *Reason* is what one produces to account for or justify an effect; *cause* is what actually produces an effect. "His *reason* for speaking is clear." "The *cause* of his leaving early is debatable." *Cause of* and *on account of* do not have the same meaning. "The *cause of* my lateness was a slow bus" is preferable to "The *cause of* my lateness was *on account of* my bus was slow." *See also* BECAUSE.

celebrant, celebrator. We *celebrate* birthdays and anniversaries, meaning that we observe them as occasions for festivity, merrymaking, or special note. One who makes merry or acts with enthusiasm or delight is a *celebrator:* "When in New Orleans, we became *celebrators* in Mardi Gras festivities." A *celebrant* is one who participates in a religious rite or other solemn ceremony: "The Reverend Samuel Barry was a *celebrant* at the funeral services."

"Members of both houses of Congress were *celebrants* at the placing of wreaths on the Tomb of the Unknown Soldier."

cement, concrete. These terms are used interchangeably by many people but not by persons in construction industries. *Cement* is an adhesive consisting of clay and rock materials that form a paste when mixed with water. *Concrete* is a construction material made up of such items as gravel, slag, and pebbles held together by *cement*. That is, *cement* is the binding element in *concrete:* "The contractor failed to put enough *cement* into his *concrete* mixture."

censer, censor, censure. A *censer* is an incense burner. To *censor* is "to examine." To *censure* is "to condemn" or "to find fault." "He bought a lovely ornamented *censer.*" "The authorities *censor* all mail." "The superintendent will *censure* you for laziness."

centenary, centennial. As both adjective and noun, each of these words refers to a period of 100 years, a hundredth anniversary, or recurring once every 100 years. The words are interchangeable; the former is more often used in Great Britain than in the United States. "In 1876, the United States celebrated the *centennial* of the signing of the Declaration of Independence."

center around. This is a wordy phrase in which *around* can always be replaced by the shorter and more accurate *on.* Both *center about* and *center around* are informal ways to say *focus.*

ceremonial, ceremonious. Both of these adjectives have to do with *ceremony,* a formal act or deed performed in accordance with custom or ritual. *Ceremonial* is usually applied to things, *ceremonious* to persons or things: "Weddings are *ceremonial* occasions." "In dress, manner, and speech Dr. Smart is a *ceremonious* person."

certain, certainly, sure, surely. *Certain* and *sure* are adjectives; *certainly* and *surely* are adverbs. Say "I *certainly* (or *surely*) am going" and "Bob is a *certain* (or *sure*) winner in that contest." *Certainly* and *surely* are rarely misused, but *sure* and *certain* constantly occur in statements requiring adverbs.

chair. In the sense of presiding over a meeting, *chair* is widely used as a verb: "The delegate was asked to *chair* the first session." Some linguists feel that *chair* may be used only informally in this function. They argue that if one can *chair* a meeting, one might "pulpit" a sermon or church or "dais" a dinner. Widespread usage, however, has made *chair* a respectable substitute for *chairman*. One may *chair* a meeting or act as *chairman* of it. The term *chairperson* is coming into use as an inclusive synonym for *chairman* and *chairwoman*.

change, alter. *Change* is the simpler and more often used of these words, but *alter* is more exact in the primary sense of "to modify" or "to make different." Actually, *change* conveys these meanings, but it also means "to convert," "to substitute," "to interchange," "to make an exchange" and conveys a half-dozen other impressions and ideas. When one *changes* his habits, he may perform any of several acts, but when he *alters* something, he preserves its identity while changing its appearance. When one *alters* his clothing, he does one thing; when he *changes* it, he may do several quite different things.

cheap, inexpensive. These words agree in their meaning of "low-cost" but differ in application. *Cheap* suggests inferiority, shoddiness, poor workmanship, small value: "This is a *cheap* piece of workmanship." "This coat was made with *cheap* fur." *Inexpensive* indicates "more expensive than cheap" and suggests that, although low in price, an *inexpensive* article is worth its cost: "She bought an *inexpensive* but attractive suit." "Jock purchased an *inexpensive* car whose value equaled its cost." In stores, merchants recognize the distinction between these words: they invariably refer to low-cost items as *inexpensive*, never as *cheap*.

check, check into. As a verb meaning "to investigate," "to inquire," "to verify," *check* is tiresomely overused. *Check into* is a wordy phrase from which *into* can nearly always be omitted.

check, curb, restrain, constrain. These words refer to putting some control on action, movement, development, or progress, but they differ in minor ways. *Check* means "to arrest suddenly," "to halt": "The rider *checked* his horse and leaped from the saddle." *Curb* implies the use of a chain, strap, rope, or similar device for guiding, controlling, or forcing within boundaries: "The rider used a heavy bridle to *curb* his mount." *Restrain* suggests the use of actual force to hold back or control: "The referee *restrained* the angry player by grasping his arms." *Constrain* is related to *restrain* but also implies the idea of compulsion: "His conscience *constrained* him to return the money." In ordinary conversation, however, one may *curb* or *check* his tongue, and one may *check, curb, restrain,* or even *constrain* his impulses and desires.

chiefly. *See* LARGELY.

childish, childlike. The suffix *-ish* often has unfavorable connotations. *Childish* refers to undesirable characteristics (*childish* temper, *childish* selfishness). The suffix *-like* frequently causes neutral or pleasing reactions (*childlike* innocence, *childlike* faith). *Childish* and *infantile* are only approximate synonyms; their antonyms are *adult* and *mature*.

choral, chorale. Each of these terms may be used to refer to a chorus (a choir, or group of singers), but *chorale* more specifically applies to (1) a *choral* composition, (2) a sacred tune, or (3) a group of singers specializing in singing hymns. That is, any band of singers may be referred to as a *choral* group, but only a group specializing in some particular form of music is a *chorale*. Also, *choral* is nearly always used as an adjective, *chorale* as a noun: "Judy is a member of a *choral* group." "Jessie belongs to a *chorale* that sings under the direction of a former concert artist."

chord, cord. A *chord* is a combination of musical tones: "The pianist played the opening *chords.*" A *cord* is a string or a rope: "Tie your packages with sturdy *cord.*"

circumlocution. *See* LOCUTION.

city, town, village. No specific guidelines exist for deciding what one should call a populated area. Size is relative, and importance is largely in the eye and mind. One can fairly say that a *town* is smaller than a *city* and larger than a *village*, but no reliable regulations suggest just what is needed to make a *town* a *city* or a *village* a *town*. A suburb may be a *village* within a *town*, itself one of a group of *towns* making up a thickly populated area that in turn is called a *city*. A *village* may be either a small *town* or a group of houses and other buildings in a rural area; in some states, a *village* is a *settlement* or *hamlet* until it is incorporated and forms its own local government. A *town* or *township* has fixed boundaries and local government, often deriving its legal existence from its incorporation as a municipality. A *city* is a large *town*, one considered important because it is a trading center or a focus of attention from outlying areas. A suggestion: call the area in which you live whatever you and your neighbors agree on; call other settlements of less than 5,000 population *villages;* refer to populated areas of from 5,000 to 50,000 persons as *towns* and to all clusters larger than that as *cities*. In usage, *city* and *village* require an article; one goes to or comes from *a city* or *a village*. *Town* needs no article.

claim. *See* DEMAND.

class. *See* CATEGORY.

classic, classical. *Classical* refers to the art and culture of Greek and Roman antiquity: "The *classical* period in ancient Greece lasted for more than two centuries." *Classic* means "of the first or highest class": "Homer's *Iliad* is a *classic* piece of work." "Homer's *Iliad* is a *classic.*" Contemporary speakers and writers overuse *classic* in describing sports events, books, television shows, and the like; the term should be applied only to works and performances of the first rank that adhere to established standards.

clean, cleanse. Each of these words means "to make clean," "to free from dirt." *Cleanse* usually has spiritual, moral, or ceremonial application. One washes with soap and water to *clean* his hands; one may experience a religious ceremony to *cleanse* himself from guilt or sin. Soap and detergent manufacturers, as well as dry cleaners, often use *cleanse* or *cleanser* when only *clean* or *cleaner* is meant, but such use is justified by neither custom nor high prices.

clench, clinch. As verbs, both of these words apply to the act of holding or securing. One is occasionally mispronounced for the other; also, they differ somewhat in meaning. *Clinch* should be used for the securing of an agreement, argument, or verdict and to mean "to hold" in boxing. One *clenches* an object with hands, fingers, jaws, or teeth.

clew. *See* CLUE.

client, customer, patron. When you enter a clothing store or beauty shop, are you a *client,* a *customer,* or a *patron?* You may be called any of these terms or something worse, but really you are a *customer* or a *patron.* A *customer* or a *patron* is a buyer, someone who purchases something from another: "Jeff was a good *customer* of the clothing store." "Sue was a *patron* of every beauty shop in the village." *Patron* also has the additional meaning of "one who supports with money or gifts": "You should be a *patron* of the arts." *Client* refers to one who seeks the advice of a lawyer or other professional person: "When I was charged with the crime, I became the *client* of an excellent firm of lawyers." "In his need, he became the *client* of a social service agency."

climactic, climatic. *Climactic* pertains to *climax*, the final and most forceful one of a series of ideas or events: "The duel was the *climactic* scene of the drama." *Climatic* pertains to *climate*, or weather conditions: "Edith likes *climatic* conditions in the Virgin Islands."

climax. *See* ACME.

clinch. *See* CLENCH.

clique, coterie. A *clique* (preferably pronounced "kleek") is a small, exclusive group or set of people. So is a *coterie*. But *clique* is usually a term of contempt or derision applied to persons who take themselves too seriously, set themselves up as authorities, and act selfishly. *Coterie* is less often used as a term of contempt and is more likely to apply to groups in the world of art than to those in society generally. "Barbara belongs to a snobbish *clique* of the country club set." "This performance is designed for a *coterie* of dedicated lovers of music."

close. *See* NEAR, CLOSE.

close, shut. These words mean "to cause something not to be open," "to stop or obstruct." *Close* is somewhat more refined and less blunt than *shut*. For instance, you might tactfully suggest to a child that he *close* his mouth while chewing but would say "*Shut* your mouth" or "*Shut* up" if you were angry, rude, or annoyed. Signs on public structures are more likely to read "This building is *closed* on Sunday" than "This building is *shut* on Sunday." *Shut,* however, derived from an Old English word related to *bolt* and *shoot,* is vigorous and emphatic and should be used when you really mean that something should be barred, bolted, or blocked.

clue, clew. These words derive their meaning from the use of a ball of thread that enabled a mythical character to find his way out of a puzzling place (a labyrinth). A *clew* or *clue* is anything that helps to guide or direct in the solution of a mystery or problem. Both spellings are acceptable, although *clue* is more generally used. In fact, "*Clue* me in" is a tiresome, overused, and weary phrase.

cohere. *See* ADHERE.

college. *See* UNIVERSITY.

collusion, connivance. *Collusion* means a secret agreement for some tricky, underhanded, or fraudulent purpose: "Drivers acted in *collusion* with warehousemen to rob the manufacturer." *Collusion* is close in meaning to *conspiracy* and should not be confused with *collaboration. Connivance,* from a Latin word meaning "to wink at," signifies avoidance of noticing something, assisting wrongdoing by not acting or speaking: "The *connivance* of museum guards circumvented regulations forbidding smoking." When one acts in *collusion,* he does something; when he *connives,* he ignores or overlooks something.

combat, contest. *Combat* suggests a direct encounter, one actually involving physical force: "The FBI is supposed to *combat* crime." "The fight between the boxers was a frightful, bloody *combat.*" *Contest* applies to either a friendly or a hostile struggle for a prize or goal. A baseball game is a *contest;* a battle between armed forces is both *contest* and *combat. Contest* should be associated with *struggle* and *contention; combat* should be related to *conflict* and *fight.*

come and. The verbs *come, go,* and *try* are often followed by *and* (*come and* get your food, *go and* get your ticket, *try and* get some rest). In such expressions *and* is a substitute for *to.* These phrases are idiomatically sound but are informal and, although widely used, are not recommended.

comely. *See* HOMELY.

commence. *See* BEGIN.

commentate, commentator. Since the word *commentator* has become well known because of radio and television, people generally have felt the need for a verb to describe what a *commentator* does. Thus a neologism has been born. The phrase "to *commentate* a game (or fashion show)" is considered dubious usage by most authorities. Why not stick with *comment, comment on, describe, or narrate?*

common, mutual. These words are loosely interchangeable, but they do have distinct meanings. *Common* refers to something shared by two or more persons (our *common* heritage). *Mutual* refers to something done or felt by each of two persons toward the other: "Jack and Bill share a *mutual* dislike." Many good speakers and writers, however, do not preserve this distinction.

common, ordinary. *Common* has specific meanings such as "shared," "belonging," and "united" (*common* goals, *common* property, a *common* purpose). It is often confused with *ordinary,* which means "commonplace," "plain or undistinguished," "of the usual kind." Thus one should refer to "the *common* lot of mankind," "the *common* desires of all dedicated parents for their children," "the *ordinary* suit worn by businessmen," and "an *ordinary* day at the office."

compact. *See* PACT.

comparatively. *See* RELATIVELY.

compare, contrast. These words are often confused, perhaps because they are related in meaning. To *compare* is to examine in order to note similarities more than differences; to *contrast* is to set in opposition in order to show differences more than similarities. Idioms are *compare to* and *compare with.* As a verb, *contrast* is usually followed by *with;* as a noun, *contrast* often takes *between.* The phrase "in *contrast*" may be followed by *to* or *with.* Examples: "How can you *compare* a man *with* (or *to*) a mouse?" "It is easy to *contrast* one's life in peace *with* that in war." "Let's *compare* this hat *with* that one." "The *contrast between* yesterday and today is astonishing."

compel, impel. These words agree in the idea of using physical or other force to result in a course of action, to cause something to be done. *Compel* has a greater sense of coercion, of actual force, than does *impel:* "My mounting debts *compelled* me to seek a loan." "Heavy fines *compel* drivers to obey traffic signals." *Impel* involves the idea of motive or incentive or inner drive: "His conscience will *impel* him to confess his guilt." "I feel *impelled* to question that statement." *Impel* may involve the concept of pushing forward (Wind *impels* the small boat), but usually it suggests pressure in a figurative sense (I was *impelled* by a sense of obligation). *See also* IMPEL, INDUCE.

complement, compliment. *Complement* implies something which completes: "This jewelry will *complement* your dress." A *compliment* is flattery or praise: "Beulah enjoyed the *compliment* paid to her."

complementary. *See* SUPPLEMENTARY.

compose, comprise, include. Each of these words involves the idea of containing, embracing, comprehending, or surrounding as, for example, a whole in reference to its parts. *Compose* has the additional meaning of making, or forming, by combining things: "This chemical compound is *composed* of five elements." *Comprise* suggests including or containing: "This section of the book *comprises* ten different subjects." To *include* is to contain as a part or member: "The list of names *includes* yours and mine." Use *comprise* when all parts are named or referred to and *include* when only some are. "*Comprised* of" is a wordy expression. Omit the *of*. *See also* CONSIST OF.

comprehend. *See* APPREHEND.

comprehensible, comprehensive. Although these words have different spellings, pronunciations, and meanings, they are sometimes confused. The first means "intelligible," "capable of being known or understood." *Comprehensive* means "including much," "large in content or scope." Examples: "What you say is so exaggerated as not to be *comprehensible.*" "This book provides a *comprehensive* study of the topic."

comprise. *See* COMPOSE.

concave, convex. *Concave* means "curved inward," and *convex* means "curved outward." That is, *concave* means having a surface that is curved or rounded inward, like a segment of the interior of a hollow sphere or circle. In keeping the meaning of *concave* straight, it may help to think of a cave as something that actually turns or curves inward from the earth. *Convex* means precisely the opposite.

concept. *See* IDEA.

concise. *See* SUCCINCT.

concrete. *See* CEMENT.

condemn, contemn. The first of these words means "to censure," "to express disapproval of," "to judge unfit": "His guilty looks *condemn* him." "If the appraisers *condemn* the ship, it will be sold for scrap metal." *Condemn* also means "to acquire ownership for a public purpose": "The town *condemned* the tract of land and turned it into a public park." *Contemn,* a less-used word, means "to treat with scorn, disdain, or contempt," "to despise": "If you do that, all right-thinking persons will *contemn* you (hold you in contempt)."

confess, admit. *Confess* means "to declare, own, or admit as true" and is closely related in meaning to *grant* and *concede*. When one *confesses* some crime or wrong-doing, he *admits* it and also accepts responsibility for the soundness of that admission. "I *confess* that I have neglected you" implies that the speaker recognizes, or *admits,* guilt or shame for the neglect. When followed by the *-ing* form of a verb, *confess* takes the preposition *to:* "I *confess to* neglecting you." For further comment on *admit* and closely related words, *see* ACKNOWLEDGE, ADMIT and ADMIT, ALLOW.

confidant, confident. Confusion between these two similar words results in an impropriety. *Confidant* (kon·fuh·DANT) refers to one to whom secrets or other private matters are entrusted. A female confidant is a *confidante* (kon·fuh·DANT). *Confident,* an adjective meaning "assured, certain of success," is pronounced "KON·fuh·duhnt" or "KON·fi·duhnt." Examples of use: "Edith was my trusted *confidante.* I was *confident* that I could trust her."

confidently, confidentially. *Confidently* means "with assurance, certainty, confidence": "Joe acted *confidently,* but his speech was halting." *Confidentially* means "in secret," "intimately," "in confidence": "The postman told me *confidentially* that the letter has been destroyed."

congenial, genial. *Congenial* means "compatible," "allied in spirit, temper, and feeling," "suited to one another": "The players on this team are *congenial.*" "At the party you will find a *congenial* atmosphere." *Genial* means "cordial," "cheerful," "sympathetic": "Our host was in a *genial* mood." *Genial* also means "favorable for growth or comfort": "They enjoy the *genial* climate of Florida." A group of *genial* persons is likely to find that they are *congenial* with each other.

connivance. *See* COLLUSION.

connotation, denotation. *Connotation* applies to the overtones of words—values and meanings that are suggested rather than specifically expressed in a dictionary definition. For example, San Francisco is "a seaport city in northern California," but the name itself has such connotations as "Golden Gate," "Chinatown," "Barbary Coast," "Gateway to the Orient," and "earthquake of 1906." Connotative words have implied, suggestive, associated meanings. *Denotation* is the exact, literal meaning of a word as contrasted with its *connotation,* or suggestive meaning. Thus, *home* has a denotative meaning of "house," "apartment," "fixed dwelling place." Its connotation might be "refuge," "place of peace," "retreat," or "haven of rest."

connote. *See* DENOTE.

conscious. *See* AWARE.

consecutive, successive. These words mean "following one another in order," "marked by logical sequence." *Consecutive* suggests uninterrupted succession, whereas *suc-*

cessive means "following in a regular sequence" with one thing in relation to another. Four *consecutive* months means four months in a row without interruption: March, April, May, and June. Four *successive* months would correspond to calendar order but might mean March, May, July, and October. *See also* CONTINUAL.

consensus. Often misspelled and misused, *consensus* means "general agreement" or "collective opinion." The word is related to *sense* and has no connection with *census*. The phrase "*consensus* of opinion" has been used so freely and widely that it is a stock expression; however, it is wordy (*of opinion* is not needed to express the thought) and is now a hackneyed term.

consequent. *See* SUBSEQUENT.

conservative, moderate, radical. As they relate to ideas and opinions involving politics, morals, property, and manners, these words have widely differing applications. What one person considers *moderate,* another might term *conservative* or *radical*. In meaning, however, *conservative* refers to a person or state of mind that is disposed to favor gradual rather than sudden change, that wishes to preserve existing conditions and institutions, that is, at most, "cautiously" *moderate*. In politics and other activities, a *moderate* is one who opposes views and goals unless they are kept within what he considers reasonable bounds and are not extreme or excessive. A *radical* favors drastic reforms in politics, morals, manners, or whatever. Each of these words is an adjective as well as a noun: thus one may refer to "a *conservative* way of dressing," "a *moderate* degree of success," and "a *radical* departure from established customs."

consistently, constantly. *Consistently* is an adverb meaning "steadfastly," "unwaveringly," "without change": "He is *consistently* behind in his payments." "This student *consistently* objects to all authority." *Constantly* means "unceasingly," "without interruption," "perpetually": "My concentration was *constantly* broken by the loud ticking of a clock." "My mail is *constantly* filled with second-class matter." Related words that might express meaning more exactly than either *consistently* or *constantly* are *perseveringly, persistently, enduringly, continually,* and *unceasingly.*

consist of, contain. These words are used interchangeably, but *contain* is a synonym only of *consist of,* not *consist in. Consist of* and *contain* express the notion that something so exists that something else can be placed or noticed within it: "The can *contains* gasoline." "His appeal *consisted of* his charm, good looks, and honesty." *Consist in* is used to define an identity, to indicate a quality or ingredient that is possessed by something: "Happiness *consists in* attaining goals that are desired and then appreciating them." *See also* COMPOSE.

constantly. *See* CONSISTENTLY.

constrain. *See* CHECK, CURB, RESTRAIN, CONSTRAIN.

consul. *See* COUNCIL.

contact. As a noun, *contact* denotes "a coming together" and also "a connection," "a person who might be of use." In both senses, its use is now considered reputable. As a verb meaning "to get in touch with," *contact* is considered an informality or impropriety. One should avoid *contacting* someone else, an unfortunate recommendation since *get in touch with* says the same thing but says it wordily. Other possibilities: *telephone, call, call upon, communicate with, write, speak to.*

contagious, infectious. These words have precise scientific meanings, but in everyday usage they are often confused. As for illness, a *contagious* disease is one communicated or transferred by contact; an *infectious* disease is indirectly communicated by such agencies as water and air. An *infectious* disease is not necessarily *contagious*. *Contagious* emphasizes the speed with which contagion (contact, communication, medium) spreads: "*Contagious* fear ran through the audience." *Infectious* suggests the powerful or irresistible quality of the source of contagion: "Mark Twain's *infectious* humor stimulated prolonged laughter and applause."

contain. *See* CONSIST OF.

contemn. *See* CONDEMN.

contemplate, meditate. These words mean "to think about," "to look at with attention." Both words apply to stages of consideration in which a decision to act or not to act is thought about. *Meditate* involves deeper thought and a more serious purpose than does *contemplate*. For instance, one might *contemplate* taking a weekend trip but is more likely to *meditate* the advantages and disadvantages of changing jobs. *Contemplate* is related in meaning to *plan, devise,* and *contrive,* whereas *meditate* is close to *ponder, muse, cogitate, ruminate,* and *study*.

contemporary. This word means "existing, living, or occurring at the same time." It is not a synonym for either *present-day* or *modern* unless no other question of time is involved and the inference is "contemporary with now." If the time frame of reference is that of Queen Elizabeth I, then a lecture on *contemporary* drama would mean plays of Elizabethan times. If the frame of reference is to drama of the present day, the time of Elizabeth II, then *contemporary* would mean "now." Because *contemporary* means what it does, it is an error to use it with *more* (meaning "to a greater degree"). It is impossible for something to be *more contemporary;* probably what is meant is *more modern*. "An Elizabethan play in *modern* costume" is clearer in meaning than "an Elizabethan play in *contemporary* dress."

contentious. *See* CONTROVERSIAL.

contest. *See* COMBAT.

contiguous. *See* ADJACENT.

continual, continuous. In some senses and uses, these words are synonymous. One distinction is that *continual* implies a close recurrence in time, or rapid succession, whereas *continuous* suggests "without interruption," "constant." "The *continual* ringing of the doorbell" and "The ticking of the clock was *continuous*" illustrate this distinction. *See also* CONSECUTIVE and CONSISTENTLY.

continuance, continuation. In law, *continuance* means the adjournment of a proceeding to a later time. In other uses, *continuance* and *continuation* are generally interchangeable: one may refer to the *continuation* or the *continuance* of a state of war or period of drought. However, *continuation* means "the extending or prolonging of time or space": the *continuation* of a structure might involve adding a room or wing, whereas the *continuance* of that structure would refer to the period of its existence, its time of standing. Thus you might speak of a politician's *continuance* in office and the *continuation* of the process by which he is elected.

continue. *See* RESUME.

continue on. The word *continue* means "to go on," "to keep on." Therefore, *on* should be omitted from this phrase. Vary your word choice: why not try *persist* or *persevere* or *last* or *endure?*

continuous. *See* CONTINUAL.

contrast. *See* COMPARE.

controversial, contentious. A subject or topic is *controversial;* an individual is *contentious:* "Every political issue is *controversial* to this *contentious* man." *Controversial* means "debatable," "arguable," "disputable." *Contentious* means "quarrelsome," "argumentative."

convex. *See* CONCAVE.

convey back. The word *convey* means "to carry, bring, or take from one place to another." Omit *back* from such a statement as "Please *convey* my regards *back* to your associates."

convince, persuade. These words are related in meaning but do have different uses. *Convince* means "to satisfy the understanding of someone about the truth of a statement or situation": "Johnny *convinced* me by quoting exact figures." *Persuade* suggests winning over someone to a course of action, perhaps through an appeal to reason or emotion: "Jim *persuaded* the grocer to consult a lawyer."

cooperate together. *Cooperate* means "to work together," "to act in combination." Drop the *together;* all it adds is a useless word.

copy. *See* REPLICA.

cord. *See* CHORD.

corespondent, correspondent. These words differ in spelling, meaning, and pronunciation. It is usually safer to be a *correspondent* (KOR·i·spon·dent), one who writes letters, than a *corespondent* (KO·ri·SPON·dent), one charged with adultery in a divorce proceeding.

corpus. *See* HABEAS CORPUS.

coterie. *See* CLIQUE.

couldn't scarcely, couldn't hardly. *See* CAN'T HARDLY. *Couldn't* is a contraction of *could not*. Drop the negative part of the phrase when using it with *scarcely* or *hardly:* "He *could hardly* see the road through the heavy fog."

could of. In normal speech, *could have* sounds like *could've,* which in turn sounds like *could of.* Not only *could of* but also *may of, might of, should of,* and *would of* are illiteracies. *Of* is not a verb. "I *could have* (not *could of*) paid the bill."

council, consul, counsel. A *consul* is an official: "Robin visited the American *Consul* in Naples." *Council* means "an assembly," "a group": "This is a *council* of senior citizens." *Counsel* is both noun and verb and means "advice" or "to advise": "The physician gave me expensive *counsel.*" "The manager will *counsel* fast action by the board of directors."

councilor, counselor. A *councilor* is a member of a *council,* an assembly of persons formed for deliberation or action: "Jesse was appointed a member of the Mayor's *Council* on Mass Transportation." A *counselor* is one who gives advice or counsel (opinion, instruction): "Martha acted as a *counsel* to the Committee on Welfare." The corresponding verb form is *counsel:* "Please *counsel* me in this matter." *Counselor* is also a term applied to lawyers, although among attorneys the word is often employed humorously or sarcastically. Certain employees at summer camps are called *counselors.*

counsel. *See* COUNCIL.

country. *See* NATION.

couple. In ordinary conversation, *couple* is sometimes placed immediately before a noun (a *couple* weeks, a *couple* dollars). Although this usage follows that of *dozen* (a *dozen* roses), it is not standard; *couple* should be followed by *of* (*couple of* months). However, when such words as *less* and *more* appear, the *of* is dropped (a *couple more* seats). *Couple* may correctly be used with a singular or a plural verb: "The couple *was* dancing" or "The couple *were* dancing." "*Couple* together" is a wordy phrase. *Couple* alone expresses the idea; omit *together*.

courteous. *See* POLITE.

covert, overt. These "look-alikes" are sometimes confused despite the fact that they are antonyms. *Covert* means "covered," "sheltered," "hidden," "secret," "concealed"; *overt* means "open to view," "plain," "manifest," "apparent," "public." To keep them distinguished, associate *overt* with *open* and *covert* with *cover:* "His every act and aim was *overt,* a matter of public record." "These politicians entered into a *covert* agreement about the paving contracts."

covet. *See* ENVY, COVET, DESIRE.

credible, creditable. *Credible* means "believable," "worthy or capable of confidence and belief," "trustworthy": "The jury found the witness's statement *credible.*" *Creditable* means "deserving credit," "bringing or deserving credit, esteem, or honor": "His performance during the game was entirely creditable." The antonym, or negative, of *credible* is *incredible;* the antonym of *creditable* is *discreditable*. An allied word, *credulous,* means "willing to believe too easily," "gullible." Its opposite is *incredulous*.

credit, accredit. As a verb, *credit* means "to put faith in," "to trust," "to believe in": "I do not hesitate to *credit* you with good intentions." *Accredit* means "to certify," "to attribute to," "to invest with power or authority": "That statement was *accredited* to Winston Churchill." "When he left the Senate, he was *accredited* as Ambassador to Peru." When some act or deed is thought of as being put to someone's advantage, either word may be used: "The discovery of this virus was *credited* (or *accredited*) to Professor John O'Reilly."

creditable. *See* CREDIBLE.

creditor, debtor. A *creditor* is one to whom money is due; a *debtor* is one under financial obligation to someone else: "This wealthy mortgage holder is a *creditor* to ten property holders in this town." "Three small loan companies were able to prove that I was their *debtor.*" The usual abbreviation for *creditor* is *cr*. The abbreviation for *debtor* is *dr*.

credulous. *See* CREDIBLE.

criterion, criteria. Meaning "standard, rule, or test for forming a judgment or decision," *criterion* (KRAI·TEER·ee·uhn) is singular in form and meaning. The plural *criteria* (KRAI·TEER·ee·uh) cannot be used for *criterion* in such expressions as "a *criteria,*" "one *criteria.*" *Criterions* is a less-preferred but acceptable plural. "One *criterion* for success is hard work." "The *criteria* in judging the papers will be neatness, thoroughness, and length."

cross-section. *See* SECTION.

cue, queue. *Cue* is more widely used than *queue* in all meanings, but careful speakers and writers continue to distinguish between them. A *queue* refers to a braid of hair and to a file, or line: "She wore her hair in a *queue* which hung down to her waist." "Let's *queue* up for the next bus." A *cue* refers in the theater to an indication of following action or speech and in general use to any kind of hint or suggestion; in games, *cue* means the tipped rod used in billiards and pool: "I don't have a single *cue* as to his intentions." "When he missed the shot, the player broke his *cue* in anger."

cultured, cultivated. As applied to people, both of these words mean "educated," "refined," "interested in and acquainted with what is regarded as superior in learning and the arts." *Cultured* is considered the more elegant and refined word in this meaning, perhaps because *cultivated* is more often associated with labor, especially with the output of agricultural products. Nevertheless, a praiseworthy goal for everyone is to be either *cultured* or *cultivated*.

curb. *See* CHECK, CURB, RESTRAIN, CONSTRAIN.

curious, inquisitive. *Curious* suggests a desire to know, especially to learn about matters that are not really one's concern or business: "This resident is *curious* about the activities of his neighbors." *Inquisitive* implies the asking of questions, the act of prying, in order to satisfy curiosity: "This determined fieldworker was *inquisitive* in her research." A person can be *curious* while doing nothing more than wondering, but an *inquisitive* individual engages in spying, peeping, or prying.

curiously enough. This is a widely used expression which, *curiously enough,* has little meaning. Remove the phrase from the sentence you have just read and from your speech and writing. Nothing will be lost.

currently. *See* PRESENTLY.

custom, practice, habit. Each of these words refers to an accustomed or established way of doing things. Each can be applied to the activities of people, animals, or entire communities. *Custom* refers particularly to the practice and preservation of social activity or usage: "It is a community *custom* to go to church on Sunday." *Practice* is closely allied in meaning to *custom* but applies particularly to an unvarying procedure: "It is the *practice* of a careful man to balance his checkbook." *Habit,* applied especially to people and animals, refers to the repetition of an action so constantly that the act becomes natural or spontaneous: "John has a *habit* of counting to 10 before he answers any question." "Our dog has a *habit* of turning around before lying down."

customary. *See* USUAL.

customer. *See* CLIENT.

cyclone, hurricane, tornado. Each of these terms applies to a disturbance of intense severity. Technically, a *cyclone* is a large-scale wind and pressure system characterized by circular wind motion with low pressure at its center. In the Southern Hemisphere, motion of the wind in a *cyclone* is clockwise; in the Northern Hemisphere it is counterclockwise. A *hurricane* is a violent tropical storm occurring mainly in the western North Atlantic, with wind speeds in excess of 70 miles an hour. The term *hurricane* is applied loosely to any storm accompanied by high winds. A *tornado* is a violently destructive and usually localized windstorm occurring over land. The most visible part of a *tornado* is its long funnel-shaped cloud, filled with debris, that extends toward the ground.

D

data. This term, meaning "facts," "information," "statistics," is really the plural of *datum*. In general use, however, *data* now appears as a singular and plural collective noun. The plural construction *(These* data *are . . .)* is appropriate in formal usage, although "*This* data *is* . . ." is more often used. The use of *datum* and *data* is not entirely comparable to that of *agendum* and *agenda* (*see* AGENDUM). *Agenda* conveys such a strong sense of the singular that it has loosely developed its own plural, *agendums*. This situation does not apply to *data,* which has no coined plural. Those who use *data* as a singular obviously regard it as meaning "a body" or "a store" of information. Strictly formal writers and speakers presumably will continue to use a plural verb with *data,* but a majority will employ a singular or a plural verb as they choose.

deadly, deathly. *Deadly* has several meanings, among them "fatal" (a *deadly* disease), "relentless" (a *deadly* enemy), "like death" (a *deadly* paleness), and "boring" (a *deadly* speech). *Deathly* means "resembling death" and "utterly": "There was a *deathly* odor from the tomb." "I was *deathly* afraid of the huge guns." In general, use *deathly* when you mean "death-dealing" and *deadly* in all other senses. Both words are intensives, strongly emotional terms that should be used sparingly.

debar, disbar. *Debar* means "to shut out or exclude" (The doorman will *debar* all who are not members) and "to hinder or prohibit" (*Debar* all candidates below the age of eighteen). *Disbar* has much the same meanings but is applied specifically to the legal profession in the sense of "to expel": "The legal society decided to *disbar* both attorneys for their conduct at the trial."

debtor. *See* CREDITOR.

debut. This importation from French is pronounced "de·BYOO," "DAY·boo," and "DAY·byoo." As a noun, it means "first public appearance," "beginning of a career," or "formal presentation." *Debut* is not yet established as a verb in standard usage, although it is appearing ever more frequently in both speech and print: "The actress *debuts* tonight in a new play." "The company will *debut* its new model tomorrow." Until *debut* is accepted as a verb by reliable dictionaries, continue to use the word only as a noun.

decisive, incisive. *Decisive* means "conclusive," "final," "having the power of putting an end to something": "This was the *decisive* battle of the entire war." "The lawyer's final argument to the jury was *decisive* in arriving at a verdict." *Incisive* means "sharp," "keen," "penetrating": "The last speaker was blunt and *incisive* in his remarks. In fact, his appeal was so *incisive* that it turned out to be a *decisive* factor in the campaign."

decorum, propriety. Each of these words, as well as *etiquette,* refers to the requirements and demands of behavior in so-called polite society. *Decorum* involves the idea of dignity and reserve in speech, dress, and actions: "This school for foreign officers stresses the importance of *decorum* at all formal functions." *Propriety,* a more general term, refers to established conventions and applies to matters of taste and morals as well as dignity. It is usually used in the plural: "When in a foreign country, try to observe the *proprieties* expected of a well-bred American."

deduce, deduct. To *deduce* is to reach a conclusion from something known or assumed: "The officer *deduced* that the criminal was a man." To *deduct* is "to take away from," "to subtract": "After you *deduct* your expenses, you will have little left." *See also* ADDUCE.

deduction. *See* INDUCTION.

defective, deficient. The first of these terms should be related to *defect,* the second to *deficit.* For example, money that is counterfeit is *defective* because of its *defect.* Money is *deficient* if there is not enough of it. *Defect* is the general word for any kind of imperfection or shortcoming; *deficit* is the general word for "shortage" or "lack." Thus one might refer to a child as being "mentally *deficient*" ("lacking normal intelligence") and "physically *defective*" ("imperfect in hearing or speech").

defendant. *See* PLAINTIFF.

defer, delay, postpone. Each of these words implies keeping or preventing something from happening until a later time: "I recommend that we *defer* (or *delay* or *postpone*) this action to our next meeting." To *defer* is to make a decision to do something later: "I shall *defer* making a decision until tomorrow." To *delay* is to lay something aside, to impede or hinder, to put something off: "I'll *delay* answering this letter until I feel like writing." To *postpone* is to put something off to a particular time in the future with the intention of following up: "This election should be *postponed* until our next session." Each of these words may be followed by an *-ing* form of a verb but not by an infinitive: "He *deferred leaving* (not he *deferred to leave*), *delayed leaving, postponed leaving.*"

deficient. *See* DEFECTIVE.

definite, definitive. These words apply to that which is clearly set forth and explained, but *definitive* also has a meaning of "final," "total," or "complete": "The time of his arrival is *definite.*" "This is a *definitive* life of the author."

definitely. *See* ABSOLUTELY.

degenerate, deteriorate. These words mean "to make or become worse," "to decline in physical, moral, or mental qualities." *Degenerate* suggests that a decline is due to some loss of virtue or worthwhile quality, whereas *deteriorate* has more the meaning of "to wear away" or "to weaken": "This able official *degenerated* into a pompous loudmouth." "The argument *deteriorated* into name-calling and squabbling." "A *degenerate* treasurer managed to *deteriorate* the cash position of his company."

degree, extent. These words have a shared meaning: "a point in any scale," "the space to which something extends." "To a *degree*" means "up to a point" or "to an extent." *Extent* also emphasizes the idea of limitation: "I agree with you to an *extent.*" Both *extent* and *degree* are overused in wasteful, wordy expressions; "to a great *extent*" means nothing more than "greatly"; "to an important *degree*" can be more economically expressed by "importantly." The phrases "by *degrees*" and "to some *degree*" are more often fillers than meaningful expressions.

deism, theism. *Deism* is a belief in the existence of God based on reason but rejecting supernatural revelation. *Theism* is belief in one God as the creator and ruler of the universe without rejection of superhuman forces and manifestations. Thomas Jefferson considered himself a *deist.* A follower of Christianity or Judaism is a *theist.*

delay. *See* DEFER.

delimit. *See* LIMIT.

delusion. *See* ALLUSION.

demand, claim. *Demand* means "to ask for with authority," "to insist boldly": "He *demanded* to see the charges against him." *Claim* means "to assert a right": "The driver *claimed* that he was entitled to a hearing." *Claim* should not be used when you mean *say, assert, state,* or *declare* unless a right is involved: "The student *claimed* his right to an examination." "The student *asserted* (or *said* or *stated* or *declared*) that he was going to college."

democracy. *See* REPUBLIC.

denotation. *See* CONNOTATION.

denote, connote. To *denote* is "to indicate," "to be a sign or mark of": "The thermometer *denotes* that he has a high fever." To *connote* is "to suggest" or "to signify": "The word *welcome connotes* hospitality." The distinction in meaning between these words is related to that between *denotation* and *connotation.* In short, *denote* "means" and *connote* "implies." *See also* CONNOTATION.

deny, repudiate. Each of these words has certain meanings that they do not share, but in the sense of stating that something is not true, *repudiate* is the stronger, more emphatic term. One might *deny* that water seeks its own level; he might *repudiate* all of mankind's accumulated observation and experience. Similarly, a father might *deny* a daughter use of the family automobile, but he would *repudiate* her only if he disowned her or threw her out of the house. *See also* REFUTE.

depositary, depository. Each of these terms can correctly be used to refer to a place where something is deposited for safekeeping. A safe deposit box stored in a bank vault is a *depository* or *depositary*. The latter word, however, is more often used to refer not to a place for safekeeping but to a group or even an individual entrusted with the preservation of something. The officers of a bank or the trustees of a museum, for instance, would more likely be called *depositaries* than *depositories*.

deprecate, depreciate. *Deprecate* means "to express disapproval of," "to plead against," "to protest." *Depreciate* means "to belittle," "to lower in value." Because the two words look somewhat similar, *deprecate* is sometimes carelessly used in the sense of "to belittle" (Jesse *deprecated* his contribution to the cause). "The teacher *deprecated* the laziness of his students." "The property *depreciated* in value."

desert, dessert. As a noun, *desert* differs in spelling, pronunciation, and meaning from *dessert*. The term for an arid region is pronounced "DEZ·uhrt." The term for a pastry, pudding, or other final course of a meal is pronounced "di·ZUHRT," as is the verb *desert:* "While roaming in the *desert* he had to do without *dessert.*" "Do not *desert* your job now." The word *desert,* as in "just *deserts,*" has nothing to do with either arid regions or sweet concoctions. It derives from the same root as *deserves* and means "rewards or punishments": "Every contestant will receive his just *deserts.*"

desire. *See* ENVY, COVET, DESIRE.

deteriorate. *See* DEGENERATE.

determinism. *See* FATALISM.

devoted. *See* ADDICTED.

dialect. *See* VERNACULAR.

dialogue. *See* MONOLOGUE.

diction, vocabulary. *Diction* is the choice and use of words for the expression of ideas. The word comes from Latin *dictio,* which means "saying," "word," and which appears in such familiar terms as *dictionary, dictator,* and *dictate*. *Diction* has been broadened in meaning to refer to one's whole style of speaking and writing: "This speaker was distinguished for his forceful, precise *diction.*" *Vocabulary* refers to the complete stock of words used or known by an individual or nation: "Joan's German *vocabulary* is limited, but she has a wide-ranging knowledge of Italian." *Vocabulary* is a more embracing term than *diction:* the latter refers to only words and expressions chosen and used by a speaker or writer, but the former includes not only the terms one uses but those that are in his recognition and reading store of words as well.

dictionary, glossary, thesaurus. A *dictionary* is a book containing a selection of words, usually arranged alphabetically, concerning which information about meanings, pronunciations, etymologies, and a wealth of other detail is provided: "The Frenchman purchased a *dictionary* of the English language." A *glossary* is a specialized dictionary, a list of terms in a particular subject, area of usage, or field of study: "This is a *glossary* of recent American slang." "At the end of this volume you will find a *glossary* of terms that may be unfamiliar to you." A *glossary* is designed to explain or define terms but usually does not deal with pronunciation, derivation, and other information provided by a dictionary. A *thesaurus* is still another kind of specialized dictionary, one that usually confines itself to a treatment of synonyms and antonyms: "Roget's *International Thesaurus* is a helpful book for everyone who writes, speaks, or reads."

die of, die from, die with. In its customary sense of "to cease living," *die* is preferably followed by *of:* "He *died of* (not *from*) a coronary attack." *Die with* expresses an idea not related to a cause of death: "He *died with* courage."

different. This word is an adjective, not a noun. "He doesn't know any *different*" is standard informal usage, but "He doesn't see any *different* between them" is an illiterate statement. In a remark such as "I consulted three *different* lawyers," *different* is superfluous. It is also unneeded in "I bought three *different* kinds of soap."

different from, different than, different to. The first two of these expressions are widely used, but *different from* is preferred by careful, educated writers and speakers: "This specimen is *different from* (not *than*) that." Unfortunately, but correctly, *different from* often leads to extra words because *than* is a convenient shortcut for *from that which.* Even so, say *different from* rather than *different than* until widespread usage sanctions the latter term. *Different to* appears more often in British than in American usage.

differentiate, distinguish. Each of these words suggests an attempt to note and analyze characteristic features of some item or person. *Differentiate* involves pointing out exactly and in detail the differences or partial similarities of two things being considered: "It is difficult to *differentiate* between the symptoms of pneumonia and influenza." "One who takes up the study of cells must quickly learn to *differentiate* among them in size and structure." *Distinguish* has much the same meaning as *differentiate* but implies general recognition of characteristics that establish the identity of something without giving attention to specific details: "It is easy to *distinguish* an elephant from a buffalo."

dilemma. *See* PREDICAMENT.

diminish, minimize. *Diminish* means "to make smaller, less, or less important," "to reduce, shrink, decrease, or contract": "Two aspirin tablets will *diminish* your pain." *Minimize* means "to reduce to the smallest possible amount, degree, size, or extent" and also means "to belittle": "It is always unwise to *minimize* the horrors of war." "Since I am doing the best I can, you should not try to *minimize* my efforts." *Minimize* is an absolute term and should not be accompanied by adverbs such as *somewhat* and *greatly*. Instead of writing *greatly minimize,* write *diminish* or *reduce*.

direct, directly. As an adjective, *direct* means "straight," "by the shortest course," "not turning aside": "This is a *direct* route to the house." As an adverb, *direct* is interchangeable with *directly* when used in this sense ("in a straight line") and when it means "without anything intervening": "The team went *directly* (or *direct*) to the locker room." "These vegetables came *directly* (or *direct*) from a nearby farm." But one cannot say "I was *direct* concerned" or "I will be there *direct.*" In the first sentence, use *directly* or *immediately* or *clearly*. In the second, say *directly* or *soon* or *immediately* or even *in a short time*.

disability. *See* INABILITY.

disassemble. *See* DISSEMBLE.

disaster, holocaust, tragedy. A *disaster* is an event causing damage or hardship. The word comes from Greek and Latin terms suggesting "from the stars" and hence has a connotation of bad luck: "Lillian felt that the loss of all her money was a minor *disaster.*" "The collision of the cars was a *disaster*, but not a fatal one." *Holocaust* comes from a Greek word meaning "burnt" or "burned" and refers to complete devastation or destruction. That is, a *holocaust* is a *disaster*, but a *disaster* is not necessarily a *holocaust*. Floods, collisions, train wrecks, and accidents of many kinds are *disasters*, but *holocaust* is a term that should be reserved for immense destruction and widespread devastation: "The bombs falling in the crowded area resulted in a *holocaust.*" *Tragedy,* a more general term, refers to any calamity or disaster, any dreadful or fatal event. One may, for instance, refer to the *disaster* or *holocaust* or *tragedy* of modern warfare.

disbar. *See* DEBAR.

disc, disk. These words are spelled differently but mean the same thing: "a thin, flat, circular plate or object." One refers to a "*discus* thrower" but may call a person who conducts a broadcast consisting of recorded music a "*disc* jockey" or a "*disk* jockey."

disclose. *See* DIVULGE.

discomfort, discomfit, discomfiture. The first of these words is widely used to refer to lack of comfort, uneasiness, and even mild pain: "His wet clothing caused him considerable *discomfort.*" "Her distress over missing the train made her feel some *discomfort.*" *Discomfiture,* a much stronger term, means "rout," "complete overthrow," "utter defeat": "The downfall of the government caused *discomfiture* throughout the nation." When you suffer *discomfiture,* you also experience *discomfort,* but *discomfort* alone rarely results in *discomfiture. Discomfit,* a verb only, means "to defeat," "to thwart," "to confuse," "to disconcert": "This direct question will *discomfit* the speaker."

discover, invent. *Discover* means "to get knowledge of," "to find out," "to learn of something previously unknown" (*discover* America, *discover* uranium). To *invent* is "to originate," "to conceive of or devise first": "*invent* the sewing machine." Synonyms for *discover,* none of which apply to the basic meaning of *invent,* are *detect, discern, notice, ferret out,* and *espy.*

discreet, discrete. These words, pronounced alike, have entirely different meanings. To be *discreet* is to be prudent, cautious, careful, trustworthy, circumspect: "Never one to talk much, she kept a *discreet* silence." "The late President Truman often referred to George Marshall as a *discreet* official." *Discrete* means "separate," "distinct," "apart," "detached": "This question consists of six *discrete* parts." "Manufacturing, advertising, selling, and collecting payment are *discrete* divisions of this business."

disinterested, uninterested. *Disinterested* means "impartial," "unbiased," "not influenced by selfish motives." *Uninterested* suggests aloofness, indifference, or lack of interest. Say "The judge rendered a *disinterested* verdict" and "The judge was *uninterested* in the courtroom behavior of the accused."

dislike. *See* HATE.

disorganized. *See* UNORGANIZED.

disparage. *See* BELITTLE.

displace, misplace. These words suggest putting something in a place where it should not or ought not to be. To *displace* is to shift something (usually solid) more or less permanently from its accustomed place: "The flood *displaced* every structure in that section of town." To *misplace* is to put an object in a wrong place so that it is difficult to find: "She could no longer sew, for she had *misplaced* her scissors." A person who has been compelled to leave his home or country is *displaced;* a worker in a position for which he is unsuited is *misplaced*.

disposal, disposition. *Disposal* refers to the act of getting rid of something by throwing away, giving away, burning, or assigning: "The problem of waste *disposal* in this village is acute." "What *disposal* will you make of these old clothes?" *Disposition* also conveys the idea of placing, arranging, and ordering, but only when such acts are performed according to a plan: "The general ordered a strategic *disposition* of his troops." "The deceased man's will arranged for the *disposition* of his property." Think of *disposal* as "disposing of," of *disposition* as "disposing."

disqualified. *See* UNQUALIFIED.

disregardless, irregardless. Both words are illiteracies. The prefixes *ir-* and *dis-* are superfluous. Say *regardless, unmindful, heedless, anyway,* or even the wordy *in spite of everything* and thus avoid a double negative *dis-* and *ir-* plus *-less): "Regardless* (not *disregardless* or *irregardless*) of what you say, I shall do as I wish."

disremember. This word is dialectal rather than illiterate, but good speakers prefer *forget* or *fail to remember:* "Did you *forget* (or *fail to remember*) what I said?"

dissatisfied. *See* UNSATISFIED.

dissect. *See* BISECT.

dissemble, disassemble. *Dissemble* means "to conceal," "to give a false appearance," "to feign": Try to *dissemble* your lack of interest by looking alert." "Roy *dissembled* his guilt by grinning broadly." *Dissemble* is a synonym of *dissimulate. Disassemble* means "to take apart": "He *disassembled* the motor and then found he could not put it together again." *Disassemble* is the antonym of *assemble.*

dissimulate, simulate. To *dissimulate* is to conceal or hide; to *simulate* is to pretend: "He *dissimulated* his injury by waving his arms." "She *simulated* pain by writhing on the grass."

distinctive, distinct, distinguished. These words are related but not interchangeable in meaning. *Distinctive* means "characteristic," "individual," "set apart": "the *distinctive* roar of a lion." *Distinct* means "clear," "plain," "definite," "unmistakable in its identity": "Oxygen has properties *distinct* from those of helium." *Distinguished* stresses the quality or characteristic of being eminent, outstanding, renowned: "This official has had a *distinguished* career in public service." What is *distinct* is clearly seen and not easily mistaken for something else; what is *distinctive* is something so set apart as to be conspicuous; what is *distinguished* is conspicuous by reason of excellence and distinction.

distinguish. *See* DIFFERENTIATE.

divert. *See* AVERT.

divide. *See* SEPARATE.

divulge, disclose. These terms mean "to make known to others what was intended to be kept secret, private, or confidential." *Divulge* is more likely to be used when something previously secret is revealed to a small number of people or a particular group; *disclose* usually refers to a general sharing of knowledge or information with others: "Barbara *divulged* to her roommates her plan to be married within a month." "The Warren Commission attempted to *disclose* the facts concerning President Kennedy's assassination." Neither word is widely used, perhaps because *reveal, tell,* and *expose* convey much the same meaning.

doctor. *See* PHYSICIAN.

dominate, domineer. The first of these words means "to control, govern, regulate, or tower above": "The superintendent *dominated* the hospital staff." "The tall pine *dominated* the coastline." *Domineer* means "to rule or govern arrogantly and tyrannically," "to regulate like a despot": "Mussolini *domineered* (or *domineered over*) his countrymen for some twenty years." *Domineer* has more unpleasant and unfavorable connotations than *dominate,* but neither suggests a happy situation for those being regulated.

donate, give. These terms mean "to make a present of," "to bestow," "to contribute": "This company *donates* (or *gives*) to the Red Cross every year." *Donate* is considered a genteel and polite word; it has been suggested that one *gives* a small sum and *donates* a large one. Both words are standard, but using *give* is recommended because the word is shorter and simpler and is fully as meaningful as *donate*. Only when referring to services (The actor *donated* his services) is *donate* preferable to *give*.

don't, don't think. *Don't* is a contraction of *do not*. Avoid such illiteracies as *"he don't," "they don't got,"* and *"it don't* seem." *Do* is a verb in the present tense and is never used in the third-person singular; use *does*. *Don't think,* a familiar, widely used expression, is not wholly logical. When one says "I *don't think* I want to leave," what he is really saying is that he *does think* that he *doesn't* want to leave or he thinks that he wants to stay. *Don't think* is not ungrammatical, but it is a wordy, careless expression.

double negative. The phrase "double negative" is not itself an error of any sort, but it does name a construction considered illiterate or narrowly dialectal. Such a construction employs two negatives to express a single negation. Illiterate or careless speech abounds with such expressions as "can't hardly," "haven't scarcely," "can't scarcely." Such double negatives have been allowable in past centuries, but they are now out of style and unacceptable. You are not likely to say, "I *didn't* get *no* money" or "I *haven't* seen nobody," but you should be careful to avoid using *not* with such negative words as *no, but, nor, only, hardly, barely, scarcely,* and *except:* "I did *not* have *but* five hours' sleep." "You *can't* help *but* love that child."

doubt if, doubt whether, doubt that. Both *doubt* and *doubtful* are often followed by clauses introduced by *if, whether,* and *that.* A choice among the three depends upon the kind of sentence involved. *That* is used when a negative or interrogative idea is involved: "There is little *doubt that* you are mistaken." "Can you any longer be *doubtful that* you are mistaken?" *Whether* is used in statements conveying genuine doubt and uncertainty: "It is *doubtful whether* he will live." "They *doubt whether* he was ever there." *If* is usually to be avoided after both *doubt* and *doubtful,* although some accomplished speakers feel that *if* and *whether* are interchangeable. Since the use of *if* is debatable in *doubt* constructions and the use of *whether* is limited, why not always use *that?*

doubtlessly. *See* UNDOUBTEDLY.

draft, draught. A *draft* is (1) a drawing, sketch, or design; (2) a current of air; (3) the act of drawing or pulling loads; (4) the taking of money or other supplies from a source; (5) selection by lot. A *draught* refers to (1) drawing liquid from a container; (2) the act of drinking; (3) a drink. Both terms refer to air currents but otherwise have distinct meanings, although in Great Britain *draught* is the preferred spelling for several of the meanings listed under *draft.* Examples: "Suddenly she felt a cold *draft* (or *draught*) of fresh air." "Jim took a long *draught* of cold beer." (In recent years, *draft* has been more frequently used in this sense.) "I shall issue a *draft* against your account at the bank." "He owns two heavy *draft* horses." "When a *draft* of fresh air entered the room, he took a *draught* of it into his lungs."

dreamed, dreamt. The past tense and past participle of *dream* are either *dreamed* or *dreamt:* "She *dreamed* a lovely dream last night" or "She *dreamt* a lovely dream last night." One may say *has dreamed* or *has dreamt* with equal correctness. *Dreamed* is more often used in the United States, *dreamt* in Great Britain. Both forms of the verb require the preposition *of* when followed by a verb form ending in *-ing:* "She *dreamed* (or *dreamt*) *of taking* an exciting journey to Europe."

drought, drouth. These words with different spellings refer to dry weather, lack of rain or other precipitation, and to any extended shortage. *Drought* is pronounced "drout"; *drouth* is pronounced with a *th* ending. *Drought* is the preferred spelling. Examples: "The *drought (drouth)* extended for three months, ruining all hopes for a good crop of vegetables." "The team went without a victory for the entire season, a long period of *drought (drouth).*"

due to. The phrase *due to,* when used in a prepositional sense meaning "owing to" and "caused by," is in common and reputable use: "His accident was *due to* a fall on the icy pavement." Many careful speakers avoid *due to* in introducing an adverbial construction (He began to shake *due to* his fear), but actually *due to* is grammatically as sound and correct as the phrases it replaces: *owing to, because of, on account of,* and *through*. However, *due to* and, especially, *due to the fact that* are wordy ways of saying *since* and because.

dwell. *See* RESIDE.

E

each. This pronoun is singular and implies *one* even when not followed by *one*. Plural words used in modifying phrases do not change the number: "*Each has* his own reasons." "*Each* of the girls *has* her own reasons." When *each* appears after a plural subject to which it refers, the verb should be plural: "Bill and Jack *each have* their own reasons."

each and every. This is a redundant (wordy) phrase; when used, it requires a singular verb: "*Each and every* one of you *has* his own reasons." Preferably, use *each* or *every*, not both.

each other, one another. In standard speech, *each other* is used when two persons are involved; *one another* is preferred when three or more persons are concerned: "The man and his wife spoke to *each other* excitedly." "The six motorcyclists were arguing with *one another.*" Common usage (not recommended, however) permits such a statement as "The five culprits regarded *each other* with distrust." Be safe: use *one another* when three or more persons are involved.

eager. *See* ANXIOUS.

early, soon. These words have a shared meaning, "in the near future." One can say, "An *early* departure time has been scheduled for the flight" or "The flight will arrive *soon*." Something referred to as *early,* however, also means something that comes or appears before the appointed or scheduled time: "One plane arrived *early* and had to wait for the other." *Soon* means "within a brief period after a specified time or event": "Once the second plane arrived, welcoming ceremonies *soon* began." *Early on,* a British expression that has become popular in the United States, is now a trite phrase. It is also a wordy one. Omit the *on* and say *early, soon, quickly,* or *immediately.*

earthy, earthly. These words have a common origin but different meanings. *Earthly* means "of or pertaining to the earth," "possible or conceivable in this world": "The travel folder claims that this resort is an *earthly* paradise." "Your help can be of no *earthly* use to me." *Earthly* is concerned with the earth, either literally or figuratively, and nearly always implies a contrast to that which is not of the earth, that is, *heavenly*. *Earthy* means "characteristic of earth or soil": "These roots have an *earthy* smell." *Earthy* also means "realistic," "practical," "coarse," and "unrefined": "His sense of humor is *earthy*." "His goals in life are *earthy* rather than idealistic."

easy, easily. These words are not interchangeable in standard speech and writing. *Easily* is an adverb; *easy* is an adjective. Such expressions as "Take it *easy,*" "Go *easy,*" and "Travel *easy* by bus" are informal, although widely used. Examples of standard use: "This is an *easy* task." "You can do that *easily.*" Because they are trite or highly informal, avoid such expressions as "*Easy* does it," "go *easy* on," "*easier* said than done," "slow and *easy,*" "*easy* money," and "on *easy* street."

eatable, edible. These words, both in standard usage, have a shared meaning of "not poisonous or harmful," "fit to be eaten": "This food does not look appetizing, but it is *eatable* (or *edible*)." *Edible* is more formal and somewhat more refined than *eatable,* a word often used in the plural: "The sack contained a quantity of various *eatables.*" Edible is preferable in a statement such as "These berries were once thought poisonous, but they are *edible.*"

economic, economical. *Economic* applies to material wealth and to business or household enterprise. *Economical* means "prudent in management," "not wasteful," "thrifty." Thus one refers to "*economic* resources" and "*economical* management," to "*economic* problems" and "*economical* living." Examples: "The Brown family moved to a smaller house for *economic* reasons." "Mrs. Brown learned to be *economical* in budgeting household expenses."

edible. *See* EATABLE.

edition, impression, printing. These terms are frequently used interchangeably, but they have distinct meanings. *Edition,* from a Latin word meaning "to give out," refers to (1) the format (size and shape) in which a work is published; (2) the entire number of copies *(impressions)* of a published work (book, magazine, newspaper) printed from a set of type in one continuous run; (3) a version of any work, printed or not, that is publicly presented, as, for instance, the latest *edition* of a play or opera. If a new *printing* involves no changes in the text or illustrations of a work, or only minor corrections, the result is not a new *edition* but a new *impression.* A thorough revision resulting in a noticeably different version is a *new edition.* A *first edition* is a work as it is or was originally published. An *impression* is one of a number of *printings* of the same *edition* made at different times from the same set of type.

effect. *See* AFFECT.

effective. *See* AFFECTIVE.

effective, efficient, effectual. *Effective* refers to something that has the power to produce, or that actually does produce, an effect or result: "This medicine is an *effective* remedy for acid indigestion." *Efficient* implies the use of energy, skill, or industry to accomplish a desired result: "This foreman is an *efficient* executive." *Effectual* refers to any agency or force that produces an intended or desired result: "Neighbors, making an *effectual* search of the area, found the lost children." An *efficient* salesman is an *effectual* agent for a company that desires to make its public image *effective* throughout the country.

egoism, egotism. Both words and their adjectival forms, *egoistic* and *egotistic,* refer to preoccupation with one's own self, or ego. *Egoism,* less commonly used than *egotism,* emphasizes self-importance in relation to other things: "Joe has quite enough *egoism* to understand his role in society." *Egotism* is an often-used word for excessive or boastful reference to, or emphasis upon, oneself: "His *egotism* made it impossible for him to hold many friends." An *egoist* is one devoted to his own interests; an *egotist* is a conceited, boastful person.

either . . . or, neither . . . nor. *Either* means "one of two"; *neither* means "not one of two." *Or* goes with *either, nor* with *neither: "Either* Sarah *or* I will go, but *neither* Bill *nor* Jane will." When used alone, both *either* and *neither* take verbs in the singular: *"Either is* ready to go with you." *"Neither is* now ready." The use of *either . . . or* and *neither . . . nor* to coordinate more than two words, phrases, or clauses is considered permissible by some authorities but not by the majority: *"Either* telephone *or* write." *"Neither* Jack *nor* Jill knows." "He is studying mathematics, chemistry, and physics, but he is proficient in *none* (preferably not *neither*)." In *either. . . or* and *neither . . . nor* constructions, these conjunctions are properly followed by similar parts of speech or similar structures. That is, write "*Either* he keeps quiet *or* he leaves the room," not "He *either* keeps quiet *or* . . ."

elapse, lapse. *Elapse,* once used as a noun and a synonym for *lapse,* is now in standard usage as a verb only: "Ten minutes have *elapsed* since the fire alarm sounded." *Lapse* is properly used both as a noun meaning "an interval of time," "a slip or failure," and "a decline" and as a verb meaning "to cease to exist": "No one could account for the *lapse* between the alarm and the arrival of firemen." "I must have suffered a *lapse* of memory." "The policy will *lapse* if the premium is not paid promptly."

elder, eldest, older, oldest. The first two words of this group apply only to persons, whereas *older* and *oldest* may apply to persons or things. Also, *elder* and *eldest* (much less common than the other two terms) apply principally to members of a given family or business establishment and indicate age or seniority (*elder* brother, *eldest* partner). However, say "He is *older* (not *elder*) than his brother."

elemental, elementary. Although these words have a shared meaning of dealing with, or referring to, agencies and forces of nature, they are distinguished in ordinary usage. *Elemental* is applied to basic elements such as power, size, or strength (the *elemental* force of the wind). *Elementary* is used to refer to that which is simple, introductory, or easy: "This is a book on *elementary* arithmetic."

elicit. *See* ILLICIT.

else, else's. *Else* is an adjective meaning "other" or "different" or "more," as in the statement "She wanted something *else*." *Else* can also be an adverb (Walk carefully on the ice or *else* you will slip), but it appears most often in compound pronouns such as *somebody else, everybody else,* and *who else*. In such constructions, the possessive is formed by adding an apostrophe and *s* to *else:* "She is *someone else's* girl." The construction is not entirely logical, but it is idiomatically correct; never say or write "someone's *else,*" "everybody's *else,*" or "anyone's *else.*" However, the possessive form of *who else* can be written as *who else's* or *whose else* but not as *whose else's:* "Is this hat yours? *Whose else* (or *who else's*) could it be?"

elude. *See* ALLUDE.

elusion. *See* ALLUSION.

emend. *See* AMEND.

emerge, emerse, immerge. *Emerge,* meaning "to come forth," "to rise up," and "to come into sight," is followed by the preposition *from:* "Martha *emerged from* the pool with her hair dripping." "The sun *emerged from* behind fleecy clouds." *Emerse* no longer appears in the language except in an adjectival (past-participle) form used in botany: A water lily standing out of water and surrounding leaves is said to be *emersed. Immerge* means "to plunge into" and "to disappear." In the former meaning it is synonymous with *immerse:* "The chemist *immerged* (or *immersed*) the solution in acid." The other meaning of *immerge* is illustrated in a statement such as "The faint moon *immerged* into the shadow of the sun."

emerge, issue. The basic meanings of *emerge* are stated in the preceding entry. *Issue* also means "to come forth," but it is applied in situations involving a forceful breaking out of something that has been confined or enclosed: "Fire-streaked smoke began to *issue* from the chimney."

emerse. *See* EMERGE, EMERSE, IMMERGE.

emigrant, immigrant. These words, together with *emigrate* and *immigrate, emigration* and *immigration,* are related to the basic verb *migrate,* which is used with reference to place of departure and to destination. *Emigrant* and *emigrate* refer specifically to a place of departure and emphasize movement from that place. *Immigrant* and *immigrate* refer mainly to destination and are followed by *to,* as *emigrate* and *emigrant* are by *from:* "Johnson *immigrated to* England in 1965." "Johnson *emigrated from* Sweden in 1965." A person moving from one country to another is an *emigrant.* One who has already moved to another area is an *immigrant.*

eminent, imminent. *Eminent* (pronounced "EM·uh-nuhnt") means "distinguished," "high in rank," "noteworthy" (an *eminent* statesman). *Imminent* (pronounced "IM·uh·nuhnt") means "about to occur," "impending" (an *imminent* rain squall).

empathy, sympathy. *Empathy,* a more specific word than *sympathy,* refers to actual identification with the thoughts and feelings of someone else or to a sharing through vicarious experience with the attitudes and emotions of another: "*Empathy* is more meaningful in this time of sadness than is any letter or gift of flowers." "Through *empathy* the young reader felt that Maugham's novel *Of Human Bondage* was a mirror of his own life." *Sympathy* refers to a general feeling of harmony or agreement between persons, a fellow feeling of understanding: "The mechanic expressed his *sympathy* but said that his garage was closed for the night."

empty, vacant. These words mean "containing nothing," but they have different applications. Something that is *empty* is lacking in its usual or customary contents: an *empty* house contains no furniture; an *empty* store contains no merchandise. *Vacant* is applied to something that is temporarily unoccupied: a *vacant* bed (no one is in it at the moment); a *vacant* house (it is unoccupied at the time). A *vacant* apartment would contain all its furnishings but would house no occupants. If a position is not filled, it is said to be *vacant,* not *empty*. A look which lacks expression would be called a *vacant* stare because the implication is that the absence of feeling is only temporary.

enclose, inclose. These words mean "to shut in," "to close on all sides," "to surround," and "to insert": "High mountains *enclosed* (or *inclosed*) the valley." "*Enclose* (or *inclose*) a check with your letter." *Enclose* is the preferred spelling. So is *enclosure* rather than *inclosure*. Expressions such as "*enclosed* herewith" and "*enclosed* herein" are wordy because *enclose* conveys the idea of *herewith* and *herein*. "*Enclosed* please find" is a piece of business jargon not only wordy but also silly. Say, rather, "I am *enclosing* . . ."

end, ending, ended. Both *end* and *ending* refer to a termination or close of something, a conclusion, the final part of an action or happening. Thus one may refer to the *end* or the *ending* of a war, a book, a play, or a love affair. *End,* however, is more often applied to the actual completion of an action, whereas *ending* refers to the process of completing or winding it up. That is, the *end* of a novel is the final line of the narrative; the *ending* of a novel can have the same meaning but may also apply to the final pages, the last full episode. The *end* of a war refers to that moment when hostilities cease; the *ending* of a war may equally apply to a longer period during which a war is winding down while negotiations for a cease-fire or armistice are in progress. That is, what is *ending* is "coming" to an *end* or is "about" to *end*. What is *ended* has actually come to an *end* at some time in the past. "He never left town during the six months *ended* last June." "He hopes to make several trips during the period *ending* next December."

Although the practice is widespread, avoid the use of *ending* to refer to any period of time other than one to be completed in the future. Also, remember that *end* itself is an overworked word, appearing in numerous trite, wordy, or illogical expressions. *End* is informal when used to mean "duty," "obligation," or "part" (your *end* of the bargain). It appears often in such trite expressions as "go off the deep *end*" ("behave recklessly or impulsively"); "make both *ends* meet" ("manage to live within one's means"); "no *end*" ("a great deal"); "hold one's *end* up" ("care for one's own responsibility"); "at loose *ends*" ("unsettled"); "at one's wit's *end*" ("at the *end* of one's resources"); "put an *end* to" ("finish," "terminate"); "*ends* of the earth" ("remote regions," "everywhere"). "*End* result" is a wordy phrase; *result* conveys the idea of *end*. Since a *result* is an *end*, avoid this trite, redundant expression.

endemic. *See* EPIDEMIC.

endless, innumerable. These words are often used interchangeably, but they have distinct meanings. *Endless* means "without an end," "boundless," "interminable," "continuous": "The *endless* prairie stretched before his eyes." "During his recent illness, he felt that his pain was *endless.*" "The workmen are replacing an *endless* conveyor belt." *Innumerable* means "too many to count," "countless," "numberless": "The daisies in that huge field were *innumerable.*" The tasks of a housewife may seem *endless,* but they are hardly *innumerable.* The leaves on a tree may be *innumerable* but they are not *endless;* neither are the *innumerable* snowflakes falling in a winter storm.

endorse, indorse. Both of these words are in standard use, although *endorse* is generally preferred. Each has two primary meanings: (1) "to support or approve" (Please *endorse* my campaign); and (2) "to write one's signature" (Please *endorse* this check). The second syllable, *dorse,* means "back," as one might refer to the *dorsal* fin of a marine mammal. Therefore, "*Endorse* on the back" is a wordy, unacceptable phrase. If you are fortunate enough to receive a check, write your name on it or *endorse* it, but don't "*endorse* it on the back."

enervating, invigorating. Possibly because *enervate* looks and sounds something like *energy,* some writers and speakers confuse the meanings of *enervating* and *invigorating,* which are almost antonyms. *Enervating* means "weakening, devitalizing, sapping the strength of" (a humid, *enervating* climate); *invigorating* means "animating, giving energy or vigor" (a brisk, *invigorating* climate).

enigma. *See* RIDDLE.

enough, sufficient. These words are interchangeable, as is pointed out under AMPLE, ENOUGH. Each means "adequate," "equal to the required amount": "We have *enough* food to last us for a week." "We have *sufficient* money to buy more when we need it." These words should not be used together; "sufficient enough" is a wordy expression. *Sufficient* is felt to be more refined and elegant than *enough,* but the words are equally acceptable. *Enough,* which can be used as a noun, adverb, and adjective, can also be overused as a conversation filler. These are trite phrases: "oddly *enough,*" "strangely *enough,*" "peculiarly *enough.*" If a modifier is needed, then omit the *enough. See also* CURIOUSLY ENOUGH.

enquire, inquire. Both spellings of this word are acceptable, although *inquire* is more widely used. Similarly, the noun inquiry is preferable to *enquiry. Enquire (enquiry)* is sometimes used for the act of questioning, whereas *inquire (inquiry)* refers to a more detailed or prolonged questioning, an investigation. This distinction hardly seems worthwhile: "The cashier made an *inquiry (enquiry)* into the cash shortage."

enrage, incense. These words alike mean "to anger," "to put in a rage," "to infuriate," "to cause to be angry." "A woman is *enraged* when she is provoked to violent anger." "Susan was *incensed* by the rude remark of her companion." *Incensed* has these characteristics: (1) it suggests greater dignity and self-restraint than does *enraged;* (2) it implies a greater degree of provocation than does *enraged;* (3) it is used to refer to someone toward whose anger we feel sympathetic.

ensure. *See* ASSURE.

entail. *See* INVOLVE.

enthuse. Meaning "to show enthusiasm," *enthuse* is nonstandard. Instead of saying "She *enthused* over the dance," say "She *was enthusiastic* over (or about) the dance."

entrance, entry. As a noun meaning "entering" or "a passage that affords entry," *entrance* is pronounced "EN·trans." As a verb meaning "to put into a trance" or "to delight," the word is pronounced "en·TRAHNS": "The *entrance* to the cave was 7 feet wide." "The audience was *entranced* by her performance." *Entry* has the same basic meanings as the noun *entrance,* and the two words may be used interchangeably. In law, *entry* has the special meaning of "something recorded" (an *entry* in the register of deeds) and "the act of taking possession by means of entering" (the landlord's right of *entry* to the property).

enure. *See* INURE.

envelop, envelope. The first of these words, a verb meaning "to encase, enclose, or surround," is pronounced "en·VEL·uhp." The noun *envelope,* meaning "something that envelops," "an enclosing wrapping," is pronounced "EN·vuh·lohp," "ON·vuh·lohp," or "ANH-vuh·lohp": "Clouds will soon *envelop* the mountaintop." "Put a stamp on the *envelope* before mailing it."

enviable, envious. *Enviable,* meaning "desirable," is a milder (less strong) word than *envious,* which has the same basic meaning but suggests strong discontent and resentment. *Enviable* may even be used as an expression of praise: "His solid strength of character is *enviable.*" *Envious* never implies praise, since it involves both resentment and desire: "Because Bill was *envious* of his supervisor's position, he tried hard to undercut him."

environment, environs. These related words, each meaning "surroundings," "surrounding area," are pronounced respectively "en·VAI·ruhn·muhnt" and either "en·VAI·ruhnz" or "EN·vuh·ruhnz." Although not a true plural and without a singular form, *environs* should not be used with any word involving number: one cannot say "three *environs* of the city" or "many *environs* in this state."

envision, envisage. These words are so often used interchangeably by knowledgeable speakers and writers that distinctions in meaning have vanished. In strict usage, *envision* means "to have a vision," "to foresee," whereas *envisage* has more a meaning of facing, seeing face to face, or confronting: "Even when desperately ill he could never envision a life of inactivity." "In his outlook for the city, the mayor *envisaged* definite plans for slum clearance." Both words are so ponderous that neither should be used in ordinary circumstances.

envy, covet, desire. Both *envy* and *covet* suggest resentment of another's fortune or condition and a desire to have that condition or situation for oneself. *Desire* is a weaker word than either *envy* or *covet,* since it expresses "wishing" or "longing for" without necessarily implying spite, malice, or resentment of another's possessions. *Envy* is broadest in meaning of the three terms because it combines desire and ill will. "Because he will never be well, he will always *envy* persons in good health." "This is a prize which everyone in the club should *covet.*" "He *desires* a good reputation more than fame or money."

envy, jealousy. These words are often used interchangeably, although *jealousy* is much more common. They do have distinct meanings. *Envy* suggests a discontented, unhappy longing for what someone else has; *jealousy* implies suspicion, fear, and uneasiness. "Her youthful beauty was the *envy* of everyone in the room." "His attitude toward his favored rival in the race changed from sympathy to dislike to outright *jealousy.*" That is, if one's attitude toward the possessions or attainments of others is mildly desirous, use *envy;* if resentment and spite are involved, use *jealousy*.

epic. This short word with powerful meanings and associated meanings should not loosely be used to refer to events, spectacles, or other matters unless they are notable for grandeur, scope, majesty, and heroism. It is doubtful that many sports events, films, TV shows, or books should really be called *epic*.

epicure. *See* HEDONIST.

epidemic, endemic. *Endemic* means "peculiar to a given country or people"; in medicine, the term is applied to a disease characteristic of, or confined to, a particular locality: "Malaria is *endemic* in certain warm, humid countries." *Epidemic,* much more often used, means "breaking out suddenly in such a way as to affect many individuals at the same time"; the term is used especially to refer to contagious diseases (*see* CONTAGIOUS): "In that year an *epidemic* of cholera broke out." *See also* PANDEMIC.

episode. *See* EVENT.

epitaph, epigraph. Both of these terms refer to an inscription on a monument or tomb or a brief piece of writing in praise of someone now dead: "The visitor paused in front of the shaft erected in memory of Queen Victoria and read the *epitaph* (or *epigraph*) carved on its face." *Epigraph* has the additional meaning of a quotation at the beginning of a book or chapter of a book: "The *epigraph* preceding this section is from the Book of Genesis."

equable, equitable. *Equable* means "uniform," "free from variations," "unchanging," and "tranquil": "The climate of Puerto Rico is *equable.*" "Marsha is well liked because of her *equable* temperament." *Equitable* means "just," "right," "fair," "reasonable": "The speaker claimed that he would campaign for *equitable* treatment of all citizens." "Both sides insisted that the settlement of their dispute was *equitable.*"

equal. Like *unique, perpendicular,* and other words with absolute meaning, *equal* should not be preceded by *more* or *most* because it is not capable of comparison. "More nearly *equal*" and "more *equitable*" are more acceptable and precise expressions than "more *equal*": "The Governor sought a *more nearly equal* distribution of state funds."

equally as. The adverb *equally* is redundant (wordy) when combined with *as*. Omit *equally* in a statement such as "Hard work is *(equally) as* valuable as ability." Delete *as* from a remark such as "*Equallly (as)* significant is one's desire to improve his lot."

equitable. *See* EQUABLE.

equivocal. *See* AMBIGUOUS.

erratum, errata. *Erratum,* derived from a Latin verb meaning "to wander," means "an error," one usually resulting from a misprint in a book or any mistake in something written by hand. *Errata* is the plural form of this noun and requires a plural verb: "The *errata* in this volume are numerous." *Errata* may also mean a list of errors or corrections, but even in this meaning is preferably followed by a verb in the plural. The word *erratas* is sometimes found in print, but the form is not generally approved. "The one important *erratum* in the volume *was* noted on an inserted page." "The major *errata* in this work *have* been listed in an appendix."

eruption, irruption. An *eruption* is a violent breaking *out;* an *irruption* is a violent breaking *in.* The discharge of lava from a volcano or of water from a geyser is an *eruption.* An invasion by an army is an *irruption.* In ecology, an *irruption* has the specialized meaning of an "increase," such as of the population of a country: "Improved health care and an increased birth rate resulted in an *irruption* during the past decade."

esoteric. *See* EXOTIC.

especial, special. These words are widely used interchangeably, with *special* being more common. There is a distinction in meaning, however. *Especial* means "exceptional," "outstanding," and *special* means "of a distinct kind," "particular," "individual": "This rule is of *especial* importance to all members of the club." "Jack is a *special* friend of mine." The adverb *especially* is more widely used than *specially,* perhaps because it embraces the meanings of "chiefly," "principally," "notably," and "mainly": "Last year we had an *especially* severe winter."

essay. *See* ASSAY.

essential. *See* NECESSARY.

essentially, substantially. As ordinarily used, these words are interchangeable: There is no difference between saying "This report is *essentially* the same as that one" and "This report is "substantially . . ." Each word conveys the idea of "basic" and "of the essence." Adjectival forms do differ, however: an *essential* service is an indispensable one, such as health care or fire fighting. A *substantial* service may or may not be indispensable, but it is always of considerable amount, quality, or size. "This drive raised a *substantial* amount of money for the hospital."

estimate, estimation. An *estimate* is a calculation or judgment as to the value, size, or qualities of something. Because an *estimation* is the forming of an *estimate*, the two words are often used interchangeably, although *estimate* is more often applied to things and *estimation* to persons, especially in the sense of opinion or belief. "His *estimate* of the storm-related damages ran into the millions." "In the *estimation* of his countrymen, he was a great man." In most instances, the words *opinion* and *judgment* are effective synonyms for *estimation*.

etc. *See* AND ETC.

eternal. *See* EVERLASTING.

ethics, morals. *Ethics* is used to refer to a system of moral principles, as one might mention "legal *ethics*," "medical *ethics*," or "the *ethics* of this community." *Morals* refers to standards or accepted customs of conduct and generally applies to right living in a society. It is not incorrect to refer, as one linguist has done, to *ethics* as the science, business, and practice of *morals* and to *morals* as the practice of *ethics*. Today, *morals* is more likely to have a religious application than *ethics* and often has a sexual connotation that *ethics* rarely has. To say that someone is a person of the highest *ethics* implies that he or she is honorable and upright in his or her private life and business dealings. To call someone a person of the highest *morals* would likely suggest that he or she is not guilty of sexual laxity. When meaning the moral sciences as a whole, *ethics* is a plural noun. It may be used with a singular verb when it refers to fitness or propriety: "The ethics of his decision *is* (or *are*) debatable." The adjective form is always *ethical,* not *ethic,* which is the singular form of the noun.

evenings. *See* AFTERNOONS.

event, incident, episode. Each of these words refers to something that happens or is regarded as happening, to some action or occurrence. An *event* is an important happening, one connected with previous happenings: "The principal *event* of the meeting was the report from the treasurer." "The historical *events* of the conflict are well established." An *incident* is a minor happening that takes place in connection with a more important event or series of occurrences: "The groom's dropping the ring was an amusing *incident* in the wedding ceremony." An *episode* is one of a series of occurrences, an action distinct from the main course of events but nevertheless interesting in itself: "His first trip to Europe was an exciting *episode* in the life of Senator Bottomley."

ever. *See* NEVER.

ever, every. *Ever* means "constantly," "always," "at any time," "repeatedly." *Every* means "each and all without exception." Few speakers confuse these words except in the phrases "*ever* so often" and "*every* so often." *Ever so often* means "frequently," whereas *every so often* means "occasionally," "now and then." Trite phrases involving *ever* and *every* include "*ever* and *ever,*" "*ever* and anon," "for *ever* and a day," "*every* which way," and "*every* now and then."

everlasting, eternal. *Everlasting* means (1) "lasting forever"; (2) "incessant," "never-ceasing"; (3) "boring," "tedious": "The *everlasting* hills were inspiring to the artist." "His severe illness caused him *everlasting* agonies throughout his body." "Children, please stop your *everlasting* chatter." That which is *eternal* is without beginning or end, is always existing: "She thought of God as the *eternal* father of everyone." Related words which might come closer to expressing a given meaning are *permanent, unending, perpetual, ceaseless, endless,* and *enduring.*

every. *See* EVER.

everybody, everyone. These words are interchangeable in their meaning of "every person," although *everyone* is considered by some speakers as more refined and euphonious than *everybody*. Both pronouns, when used as subjects, require singular verbs; accompanying pronouns should also be singular: "Everyone *has* (not *have*) an obligation to cast *his* (not *their*) vote." Spelled as one word, *everyone* means "everybody." *Every one* (two words) refers to each person of a group and is followed by *of: "Every one of* them is loafing on the job."

everyplace. This word is informal when used to mean "everywhere." Spelled as one word or two, *everyplace* is less standard than *everywhere.*

everyway. This adverb is a correct word when used to mean "in every way," "in every direction or manner": "We tried *everyway* we could to convince him of his error." There is no standard word *everyways*. "In *every* which *way*" is not a standard expression; omit *which.*

evidence, proof, testimony. These words are occasionally used as synonyms, but they do have distinct meanings. *Evidence* is information given in an investigation to support a contention: "At the trial, the witness presented *evidence* to convict the accused." *Proof* is that kind of evidence which is so weighty as to remove any possible doubt: "His signed confession is *proof* of his guilt." *Testimony* is the statement of a witness, usually given under oath: "The jury listened attentively to the *testimony.*" *Evidence* and *testimony* are often confused, but *testimony* should be used to refer only to statements and *evidence* to any ground for belief that is spoken, written, or presented in any other form.

evident. *See* APPARENT.

evidently. This word, meaning "obviously" or "apparently," is frequently mispronounced. It has only four syllables, pronounced "EV·uh·duhnt·lee" or "EV·i·duhnt·lee." The ending of the word is not pronounced "TAL·li" or "TUH·lee."

example, instance, sample. An *example* is a part of something, one of a number of things: "This is an *example* of his better work." The word also means "pattern," "model," or "specimen": "His devotion to work set an *example* for all of us." An *instance* is that kind of *example* used to prove or illustrate: "His bad behavior that day was an *instance* of his surly character." A *sample* is a small part of something and has the basic meaning of "specimen": "This *sample* of cloth is lovely." Although "for *instance*" and "for *example*" are interchangeable, *instance* and *example* are not: your behavior can set a good *example* for others but not a good *instance*.

exceedingly, excessively. The first of these words means "to an unusual degree," "extremely," "very much": "Everyone in the class is studying *exceedingly* hard." *Excessively* means "too much," "beyond proper or normal limits": "It was *excessively* cold for a day in spring."

except. *See* ACCEPT.

exceptionable, exceptional. These often-confused words are not interchangeable. The former means "objectionable"; the latter means "extraordinary," "uncommon," "unusual": "The judge ruled the behavior of the witness *exceptionable* and had him removed from the courtroom." "Martha has always been an *exceptional* student."

excerpt, extract. These words have several different meanings as both noun and verb, but each may refer to a passage or scene selected from a book, play, or article.

Basically, to *excerpt* is "to pick out," "to pluck," whereas to *extract* is "to remove, often with force": "The professor read us an *excerpt* from the novel." "From this poem, please *excerpt* your favorite lines." "Don't extract the wrong meaning from my remarks." "The dentist will soon *extract* this bad tooth."

excessively. *See* EXCEEDINGLY.

excuse, excuse me. *See* APOLOGY.

execrable, inexecrable. *Execrable* means "very bad," "abominable," "detestable": "The drunken actor gave an *execrable* performance." "Your rude behavior is *execrable.*" *Inexecrable* occasionally appears in print, but it is obsolete and is probably mistaken for some such word as *inexorable*.

exercise, exorcise. When these two words are misused, the mistake is probably due to misspelling or mispronunciation. *Exercise* means "something done or performed," "bodily or mental exertion," "to train, develop, or condition": "This is an *exercise* to strengthen one's back." "*Exercise* your mind or it will become slack." *Exorcise,* a verb only, means "to cast out," "to expel," "to deliver from": "The faith healer tried to *exorcise* an evil spirit from the sick man."

exhaustive, exhausting. *Exhaustive* means "thorough," "comprehensive," "completely consuming": "This is an *exhaustive* study of the subject." *Exhausting* means "using up fully," "expending the whole of," "exerting to the point of fatigue": "Digging trenches is an *exhausting* task."

exhibit, exhibition. An *exhibit* is a display of items or a collection of articles in an *exhibition*. An *exhibition* is a large-scale display, such as a fair, an exposition, or an art showing. One or more paintings by one artist might be an *exhibit* in an *exhibition* of modern art.

exist, subsist. To *exist* is "to live," "to be," "to have life": "Raccoons *exist* in that forest." "Hatred of war *exists* in all nations." To *subsist* also means "to have life" but with the additional idea of doing so by dependence upon something else, such as food, water, and shelter: "Only an experienced explorer can *subsist* in the Arctic."

exorcise. *See* EXERCISE.

exotic, esoteric. *Exotic* means "of foreign origin," "striking," "unusual," "strange," "exciting": "Mac loved the *exotic* food, *exotic* dress, and *exotic* speech which he encountered in Singapore." *Esoteric* means "understood or appreciated by only a few," "private," "secret": "It is difficult to grasp this *esoteric* poetry because of its many allusions to ancient mythology."

expertise. This widely used synonym for *skill, knowledge,* and *expertness* has become as trite as *know-how*. *Expertise* is acceptably used in formal and informal speaking and writing, but a synonym can always be found for this now-hackneyed term.

explicit, implicit. *Explicit* means "distinct," "specific," "clearly defined": "The foreman gave us *explicit* instructions." *Implicit* means "understood though not expressed": "A commitment to duty was *implicit* in his every act and thought." *Implicit* may also mean "complete," "unreserved" (*implicit* faith in our system of government).

explosion, implosion. An *explosion* is a violent expansion of some sort, a bursting out of gas, air, fuel, or other substances. An *implosion* is a similar bursting but one that is directed inward. When a gas tank *explodes,* debris is hurled outward; when it *implodes,* walls collapse and fall inward. A similar distinction is found in the words *eruption* and *irruption* (*see* ERUPTION).

expostulate, postulate. *Expostulate* means "to reason earnestly," "to remonstrate," "to demand": "The policeman *expostulated* with the motorist about the dangers of fast driving." *Postulate* is derived from the same Latin word as *expostulate* but means "to claim, assume, ask, or request without any degree of urgency or force": "The lecturer *postulated* the idea that all of us are selfish."

expurgated. *See* UNABRIDGED.

extant, extent. *Extant* (pronounced "EKS·tuhnt" or "ek·STANT") means "still in evidence, not destroyed or lost." *Extent* (pronounced "ek·STENT" or "ik·STENT") means "scope," "range," "comprehensiveness." "The *extent* of the land can be determined by *extant* property lines."

extemporaneous, impromptu. These words are applied to something said or done without special or advance preparation, as one might make a speech or perform some act on the "spur of the moment" (the meaning of *extemporaneous* in Latin). *Extemporaneous* is especially applied to an unmemorized speech given from notes or an outline: "Following the main address, someone in the audience began a heated *extemporaneous* discussion of the issues." *Impromptu,* derived from a Latin phrase meaning "in readiness," is applied to a speech given, a poem recited, or a song sung without advance notice or warning: "Although she was startled, Cissy gave an excellent *impromptu* talk."

extemporize. *See* TEMPORIZE.

extended, extensive. *Extended* means "stretched-out," "prolonged," "widespread," "outstretched": "When the basketball player's body was fully *extended,* he was nearly 7 feet tall." "The wires were then *extended* from one post to another." "His *extended* remarks lasted for nearly an hour." *Extensive* shares these meanings with *extended* but more specifically means "wide," "of great extent," "broad," "far-reaching": "His influence is *extensive* throughout the region." "As he continued to purchase acreage, his holdings became more and more *extensive.*" "Although his knowledge of the subject was *extensive,* the speaker's remarks seemed boringly *extended.*"

extent. *See* DEGREE and EXTANT.

exterior, external. These words share meanings of "out," and "outer," "outside," and "outward," but they do have a few different applications. One might say of a liniment, for example, that it is designed for *external* use but would not say that it is intended for *exterior* use. Also, *external* is an adjective only, whereas *exterior* is also a noun: "The *exterior* (not the *external*) of this house needs repairing." Use *exterior* to refer to "outer surface" and *external* as the opposite of *internal:* "The *exterior* of the melon was firm and clear, but the fruit inside was spoiled." "He had his own code of conduct and was not swayed by *external* influences."

extract. *See* EXCERPT.

extraneous, intrinsic. *Extraneous* means (1) "coming from or introduced from without"; (2) "irrelevant," "not belonging"; (3) "foreign," "external": "Judge this matter on its merits, not on *extraneous* considerations." "Stick to the subject; don't make any *extraneous* comments." *Intrinsic* is a near-antonym of *extraneous*. Its basic meaning is "belonging to something by its very nature," "innate," "native," "without regard to added properties or qualities": "The *intrinsic* worth of this proposal should be evident to everyone." "The *intrinsic* value of this coin is only 10 cents, but its *extrinsic* worth—what it would bring at auction—is many times greater."

F

fable. *See* MYTH.

facility, faculty. These words are loosely interchangeable when used to mean "ability," "skill," and "aptitude": "Henry's *facility* in handling tools made him a competent mechanic. His *faculty* for making friends brought him many customers." *Facility* has an added meaning of something that makes possible an easy or fluent performance or action: "Sue's *facility* in playing the piano made her a welcome addition to our group." A *facility* is also a convenience or service: "An additional washroom is a much-needed *facility* for this office." A *faculty* is a power or capability of mind or body: "He used every *faculty* of his mind in wrestling with the problem." Also, *faculty* refers to a department of learning or collection of teachers: "The *faculty* of this college is distinguished."

fact. There is no such thing as a "false *fact.*" Therefore, "true *fact*" and "true *facts*" are wordy expressions. Don't say "The true *facts* are . . ."; omit *true*. *Suppositions* and *allegations* are preferable to the expression "loose *facts.*"

factitious, fictitious. The basic meanings of *factitious* are "artificial," "contrived," "not spontaneous": "Many gadgets in the home are but *factitious* conveniences."

Fictitious has a related meaning of "not real," but it is more often applied to works of the imagination, such as novels, plays, and stories: "His account of the experience was partly accurate and partly *fictitious.*" A *factitious* lawsuit is one that has been contrived with little basis in fact; a *fictitious* lawsuit is one that has a completely imaginary basis.

factor. This noun has several precise meanings, but it is loosely and vaguely used to mean "element," "condition," or "situation," which themselves are terms of jargon. "One *factor* that made me take the job was the salary offered" can better be expressed "I took the job partly because of the attractive salary." Possible substitutes for *factor* include *ingredient, component,* and *element,* although none is really precise. A *factor* is an element leading to a result, so that the expression "contributing *factor*" is a phrase from which *contributing* should be omitted. A *factor* is only an element or a cause, never an event or occurrence in itself. Omit *factor* from speech and writing as often as you can; it's a loose, vague term.

faculty. *See* FACILITY.

faker, fakir. A *faker* is one who fakes, that is, a swindler, a trickster, or a fraud. The term is also applied to a person who pretends, who conceals something in order to deceive others, who assumes a false front: "This *faker* tried to sell property that he did not own." A *fakir* is a Muslim or Hindu religious person, usually one who devotes his life to contemplation and self-denial: "This *fakir* is a member of an Islamic religious order with which I am not familiar."

famed, famous, notorious. The first two of these words have about the same meaning: "celebrated," "acclaimed," "renowned." Each, however, is overused in an exaggerated sense of "well-known." *Notorious* has a meaning of "infamous," "known widely and unfavorably." George Washington was *famed* and *famous;* Benedict Arnold was *notorious.*

fancy, fantasy. *Fancy* is a term for imagination that is light, playful, unreal, and whimsical: "I often indulge in the happy *fancy* that I am both rich and powerful." "Sue's belief that she is irresistible is merely her playful *fancy.*" "She let her *fancy* play with the idea of a luxurious trip to Paris." *Fantasy* is applied to that kind of *fancy* that is unrestrained, extravagant, and erratic: "It is a dangerous *fantasy* to believe that you can fly through the air by flapping your arms." "The *fantasy* of this artist resulted in paintings that are weird and unbelievable."

farther, further. Distinction between these words has been breaking down for many years, but careful speakers use *farther* and *farthest* to refer to a measurable distance or space: "The ball traveled 10 yards *farther.*" *Further* indicates "greater in quantity, time, and degree" and also means "moreover": "We should discuss this problem *further.*" *See also* ALL THE FARTHER.

fashion, manner, mode. In ordinary use, these three words (especially the first two) are interchangeable in their meaning of "prevailing custom" and "accepted style." Thus one can refer to someone's *fashion* in dress, *manner* of dress, and *mode* in dressing. Slight differences in meaning do exist, however. *Fashion* may be defined as that which sets apart (distinguishes) the manners, dress, and habits of a group or period of time: "That hat would have been in *fashion* thirty years ago." "Dipping snuff is not the *fashion* of today's tobacco users." *Manner* is more often applied to the actions and behavior of individuals: "This hostess has a gracious *manner* in welcoming guests." "Ned's table *manners* could stand improvement." *Mode* has to do with a method of acting, with form, with a way of doing something: "Solar heat is a new *mode* of warming buildings." "Jack tries hard to keep up with the latest *mode* in everything he does." Approximate synonyms for *fashion, manner,* and *mode* in the meanings indicated here are *style, vogue,* and *fad.*

fat, plump, obese, stout. *Fat* is the customary, everyday word applying to someone who has too much flabby tissue: "Is it true that nobody loves a *fat* man?" Whereas *fat* usually has an unpleasant connotation, *plump* and *stout* suggest a roundness that is pleasing or a heavy build that is not unpleasant: "This is a jolly *plump* (or *stout*) old man." "Her *stout* (or *plump*) figure was attractively covered by a well-designed gown." *Obese,* meaning "excessively fat," "overweight," is used more often in scientific circles than by the general public: "The physician outlined a strict diet for all his *obese* patients." If none of these terms expresses what you have in mind, consider *corpulent, well-fed, adipose, pudgy, portly, bulky, thickset, rotund, chubby,* and *fleshy.*

Fat appears in many slangy or trite expressions for which less-worn synonyms can usually be found: "*fat* chance" ("slight chance"); "*fat* lot" ("little" or "not at all"); "chew the *fat*" ("engage in informal conversation"); "the *fat* is in the fire" ("the action is started and cannot be stopped"); "the *fat* of the land" ("the best of anything"); "*fat* cat" ("wealthy or important person"); "*fathead*" ("stupid person"); "*fats,*" "*fatso*" ("overweight person").

fatal, fateful. These words, derived from a Latin term meaning "destiny" or "fate," have distinct meanings. *Fatal* means "causing death" or "capable of resulting in destruction or ruin": "The highway accident was *fatal* to four persons." "Your lack of support will be *fatal* to my campaign." Synonyms for *fatal* include *deadly, lethal,* and *mortal. Fateful* means "important," "highly significant," "involving momentous consequences": "The meeting between Hitler and Mussolini was *fateful* for the history of Europe and the entire world." *Fateful* may mean "fatal," as in the preceding example, but what is *fatal* is not always *fateful:* Your unwillingness to lend me money to buy a coat may be *fatal* to my wardrobe plans but is hardly a *fateful* occurrence.

fatalism, determinism. *Fatalism* is the belief (doctrine) that all events are in the control of fate, that everything is the result of inevitable advance arrangement. *Fatalism* also involves the acceptance of fate, a submission to all occurrences as bound to happen: "The soldier's *fatalism* helped him to face the prospect of death without terror." *Determinism* has a related but distinguishable meaning —all events and facts result from natural causes; all choices and decisions can be accounted for on the basis of sufficient cause: "Because of his faith in the doctrine of *determinism,* he felt that his lot in life had been settled by the conditions under which his grandparents lived."

fateful. *See* FATAL.

fatuous. *See* FOOLISH.

faze. This word, which may also be spelled *fease* or *feaze,* means "to bother," "to disconcert," "to disturb," "to disrupt." It is a variation of *feeze,* an obsolete and dialectal word derived from Old English meaning "to drive away," "to put to flight." At best, *faze* is an informal word; at worst, it is tiresomely overused in such expressions as "Nothing *fazes* him." Do not confuse *faze* with *phase,* a word with a completely different meaning but the same pronunciation.

feasible, possible. *Feasible* means "capable of being done"; *possible* means that something can happen. *Feasible* suggests the ease with which something can be done and implies desirability for doing it: "This is a *feasible* plan that I hope you will adopt." *Possible* refers to that which is likely to happen: "It is *possible* that prices will continue to rise." "It is *possible* (not *feasible*) that we will have rain tomorrow."

feature. This word, admittedly overused, is now acceptable as a noun (What is the *feature* of the show?), an adjective (This is the *feature* attraction), and a verb (The newspaper *featured* that story). Its use to mean "to imagine" or "to conceive of" is informal and dialectal. Avoid such statements as "I cannot *feature* his holding that job" and "He *features* himself as a great storyteller."

feel. *See* BELIEVE and SENSE.

feet. *See* FOOT.

felicitous, fortuitous, fortunate. *Felicitous* means "well-suited," "apt," "appropriate": "The speaker's *felicitous* joke put the audience in a jovial mood." *Fortuitous* means "accidental," "produced by chance," "lucky": "Our meeting today on the street is *fortuitous.*" "A typical success story is filled with *fortuitous* events." *Fortunate* means "resulting favorably," "having good fortune," "auspicious": "It is *fortunate* that you slowed down before reaching the curve." Some *fortuitous* happenings may be both *felicitous* and *fortunate,* but the three words are not usually synonymous.

female. Current usage restricts *female* to designations of sex in scientific contexts. If *female* is considered objectionable in other contexts, and it is, we lack a word to express "female human being of whatever age."

ferment, foment. In the sense of causing trouble, these words can be used interchangeably: "Rebel soldiers *fomented* (or *fermented*) unrest among the people." *Ferment* literally means "to act upon as a ferment," that is, to cause the giving off of gases that induce bubbling and rising: "The mash will *ferment* for several days." Because fermentation is a state of unrest and agitation, as a noun *ferment* means "excitement," "commotion," and "tumult": "The lover's mind was a *ferment* of emotions." To *foment* is "to cause rebellion or discord," "to incite," "to arouse," "to inflame": "The inmates of the prison tried to *foment* a rebellion against the guards." *Foment,* a verb only, conveys the idea of causing unrest; *ferment,* both noun and verb, stresses the idea of being in, rather than causing, a state of unrest.

festive, festal. These words refer to a festival or feast, but *festive* has an added meaning of "joyous" or "merry." That is, a *festal* occasion may be *festive,* but not all *festive* occasions are connected with a feast or festival: "Decorations for the dance were imaginative and *festive.*" "The reunion of our class was a *festive* occasion." Many *festal* rites are connected with such occasions as Christmas, Easter, and Passover: "Following church services, the congregation will sit down to a *festal* meal."

fewer, less. Both of these words imply a comparison with something larger in number or amount. *Fewer* is preferred when number is involved (*fewer* houses on this street, *fewer* fish in the stream). *Less* is used in several ways: it is applied to material in bulk (*less* sugar in the coffee); with abstractions (*less* honor in business dealings); with matters involving degree and value (1 is *less* than 2). Although many writers and speakers use these words interchangeably, *fewer* should be used to refer only to numbers or to units capable of being counted: "The *less* money we have, the *fewer* supplies we can bring."

fictitious. *See* FACTITIOUS.

figuratively, literally. *Figuratively* means "not literally," that is, "metaphorically" (by means of a likeness or figure of speech). *Literally* means "really," "actually." *Literally* means "in a manner true to the *exact* meaning of the words it accompanies": *figuratively* means "in a manner of speaking": "The heavy work *literally* drained his remaining energy." "This author writes *figuratively* about the terror of solitude."

figure, number. In the sense in which it is often confused with *number*, *figure* means "a numerical symbol," "an amount or value expressed in numbers": "The little boy had difficulty writing the *figure* 5." "What *figure* did you arrive at as the total?" A *number* is a symbol or word, or a combination of symbols or words, used to denote a sum: "The *number* of people at the party exceeded 100." A *number* may be expressed in words (one hundred) or figures (100). The use of *figure* as a verb to mean "to compute" is standard (*Figure* what I owe you), but its use to mean "to judge" or "to think" or "to conclude" is substandard. As a verb, *figure* is an overworked word for which the following might be substituted: *calculate, comprehend, compute, contrive, determine, reason, suppose,* and *think*. "*Figure* out" is both trite and informal, as are "cut a *figure,*" "*figure* on," and "it *figures.*"

final, finale. *Final* is primarily an adjective meaning "coming at the end," "last in place, time or order": "This is the *final* event on the program." "The decision of the Supreme Court is *final.*" As a plural noun, *finals* refers to a decisive examination or concluding series of events: "He attended the *finals* of the club tennis tournament." *Finale,* used only as a noun, means the concluding part of any performance or set of proceedings: "As the *finale* of her program, she sang an aria of her own composition."

finalize. In the sense of "to complete," "to conclude," "to make final," *finalize* has been used so often that it is now accepted by most dictionaries as a standard word. Some careful speakers avoid the word because of its associations with bureaucracy and big business: "Let's *finalize* (or *conclude*) this meeting by summing up our objectives."

first, firstly, secondly. All three of these terms are in acceptable use, but *first* is more common than *firstly*. A speaker or writer will often start with *first* and then move on to *secondly* and *thirdly*. Although these *-ly* words are in respectable use, it is simpler and more economical to employ shorter forms (*first, second, third, fourth*), especially since these short forms can be used adverbially or adjectivally: "Several points need to be stressed: *first* (or *firstly*) there is the matter of money." "Who came in *first?*" "Let us *first* (or *firstly*) consider the refugees." Numbers greater than four usually come after *first* (the *first twenty* applicants); numbers smaller than four may precede or follow *first* (the *first three* applicants, the *three first* applicants). Recommendation: drop the *-ly* forms and always use *first, second, third,* etc., or *one, two, three,* etc. No need or excuse exists for such phrases as "*first* of all" and "*second* of all." Use *first* or *firstly, second* or *secondly,* and drop the useless *of all. See also* OF ALL.

fiscal. *Fiscal* is derived from a Latin term meaning "treasury" or "basket" and is employed to refer to the monetary practices and policies of a government, company, or institution: "The *fiscal* arrangements of this store are in hopeless shape." The term "*fiscal* year" refers to any twelve-month period for which an organization plans the handling of its funds: "During this *fiscal year* the company's cash flow increased 10 percent."

fix. *Fix* has a basic meaning of "to place" and "to fasten securely," but it is overused in a variety of meanings only loosely related to establishing, securing, or repairing. As a noun, *fix* is used to refer to (1) a dilemma or predicament, (2) the position of a plane or ship, (3) bribery and collusion, and (4) an injection of heroin or some other opiate. These uses of *fix* are ranked as standard, informal, or slang by different dictionaries, but all are employed so widely that it seems useless to recommend against them. As a verb, *fix* has some thirty different meanings, most of which are vague, loose, and imprecise. Try to substitute a more exact word, because it doesn't make sense to use the same expression in such locutions as "*fix* a toy," "*fix* a drink," "get a *fix,*" "*fix* your position at sea," "*fix* your face," "*fix* your hair," "*fix* a bet on a game," "*fix* an engagement," "*fix* a sentence," "*fix* a fight," and "be in a *fix.*" *Fixings* is an informal word for "trimmings," "accessories": "turkey and all the *fixings* (or *fixin's*)."

flagrant. *See* BLATANT.

flair, flare. *Flair* means "natural talent," "aptitude," "bent," "knack," or "keen perception": "This mechanic has a *flair* for spotting engine troubles." "She lived in Europe for many years, developing her *flair* for languages." *Flare* applies to a sudden burst of flame or the act of flaming: "His quick temper *flared* at the insult." "The guide used a *flare* to show me the way to our camp."

flammable, inflammable. These words mean the same thing and are interchangeable. They are not contrasted, as are, for example, *capable* and *incapable, mature* and *immature*. Although both words are correct, *flammable* is more often used by scientists and in technical pursuits, whereas *inflammable* is more common outside manufacturing contexts. In referring to someone's temperament or behavior, *inflammable* seems more appropriate than *flammable* (his *inflammable* disposition). Possibly someday everyone will settle on *flammable*.

flare. *See* FLAIR.

flaunt, flout. These words are often used interchangeably, but they have distinct meanings. *Flaunt* means "to show off," "to make a boastful display." *Flout* means "to scoff at," "to scorn." Say: "This prisoner has continued to *flout* (not *flaunt*) the law." "The cook *flaunted* (not *flouted*) his skill in flipping flapjacks."

fleshly, fleshy. Both these words refer to flesh and the body, but they should be distinguished in use. That which is *fleshly* is "physical," "bodily," "corporeal," or "carnal," "sensual," and "worldly": "His belief in God caused him to give up all *fleshly* pursuits." *Fleshy* means "fat," "plump," "having much flesh": "The more she ate, the more *fleshy* she became." *See also* FAT.

flotsam, jetsam. These terms usually appear together to refer to that part of the wreckage of a ship and its cargo found floating on the water or washed ashore. The phrase "*flotsam* and *jetsam*" now has an extended meaning of "useless trifles," "odds and ends": "The attic was filled with the *flotsam* and *jetsam* of many years." Although the words are now inseparable, in law they have distinct meanings. *Flotsam* (from an Old English word meaning "to float") is that part of a wreck that is floating on the surface; *jetsam* (from a Latin term meaning "to throw") refers to cargo tossed overboard to lighten a ship or improve its seaworthiness. Centuries ago, the *flotsam* of a wreck belonged to the king, *jetsam* to the lord of the manor off whose property the wreck occurred.

flout. *See* FLAUNT.

fluctuate, vacillate. Each of these words means "to move back and forth," "to change continually," "to vary." What little distinction in meaning there is between them is that *fluctuate* can apply to both persons and actions, whereas *vacillate* is usually applied only to persons: "The stock market will undoubtedly *fluctuate* during the coming year." "She *vacillated* between washing her hair and going to the movies."

flurried, flustered. These words are virtual synonyms; both mean "excited," "confused," "agitated": "Constant criticism *flustered* (or *flurried*) her." In one sense, to *fluster* someone is to *flurry* him, but *fluster* is a stronger term than *flurry*. A *flurried* person is upset or confused; a *flustered* person is agitatedly nervous or wildly disturbed: "Early during the evening he was *flurried*, but he became more and more *flustered* as the party wore on."

focus, nexus. Derived from a Latin word meaning "hearth," *focus* now has a basic meaning of "gathering point," "center of attraction, attention, or interest," "point of concentration": "Their home is the *focus* of community activity." "At the dance, she was the *focus* of everyone's interest." *Nexus* comes from a Latin word meaning "binding" and refers to a tie, a link, a means of connecting: "The *nexus* of this student body is school spirit." "Respect for everyone else is the *nexus* of civilized society." "*Focus* down on" is a wordy, trite phrase from which *down* should be dropped. *See also* CENTER AROUND.

folks. This is an informal, even archaic, term for "people," "folk," "relatives," or "race." "Just *folks*" and "plain *folks*" are trite phrases implying simplicity and unpretentiousness. *Folksy* is an informal term for "sociable" or "genial": "The President is a sociable (genial, companionable, friendly) man." If he is so *folksy* as to be "of the folk," he may not deserve to be President.

follows, as follows. Regardless of the singular or plural form of the noun that precedes, one can never say "as *follow.*" This is a matter of idiom, established usage, that has no regard for grammatical convention: "His comment was *as follows.*" "Events on the schedule are *as follows.*" If *as* is omitted, use *follow* or *follows* in accordance with usual grammatical principles: "His comments *follow.*" "His comment *follows.*" "Events on the schedule *follow.*"

foment. *See* FERMENT.

foolish, fatuous. These words, along with *silly, simple, asinine, vapid, stupid, witless,* and *senseless,* mean "lacking in judgment or intelligence, or both" and may ordinarily be used interchangeably. But they do have slightly different meanings and applications. A *foolish* person lacks both judgment and common sense and in addition may have a weak mind: "Eating heavily when you are not hungry is a *foolish* thing to do." "Your remarks are not only out of place but entirely *foolish.*"

Fatuous implies being not only dull and stupid but satisfied and complacent: "Because I have only one daughter, whom I adore, I realize that I am *fatuous* about her." "The lecturer haughtily provided *fatuous* answers to our questions." A *foolish* person cannot always help himself; a *fatuous* person usually can.

foot, feet. *Foot* has many meanings, the most common of which are (1) a part of the body and (2) a unit of length. The plural of *foot* is *feet*. The singular is preferred in such expressions as "a 3-*foot* ruler" and "a 9-*foot* wall," despite the fact that the numerals involved indicate more than one. However, idiom requires that one refer to "a ruler 3 *feet* long" and "a wall 9 *feet* high." One can say "a 6-*foot* man" but should say "a man 6 *feet* tall." That is, *foot* is normally used in forming compound adjectives (*barefoot* girl), and *footed* (not *feeted*) is employed in such terms as "four-*footed*" and "sure-*footed.*" *Foot* appears in such trite phrases as "put one's best *foot* forward," "put one's *foot* in one's mouth," "always *underfoot,*" "*footloose* and fancy-free," "get off on the wrong *foot,*" "have one *foot* in the grave," "put one's *foot* down," "put one's *foot* into it." *Feet* is tiresomely used in "set someone on his *feet*" *and* "*feet* first."

forbear, forebear. These words are tricky because *forbear* is a variant but correct spelling of *forebear*. A *forebear* is an ancestor, a forefather: "Chinese are said to have great respect for their *forebears.*" "This man's *forebears* emigrated from Scotland." *Forbear* means "to desist," "to keep back," "to be patient and self-controlled": "The kind teacher will *forbear* telling us what we did on the test." "The jury decided to *forbear* in this case and rendered a verdict based on mercy, not justice." Recommendation: always spell the word for "ancestor" with two *e*'s, remembering that such a person was alive *before* you were.

forcible, forceful. These words are closely related in meaning but should be distinguished in usage. *Forcible* applies to that which is accomplished by force or violence: "The firemen made a *forcible* entry into the burning building." *Forceful* applies to that which is effective or notable because of force: "You have a *forceful* personality." "The attorney made a *forceful* plea for his client."

forebear. *See* FORBEAR.

forego, forgo. To *forego* is "to go before," "to precede." *Forego* is a rarely used word, but it would be correct, although somewhat archaic, to say "The singing of a song will *forego* the main speech." *Forgo* (also a correct variant spelling of *forego*) means "to give up," "to abstain," "to renounce": "I'm not hungry and will *forgo* dinner." Although *forgo* may be spelled "forego," *forego* may not be spelled "forgo."

foreseeable future. *Foreseeable* involves seeing beforehand, exercising foresight. *Foreseeable future,* probably meaning "the future as far as we can now anticipate or predict it," is not only trite but lacking in good sense. None of us, no matter how smart or clever, can "see" even one minute into the future.

foreword, forward. Although these words give some trouble with spelling and pronunciation, their meanings are clearly distinguishable. A *foreword* is a preface, introduction, or introductory statement: "The *foreword* of this book runs for five pages." *Forward* means "in front," "located in advance," "ahead": "Troops will move *forward* on the count of four." "His cabin is located in the *forward* part of the ship." *See also* FORWARD.

for free. This is wordy slang, often used by careless speakers who forget that *free* means "for nothing."

forget, forgot, misremember. The past tense of *forget* is *forgot*: "I *forgot* to turn off the stove." The past participle is *forgotten* or *forgot:* "You seem to have *forgotten* (or *forgot*) me recently." *Forgotten* is more widely used than *forgot* as the past participle, but both forms are acceptable. The past-tense form *forgat* is archaic. *Misremember* is an archaic or dialectal synonym for *forget* and should never be used except, possibly, for humorous effect. *See also* DISREMEMBER.

forgetful. *See* OBLIVIOUS.

forgo. *See* FOREGO.

forgot. *See* FORGET.

for instance, for example. *See* EXAMPLE.

former, latter. *Former* applies to the first of two in a series. When you refer to the first of three or more, say either *first* or *first-named*. In the sense in which it contrasts with *former, latter* refers to the second of two things mentioned. When you mention the last of three or more, say *last-named,* not *latter*. Examples of use: "Of these two solutions, I prefer the *former.*" "The *latter* of these solutions is inferior to the *former.*" "The *first-named* soldier in the company will now step one pace forward." "After I call the roll, the *last-named* student will please raise his hand."

formidable, impressive. Each of these words means "arousing feelings of admiration," "superior," "exceptional": "This candidate is a *formidable* (or *impressive*) opponent." "You are asking me to undertake an *impressive* (or *formidable*) task." *Formidable* has the additional meaning of "intimidating," "feared," "dreaded," "awesome": "His strength and quickness made him a *formidable* fighting man." *Impressive* has the added meaning of "solemn," "moving": "The funeral was an *impressive* ceremony." Approximate synonyms for *formidable* include *fearful, menacing, appalling, frightful,* and *threatening.* Words allied in meaning to *impressive* are *imposing, majestic,* and *lofty.*

fortuitous, fortunate. *See* FELICITOUS.

forward, forwards. One can say "step *forward*" or "step *forwards*" with equal correctness, although *forward* is more often used. Only *forward* can be used to apply to a following noun: one can say "a *forward* movement" but hardly "a *forwards* movement." *Forward* is also preferred in such constructions as "bring *forward,*" "come *forward,*" and "from this day *forward.*" As a verb, one can use only *forward:* "Please *forward* my mail to me." Since *forward* is never incorrect, why not always use it in preference to *forwards? See also* FOREWORD.

fragile, brittle, frail. These words are interchangeable in their meaning of "weak" and "delicate," but they do have distinct uses. *Fragile* is the opposite of *sturdy* and suggests that something must be handled carefully to avoid breakage or damage: "This beautiful china is *fragile.*" *Brittle* also refers to something that snaps or breaks into pieces but is usually applied to objects that have a hard surface or finish: "This material is as *brittle* as glass." *Frail* applies particularly to persons, rather than things, and usually refers to such matters as health, mental qualities, and temperament: "After a wasting illness, his body seemed more *frail* than ever." "His bold hopes for the future have a *frail* foundation." Bric-a-brac is *fragile,* some conversation is *brittle,* and an invalid is *frail.*

frank. *See* CANDID.

Frankenstein. This is a name for someone who creates a monster or a destructive agent that he cannot control and that brings about ruin. *Frankenstein* is often used to mean "a monster," but when this meaning is intended, the expression should be "*Frankenstein* monster." (Baron Frankenstein, a character in a nineteenth-century novel, discovered the "secret of life" and created a monster. In trying to escape from his monstrous creation, the baron lost his life.) Rigidly accurate users of language would add "monster" to a sentence such as "The administration has created this *Frankenstein* and must now deal with it."

free, gratis. *Gratis* means "freely," "for nothing," "without charge." Say *free* or *gratis,* but don't use both in the same phrase: "This excellent service is *gratis.*"

frequent. *See* RECURRING.

from whence. Although this phrase has been widely used in previous centuries (even in the King James version of the Bible), it is wordy. Omit *from* or *whence* or just say *where: "Where* did that boot come from?"

-ful, -fuls. In recipes, the plural of *cupful (cup full)* is *cupfuls,* presumably because the same container is used more than once. If you fill two cups with coffee, however, you have *two cups full.* Because the same-container rule usually applies, the plurals are *mouthfuls, armfuls, tablespoonfuls, teaspoonfuls, handfuls,* etc. Note, however, that you serve four guests four *glasses full* of iced tea.

function, work, job, position. These words have associated meanings but should be applied carefully. *Function* means the kind of activity that is suitable and proper to a person or institution: "The *function* of this committee is to approve the budget." *Work* has many meanings of which the principal one is "toil," "labor," "exertion": "At what time did you finish *work* today?" *Job* refers to a post, location, or situation of employment; in fact, it is a colloquial and widely used synonym for *position:* "What *job* do you have in this firm?" *Position* refers to any type of work above the lowest kind of labor and applies to occupation that is desired: "He sought a *position* that would pay him more money." *Work, position,* and *job* are all overworked. Perhaps one of the following might express your meaning more exactly: *station, place, rank, spot, task, project, responsibility, occupation. Job* is slang when used to mean a theft or similar crime and a person: "She was a sweet *job.*" "Lie down on the *job*" and "on the *job*" are trite expressions. As a verb, *job* is slang when used to mean "to cheat" or "to defraud": "He *jobbed* me on that deal."

funeral, funereal. These words have related meanings, but *funeral* (FYOO·nuhr·uhl) usually means "burial rites," whereas *funereal* (fyoo·NEER·i·uhl) has an additional and more regularly intended meaning of "sad," "doleful," and "gloomy" (a *funereal* expression on her face).

funny, strange, peculiar. *Funny* is much overused to mean "curious" and "odd" (I had a *funny* feeling that you would come here), but actually the word means "witty," "humorous," "droll," "absurd," "comical," "farcical," "ludicrous," or "laughable." Perhaps many of us find something amusing in that which is unusual or hard to understand. *Strange* means "curious," "extraordinary," and "unusual": "Fran's loud behavior at the party was *strange* because she is usually quiet and reserved." Approximate synonyms for *strange* are *bizarre, abnormal, queer,* and *singular. Peculiar* also means "uncommon" or "eccentric": "Your accent is most *peculiar.*" *Strange* and *peculiar* can be used interchangeably in most situations, but when you use *funny,* ask yourself "Do I mean '*funny*-peculiar' or '*funny*–ha-ha'?"

further. *See* FARTHER.

G

gage, gauge. In the sense of a standard of measurement, these words are interchangeable (a narrow-*gauge* or -*gage* railroad), although *gauge* is the preferred spelling. Only *gage* can refer to a variety of plum and to a challenge or pledge: "This is a can of *gage* (really *greengage*) plums." "The swordsman threw his glove on the ground as a *gage*." "This ticket represents a *gage* at the pawnbroker's."

gamble, wager, bet. All three of these words may be used as verbs or nouns. *Gamble* is a general term meaning "to play at any game of chance for stakes." Perhaps because it suggests risking something that should not be afforded, *gamble* has an unfavorable connotation: "The workman *gambled* away his week's wages." *Wager* means "to risk something on an uncertain event" and is closely allied in meaning to *gamble*. It has a somewhat less unfavorable connotation than *gamble*, perhaps because it conveys the idea of venture: "The foreman *wagered* that production for the day would exceed 1,000 barrels." *Bet*, the most commonly used of these three words, literally means a pledge that is to be forfeited if one's prediction, or forecast, about a future event is incorrect: "I placed a *bet* that Pounditout would win the fifth race."

gantlet, gauntlet, gamut. One may run a *gantlet* (a former kind of military punishment). One may also run a *gamut* (a series of musical notes or the whole range of anything). But one may not run a *gauntlet* because it is a kind of glove. "To take up the *gauntlet*" ("to accept a challenge") and "to throw down the *gauntlet*" ("to challenge to combat") are correct but hackneyed expressions.

garnish, garnishee. *Garnish* means (1) to decorate, to adorn, to supply with something (A good chef will *garnish* a casserole like this with parsley); and (2) to attach money or property (If you don't pay the debt, we shall have to *garnish* your salary). The verb *garnish* is more usually rendered as *garnishee,* which is also a noun meaning a person whose money or property has been attached: "The judge ordered the creditor to *garnishee* half of my pay."

gauge. *See* GAGE.

gauntlet. *See* GANTLET.

gender, sex. *Gender* is a grammatical term indicating (in the English language) whether nouns and pronouns are classed as masculine, feminine, or neuter. The number of *genders* in languages other than English varies from two to more than twenty; in some languages, *gender* disregards *sex* entirely. For example, a sexless (neuter) article, the noun *pen,* is, in French, feminine *(la plume)*. In Old English, the word for *wife* was considered neuter and *woman* was masculine. *Gender* can never be substituted for *sex*. *Sex,* a word of many meanings and applications, applies specifically to the fact or character of being male or female (*see* FEMALE). Thus we say that Bill is a proper noun in masculine *gender* and that Bill is a member of the male *sex*. Substitute *sex* for *gender* in this statement: "Students in this school are classified on the basis of age, *gender,* and previous training."

general, generally. *General* and *generally* are loosely overused in many expressions: "*generally* speaking," "in *general,*" "in a *general* way." Possible substitutes: *prevailing, customary, ordinary, regular, popular, catholic, common, universal,* and their corresponding adverbial forms (*universally,* etc.). "*Generally* always" is a wordy, trite expression. "*Generally* speaking" is usually a mere filler.

genial. *See* CONGENIAL.

genius, talent. These words have had varied meanings over the centuries, but in current use *genius* is a much stronger word than *talent* to refer to ability and aptitude. *Genius* means "exceptional natural capacity," "high intellect," "strong creative or inventive power": Shakespeare was an unquestioned *genius. Talent* is more correctly applied to ability or aptitude in a particular field: "a *talent* for making friends," "a *talent* for playing the piano." A *genius* may have many *talents,* but a *talented* person is not necessarily a *genius.*

gentleman, lady, woman. In medieval times, a *gentleman* was a man above the rank of yeoman (the owner of a small farm), but the term is now applied to a person of good manners and breeding or as a mark of respect to any man: "A *gentleman* should never give offense to others." "Will every *gentleman* please come this way?" *Gentleman* is now rarely used in everyday speech, but *gentlemen* is customary in such expressions as "What will the *gentlemen* have to drink?" and "Ladies and *gentlemen.*" *Lady,* a term originally applied to a loaf-kneader, has been used as a polite form of address. *Lady* normally has no more justification than does *gentleman* in place of *man.* True, you would say to a waiter in a restaurant "The *lady* will have" rather than "The *woman* will have," but the social distinction between *lady* and *woman* has all but disappeared. *Woman* is a general term for the adult female human being as distinguished from the male: "This *woman* just gave birth to twins."

genuine. *See* AUTHENTIC.

germ, microbe, bacteria, virus. These terms are so closely related that only a scientist would ordinarily need to differentiate among them. A *germ* is a *microbe,* a disease-producing microorganism. In biology, *germ* refers to an initial stage in development, as "a *germ* cell of such-and-such a form." By extension, *germ* also is used to refer to anything that acts as a source or initial stage: "I have the *germ* of an idea." A *microbe* is a *bacterium,* the singular form of *bacteria,* which refers to any of numerous microscopic organisms involved in such processes as fermentation, putrefaction, and disease. A *virus* is an infectious agent, especially one that reproduces only in living cells. *Virus* is really a medical term for the active element that infects with and produces a contagious disease: "the *virus* of yellow fever." *Germ* is a general term which will serve in all ordinary situations.

get. This word of many meanings has a primary one: "to obtain," "to come into possession of." It has numerous informal, idiomatic, or slangy meanings and appears in several hackneyed expressions. Among informal meanings of *get* and *got* (the past tense of *get*) are "to comprehend" (I don't *get* you); "to get the advantage of" (Overeating will *get* him); "to be forced or obliged (I have *got* to leave soon); "to strike or hit" (The bullet *got* him in the arm). Among slangy or trite uses may be mentioned "to puzzle" (That remark *got* me); "to observe" (Did you *get* that look?); and "*get* about," "*get* ahead of," "*get* across," "*get* along," "*get* by," "*get* down to business," "*get* nowhere," "*get* something off one's chest," "*get* out of," "*get* together," "*get* through to someone," "*get* up and go." Dó you *get* the idea that *get* is overused?

get up, arise. These words mean the same thing, "to sit up or stand," "to ascend or move upward": "*Get up* and move." "*Arise* and eat breakfast." *Arise* has the additional meaning of "to come into being," "to spring up": "New problems seem to *arise* every day." In the sense of sitting up or standing, *arise* is less often used than *rise*, but both words are correct, and both are considered somewhat more formal and refined than *get up*. Spelled as one word or hyphenated, *getup* (or *get-up*) is an informal and not-recommended term for *costume, style, outfit, overall arrangement,* and *format:* "You look silly in that *getup*." "What is the *getup* of our new assignment?"

gibe, jibe. *Gibe* means "to scorn," "to sneer at": "Please don't *gibe* at me." *Jibe* has the same meaning as *gibe* but may also be used to refer to changing direction: "The boat *jibed* twice on the homeward run."

gild, guild. To *gild* something is to overlay it with gold. A *guild* is an association or union. "The potter will *gild* this vase for you." "Joe belonged to a *guild* of craftsmen."

give. *See* DONATE.

glamour, glamor. *Glamour* is the preferred (really the only) spelling of that which compels charm and induces romance and excitement: "She secured a position in the theater which is loaded with *glamour*." "Joe longed for the *glamour* of becoming an astronaut." The verb form is spelled differently, however (Don't *glamorize* your job), and the adjectival form is *glamorous:* "She is the most *glamorous* woman in the entire film world."

glance, glimpse. A *glance* is a quick look; to *glance* is to direct one's gaze briefly: "Take a *glance* at the morning paper." "Read the book carefully; don't just *glance* at it." A *glimpse* is a brief or momentary sight of something: to *glimpse* is to obtain a brief view of something: "I caught only a *glimpse* as she passed." "I *glimpsed* the bird as it flew past me." What one sees in a *glance* is a *glimpse*.

gloomy, pessimistic. These words are nearly but not quite synonymous. A *gloomy* person is dejected, depressed, or sad; a *pessimistic* person is also *gloomy* but holds the opinion that everything is evil now and will continue to remain that way. A *pessimistic* person is exceptionally and excessively *gloomy* and, furthermore, tends to remain a pessimist indefinitely. One's *gloom* may soon depart; one's *pessimism* reflects a philosophical attitude that evil in the world has always outweighed the good.

glossary. *See* DICTIONARY.

glutton. *See* GOURMAND.

go and. *See* COME AND.

good, well. *Good* is an adjective: "to see a *good* play"; "to have a *good* time." *Well* is both an adjective and an adverb, but with different meanings; as an adjective, "in good health," and as an adverb, "ably": "Since my illness, I have felt *well.*" "The cast performed *well* in the first act." *Good* may be used correctly after such linking verbs as *seem, smell,* and *taste*. In such uses, *good* remains an adjective that qualifies the subject and is not an adverb that modifies the verb: "Your report seems *good* to me." But *good* cannot qualify a verb directly: "She speaks *well* (not *good*)." *Good* appears in such trite, informal expressions as "make *good,*" "*good* for nothing," "come to no *good,*" "all to the *good,*" "*good* and sick," "*good* and tired," "as *good* as new," "for *good* and all," "*good* egg," "*good* Joe," "*good*-oh," "*goodies,*" and "*goody-goody.*"

got, gotten. The principal parts of *get* are *get, got, got* (or *gotten*). Both *got* and *gotten* are acceptable words; your choice will depend upon your speech habits or on the rhythm of the sentence you are writing or speaking. *Got* is colloquial when used to mean "must," "ought," "own," "possess," and many other terms: "I *must* (not *got to*) go." "I *ought* (not *got*) to go." "I *own* (not *got*) two new suits." *See also* GET and HAVE GOT TO.

gourmand, gourmet, glutton. These words have to do with eating, but they are different in meaning. A *gourmand* is a large, enthusiastic eater (Diamond Jim Brady was a *gourmand,* often eating for three hours at a time). A *gourmet* is a fastidious eater, an epicure (As a French chef, he considers himself a *gourmet*). A *glutton* is one with a huge appetite, one who eats to excess and with little delicacy of choice or table manners. A *gourmand* is a heavy consumer of food but prides himself to some degree on his knowledge of cuisine; a *gourmet* may or may not be a heavy consumer of food but in any event is a connoisseur, an expert; only a *glutton* eats with an unrestrained appetite. The use of *gourmet* as an adjective (*gourmet* foods, a *gourmet* meal) is not considered standard, but widespread usage will likely confer reputability upon it as time passes.

grade school, graded school. Each of these terms is in widespread use, and each is acceptable. Use the phrase most prevalent in your community. Both phrases refer to an elementary school in which pupils are classified (grouped) according to their degree of advancement: "That building is a *grade* (or *graded*) school."

graduate, graduate from. Both *graduated* and *was graduated* are acceptable terms, provided *from* is also used. Say "He *graduated from* college last year" or "He *was graduated from* college last year." Do not say "He *graduated* college last year."

graffiti. This Italian word derived from both Greek and Latin means "phrases or words written on the walls of buildings, public restrooms, and sidewalks." *Graffito,* an archaeological term, refers to an ancient writing or drawing scratched on a wall or other surface. When one phrase or word is concerned, use *graffito;* when more than one is involved or mentioned, say *graffiti:* "This is an amusing *graffito.*" "Most of these *graffiti* are obscene."

grammar, syntax. *Grammar* is not a list of rules involving "do's and don'ts." As usually applied in speech and in some writing, the word *usage* should be substituted for *grammar. Grammar* itself is the science that deals with words and their relationships to each other. It is concerned with a consideration and account of the features of a language and with speech and writing according to various standards of usage but not according to correctness, as such. When someone is said to use bad *grammar,* all that can be meant is that he uses language in some way that is not currently and generally accepted or that his usage is not in line with prevailing practice. *Syntax* is a study of the signs that appear in a system and, as applied to language, deals with the arrangement of words in a sentence to show their relationship. It is a rather vague and general term but one for which our language has no adequate substitute. Although *syntax* is a branch of *grammar,* the latter term is more useful in referring to word order, parts of speech, and the like.

grateful, gratified. *Grateful* is an adjective indicating appreciation of personal kindness: "I am *grateful* for your thoughtful response to my appeal." *Grateful* is a synonym of *thankful, indebted,* and *obliged. Gratified* is a verb form, the past tense and past participle of *gratify,* a word meaning "to give pleasure," "to satisfy," "to indulge," "to humor": "He *gratified* his clothing desires by buying three new suits." "These customers were *gratified* by a refund of their money."

gratis. *See* FREE, GRATIS.

greatly. *See* MATERIALLY.

Grecian, Greek. These words refer to Greece, its language, and its culture. *Greek* is much more widely used than *Grecian,* a term most likely to be applied to architecture and statuary; many writers, however, prefer *Grecian* because of its more pleasing sound. One should refer to "the *Greek* Catholic Church," "the *Greek* language," and "a *Greek.*"

groom. This is a word for "manservant," but it is widely used as a shortened form of *bridegroom.* Actually, one should say *bridegroom* rather than *groom* when this meaning is called for, because in Old English *bryd* meant "bride" and *guma* meant "man."

guarantee, guaranty. A *guarantee* is a promise or assurance that something is of specified content or quality or that it will perform satisfactorily: "This percolator carries an unconditional five-year *guarantee.*" *Guarantee* and *guaranty* are synonymous when used to mean a warrant, pledge, or assurance that someone else's obligation or debt will be fulfilled: "This bond will serve as a *guaranty* for his appearance in court." *Guarantee* can be used as both noun and verb; *guaranty* is primarily a noun and has limited use as a verb.

guess. *See* CALCULATE.

guild. *See* GILD.

guts. This is a slang term when used to mean "courage," "bravery." The word is in such widespread use that it would be absurd to suggest that you never use it in this sense. *Intestinal fortitude* is stuffy and pretentious, but you might occasionally use *fortitude, resolution, tenacity, mettle, spirit, boldness, audacity, grit, pluck, backbone, heroism, gallantry,* or *valor.*

guy. This word has several meanings but is most often used colloquially to refer to a man, boy, or individual generally. Some experts regard this use of the word as slang; it should be avoided in standard English. "To *guy* someone" is a slangy way to express the sense of teasing or joshing.

H

habeas corpus. Translated literally from Latin, this phrase means "You have the body." In English usage, *habeas corpus* is a writ (written order) designed to secure the release of someone from unlawful restraint. In his first inaugural address, Jefferson referred to "freedom of person under the protection of the *habeas corpus.*" The term is pronounced "HA·bee·us KOR·poss."

habit. *See* CUSTOM.

habitable, inhabitable. *Habitable* means "capable of being lived in." It is applied to buildings in which people might reside: "This house is so flimsy that it is hardly *habitable.*" *Inhabitable* refers to countries or large areas in which human beings or animals can live: "Most persons feel that the Sahara Desert is not *inhabitable.*" The antonym of *inhabitable* is *uninhabitable.*

habitat, habitant. *Habitat* means (1) "a place of abode," "an area for residence"; and (2) "the native environment of an animal or plant": "This is a likely *habitat* for rabbits." "These creatures can live only in a tropical *habitat.*" *Habitant* means "an inhabitant," that is, a person or animal that lives in a specified place: "Few *habitants (inhabitants)* of this section escaped severe damage from the tornado."

habitual. *See* USUAL.

had better, had rather. *Had better* is widely used in giving advice or issuing a mild threat: "We *had better* get started before midnight." "You *had better* apologize to me for that remark." The phrase *had best* can be substituted for *had better* in such expressions. Neither is so exact as *should. Better had* (You *better had* get here soon) is dialectal or illiterate. *Had rather* (and also *would rather*) indicates a preference: "I *had rather* (or *would rather*) stay than go."

hadn't ought. This is a nonstandard expression for *shouldn't:* "You *shouldn't* (not *hadn't ought*) do that." *Had ought* is as illiterate as *hadn't ought*. Do not use it for *should* in a statement such as "You *had ought* to leave at once."

had rather. *See* HAD BETTER.

hamstring, hamstrung. A *hamstring* is one of the tendons around the hollow of the knee. (One meaning of the word *ham* applies to the part of the human leg back of the knee.) As a verb, *hamstring* means "to cripple or disable," "to render powerless": "You are trying to *hamstring* my efforts on this job." The past tense of *hamstring* is *hamstrung* or *hamstringed*. Also correct are *hamstrung* and *hamstringed* as the past participle. Because of familiarity with the principal parts of *string* as *string, strung, strung,* most writers prefer *hamstrung:* "You have consistently *hamstrung* everything I have attempted."

handicap, hindrance. The word *handicap* (derived from a game of wagering in which participants put their hands in their caps and withdrew varying amounts of money) most often is used to mean "disadvantage" or "disability": "His thin voice is a *handicap* in speaking to large crowds." "The player was *handicapped* by bruised ribs." A *hindrance* is something that impedes, prevents, or stops; it acts as a check or restraint of some kind: "His lack of money is a *hindrance* in the development of his business." A severely *handicapped* child is *hindered* from pursuing the normal activities of children. You will discover, perhaps, that youth and inexperience are *hindrances* to finding a job, but neither is necessarily a *handicap*.

handle, manage. These words are interchangeable when used to mean "to control," "to train," or "to influence": "This teacher can *handle* (or *manage*) all kinds of students. She can *manage* (or *handle*) them in all situations." *Handle* should be used when hands are actually involved; *manage* is preferable when nonphysical control or direction is indicated: "He *handled* the gun as though it were loaded." "Seth is prepared to *manage* this office when the supervisor is absent."

hanged, hung. The principal parts of *hang* are *hang, hung, hung*. However, when the word refers to the death penalty, the parts are *hang, hanged, hanged*. "The draperies are *hung*." "The murderer was *hanged*."

happen, transpire, occur. These words are frequently used interchangeably, but not by careful users of language. *Happen* means "to take place," "to come to pass": "A fatal accident just *happened* at that intersection." *Happen*, which originally indicated the taking place of something by hap or chance, should be used for events that are spontaneous or accidental. *Occur* has much the same meaning as *happen* but is more specific as to time or event: "His election *occurred* the month before." That which is scheduled (prearranged) may be said to *take place;* that which *occurs* or *happens* is more likely to be unplanned. *Transpire* is a formal word that means "to escape from secrecy" and should not be used as a synonym for *happen, occur,* or *take place*. Its literal meaning is "to be emitted as a vapor," "to be breathed out." From this meaning, *transpire* has come to suggest leaking out and becoming known. One can ask "Has anything *transpired* during my absence?" but only if he means "Has any secret leaked out?" or "Has anything come to light that was previously hidden or unknown?" Since the correct use of *transpire* is limited, why not always say *happen, occur, take place, come to pass, befall,* or *present itself?*

harangue, tirade. An *harangue* is a passionate and vehement speech, one that is usually lengthy and delivered before a public gathering: "The candidate indulged in an (or a) *harangue* that dealt more with his opponents than with the issues at hand." A *tirade* is a prolonged outburst of emotionally toned, vehement denunciation of some person or object. The distinctions between *harangue* and *tirade* are these: (1) A *tirade* is always an attack; an *harangue* may be only a long, violent speech. (2) An *harangue* is always made to an audience of some size; a *tirade* can be directed to or at one person only.

harass. *See* TANTALIZE.

harbor. *See* PORT.

hardly, scarcely, barely. These three adverbs imply the doing or accomplishing of something by the narrowest of margins: "The injured man was *hardly (scarcely, barely)* able to move his lips." What slight difference exists among them is that *hardly* suggests difficulty, the hardness of something (My lungs hurt so much that I could *hardly* breathe); *scarcely* suggests a margin so small as to be almost unbelievable (You would *scarcely* believe he could be so stupid); and *barely* stresses the idea of narrowness and thinness (He *barely* passed the examination). All three words have a negative quality and should not be used with another negative; do not say "*hardly* never," "*scarcely* never," "couldn't *hardly*," "wouldn't *scarcely*," and "not *barely*." *See also* DOUBLE NEGATIVE.

harmony, melody, tune. Each of these words refers to musical sound. *Harmony* is the study of the structure and relation of musical chords, that is, the blending or mingling of sounds. *Melody* is the rhythmical relation of successive sounds that combine to make a *tune*. A *tune* is a series of sounds forming an air. *Harmony* and *melody* are two of three basic elements of most Western music (the third element is rhythm). Examples: "In this orchestra there is complete *harmony* between the brass section and the violins." "Gene sang a tuneful *melody* while he showered." "The only *tune* he could play was 'On, Wisconsin.'" The adjectives *melodious* and *tuneful* are synonymous in their meaning of "forming a pleasing succession of sounds," "agreeable to hear."

hate, dislike. *Hate* implies strong and passionate *dislike*, a feeling of enmity, extreme aversion or hostility: "I *hate* war and every sacrifice and stupidity that it entails." "My strongest feeling about social injustice is one of *hate*." Approximate synonyms for *hate* as a verb include *loathe, despise, execrate, abhor, abominate,* and *detest*. Noun equivalents are *animosity, abomination, loathing,* and *detestation*. *Dislike* means "to regard with displeasure"; it suggests a definite but not necessarily powerful aversion: "I *dislike* having to get up so early." Close to *dislike* in meaning and tone are *distaste* and *disrelish*. It is immature to use the word *hate* when only *dislike*, lack of interest, or unconcern is involved; probably few persons *hate* nearly so many things and ideas as they *dislike*.

have got to. This phrase is a colloquial and wordy expression for *must, should,* and *ought to:* "I *must* (or *should*) do my laundry this morning"—not "I *have got to* do my laundry." "I *ought to* leave early tonight"—not "I *have got to* leave early."

healthful, healthy. These words are often used interchangeably, but *healthful* precisely means "conducive to health"; *healthy* means "possessing health." In other words, places and foods are *healthful;* people and animals are *healthy:* "I wonder whether he is a *healthy* person because he lives in a *healthful* climate."

heaps. *See* LOTS.

hedonist, epicure. These words, closely related in meaning, refer to luxurious living and sensuous pleasure. Neither conveys favorable connotations, although an *epicure* (or *epicurean*) is less frowned upon by moralists than is a *hedonist*. A *hedonist* is someone who devotes his entire life to a pursuit of pleasure because he believes that pleasure is the highest good attainable by mankind. mankind. (In psychology, *hedonism* is the theory that behavior is motivated by a desire to gain pleasure and avoid pain.) An *epicure* is someone with a cultivated, refined taste in such sensuous delights as superb food and superior wines. Because an obsolete meaning of *epicure* is identical with the present-day meaning of *hedonist* and because much of mankind apparently feels that a pursuit of pleasure is morally unjustified, it is not easy to label any one person or group as being either *epicurean* or *hedonistic*. Perhaps one might refer to a superb chef or connoisseur of wines as an *epicure* and to certain members of the so-called jet set as *hedonists*.

help, aid, assist. These words have to do with furnishing something that is needed or wanted or with assisting in the fulfillment of some purpose or end. *Help* and *aid* are usually interchangeable, although *help* suggests great effort and direct involvement in providing assistance: one might *help* someone to change a tire and *aid* him in keeping his temper while he is performing the act. *Assist* is more formal and less used than *help* and *aid;* it implies making only a minor contribution or acting in a secondary role. In frequency of use and degree of actual participation in providing what is being sought, the words rank in the order listed above: "He *helped* the ill woman into a taxicab." "This book will *aid* you in arriving at a better idea of democracy." "Although I can provide you with no active *aid* or *help,* someone should *assist* you in becoming more tolerant of other people."

help but. *See* CANNOT (CAN'T) HELP BUT.

helpmate, helpmeet. These words, of which the first is more often used, mean "a helpful companion" and usually refer to a spouse, especially a wife. In the second chapter of the Book of Genesis, God creates Eve as a "help meet" for Adam, with *help* meaning "someone to provide assistance" and *meet* meaning "suitable," "proper." Later, *help* and *meet* were joined by a hyphen and still later were run together as *helpmeet*. Because *helpmate* sounds better and more logical to the modern ear and mind, *helpmate* is preferable, but *helpmeet* is equally correct.

hence. *See* THENCE.

heterodox, orthodox. These words, derived from Greek expressions meaning, respectively, "differing in opinion" and "having the right opinion," refer to agreement with or denial of accepted beliefs, especially church doctrine and teachings. A *heterodox* person is an unorthodox individual who breaks with tradition or convention. An *orthodox* person adheres to accepted, traditional, established, and customary beliefs, practices, and attitudes. A so-called solid citizen is considered *orthodox;* a student rebel is *heterodox*.

hiccup, hiccough. These words referring to a spasm of the diaphragm are pronounced alike: HICK·up. ("HICK·off" is a regional, unrecommended pronunciation.) Both spellings are standard, although some writers apparently consider *hiccough* more genteel than *hiccup*.

hide. *See* CACHE.

high. *See* TALL.

highbrow, lowbrow. These terms are being used so increasingly in writing and speaking that presumably they will, in time, be accepted as standard usage. Their status now is that of either slang or colloquialisms, depending upon the authority consulted. For a while, at least, they should not be used in formal writing and speaking. *Lowbrow* refers to a person lacking, or considered to lack, cultivated and intellectual tastes; *highbrow,* naturally, applies to a person who does have such attainments. Both terms are frequently used in a derisive or derogatory manner.

him, himself. *Him* is the objective case of the third-person personal pronoun *he*. *Himself* is a pronoun that suggests emphasis (He, *himself,* will go) and that turns action back on the grammatical subject (He bathed *himself* carefully). Use *him,* not *himself,* in a statement such as "Sandy remarked that his aunt would spend the week with Mrs. Sandy and *him*."

hinder. *See* PREVENT.

hindrance. *See* HANDICAP.

historic, historical. The senses of these words overlap, but *historic* should be used to refer to something that is renowned, influential, or history-making (the *historic* meeting of Livingstone and Stanley). *Historical* means "concerned with or contained in history" (a specialist in *historical* studies). Pronounce them "hi·STOR·ik" and "hi·STOR·i·kal." *Historically* has five syllables: "hi-STOR·i·kal·ly." *History* should be pronounced "HIS-tuh·ri," not "HIS·try." *See also* A, AN.

hither, thither. *Hither* is a rarely used adjective and adverb that has been largely replaced by *here*. It is correct, but somewhat old-fashioned, to say "Come *hither,*" meaning "Come *here,*" and "the *hither* side of the stream," meaning "the nearer side." *Thither* is an archaic word meaning "in that direction," "there," "toward that place": "I'll meet you on the *thither* side." *Hither* and *thither* appear with some frequency in the expressions "*hither* and yon," meaning "from here to over there," and "*hither* and *thither*," meaning "here and there."

hoard, horde. A *hoard* is a store of laid-up articles or items: "This is the squirrels' *hoard* of nuts." *Horde* means "crowd": "A *horde* of picnickers descended upon the beach."

hoi polloi. This is a Greek term meaning "the masses," "the many." If you use it, do not say "*the* hoi polloi," because *hoi* is Greek for "the": "This dictator thinks of everyone in the country as *hoi polloi.*"

holocaust. *See* DISASTER.

home, house. These words identify any kind of shelter that serves as the residence of a person, family, or household. *House* lacks the associated meanings attributed to *home*, a term that suggests comfort, peace, love, and family ties. It may be said that what a builder erects is a *house* which, when lived in, becomes a *home*. Such a statement may be considered sentimental, echoing the lines of Edgar A. Guest ("It takes a heap o' livin' in a house t' make it home"). Sentiment or not, one usually speaks of "buying a *home*" and "selling a *house*." But firemen put out a fire in a *house*, not a *home*, and reference is always made to a "*house* and lot," not a "*home* and lot." Conversely, one usually refers to a "*home* for the aged," not a "*house* for the aged." Since *home* and *house* are so subtly differentiated in use, why not sometimes resort to *residence* and *dwelling* and save confusion?

homelike. *See* HOMEY.

homely, comely. Although *comely* is a rarely used word, it is sometimes confused with its direct opposite, *homely*. A *comely* person is pleasing in appearance, attractive, pretty, handsome, good-looking, or personable. A *homely* person is unattractive, not beautiful, even ugly. *Homely* can also be used to mean "plain" or "domestic":

"Jean was used to the *homely* duties of cleaning and cooking."

homesickness. *See* NOSTALGIA.

homey, homelike. These words mean "comfortable," "cozy," "familiar," "like home." Both emphasize attractiveness and peaceful security, but *homelike* is preferable because it is less sentimental and informal: "This hotel tries to create a *homelike* atmosphere for its guests."

homicide, manslaughter, murder. *Homicide,* the killing of one human being by another, is a general term that includes *manslaughter* and *murder*. *Homicide* and *manslaughter* are synonyms in general use, although, in legal terms, *manslaughter* is referred to as the unlawful killing of a human being but without premeditated (aforethought) intent. *Murder* is the killing of a person with malice aforethought. Special statutory definitions and degrees of murder are common in the United States. The killing of someone, whether accidental or planned, is *homicide:* an accidental death from a traffic occurrence is *homicide*. Some legal jurisdictions would hold that a traffic death caused by careless driving would be *manslaughter* but one resulting from the fault of the victim would be *homicide*. *Murder* is generally a killing planned ahead and committed with deliberate intent.

homonym, homograph, homophone. These words are based on a common element, the Greek term *homo,* meaning "same." A *homonym* is a word like another in sound and spelling but different in meaning: "the *bow* of a boat" and "to make a *bow*"; "the *bark* of a dog" and "the *bark* on a tree." A *homograph* is a word of the same written form as another but of different origin and meaning and possibly of pronunciation: *sole* ("only," or part of a shoe); *wound* ("injury," and the past tense of *wind*). A *homophone* is a word pronounced the same as, but differing in meaning from, another, whether spelled the same way or not: *key* and *quay, tear* and *tier, heir* and *air*.

honorarium. This word is occasionally used to refer to a fee (payment) for services rendered by an eminent or professional person. An *honorarium* is considered a reward for some act for which custom or tact forbids the setting of a fixed amount, or fee: "The ambassador received a small *honorarium* for speaking at our meeting." The word is a kind of euphemism for fee; an *honorarium* is not considered a recognition in money so much as a token of the honor conferred by the presence of the person rendering the service.

horde. *See* HOARD.

horrible, horrid. Each of these words means "dreadful," "extremely unpleasant or disagreeable," "abominable." One can speak of "a *horrid* disease" or "a *horrible* disease" with equal meaning and emphasis. Both words are intensives, that is, terms that have a strong emotional meaning and that usually exaggerate what is actually in mind. Consequently, *horrible* and *horrid* should be used thoughtfully and sparingly. Few acts, conditions, or thoughts can truly be said to cause *horror,* an overwhelming and painful feeling caused by something frightfully shocking, terrifying, or revolting. Perhaps slightly less forceful words may, on occasion, be more apt: *shocking, fearful, horrendous, dismaying, frightening, startling, intimidating, scary, alarming.*

house. *See* HOME.

huh-uh, hunh-uh. *See* UH-UH.

human, humane. *Human* refers to the form, nature, or qualities characteristic of man. Formerly, *human being* was recommended over *human,* but both expressions are fully acceptable now. *Humane* refers to such good qualities in man as mercy, compassion, and kindness (a *humane* citizen of this town). *Human* is pronounced "HYOO·muhn"; *humane* is sounded "hyoo·MAYN."

humbleness, humility. *Humbleness* is a standard word but one now rarely used. It denotes a state of feeling inferior or insignificant, of holding oneself low in rank, position, and importance. *Humility* is as much overused as *humbleness* is neglected; it means about what *humbleness* does: a modest estimate of one's rank or significance. *Humility* suggests acceptance of one's low station, whereas *humbleness* merely identifies that position. We acknowledge the *humbleness* of a man's birth and honor his *humility* in accepting that origin.

humor, wit. *Humor* may be defined as a comic quality causing amusement: "The *humor* of his predicament caused him to laugh at himself." *Humor* is also applied to the abilities and faculties of seeing, understanding, appreciating, and expressing what is amusing and laughter-producing and to a frame of mind (in a good *humor* that day). *Humor* consists largely of a recognition and expression of oddities, peculiarities, and absurdities in an act or situation. *Wit* is derived from an Old English word, *witan*, meaning "to know," and still possesses the idea of understanding and recognizing. *Wit* is an intellectual display of cleverness and quickness of perception, whereas *humor* is less obviously mental in its approaches to absurdity and incongruity. *Wit* plays with words; *humor* rises from situations or incidents and involves a sympathetic and even kindly recognition of the follies and stupidities of mankind. In Shakespeare's *Henry IV*, Part I, Falstaff demonstrates his *wit* through the use of puns and verbal fencing. His bluffing, his laughter at himself, and his recognition of the ludicrousness of various situations are examples of *humor*.

hung. *See* HANGED.

hurdle, hurtle. *Hurdle* means "to leap over," "to overcome": "I can easily *hurdle* that small stream." "He is determined to *hurdle* every obstacle in his path." *Hurtle* means "to move with great speed," "to rush," "to go violently": "The motorcycle *hurtled* down the road." "An avalanche will soon *hurtle* down the mountainside."

hurricane. *See* CYCLONE.

hypothecate, hypothetical. These words look as though they are related, but they have different origins and different meanings. *Hypothecate* means "to mortgage," "to pledge to a creditor as security": "To complete this transaction you will have to *hypothecate* your stocks and bonds." *Hypothetical* means "assumed," "supposed," "conjectural": "This is only a *hypothetical* example." To *hypothesize* is to form an *hypothesis* (a proposition, premise, or assertion).

I

idea, concept, notion. Any thought existing in the mind may be called an *idea, concept,* or *notion.* The most widely used of these words, *idea,* should be applied to thoughts that are serious or elaborate: "The surgeons weighed the *idea* of an immediate operation." "The *idea* of armed conflict is frightening." A *concept* (or *conception*) suggests a thought that is complete, detailed, and even intricate: "The artist's *concept* of portrait painting is highly unorthodox." A *notion* is a fleeting, vague, hastily formed, or imperfect thought: "I had no *notion* this is what you were planning." Recommendation: use *notion* for an idea that has not been pondered and weighed; use *idea* or *concept* for important thoughts that have been given serious attention. Occasionally try substituting for *idea* (the generally used term) such words as *opinion, belief, view, conviction, theory, hypothesis,* or *whim.* Any word that you use may be as vague as *idea,* but you will avoid overworking a threadbare term.

idiot. *See* MORON.

idle. *See* LAZY.

if, whether. In formal use, *if* introduces one condition only; *whether* introduces alternate conditions, usually with *or not* expressed or implied: "*If* we try hard, we can do the work." "We were wondering *whether* we could do the work." In less precise use, both *if* and *whether* are used to introduce clauses of various kinds, but *if* is not used when it causes doubt about meaning; for example, the sentence "The physician asked to be telephoned *if* the patient was in a coma" could mean *at what time* or *whether* the patient was in a coma. Also, prefer *whether* in a sentence such as "*If* I was going to pay the bill was the question raised by the letter."

if and when. This is a hackneyed and wordy phrase from which *and when* can be dropped without loss of meaning. Other related wordy phrases that need excision are *when, as, and if* (only *if* is needed) and *unless and until* (*unless* expresses the thought).

if not the. *See* ONE OF THE . . . IF NOT THE.

ignorant. *See* ILLITERATE.

ill, sick. These terms mean "of unsound physical or mental health," "unhealthy," "diseased," "afflicted," "not well." In the United States, they are used interchangeably, with *ill* being considered the more formal and sometimes applied only to more serious maladies and afflictions: "This patient is *ill* with pneumonia. That one is *sick* with a cold." In Great Britain, *sick* is used almost exclusively to mean "nauseated," but that restriction does not apply in American usage. *Sick,* the more often used word, appears in such trite terms and phrases as "*sick* at heart," "*sick* to (or at) the stomach," "a *sick* headache," "*sick* for home" ("suffering from nostalgia"), "*sick* humor," and "*sick* smell." Possible substitutes for *sick* are *ailing, indisposed, nauseated,* and *infirm.*

illegal, unlawful. These words mean "contrary to statutes and regulations," "not legal." *Illegal* is restricted to these meanings, but *unlawful,* a more general term, is also applied to acts that are not only against the law but generally unauthorized or unacceptable. That is, something *unlawful* may go against not only the law but also moral standards; a synonym for *unlawful* is *illicit*. For example, gambling is not *illegal* in some states, but in every state some persons consider it *unlawful*. An *unlawful* act may or may not be *illegal*, but it is always "not approved," "not sanctioned." *See also* ILLICIT.

illegible, unreadable. These words have a shared meaning of "difficult to read," "hard to make out or decipher": "Your handwriting is *illegible* (or *unreadable*)." "The manuscript was so faded and worn that it was *unreadable* (or *illegible*)." *Unreadable* has additional meanings of "dull," "tedious," "not interesting": "I quickly became bored with what seemed to me an *unreadable* book." "The professor handed me an *unreadable* treatise on metaphysics."

illegitimate, legitimate. *Illegitimate* means "illegal," and *legitimate* means the precise opposite, "legal" (*see* ILLEGAL). *Illegitimate* also has these specialized meanings: (1) "born out of wedlock (born a bastard)"; (2) "irregular" (an *illegitimate* forward pass); (3) "invalid" (a logically *illegitimate* conclusion). *Legitimate* is the antonym of *illegitimate* in each of these three meanings and is also used to mean "rightful" (a *legitimate* sovereign); "genuine" (a *legitimate* claim); and "pertaining to professionally produced stage plays" (the *legitimate* theater), as opposed to radio, television, films, and other forms of entertainment.

illicit, licit, elicit. As is suggested in the entry ILLEGAL, *illicit* means "unlawful," "not sanctioned or authorized," "improper": "Millie was accused of being an *illicit* trader in cigarettes." "You are in *illicit* territory because this area is off bounds to all personnel." *Licit* means the direct opposite of *illicit*. *Elicit* means "to bring out," "to draw forth": "The judge tried to *elicit* the truth from this defendant." "The politician tried hard to *elicit* a favorable response from the assembled crowd."

illiterate, ignorant. An *illiterate* person is someone unable to read. The term has been broadened to mean "unable to read or write." Somewhat loosely and inexactly, *illiterate* is now used also to mean not only "unlettered" but "lacking knowledge or culture" either in general or in some particular subject or area: "Because he was *illiterate*, he had to sign his name with an X." "Because the old woman was *illiterate*, the nurse had to read the letter to her." "I am a musically *illiterate* person." An *ignorant* person is one lacking in training or knowledge, either generally or in some particular subject: "Although an *ignorant* man can be dangerous, he is not to be despised or feared." "Trish considered herself *ignorant* in mathematics." *Ignorant* is a broader and more inclusive term than *illiterate*, but the latter is rapidly acquiring all the meanings of the former. Possible substitutes to avoid overusing either: *untaught, uninstructed, uneducated, unlettered, uninformed, unaware. See also* LITERATE.

illusion. *See* ALLUSION.

imaginary, imaginative. *Imaginary* means "not real," "fancied," "existing only in the imagination": "Jock is acting: his illness is only *imaginary*." "This novelist makes *imaginary* characters seem more real than actual people." *Imaginative* applies to someone who can form mental images of what is not actually present to the senses. An *imaginative* person imagines or conceives ("dreams up") matters that are not real; an *imaginary* man does not exist at all but is the product of some *imaginative* person's mind.

imagine, suppose. These words are so constantly used interchangeably by so many people of all degrees of education that it seems useless to attempt differentiating between them. You can say "I *imagine* that's true" or "I *suppose* that's true" with equal correctness. If you wish to be precise, use *imagine* to mean "to form a mental image of something that is not actually available to one's senses": "I *imagine* that Napoleon was a vain and pompous little man." Use *suppose* to mean "to assume something without reference to its truth or falsity": "*Suppose* the cost to be more than we have in hand." "I *suppose* that you will use *imagine* and *suppose* to mean the same thing."

imbecile. *See* MORON.

immanent, imminent. *Immanent* is a rarely used word meaning "remaining within," "indwelling," "inhabiting," "inherent": "Some people believe that God is *immanent* in everything." "The *immanent* and controlling force of logic is reason." *Imminent,* which means "impending," "likely to occur now or soon," is further discussed under EMINENT.

immature, premature. *Immature* means "not perfected," "not developed," "not ripe," "not complete": "All infants are *immature.*" "Thinking that the world owes you a living is an *immature* concept." *Premature* means "too soon," "not yet ready": "The society editor made a *premature* announcement of the wedding." Some newborn babies are *premature;* all newborn babies are *immature*.

immerge. *See* EMERGE, EMERSE, IMMERGE.

immigrant. *See* EMIGRANT.

imminent. *See* EMINENT and IMMANENT.

immoral. *See* AMORAL.

immunity, impunity. These "look-alikes" mean "exemption," but *immunity* has a larger number of applications. *Impunity* means only "exemption from punishment" or "freedom from unpleasant consequences": "You cannot disobey the law with *impunity.*" "No one can exhaust himself physically with *impunity.*" *Immunity* shares these meanings with *impunity* but also means a state of being exempt from (not subject to) a disease and from any liability, obligation, or service: "He was granted *immunity* from local taxation." "He was healthy enough to think that he possessed *immunity* from all diseases."

immured, inured. *Immured* means "confined," "shut in," "imprisoned," or "enclosed": "The flower beds were *immured* between gravel walks." "A country boy, he felt *immured* in his small room in the city." *Inured* (which may also be spelled *enured*) means "accustomed," "habituated," "hardened by exercise or custom": "His rugged early life *inured* him to labor and pain." "Recruits quickly become *inured* to the rigors of army life." "In later life, the benefits of social security *inured* to him and his family." *See also* INURE.

impeach. This word means "to accuse" (especially an official), "to bring charges against," "to challenge the credibility of someone," "to call to account." *Impeach* comes from a Latin term meaning "to trap," and, contrary to widespread opinion, does not mean "to convict," "to find guilty." President Andrew Johnson was *impeached;* that is, charges were brought by the House of Representatives, but he was not convicted (found guilty) by the Senate. To *impeach* is to indict, not to convict. Impeachment is followed by a trial to determine guilt or innocence.

impediment. *See* OBSTACLE.

impel. *See* COMPEL.

impel, induce. Does one say "I wonder what *impelled* him to do that" or "I wonder what *induced* him . . ."? *Impel* means "to drive or press on," "to incite," "to propel": "The angry speaker was *impelled* by his sense of injustice." "The coach's fiery talk to his players *impelled* them to play harder." *Induce* means "to lead or move by persuasion," "to bring about": "This medicine will *induce* sleep very quickly." "Your remarks have *induced* me to change my attitude." In the first sentence of this entry, use *impelled* if some force or outside influence was operating; use *induced* if some inner conviction led to action.

imperious, imperial. These words are derived from the same Latin term and share a meaning of "domineering," "overbearing," "dictatorial": "The judge had an *imperious* (or *imperial*) manner in court." Originally, *imperious* meant "befitting or suitable to an emperor or ruler," as in Shakespeare's lines from *Hamlet: "Imperious* Caesar, dead and turned to clay,/ Might stop a hole to keep the wind away." Now *imperious* is more often used to mean "imperative" or "urgent": "There is an *imperious* need for food in this stricken area." One might speak of an *imperious* dictator who lives in the *imperial* capital city of his country.

impertinent. *See* IMPUDENT.

implicit. *See* EXPLICIT.

implosion. *See* EXPLOSION.

imply, infer. To *imply* is to suggest a meaning only hinted at, not explicitly stated. To *infer* is to draw a conclusion from statements, evidence, or circumstances. "Your remark *implies* that Bill was untruthful." "The officer *inferred* from the fingerprints that the killer was left-handed."

imply, insinuate. To *imply* is to indicate without actual statement something that is to be inferred (*see* IMPLY, INFER). To *insinuate* is to hint slyly or subtly, to instill an idea by tricky, subtle, or underhanded means. *Insinuate* also means "to enter or introduce by devious ways." "Sis *insinuated* herself into the group over the protests of some members." "This is propaganda *insinuated* into the unsuspecting minds of citizens." "Did the speaker intend to *imply* that we have *insinuated* in people's minds doubt about the real purpose of his actions?"

impractical, impracticable, unpractical. Distinctions in the meanings of these words have largely broken down, but *impractical* actually means "theoretical" or "speculative." *Impracticable* means "not capable of being used," "unmanageable." "The architect's recommendations are *impractical*, and his blueprints are *impracticable.*" *Unpractical* is interchangeable with *impractical* but is considered less formal.

impression. *See* EDITION.

impressive. *See* FORMIDABLE.

impromptu. *See* EXTEMPORANEOUS.

impudent, impertinent. These words refer to bold, rude, and arrogant acts or speech. *Impudent* suggests shameless impertinence: "an *impudent* young person," "an *impudent* response to a friendly suggestion." *Impertinent* has a primary meaning of "inappropriate," that is, "not pertinent," and therefore implies unwarranted, uncalled-for intrusion into something that does not concern one, that is none of one's business: "This is an *impertinent* interruption of a serious meeting." The opposite (antonym) of *impudent* is *courteous;* that of *impertinent* is *polite*. Approximate synonyms for one or the other of these words are *fresh, insulting, pert, saucy, brazen,* and *officious*.

impunity. *See* IMMUNITY.

in, at. *See* AT, IN.

in, into. *In* has a basic meaning of "within a space or a place": "The family was sitting *in* the room." As distinguished from *in, into* indicates movement or direction *to* an interior location. Say "Molly was *in* the kitchen" and "Molly walked *into* the kitchen." If you pause between *in* and *to* (say *in to* rather than *into*), *in* becomes an adverb: "You may now go *in to* see the new baby." *In* is an indispensable word, but perhaps one does not have to use it so often in such trite expressions as "have it *in* for" ("hold a grudge"), "*ins* and outs" ("twists and turns," "changing conditions"), "all *in*" ("fatigued"), "*in* for" ("guaranteed," "about to receive"), "*in* that" ("since"), "have an *in*" ("possess access or favor"), "*in* group" ("incumbent or favored group"), "*in* with" ("on friendly terms"), "*in* apple-pie order," "*in* black and white," "*in* the last analysis," "*in* the same boat," and "*in* spite of the fact that" and in a rash of new terms such as *laugh-in, teach-in, talk-in, sit-in, be-in*.

inability, disability. *Inability* means "lack of ability," "lack of capacity, power, or means": "His *inability* to pass a driver's test disturbs him." *Disability* also implies lack of power or ability, but a lack due to some permanent flaw, weakness, or handicap, either mental or physical: "Jeb was excused from service in the armed forces because of a serious physical *disability*." *Inability* is traceable to some inherent lack of talent or power that may or may not be due to actual *disability:* One's *inability* to speak may have been caused by a birth defect; his *disability* in speaking may have been caused by an injury.

inapt, inept, unapt. *Inapt* and *inept* mean "not apt," "not fitting," "without aptitude or capacity": "This person is *inapt* in computing the sales tax on purchases." "Tom is a good mechanic, but he is *inept* in keeping customers satisfied." *Inapt* and *inept* share such approximate synonyms as *unsuited, inappropriate, awkward,* and *clumsy*. The exact opposite (antonym) of *inapt* is *capable;* that of *inept* is *suited*. *Inapt* is more commonly used than *inept* in the meaings indicated above. *Unapt* also has meanings of "inappropriate" and "unsuitable" but is more often used to mean "not likely" or "not disposed": "The supervisor is *unapt* to let you leave early."

in back of. *See* BACK OF.

incapable, unable. These words mean "without the necessary power, capacity, or ability" to perform some particular act. "The speaker was *incapable* of making himself heard in the rear of the hall." "The speaker was *unable* to make himself heard in the rear of the hall." *Unable* is always followed by *to, incapable* by *of. Incapable* usually refers to a permanent or long-standing lack of some sort; *unable* refers to a temporary inability: "This truck is *incapable* of carrying more than 2 tons." "For several minutes he was *unable* to breathe normally."

incense. *See* ENRAGE.

incentive. *See* MOTIVE.

incident. *See* EVENT.

incidentally, incidently. Although *incidentally* has a primary meaning of happening in connection with something else, it is more often used to mean "apart from the main point" and "by the way": "*Incidentally,* I forgot this minor matter." "Whether you come or stay is *incidentally* unimportant." Although *incidently* was once in good use, it no longer appears in the language and is considered an illiteracy. *Incidentally* should be spelled and pronounced with five syllables.

incisive. *See* DECISIVE.

inclose. *See* ENCLOSE.

include. *See* COMPOSE.

incomparable, uncomparable. *Incomparable* means (1) "unequaled" and "matchless" and (2) "incapable of being compared." *Uncomparable* shares the second of these meanings but not the first. "Helen of Troy's beauty was said to have been *incomparable.*" "Bananas and potatoes are *uncomparable.*"

Incomparable is also a term applied to certain words that are considered absolute in meaning and that cannot be used in a comparative or superlative sense. Some students of language have turned *incomparable* into a noun and list as *incomparables* such words as UNIQUE. If one says "more *unique*" or "most *unique,*" what becomes of this word that is used to designate the only one of a kind? If something is *perfect,* how can it be "more *perfect*"? A short list of incomparables would contain these words with absolute meaning: *eternal, equal, final, total, supreme, infinite, absolute,* and *fatal.*

inconceivable, unthinkable. *Inconceivable* means "incredible," "incapable of being explained," "incapable of being conceived or visualized in one's mind": "It is *inconceivable* that he would have done this to me." "It is *inconceivable* that water should not be wet." *Unthinkable* refers to something that cannot be made an object of serious thought, but the word is more often applied to matters that are improbable or difficult to accept: "It is *unthinkable* that he would have left me no money for food." "No matter what the minister says, I consider eternity to be an *unthinkable* subject."

in connection with, in this connection. The first of these phrases is a wordy, wasteful way of saying *about* or *concerning*. Substitute either of these shorter words for *in connection with* in a sentence such as "The insurance adjuster and the driver had an argument *in connection with* the damages involved." *In this connection* is an all-purpose phrase that really has no purpose and can usually be omitted entirely.

incredible, incredulous. *Incredible* means "unbelievable"; *incredulous* means "skeptical," "unbelieving." "The story Bill told us was *incredible.*" "The speaker's remarks left his audience *incredulous.*"

incubus, succubus. The first of these words appears frequently, the latter rarely. A *succubus* was originally an imaginary demon in female form that descended upon sleeping men and had intercourse with them. Similarly, an *incubus* was an evil male spirit that descended upon women. By extension, *incubus* (but not *succubus*) has come to mean something that weighs upon one's mind or anything that oppresses. A nightmare is a kind of *incubus,* but the word means any kind of burden or obstacle: "His mortgage was an *incubus* that he could not shake." "Knowledge of his guilt weighed upon the murderer like an *incubus.*"

inculcate, indoctrinate. These words mean "to teach," but to teach by repeated statements, by direct advice, by pointed suggestion: "By lecturing earnestly and persistently, the professor *inculcated* in his students a love for good literature. He *indoctrinated* them with the underlying theories of creative imagination." The Latin word from which *inculcate* is derived means "stamped" or "trodden," thus emphasizing the idea of forceful instruction. *Indoctrinate* suggests *doctrine,* so that the word is usually applied to teaching that involves principles and ideas, especially religious or moral doctrines and beliefs.

indention, indentation. These words mean "a cut, notch, or recess." Either spelling is correct. Reference is usually to the setback from the margin which appears in the first lines of paragraphs as they are normally written or printed: "The *indention* of paragraphs was uniform throughout the manuscript."

indict, indite. *Indict* means "to accuse" or "to charge with crime": "Bolo was *indicted* for manslaughter." *Indite* means "to write," "to compose": "Lincoln *indited* a beautiful letter to the Widow Bixby."

individual, party, person. *Individual* is loosely overused to refer to "one person only" and often has a humorous or contemptuous meaning: "Who is that *individual* with the loud mouth and wide grin?" Except in legal and telephonic language, *party* is not recommended as a reference to one person. *Party* refers to a group (a supper *party,* the Socialist *party*) and is dubious in a sentence such as "Who is the *party* that brought you to the store?" In most situations, *person* should be preferred to either of the other two terms when reference is being made to one. Phrases such as "*individual* person," "each *individual* member," and "*individual* self" are wordy.

indoctrinate. *See* INCULCATE.

indolent. *See* LAZY.

indorse. *See* ENDORSE.

indubitably. *See* UNDOUBTEDLY.

induce. *See* IMPEL, INDUCE.

induction, deduction. The common methods of thinking are *deduction* and *induction.* The former method tries to establish a specific and limited conclusion by showing that it is allied with, or conforms to, a general truth or principle. In *deduction,* thought moves from the general to the particular: "From the general principle (fact) that most Scandinavians have blue eyes, the *deduction* may be made that Lars, a Scandinavian, probably has blue eyes." *Induction* seeks to establish a general truth, a principle. In *induction,* one observes a number of facts, classifies them, and arrives at a conclusion, or principle: "From observation of hundreds of Scandinavians, most of whom have blue eyes, one may *induce* (make an *induction*) that most Danes have blue eyes." Through *induction,* the laws (principles) of science have been arrived at. Through *deduction,* these principles (laws) are applied in specific situations, such as the development of a vaccine or the manufacture of a synthetic fiber.

inedible. *See* EATABLE and UNEATABLE.

ineffective, ineffectual. These words mean "not effective," "incompetent," "futile": "I tried hard, but I turned out to be an *ineffective* speaker." "All the remedies for a cold that I have tried seem *ineffectual.*" The only distinction between the meanings and uses of these words is this: an *ineffective* person may be "powerless" or "futile" or "incompetent" in only one endeavor or undertaking, whereas an *ineffectual* person is likely to be "not competent" in everything he undertakes. The distinction hardly seems worthwhile. Possible substitutes for either or both words include *useless, worthless, valueless, vain, unavailing, pointless,* and *feeble.*

inept. *See* INAPT.

inexecrable. *See* EXECRABLE.

inexpensive. *See* CHEAP.

infectious. *See* CONTAGIOUS.

infer. *See* IMPLY, INFER.

inferior than, inferior to. Although *inferior than* is widely used, idiomatic usage decrees the proper expression to be *inferior to.* This usage is not a matter of grammar but of idiom, a speech form that is peculiar to itself: "This automobile is *inferior to* (not *inferior than*) that one." *See also* SUPERIOR THAN.

inflammable. *See* FLAMMABLE.

inflict, afflict. These words have different meanings and applications, although the base *flict* is common to both.

(*Flict* is derived from a Latin word meaning "to beat down," "to strike against.") *Inflict* means "to lay on," "to impose," and always has a connotation of something burdensome or unwelcome: "Don't *inflict* any more work on me today." "Society *inflicts* penalties and punishments upon some wrongdoers, but not upon all of them." *Afflict* means "to trouble," "to distress," "to lay on bodily or mental pain": "Several of the boys were *afflicted* with boils." "Severe depression *afflicts* many persons who are mentally ill."

inform. *See* TELL.

informer, informant. Each of these words identifies someone who communicates information or news. An *informer*, however, is one who informs (that is, tells on) someone else for the purpose of collecting money or other reward. An *informer* can be anyone who supplies facts or alleged facts: newspaper reporters and radio and television broadcasters are *informers*. An *informant* conveys to authorities information about criminal acts or other wrongdoing that is designed to lead to prosecution of the guilty person. The Internal Revenue Service, for example, relies on *informants* to supply information about persons who have not fully declared their incomes.

infra dig. This Latin phrase, an abbreviation of *infra dignitatem*, means "beneath one's dignity," "undignified," and is pronounced "IN·frah DIG": "The winner of the prize considered it *infra dig* to accept it."

infrequent. *See* UNFREQUENT.

ingenious, ingenuous, naïve. *Ingenious* means "inventive," "resourceful," "talented," "imaginative." *Ingenuous* means "naïve," "frank," "unsophisticated," "artless." "Alex's suggested solution is *ingenious*." "She is an *ingenuous* little child." *Naïve* (correctly spelled with a dieresis over the *i* but also considered correct without this mark or spelled *naïf*) has much the meaning of *ingenuous*. It is applied to persons who reveal natural simplicity, artlessness, and innocence. *Naïve* usually suggests traits that are amusing to the user of the word but not to the person so described. Probably no one would like to be Diane in a statement such as "Diane is so *naïve* she believes everything her boyfriend tells her." *See also* UNSOPHISTICATED.

inhabitable. *See* HABITABLE.

inhibit, prohibit. These words mean "to prevent," "to hinder," "to restrain," and "to forbid." Each suggests a command, law, or impulse to refrain from some action. *Inhibit* is preferable when the checking or hindering of acts or impulses comes from some inner feeling or condition: "His conscience will *inhibit* his taking advantage of weak persons." "Fear of cancer may *inhibit* his continuing to smoke." *Prohibit,* a more formal word, is preferably used when something is forbidden by law or other authority: "Library regulations *prohibit* smoking in the main reading room." "State law *prohibits* the sale of alcoholic beverages after 8:00 P.M."

inhuman, unhuman. *Inhuman* means "cruel," "brutal," "lacking normal human compassion, pity, sympathy, and kindness": "Treatment of prisoners in that jail was was considered *inhuman.*" "Nero is usually described as having been an *inhuman* Emperor." *Unhuman,* a much less common word, is occasionally used, somewhat loosely, in the above-mentioned meanings of *inhuman.* Careful use confines *unhuman* to the meaning of "not human," "without the characteristics and attributes of human beings": "The sounds issuing from the wounded man's throat were *unhuman.*" "To make mistakes is human; never to make a mistake is *unhuman.*"

innumerable. *See* ENDLESS.

inquire. *See* ENQUIRE.

inquiry. *See* QUERY.

inquisitive. *See* CURIOUS.

in re. *See* RE.

insanitary. *See* UNSANITARY.

inside, inside of, outside of. *Inside* is an adverb, adjective, noun, and preposition. In each of its grammatical functions, *inside* suggests meanings of "inner" or "within": "*inside* the room" (preposition); "step *inside*" (adverb); "an *inside* seat" (adjective); "the *inside* of the building" (noun). *Outside,* with a meaning directly opposite that of *inside,* is also used as four parts of speech. Except when functioning as nouns, neither *inside* nor *outside* should be followed by *of:* One should say "*inside* the room," not "*inside of* the room" unless the meaning is "*the inside of* the room." The correct phrase is "*outside* the house" unless the meaning is "*the outside of* the house." *Inside of* does have an informal use in reference to distance or time: "We passed the car *inside of* a mile." "The doctor arrived *inside of* ten minutes." *Outside of* can also be used to mean "with the exception of," "except for": "He cares for nothing *outside of* his stamp collection." "*Outside of* giving you some money, there is nothing I can help you with."

insignia, insigne. *Insignia,* meaning "a distinguishing mark, sign, or badge," is both singular and plural in number and has an additional plural form, *insignias:* "A black armband is an *insignia* of mourning." "Flags flying above the building are *insignia* (or *insignias*) of national identity and pride." In Latin, the singular form is *insigne,* a form occasionally appearing in English: "The official wore the *insigne* of his position." General use suggests that *insignia* be employed in both singular and plural functions and that *insigne,* if used at all should appear only as a singular.

insinuate. *See* IMPLY, INSINUATE.

insipid. *See* VAPID.

instance. *See* EXAMPLE.

instinct, intuition. These words are used interchangeably to apply to an inborn tendency, natural impulse, or inner perception. "My *instinct* was not to trust that man" probably means the same thing as "My *intuition* told me not to trust that man." An *instinct* is something inborn and natural, not dependent upon any thinking process of any kind (an *instinct* to fear falling from a height); *intuition* does not depend upon reasoning either but does convey the idea of knowledge and awareness: "a woman's *intuition*"; "a speaker's *intuition* that his talk is too intellectual." An infant is born without *intuition* but forms opinions and judgments as he experiences life. A baby is born with the *instinct* to survive. Later, that baby becomes aware (has an *intuition*) that survival requires effort.

insure. *See* ASSURE.

integration, segregation. These words, despite being antonyms, are sometimes confused. *Integration* means "combining"; *segregation* means "separating." An *integrated* school is one in which students are drawn from various ethnic groups, races, and religions. A *segregated* school is one from which one or more racial, religious, or ethnic groups is separated, set apart, withdrawn. In an *integrated* prison, all inmates are housed together; in a *segregated* prison, hardened criminals might be placed in separate quarters.

intelligent, intellectual. An *intelligent* person is quick to comprehend and understand, has a high mental capacity, has the ability to reason clearly. An *intellectual* person has not only a high degree of understanding but also a clear, distinct, and active taste and capacity for higher forms of knowledge. An animal can be *intelligent* but not *intellectual;* a distinguished professor is *intellectual* and is presumed to be *intelligent.*

intend. *See* AIM.

intense, intensive. *Intense* means "strong," "acute" (*intense* fear); "to a high or extreme degree" (*intense* cold); "severe," "great" (*intense* sunlight); "strenuous" (*intense* activity); and "emotional" (an *intense* person). *Intensive* has several of the meanings of *intense*, but it is usually used to indicate concentration or compression: "The chemist spent a year in *intensive* research on this compound." "The attorney directed *intensive* questioning at his client." "That battalion received *intensive* shelling from the enemy." That which is *intensive* is usually *intense*, but what is *intense* need not be *intensive:* "The fire chief will make an *intensive* search for causes of this *intense* fire."

intentionally. *See* ADVISEDLY.

inter-, intra-. These prefixes, appearing in hundreds of words commonly used, are often confused. *Inter-* is a prefix occurring in loan words from Latin where it was used to mean "between," "among," "mutually," and "together." English words include *interact, intergroup, intercept, intercollegiate, interfere, international, intermarriage, interview, intersection,* and *interrupt. Intra-* is a borrowing, also from Latin, meaning "within" and appearing in such words as *intramural, intramuscular, intrastate,* and *intravenous*. When a college fields athletic teams to play against other colleges, it engages in *intercollegiate* athletics. When athletes in a college play against each other (that is, within their walls) they engage in *intramural* athletics. "*Intrastate* commerce" refers to commerce within a state; "*interstate* commerce" means "commerce between and among states."

interest. *See* INTRIGUE.

interject, interpolate. These words are related in meaning because of their common prefix (*see* INTER-). To *interject* is "to put between," "to introduce between parts": "Let me *interject* another topic at this point." "The speaker then *interjected* several remarks that he hoped would amuse his hearers." *Interpolate* conveys much the same meaning as *interject* but is usually applied to the insertion in written matter of material that is false, deceptive, or extraneous: "Someone has *interpolated* several passages in the court records."

interpretative, interpretive. Both of these words mean *explanatory,*" "serving to make clear and explain," and both are correct: "We attended a program of *interpretative* (or *interpretive*) dancing." *Interpretative* is more commonly used, but follow your own preference.

in this connection. *See* IN CONNECTION WITH.

into. *See* IN, INTO.

intra-. *See* INTER-.

intrigue, interest. Each of these words means "to cause to become involved with," "to arouse the curiosity or hold the attention of": "Your plan *interests* me." "Your plan *intrigues* me." However, some experts object to the use of *intrigue* for *interest* on the ground that it suggests an often-unwarranted sense of mystery and suspense. One should use *interest* unless a suggestion of drama, secretiveness, or underhandedness is involved. A love story *interests;* a suspense story *intrigues*.

intrinsic. *See* EXTRANEOUS.

intuition. *See* INSTINCT.

inure, enure. *Inure* is the preferred spelling of this word meaning "to accustom," "to habituate," "to make used to something by exercise": "His poverty-stricken early life *inured* him to the hardships of old age." "The food was poorly prepared, but after several weeks I became *inured* to it." "His muscles soon became *inured* to the heavy lifting involved." *See also* IMMURED.

invent. *See* DISCOVER.

invigorating. *See* ENERVATING.

involuntary, voluntary. The meanings of these words are so different that they should never be confused, but they often are. *Involuntary* means "unintentional" or "unconscious" (an *involuntary* movement of the eyes); "independent of one's will," "made or done other than by one's own choice" (an *involuntary* witness to the crime). *Voluntary* means "undertaken or brought about by one's own choice, one's free will (a *voluntary* contribution to the campaign); "according to one's own will or desires" (*voluntary* cooperation with the police). *Voluntary* implies the previous use of judgment and consideration (a *voluntary* admission of guilt); *involuntary* implies lack of conscious control and is the direct opposite of *intentional* (*involuntary* twitching of tired muscles).

involve, entail. These words are closely related in meaning but have slightly different applications. *Involve* means "to contain or include," "to have as an essential feature or necessary consequence," "to absorb," "to complicate": "My work *involves* a lot of hard work." "This contract *involves* monthly payments for services rendered." "Do not try to *involve* me in your problems." *Entail* shares these meanings of *involve* but more particularly means "to impose as a burden or problem," and, in legal use, "to limit and direct the succession of property": "Losing weight usually *entails* controlling one's appetite." "The attorney will so *entail* the estate that you can inherit nothing."

irony, satire, sarcasm. Each of these words indicates ridicule, contempt, or mockery of someone or something. *Irony* is a figure of speech in which the literal (exact, denotative) meaning of a word or statement is the opposite of that intended. Cicero defined *irony* as "the saying of one thing and meaning another." A person uses *irony* when, on a miserable day, he says "Nice day today, isn't it?" Considered the most ironic writing in all literature is Jonathan Swift's *A Modest Proposal*, in which the author "recommends" that the Irish sell their babies to English landlords for food. *Satire* is the ridiculing of stupidity, vice, or folly; it often employs *irony* and *sarcasm* to denounce the frailties and faults of mankind. *Satire* blends wit and humor with a critical attitude toward human activities and institutions. An attack on man's overconsumption of electricity and fuel would be a *satire* (satirical treatment) of man's folly in exhausting his supplies of energy. *Sarcasm* is a form of *irony* that consists of bitter and often cruel derision. *Sarcasm* is always personal, always jeering, and always intended to wound: "What a great friend you turned out to be!" "You couldn't tell the truth to save your life!"

irrefutable. *See* REFUTABLE.

irregardless. *See* DISREGARDLESS.

irrevocable, irreversible. *Irrevocable* means "unable to be repealed or annulled," "not to be called back": "The judge declared that the fine was *irrevocable.*" "After jumping from an airplane, one realizes that his act is *irrevocable.*" (Irrevocable should be pronounced with emphasis upon the second syllable: ir·REV·o·ca·ble.) *Irreversible* has much the same meaning: "incapable of being changed or reversed." What little distinction there is between the words is that *irrevocable* is more often applied to statements, single acts, and decrees and *irreversible* to a course or pattern of action: "His decision to resign was *irrevocable.*" "The life-style of a hardened criminal is sometimes considered *irreversible.*"

irritate. *See* AGGRAVATE.

irruption. *See* ERUPTION.

Israel, Israeli. *Israeli* should be used to refer to a native or inhabitant of the state of *Israel*. Some *Israelis* prefer using the adjective *Israel* to mean "pertaining to the state of Israel," but *Israeli* is more often used in this context in cultural and historical applications. An *Israelite* was a descendant of Jacob, especially a member of the Hebrew people who lived in the ancient kingdom of Israel.

issue. *See* EMERGE, ISSUE.

is when, is where. The use of *is when* and *is where* in explaining and defining something is a common error in speech and writing. Rather than misuse an adverbial clause (Anemia *is when* the blood is deficient), employ a noun or a noun with modifiers (Anemia is a disease in which deficiencies appear in the blood.) To say, for instance, "Stealing *is where* you take . . ." instead of "Stealing is the act of taking . . ." is to be awkward, if not illiterate.

it, its, it's, It's me. *It* is a short, necessary word often used in a vague or indefinite way to stand for, or refer to, a variety of things and ideas. The term also appears in expressions that are trite or slangy, such as "to get with *it,*" "be with *it,*" "have *it*" ("be attractive"), "had *it*" ("reached the end of endurance or patience"). *It* is a singular pronoun in the third person; "*it* don't" and "*it* weren't" are illiteracies. *Its* is the possessive form of *it*. "The dog has lost *its* collar." "I'm sorry about *its* arriving too late for your birthday." *It's* means "it is" (*It's* raining) and "it has" (*It's* been raining). Awkward and stilted though the expression may sound, one should say "It's *I*" rather than "It's *me*," because a predicate complement is in the nominative case. If you don't like to say "It's *I*" (or "It is *I*" or "This is *I*"), then say "This is" followed by your name. Similarly, watch out for such expressions as "*It's* us," "*It's* them," "*It's* her," "*It's* him." If you think the correct forms of *we, they, she* and *he* in these constructions sound strained, then use names: "*It's* Jane," "*It's* Jim."

-ize. This suffix has aided in the creation of hundreds of standard words such as *pasteurize, dramatize, sterilize,* and *hospitalize*. Unfortunately, many weird improprieties have also resulted, such as *powerize, concertize,* and *headlineize*. Most verbs and adjectives in the language *can* be treated with *-ize,* but it would be well not to *finalize* or *permanentize* or *concretize* or *definitize* an attachment to them until such coinages are widely accepted.

J

jealous, zealous. A *jealous* person feels resentment or suspicion because of rivalry or competition of some sort: "Sue was *jealous* of her beautiful sister." A *zealous* person is active, diligent, devoted: "He was the most admired, *zealous* worker in the plant." *Jealous* is pronounced "JEL·uhs"; *zealous* is sounded as "ZEL·uhs."

jealousy. *See* ENVY, JEALOUSY.

jetsam. *See* FLOTSAM.

jibe. *See* GIBE.

job. *See* FUNCTION.

jocular. *See* JOLLY.

join together. *Join* means "to unite," "to connect," so that *together* is here wordily unnecessary. Since marriages are sometimes shaky, perhaps they require the statement, "What therefore God hath *joined together,* let not man put asunder," but in other instances avoid redundancy.

jolly, jocular, jovial. These words are closely related in meaning to each other and to such adjectives as *merry, convivial, gay, mirthful, jocund, jocose, gleeful, happy,* *cheerful, blithe, sportive, sprightly, airy, lighthearted, lively, vivacious,* and *frolicsome. Jolly* especially denotes a natural, good-humored, expansive gaiety of mood or disposition: "We had a *jolly* crowd at the last party." "For he's a *jolly* good fellow." *Jocular* suggests "joking," "jesting," "waggish," "facetious": "Many *jocular* remarks were addressed to the bridegroom." "Being in a *jocular* mood, the speaker told several amusing stories." *Jovial* suggests a hearty, earthy, joyous humor, a spirit of good-fellowship: "He was a *jovial* host who made everyone feel welcome."

judge. *See* JURIST.

judge, adjudge. As a verb, *judge* shares with *adjudge* the meanings of "to think," "to consider," "to guess," and "to estimate": "We *judged (or adjudged*) our best move was to get away as soon as possible." *Adjudge,* a more formal term than *judge,* is usually reserved for such meanings as "to announce formally" and "to decree" (The court *adjudged* the will to be valid) and "to award judicially" (The verdict was *adjudged* to the plaintiff). *Judge* has a variety of meanings, as suggested by uses such as these: "The coach will have to *judge* between us." "Listen to both of us and *judge* accordingly." "You shouldn't *judge* a magazine by its cover." "The foreman *judged* me to be right." "The pilot *judged* the distance to be 1 mile."

judicial, judicious. Although these words have a common Latin base meaning "judgment," they have different uses today. *Judicial* refers only to justice, courts of law, and judges: "*Judicial* proceedings are likely to be slow and involved." "The attorney tried to assume a look of *judicial* gravity." "There is a difference between the *judicial* and legislative operations of a government." *Judicious,* like *judicial,* refers to wise and balanced judgment but is not restricted to concerns of law and justice and has added meanings of "discreet," "prudent," and "expedient": "Try to make *judicious* use of your money." "After careful examination of those present, Sam made a *judicious* choice of a dancing partner."

juncture, junction. These words have a primary meaning, "the act of joining": "The torn cartilage lies at the *juncture* (or *junction*) of these bones." In this sense, *junction* is more widely used and is preferred: "the *junction* of tributary and river"; "the *junction* of a railway and bus line." *Junction* is favored when reference is to a point of time and to a serious state of affairs: "At this *juncture,* we must decide whether to advance or retreat." "We must decide now, for the affair has reached a critical *juncture.*" In linguistics, *juncture* is a term for a distinctive sound feature of the language such as, for example, the difference in sound between, and time required to pronounce, *already* and *all ready*.

jurist, judge. Although these words are often used interchangeably, they are not synonyms. A *judge* is an official authorized to hear and determine cases in a court of law. A *jurist* is someone acquainted with the law and versed in it: a lawyer, for instance, or a person who writes on the subject of law. A *judge* is a *jurist,* but a *jurist* may or may not be a *judge*.

just, justly. *Just* is an adjective with the primary meaning of "guided by fairness, truth, and reason." *Justly* is an adverb conveying this same meaning: "A *just* man is *justly* honored by others." *Justly* should never be used as a noun. In its adverbial use, *just* has additional meanings. It is used to mean "precisely" (*just* perfect), "narrowly" (*just* missed the bus), "recently" (*just* got here), and "only" (*just* a taste). Phrases such as "*just* exactly" (I have *just exactly* $10) and "*just* recently" (He *just recently* got here) really say the same thing twice. "*Just* about" (I'm *just about* to leave) seems self-contradictory, since the words mean "precisely approximately." However, this book is not *just about* going to deny that the idiom is common and deep-rooted, although one might occasionally say *very nearly* or *almost*, instead of the idiomatically (but not logically) acceptable "*just* about."

K

karat. *See* CARAT.

ketchup. *See* CATSUP.

kid, youngster. *Kid* means "a young goat," in which sense it is rarely used. But *kid* in two other senses is one of the most ubiquitous words in the language. We use it to refer to a "child or young person" and we use *to kid* when we mean "to tease, banter, jest with." In both uses, the word is slangy and should be employed sparingly. *Youngster* is always acceptable for reference to a child or young person, whether boy or girl. Other names for young males are *youth, lad,* and *stripling*.

kin. *See* KITH AND KIN.

kind. This word has many meanings, among them "class" (a *kind* of preacher), "subdivision of a category" (that *kind* of orange), and, with *of,* "rather" or "somewhat" (*kind of* sorry). *Kind* is singular, so that one should not say "*these* (or *those*) *kind* of shoes" but "*this kind of* shoes" or "*these kinds* of shoes." (The same principle applies to *sort* as to *kind.*) Both "*kind* of a" and "*sort* of a" are wordy phrases from which *a* should be omitted. *See also* SORT OF.

kindly, please. In a statement such as "*Kindly* answer my letter soon," one with equal correctness and propriety could write "*Please answer. . . .*" In such use, *kindly* and *please* are courteous formalities that convey a primary meaning of "obligingly." Each, a polite addition to a request, no more conveys exact meaning than the *dear* in the salutation of a letter expresses affection. *Please* is the more commonly used word in this situation, possibly because *kindly* seems to some people to carry an air of affectation or smugness. Take your pick.

kind of a. *See* KIND.

kingly, royal, regal. Each of these words refers to anything that is suitable for a king or closely associated with one: "The tall old man with a long white beard had a *kingly* (or *regal* or *royal*) look about him." Each also has a meaning of "stately, splendid": "The ambassador and his staff made a *regal* (or *royal* or *kingly*) entrance into the ballroom." *Kingly* is a word closely associated with a monarch (a *kingly* crown); *regal* refers to the grandeur and majesty of the office of kingship (*regal* authority, *regal* robes); *royal* applies particularly to the person (body) of the king (*royal* residence, *royal* bedchamber).

kith and kin. This is a tiresomely overworked phrase meaning "acquaintances and relatives." *Kith* and *kin* are not synonymous: *kith* means "friends, neighbors, and the like"; *kin* means people actually related through family ties, persons descended from a common ancestor. When properly used, both *kin* and *kith* are plural, so that one relative cannot be called *kin* and is not *kith* at all.

knot. It is an error to mention "*knots* an hour" or "*knots* per hour." A *knot* in this sense refers to a unit of speed, "1 nautical mile an hour." Consequently, the word *knot* should never be followed by *an hour*. A ship can travel "at 10 *knots*" or "at 10 nautical miles an hour," but not "at 10 *knots* an hour." Nor can a ship "cover such and such a number of *knots*. It speeds (or crawls) at so many *knots* and covers so many nautical miles in a day.

know. *See* REALIZE.

Kodak. Trademark for a portable camera, belonging to the Eastman Kodak Company. The word should not be used to refer to any and all portable cameras and should never be used as a verb.

kudos. This is a word taken from Greek meaning "glory," "renown," "praise," and "approval." The final *s* in *kudos* is not the sign of a plural; there is no such thing as a *kudo:* "The diplomat received *kudos* for his role in bringing about peace."

L

lack, want, need. *Lack* refers to a deficiency, to the absence of something desirable, customary, or needful: "He feels a *lack* of confidence among his followers." "I am suffering from a *lack* of money and time." *Want* and *need,* as nouns, may have much the same meaning: "a necessity," "something that is required or demanded." One may say "My *wants* (or my *needs*) are few." *Need* has connotations that give it an emotional appeal (a *need* to be loved). Approximate synonyms for *lack* and *want* include *death, scarcity, inadequacy, deficit,* and *insufficiency*. Distinctions among these words when used as verbs can be suggested by these sentences: "These plants *lack* water." "These plants *want* water." "These plants *need* water." In the first sentence, *lack* suggests deficiency; in the second, *want* suggests desire; in the third, *need* implies necessity.

lady. *See* GENTLEMAN.

laid, lain. *Laid* is the past tense and past participle of lay. *Lain* is the past participle of *lie*. Choice between *laid* and *lain*, therefore, depends upon which verb is involved. The primary meaning of the verb *lay* is "to set down," "to put or place in a horizontal position." *Lay* implies both a subject (an active agent) and an object: "The girl *laid* the book on the table." "The storm had *laid* the grain flat." The verb *lie* has two basic meanings, "to make a false statement" and "to be in a prostrate position." When a falsehood is involved, the principal parts are *lie, lied, lied:* "I *lie* today." "I *lied* yesterday." "I have *lied* every day this week." When *lie* is used in its second meaning, the principal parts are *lie, lay, lain:* "I *lie* down." "I *lay* down yesterday." "I have *lain* down every day this week." *Lay* always takes a direct object; *lie* never does. These sentences reveal correct uses of *laid* and *lain* and other forms of *lie* and *lay:* "She *laid* the towel on the bed." "She has *lain* in bed for three days." "The pen is *lying* on the desk." "*Laying* wallpaper is difficult work." "The doctor *lies* down every day after lunch." "This hen *lays* lots of eggs." "The garbage has *lain* there for a week." "Bill enjoys *lying* in bed on a rainy day." "The dinner table was *laid* for six people." "Are you *lying* down on the job?" "The river *lies* between two hills; it has *lain* there for centuries." *See also* LAY.

lapse. *See* ELAPSE.

large. *See* BIG.

largely, chiefly. *Largely* means "to a great extent," "generally," "in great part": "That opinion is *largely* incorrect." "My reaction will depend *largely* on the kind of answer I get." *Chiefly,* a stronger word than *largely,* means "principally," "mainly," "essentially": "My interest is *chiefly* in the salary." Related words include *notably, signally, especially, markedly,* and *exceptionally*.

last, latest. The adjective and adverb *late* has *later* for its comparative degree and *last* and *latest* as the superlative. Both superlatives mean "coming after all others," but *last* has more extended meanings than *latest*. *Latest* is restricted to a meaning of "current" and "most recent": "This is the *latest* bulletin on the disaster." "His suit was cut in the *latest* style." *Last* means "final" (in his *last* illness); "conclusive" (the *last* word in the argument);

"extreme" (the *last* degree of agony); "pertaining to the end" (the *last* day of the year); and "single" (every *last* seat in the house). Remember that *last* suggests an end, a finality, that *latest* does not: "Let's hope his *latest* mistake will be his *last*." "When I *last* saw her, she was excited about her *latest* boyfriend."

latter, later. As is mentioned in the entry FORMER, *latter* means "the second of two": "I prefer your *latter* suggestion to your first." *Latter* also has the meaning of "more advanced in time" and "near the end": "In the *latter* years of his life, he was a happy man." "In these *latter* months she has become angry and frustrated." In sentences such as these two, *later*, being the comparative degree of *late*, could be substituted for *latter*. However, *later* is more likely to be used to refer largely or solely to time references, whereas *latter* can refer not only to time but to any kind of series: "I may be free or occupied in the morning; in the *latter* event, I shall have to see you *later* in the day."

laudable, laudatory. *Laudable* means "praiseworthy," "commendable," "deserving approval": "Your suggested plan is both practical and *laudable*." *Laudatory* means "containing or expressing praise": "The speaker addressed several *laudatory* remarks to the class before he handed out diplomas."

lavish, profuse. These words refer to that which exists in great quantity. *Lavish* implies excessive openhandedness and generosity: "The food, decorations, and entertainment at the party were *lavish*." *Profuse* suggests exaggeration and overstatement: "Please accept my *profuse* thanks for your hospitality." Related words are *excessive, unstinted, improvident, generous,* and *openhanded*.

lawful. *See* LEGAL.

lay, lie. *Lay* means "to place" and is a transitive verb requiring an object. *Lie*, in the context here, means "to recline," is intransitive, and takes no object. "I shall *lay* the rug on the floor." "Please *lie* down here." The principal parts of *lay* are *lay, laid, laid, laying;* the principal parts of *lie* are *lie, lay, lain, lying*. Among hackneyed expressions employing *lay* and *lie* may be cited "*lay* down the law," "*lay* of the land," "*lay* oneself open," "*lay* by the heels," "*lay* down one's life," "*lay* heads together," "*lay* one's cards on the table," "*lay* a course," "*lay* about one," "*lay* for," "*lay* it on with a trowel (or shovel)," "*lay* it on thick," "*lie* down on the job," "*lie* low," "take *lying* down," "*lie* in wait," and "Uneasy *lies* the head that wears a crown." *See also* LAID.

lazy, idle, indolent. These words mean "not active," "not in use or operation," "doing nothing." Although *lazy* can be used without implying reproach or condemnation, as in "*lazy* afternoon," it usually suggests criticism: "That boy is too *lazy* to learn." "I'm looking for a helper who is not incurably *lazy*." *Idle* suggests temporary inactivity or doing nothing through necessity, and hence carries no implication of faultfinding: "The machines are *idle* during the noon hour." "Because supplies did not arrive that day, the work crew was *idle* for several hours." *Indolent* is applied to someone who not only avoids effort but likes to indulge in relaxation: "Jon was a contented, *indolent* fisherman." "Selling from door to door is no occupation for an *indolent* person." Related words that convey greater degrees of reproof than either *lazy* or *indolent* are *sluggish* and *slothful*.

lead, led. These words are sometimes confused because the past tense of *lead* is *led*, which is pronounced like the metal *lead*. When an object is covered or treated with *lead* (the metal), it is *leaded*, but such a condition bears no relationship to the verb that means "to show the way," "to conduct or escort": "If you *lead* the way, I'll follow you." "You have *led* me to make a foolish mistake." "This experiment has *led* me to believe that *lead* is a heavy, soft, malleable metal."

leaflet. *See* BROCHURE.

learn, teach. In standard usage, *learn* (meaning "to gain knowledge") is never acceptable in the sense of *teach* ("to instruct," "to impart knowledge"). One can *learn* something, but he cannot *learn* someone else anything: "This should *teach* (not *learn*) you to stay out of trouble." "If you will take the time to *teach* me, I'll try to *learn.*"

least, less, lest. *Least* is the superlative degree of *little; less* is the comparative: "Toby has *less* money than I have; in fact, she has the *least* money of any girl in our group." Both *least* and *less* always refer to amount, size, or importance: "*less* value," "*least* importance," "*least* influence," "*less* distance." (For the distinctions between *less* and *fewer, see* FEWER.) "At *least*" and "not in the *least*" are frequently mere fillers in conversation and are overworked phrases. Neither *least* nor *less* should be confused with the conjunction *lest,* which means "for fear that": "He kept moving his fingers *lest* they freeze in the bitter cold." *Lest* also conveys the meaning of "so that" when used to introduce a statement suggesting a need for caution: "Don't say much *lest* the opposition steal your plan."

leastways, leastwise. These words are dialectal, appearing only in regional speech and never in formal writing. They mean "at any rate," "in any event," or "at least": "*Leastways,* that's what I thought he said." "You could *leastwise* try harder." Both words are highly informal conversation fillers and should not be used in writing or speech unless employed for the purpose of characterizing an uneducated person.

leave, let. These words are interchangeable only when accompanied by *alone:* "*Leave* (or *let*) Eleanor alone." In correct usage, *let* normally means "to allow," "to permit," "to cause": "*Let* me do that for you." *Leave* usually means "to go away from" or "to cause to remain": "If you *leave* me undisturbed, I can finish the work quickly."

led. *See* LEAD.

legal, lawful. The basic meanings of *legal* and *lawful*, as well as the distinctions in meaning between them, are explained in the entry ILLEGAL. *Legal* means "according to human law," but *lawful* has further meanings of "conforming to moral principle" and "in line with religious or ethical doctrine." Thus one refers to *"legal* rights" or *"lawful* rights" but is more likely to say *"lawful* marriage" than *"legal* marriage" and *"lawful* living" than *"legal* living."

legend. *See* MYTH.

legible. *See* READABLE.

legitimate. *See* ILLEGITIMATE.

lend, loan. *Loan* has long been established as a verb, especially in business circles (*loan* the firm some money), but *lend* is considered preferable by many careful writers and speakers: "I refused to *lend* (not *loan*) him my car for the evening." *Loan* (not *lend*) should be used as a noun. If you prefer to use *lend* rather than *loan* as a verb (perhaps because "Distance *loans* enchantment" sounds odd), remember that the past tense and past participle are *lent:* "The bank *lent* him money yesterday." "The bank has *lent* him money many times."

lengthy, long. The serviceable and most often used word to indicate "extending in space," "of considerable duration," "not short," and "not brief" is *long:* "London is a *long* distance from Budapest." "The lovers had a *long* conversation about their plans." "This book is 500 pages *long.*" *Lengthy* has much the same meanings: "a *lengthy* journey," "a *lengthy* conversation," "a *lengthy* book."

Perhaps because there is no real need for *lengthy* (one expert has scornfully compared it to *thicknessy* and *breadthy*), it has taken on associated meanings not conveyed by *long*. *Lengthy* is most often applied to speeches, writings, or programs in general that seem "overlong," "tedious," "wordy," "longer than need be": "The *lengthy* proceedings dragged on for weeks." Try to keep your remarks from being *lengthy*.

less. *See* FEWER and LEAST.

lessee, lessor. These words are based on *lease*, a term for a contract renting property to another. A *lessee* is one to whom a lease is granted (the renter); a *lessor* is one who grants a lease (the owner or manager): "The *lessor* demanded that the *lessee* pay two months' rent in advance."

lest. *See* LEAST.

let. *See* LEAVE.

let's. As a contraction of *let us*, *let's* is informal but standard. "*Let's* us" ("*Let's us* leave early") is a wordy expression; omit *us* or *'s*.

liable. *See* APT.

libel, slander, scandal. Both *libel* and *slander* mean "defamation," "injury to the reputation of someone." *Libel*, however, is restricted to defamation by written or printed words, pictures, or any form other than speech: "The attorney feels that this article is a clear case of *libel* and that you should sue." "Be careful; do not publish a *libel* against someone more powerful than you are." *Slander* is oral defamation: malicious, false, or harmful statements that are made but not put into print or graphic form. When someone tells lies about you, that is *slander;* when he prints or writes them, that is *libel*. In this context, *scandal* is a milder word than either *libel* or *slander*. It does mean "malicious gossip," "defamatory talk," but it conveys the idea that the charges leveled may be true or false. That is, much *scandal* is mere rumor: "The old men sitting on the courthouse lawn spent their days chewing tobacco and exchanging *scandal*." "No *scandal* ever touched this upright citizen."

licit. *See* ILLICIT.

lie. *See* LAY.

lifelong, livelong. *Lifelong* means "continuing for a lifetime": "Johnson dwelled in *lifelong* poverty." *Livelong* (pronounced "LIV·lawng") means "long in passing," "whole": "She spent the *livelong* day on the beach."

lighted, lit. The past tense of *light* is *lighted* or *lit*. Thus, it is correct to say "Bill *lighted* a cigar" and "Bill *lit* a cigar." Take your choice; one is as standard as the other. True, you are more likely to refer to a "*lighted* cigarette" than a "*lit* cigarette," but you are also more likely to say "Bill *lit* the match" than "Bill *lighted* the match." Since *light* may also mean "to descend" or "to land," either *lighted* or *lit* may be used to refer to all things that come down, whether planes, snow, or birds: "The bird *lighted* (or *lit*) on the roof."

lightening, lightning. *Lightening* (pronounced "LAIT·unning") means "making lighter in weight," "lessening." *Lightning* (pronounced "LAIT·ning") is an electrical discharge. "By *lightening* the load, we can travel faster." "What is your opinion of the story about Ben Franklin and *lightning?*"

like. In recent years, *like* has been used so increasingly for *as* or *as if* that this usage is now accepted as popular or informal in constructions formerly considered nonstandard. When *like* precedes a noun that is not followed by a verb, its use is standard: "He talked *like* an expert." The use of *like* as a subordinating conjunction is not recommended, however (He drank beer *like* it was going out of style). In standard usage, say *as* or *as if* in clauses of comparison: "You should do *as* I tell you," not "You should do *like* I tell you." No longer do you need to avoid *like* "like" you once did, but it is preferable to use it only in a prepositional sense. In other situations, use *as if, though,* and *as though* not only for correctness but for effective variety. You will then speak *as* (not *like*) a good speaker should.

In recent years, *like* has become a filler, a throwaway word used constantly in the speech of many persons, especially young people: "You know, I want to, *like* I said, try to do better, but something always, *like,* gets in the way." One can sympathize with the nervousness or ignorance that presumably causes this misuse and overuse, but one can also avoid the practice himself. *See also* AS IF.

like for, like to. These phrases are nonstandard in expressions such as "I'd *like for* you to have it" and "She *likes to have* drowned." From the first example, omit *for;* for *like to have* in the second, substitute *nearly* or *almost.*

likely. *See* APT.

likes of. This is a nonstandard expression when used to mean "of a kind," "of a sort." Avoid a statement such as "She wore a hat the *likes of* which I'd never seen before." Use *like* or omit the expression entirely.

like to. *See* LIKE FOR.

likewise. This is a standard adverb meaning "moreover," "in addition": "Mrs. James is *likewise* our best hostess." *Likewise* also means "similarly," "same here," "in the same way." It must be this latter meaning that causes a person to acknowledge an introduction to someone who says "I'm glad to meet you" with the silly comment "Likewise." Why not respond "I am, too" or with the ungrammatical but familiar "Me, too"?

limit, delimit. To *limit* is to restrict, contain, or keep within bounds: "The chairman will *limit* each speaker to five minutes." "Please *limit* your expense accounts for the next few weeks." To *delimit* is to mark off boundaries, to separate by fixing lines: "The line of demarcation will *delimit* the fighting areas." "A stone wall *delimits* my property on the south."

lineage, linage. Confusion between these words is due to spelling and pronunciation. *Linage* is a word of two syllables (LIE·nij) meaning the number of printed lines covered by an article, story, advertisement, or the like and also the amount charged or received for each printed line. It is always pronounced in two syllables but may also be spelled *lineage,* a word preferably reserved to mean "ancestry" or "line of descendants." In this meaning, the word (however spelled) is pronounced in three syllables (LIN·e·ij). "The *linage* in this issue of our magazine is down by 10 percent from last month." "She tried to trace her *lineage* to early settlers in Jamestown, Virginia."

liqueur, liquor. These words refer to alcoholic beverages, but a *liqueur* is a sweet, strong, highly flavored alcoholic drink such as crème de menthe (literally, "cream of mint") or chartreuse. Another name for *liqueur* is *cordial.* A *liquor* is a distilled or spirituous beverage, such as brandy or whiskey, which is distinguished from fermented beverages like beer and wine. The broth from meats or vegetables is also called *liquor.* "The partygoers had several drinks of *liquor* before dinner and turned to *liqueurs* after dessert." "His favorite *liqueur* is Drambuie; his favorite *liquor* is bourbon." "The *liquor* from these greens is rich in vitamins."

lit. *See* LIGHTED.

litany, liturgy. A *litany* is a ceremonial form of prayer. It consists of a series of invocations (calls) or petitions followed by responses: "The language of the *litany* in the Book of Common Prayer is considered beautiful." *Litany* may also refer to any recitation or recital of lines and to a prolonged or monotonous account: "His recital of mishaps was a *litany* of bad luck." *Liturgy* refers to a form of public worship, to a ritual of services. It is applied especially to what is known as the Eucharist in the Eastern Church and as the Mass in the Western Church. "At the seminary, he studied liturgics, the art and science of conducting public worship that is known as *liturgy.*"

literally. *See* FIGURATIVELY.

literate, illiterate. The basic distinctions between these words are treated in the entry ILLITERATE. In addition to meaning "able to read and write," *literate* means "literary" and "possessing skill, polish, and refinement": "Everyone should be able to read and write, but it requires hard work and much study to become truly *literate.*"

liturgy. *See* LITANY.

live. *See* RESIDE.

livelong. *See* LIFELONG.

loan. *See* LEND.

loath, loathe. *Loath* is an adjective meaning "reluctant," "unwilling," "averse," "disinclined": "I am always *loath* to admit my mistakes." *Loathe* is a verb meaning "to detest," "to abhor," "to abominate," "to feel disgust for": "Most people *loathe* the rude jangling of an alarm clock."

locality, location. These words have much the same general meaning: "a place, district, or spot." *Location* is much more often used, however, when people are involved in the reference. That is, *locality* is usually restricted to its geographical meaning, whereas *location* specifically means "a place or residence or settlement": "Many mines were once worked in that *locality.*" "This valley is a good *location* for you to settle in." Motion picture companies leave studios to film not "in or at a *location*" but "on *location,*" meaning a place or spot where action can be filmed.

locate, settle. Each of these words is used to mean "to establish oneself, one's residence, or one's business in a place": "He *located* (or *settled*) in a small Western town." *Settle* is preferred when reference is to the residences, or living quarters, of people: "The soldiers *settled* into the fort quickly." "Government authorities will *settle* this area with newly arrived immigrants." Although *locate* is not incorrect in this meaning, it is considered less refined and more dialectal than *settle*. In other words, *settle* has the connotation of location, *locate* that of locality. *See also* LOCALITY.

location. *See* LOCALITY.

locution, circumlocution. *Locution* means "a style of speech," "a manner of oral expression," "phraseology," "a particular form of expression": "The *locution* of native-born speakers differs from that of immigrants." "The *locution* of deaf persons sometimes seems strained and awkward." *Circumlocution* derives its meaning from its prefix, *circum-*, an element meaning "around" and "about." That is, *circumlocution* is *locution* that is roundabout, indirect, or wordy. "At this point in time" is a *circumlocution* for *now* or *today*.

lofty. *See* TALL.

lonely, lonesome. These words mean about the same thing and are frequently used interchangeably. A *lonely* person is likely to be *lonesome* because he is "without companions" or "remote from places of human habitation." *Lonesome,* rather than *lonely,* is more often used to mean "isolated," "desolate," and "unfrequented": "This is a *lonesome* part of the forest." "The narrow path wound through a *lonesome* stretch of country." *Lonely* conveys a feeling of dejection, depression, or sadness: "Janet was almost in tears because she felt so *lonely.*" In the sense that *lonely* and *lonesome* mean "alone," one of man's greatest achievements is to be alone and yet possess such inner resources that he feels neither *lonely* nor *lonesome.*

long. *See* LENGTHY.

longshoreman, stevedore. These words are used interchangeably, but to discriminating users of language a *longshoreman* (the word *longshore* is a variant of alongshore) is someone employed to load and unload vessels. A *stevedore* (a word derived from a Spanish term meaning "to pack," "to stow") is an employer of *longshoremen.* A *stevedore* is a hiring firm or group of men; a *longshoreman* is a laborer on wharves.

lots, heaps. In the meaning of "a great many" or "a great deal," these words are informal: "*lots* of trouble," "a *lot* of money," "*heaps* of food," "*heaps* of good times." When used in this sense (an indefinitely large amount), both *lot* and *lots* are singular when appearing alone and plural when followed by *of* and a plural noun: "This *is* a lot." "Help yourself to the food; *lots is* here." "*Lots* of girls *are* at the party." *Lot* and *lots* require a singular verb when followed by *of* and a singular noun: "This *is* a *lot* of money." "There *is lots* of news on the radio tonight." Nearly always, *many* or *much* can be substituted for *a lot, lot of,* and *lots of.* Meaning "all," "the *lot*" is informal: "I'll disregard *the lot.*" *Heaps* is at least as casual as *lots* when used to mean "a great deal." Avoid saying "*heaps* of people" and "a *heap* of misery" unless you are striving to create a homespun, folksy atmosphere. *Heap* is slang for an old run-down automobile, but *rattletrap* is a more colorful term.

loud, loudly. *Loud* can be both an adjective and an adverb, but *loudly* may be used only as the latter. It is permissible to say "Shout out *loud*" or "Shout out *loudly.*" Such optional usage is common after such verbs as *sing, talk, say, scream,* and *laugh,* but among careful speakers and writers, *loudly* is preferred. Also, one "boasts *loudly* (not *loud*)," and *loudly* is accepted idiomatic usage with such other verbs as *insist, brag, state,* and *exclaim.* It is safer to use *loud* only as an adjective (a *loud* noise, the noise was *loud*).

louse, lousy. *Louse* is a slang term for a contemptible person. "*Louse* up" is slang for "botch" and "spoil." *Lousy* is slang for "well-supplied" (*lousy* with money) and "unpleasant," "inferior," "worthless" (a *lousy* cold, a *lousy* meal, a *lousy* show). *Lousy* also means "infested with lice"; if you wish to impress friends, say *pediculous.*

lowbrow. *See* HIGHBROW.

lunch, luncheon. These words refer to a light meal eaten at some time between breakfast and dinner (or supper). *Lunch* is considered more informal than *luncheon.* If the meal is customary and uneventful, use *lunch.* If it is an occasion, a formal occurrence, say *luncheon.* "Pick me up for *lunch.*" "The annual *luncheon* for employees will be given next week." *Lunch* can also serve as a verb (*lunch* with me), but *luncheon* is a noun only.

lustful, lusty. These words are derived from an Old English word meaning "desire" and "pleasure," but they have different meanings and applications in modern usage. *Lustful* means "full of greed": "This politician is *lustful* for power." *Lustful* also means "lecherous," "having lewd desires," "sexually desirous": "Persons who like X-rated films are usually *lustful.*" "Young girls often claim to fear *lustful* males." *Lusty* means "full of vigor," "hearty," "robust," "sturdy," "strong": "This is a *lusty* young athlete." "He has a *lusty* attitude toward life." A *lusty* person may be *lustful,* but not necessarily. A *lustful* person may not be *lusty* at all.

luxuriant, luxurious. *Luxuriant* means "growing abundantly," "flourishing vigorously": "The tropical foliage was *luxuriant.*" *Luxurious* means "fond of, or given to, luxury": "These hotel rooms are *luxurious.*" Approximate synonyms of *luxurious* are *sensuous, voluptuous, sumptuous, self-indulgent, epicurean,* and *rich.* Approximate synonyms of *luxuriant* are *lush, teeming, fruitful,* and *prolific.*

lyric, lyrical. These two adjectives may be used interchangeably to refer to anything that is characterized by spontaneous feeling, by an outpouring of emotion. Both words are applied to poetry that has the musical quality of song and to any kind of writing or speech reflecting sensation and mood: "*lyric* (or *lyrical*) poetry," "*lyric* (or *lyrical*) song," "*lyric* (or *lyrical*) love letters." *Lyric* is more often used, and is preferred, except when the feeling to be conveyed is somewhat unformed and vague: "The mother was *lyrical* in praise of her daughter's performance." Use of *lyric* to refer to the words of a song (The melody is great, but the *lyrics* are poor) is informally colloquial.

M

machismo. This term from Spanish is now commonly used to indicate such qualities as courage, virility, and aggressiveness. It may also be used to mean an attitude of male superiority. *Machismo* is a useful, colorful, acceptable term, but widespread employment is rapidly turning it into a trite expression.

mad. *Mad* is informal when combined with *about* or *over* to indicate enthusiasm (*mad* about football). It is slang when used to mean "unusual" or "pointless" (*mad* conversation) and "gay" or "frantic" (a *mad* dash for the train). "Like *mad*" is slang for "wildly" (driving *like mad*). "To have a *mad* on" is slang for "to sulk," "to be angry." "*Mad* as a hatter" is a hackneyed expression. *See also* ANGRY.

madam. Spelled as *madam* and pronounced "MADuhm," the term is a title of respect and a form of address to a woman. Spelled as *madame* and pronounced "mah·DAHM," the word is a French title of courtesy and is roughly equivalent to *Mrs.* The plural of both *madam* and *madame* is *mesdames* (MAY·dahm). It is safe enough to call any woman *madam,* but you should be careful not to refer to one as "*a* madam," unless you are in a brothel. *Ma'am* is an informal abbreviation of *madam* and *madame*. *Missus* and *missis* are illiteracies. *Mrs.* (pronounced "MIS·iz") has a plural of *Mmes.* and is a title prefixed to the names of married women only. The title *Ms.*, prefixed to the names of women, married or single, is being used more and more often. *See also* MR.

magic, magical. As a noun, *magic* refers to producing results through mysterious influences or unexplained powers. It involves the control by persons skilled in magic of supernatural agencies and the forces of nature. In view of this meaning, *magic* seems loosely used and overused to refer to occurrences that might correctly be labeled "unusual," "effective," or "spectacular." "His piano playing was *magic*" and "When she smiled, the effect was *magic*" are examples of such misuses of a powerfully charged word. As an adjective, *magic* means much the same as *magical*, but here again exaggeration is usually apparent: "The lovers spent a *magical* (or *magic*) night" and "This baritone has a *magic* (or *magical*) range to his voice" are examples of overemphasis. Recommendation: use both adjectives sparingly and always place *magic* directly before the word it modifies: "*magic* number," "*magic* square," "*magic* lantern," "*magic* artistry." If this can't be done, use *magical*.

maintain, repair, service. Use of these words reflects the social attitudes of those who use them fully as much as the basic meanings of the terms themselves. Presumably because many persons feel that the word *serve* suggests something menial and degrading, such terms as *maintenance engineer* and *appliance custodian* have replaced the concept of serving in such terms as *repairman* and *serviceman*. (*Serviceman* is a term still in general use for a member of the armed forces of a country.) *Maintain* means "to preserve," "to keep in due operation and condition": "The crew is expected to *maintain* this highway throughout the winter." The act of maintaining may involve making repairs but is usually restricted to mean "watching over," "preventing trouble." *Repair* suggests restoration or renewal: "The doctor sent him to a dry climate so that he could *repair* his health." "The only way to *repair* this refrigerator is to install a new motor." *Service* is an inclusive word with the meanings of both *maintain* and *repair* as well as that of inspection: "This company will *service* all parking meters in the city." *Service* is incorrectly used for *serve* in a sentence such as "This bus line *services* four counties."

majority, plurality, minority. One meaning of *majority* is "more than half." *Plurality* means "the highest number within a given number," "the excess of votes received by the leader over the next candidate when three or more are competing." If Joe got eighty votes, Jack sixty, and Bill forty, Joe would have a *plurality* of twenty but not a *majority* because he received fewer than half the votes cast. *Majority* is often used as a loose substitute for *many*. In this context, *minority* means a number, amount, or part forming less than half of the whole. *Minority* also applies to a group differing in ethnic background, race, or religion from the *majority* of a population. "The Democrats form the *majority* party in this county." "To win this election, you will need a *plurality* of the votes, not necessarily a *majority*." "In this state, Chinese-Americans are a *minority* group." *See also* BULK.

male, manly, masculine. These words are closely related but have distinct meanings and applications. *Male* always refers to sex: "Jim belongs to a *male* choir." *Manly* implies possession of the most desirable qualities a male can have. *Masculine* refers to the qualities of a male as contrasted with those of a female. *Male, manly,* and *masculine* have the shades of meaning concerning men that *female, womanly,* and *feminine* have for women. *See also* FEMALE.

malodorous. *See* ODOROUS.

manage. *See* HANDLE.

manifold, multiform, multiple. *Manifold* means "of many kinds," with the added suggestion that the number involved is not only large but varied and complex: "The superintendent of the apartment building had duties that were *manifold.*" *Multiform* means "having many forms of many different kinds": "The obstacles to saving money are *multiform,* but a strict budget will help overcome them." *Multiple* means "consisting of many parts or elements": "There are *multiple* risks in starting a new business." Related words include *numerous, multifarious, myriad, sundry, various,* and *multitudinous.*

manly. *See* MALE.

manner. *See* FASHION.

manner born. This expression has come to mean "accustomed by birth to a high position." In this expression, *manner* is frequently spelled *manor,* through the mistaken idea that "*manor* born" means "born to high estate, to the aristocracy." The word should be *manner,* meaning "custom," "habitual practice." One should have no trouble with the expression if he will recall the Shakespearean passage in which it originated. In *Hamlet,* Horatio asks about the sound of trumpets, guns, and drums. Hamlet tells him that each time the King (Claudius) takes a drink, the act is followed by this outburst. When asked if this uproar is a custom, Hamlet replies: "Ay, marry, it is;/ But to my mind, though I am native here/ And to the manner born, it is a custom/ More honored in the breach than the observance."

manslaughter. *See* HOMICIDE.

manuscript, typescript. A *manuscript* is a letter, document, or book written by hand; it is writing as distinguished from print. *Manuscript* comes from Latin words meaning "written by hand," but the term is now applied to an author's copy of a work, whether in longhand or typewritten, that is used as the basis for typesetting. *Typescript* is a typewritten copy of a composition; it refers to such matter as distinguished from handwritten or printed material. "This *manuscript* is written in pencil." "The *typescript* of this short story is twenty pages long."

marital, martial. *Marital* pertains to marriage, *martial* to war. Only cynics would maintain that the words are interchangeable. Note both spelling and pronunciation: MAR·uh·tuhl and MAHR·shuhl. "*Marital* disagreements sometimes lead to separation and divorce." "The ancient Spartans were considered a *martial* people."

marriage, nuptials, wedding. Each of these words applies to the ceremony of joining couples in matrimony, uniting them in wedlock. *Marriage* is the most commonly used word; it refers not only to the ceremony itself but to the union of a couple as long as that union lasts: "The proud parents recently announced the *marriage* of their daughter." "The Blakes' *marriage* lasted for fifty years." *Nuptials* is a formal word usually applied to a ceremony involving persons of high social standing, wealth, or nobility: "The royal *nuptials* of Elizabeth and Philip were celebrated by millions of people." *Wedding,* a term applying only to the ceremony (unlike *marriage*), has emotional and sentimental connotations: "Her *wedding* was so beautiful that it had many guests in tears."

martial. *See* MARITAL.

martyr, victim. A *martyr* is someone who (1) willingly suffers death because of his beliefs and attitudes or (2) is tortured or killed because of his principles or unwillingness to give up a cause or faith. The word is loosely overused to refer to anyone who undergoes severe suffering or hardship or who seeks attention by pretending pain or loss. A person who dedicates his life to some cause at the expense of his health or financial standing may be called a *martyr:* "He lived his adult life as a *martyr* to the cause of equal rights for everyone." A parent who stays at home to care for children rather than going out to play bridge or engage in hanky-panky is something less than a *martyr.* A *victim* is a sufferer from any injurious or destructive action or event or one who is cheated and deceived by others: "The hospital is filled with accident *victims.*" "Joe was the *victim* of his own stupidity." "Because of his immaturity, he is often the *victim* of misplaced confidence."

masculine. *See* MALE.

masterly, masterful. These terms imply having the skill or art of a master. *Masterly* is usually restricted to a meaning of "skillful," however, whereas *masterful* suggests authority, dominance, and force: "Napoleon, a *masterful* man, deployed his troops in a *masterly* way."

material, matériel. The more common of these words, *material* (muh·TIR·i·uhl) means "matter," "substance," "constituent element." *Matériel* (muh·TEER·i·el) is usually limited to equipment or supplies and is distinguished from *personnel* (people). "The *material* in this dress is shoddy." "The retreating army left behind vast quantities of *matériel.*"

materialize. This word means "to give form to," "to make physically apparent": "The money we hoped to make in this venture never *materialized.*" *Materialize* is overused as a polysyllabic synonym for "to take place," "to develop," or "to happen" and should not be used in a sentence such as "The anxiety which I expected to feel never did *materialize.*"

materially, greatly. *Materially* means "considerably," "to an important degree": "The small check he sent did not help my problem *materially*." *Materially* also means "physically" when used with reference to material matters and conditions: "Because of the condition of the roads it was *materially* impossible to make good time." In nearly every situation arising in speech or writing, *greatly* can effectively substitute for *materially* and is less likely to be misunderstood. "My health is *materially* improved" can just as effectively be stated "My health is *greatly* improved."

matériel. *See* MATERIAL.

matinee performance. A *matinee* (derived from a French word meaning "morning") is a performance or entertainment presented in the daytime, usually in the afternoon. To say "There will be an extra *matinee performance* next week" is to be unnecessarily wordy. Omit *performance*.

matricide. *See* PATRICIDE.

maunder, meander. *Maunder* means "to talk in a meaningless, rambling, foolish way": "The speaker *maundered* on and on for what seemed hours." *Meander* means "to ramble," "to wander aimlessly," "to go by an indirect course": "The stream *meandered* down the mountainside." It is true, however, that one can *meander* in speech as well as in movement, so that a speaker can be said to *meander* or *maunder*. If the wandering in speech is clever or brilliant, call it *meandering;* if it is dull and pointless, call it *maundering*.

may. *See* CAN.

maybe, may be. *Maybe* is an adverb meaning "possibly," "perhaps": "*Maybe* it will snow tonight." *May be* is a verb phrase, two words that express possibility or likelihood: "It *may be* that it will snow tonight."

mean. *See* AVERAGE.

meander. *See* MAUNDER.

media, medias. *See* MEDIUM.

median. *See* AVERAGE.

mediate. *See* ARBITRATE.

meditate. *See* CONTEMPLATE.

medium, media, medias. These words refer to an agency, means, method, or instrument by which information and advertising may be made public. Such agencies and means include principally newspapers, magazines, radio and television broadcasting, and films. The singular is *medium:* "Television is an important *medium* for national advertisers." The plural is *mediums* and *media:* "In his campaign, the congressman used such *media* (or *mediums*) as spot announcements on radio and television and paid newspaper advertisements." It is nonstandard to refer to *"a mass media* such as television." *Medium* means "one method of mass communication." *Media* (or *mediums*) means "more than one method." *Medias* is an incorrect plural.

meet, meet with. In the sense of "to come into the company of," *meet* and *meet with* have different meanings: "The mayor wishes to *meet* the new members of the council." "The mayor wishes to *meet with* the new members of the council." In the first sentence, *meet* means "to make the acquaintance of"; in the second, "to join the company of." Both *meet* and *meet with* can mean "to come across," "to encounter": "I rarely *meet* her on the street since her illness." "My plan will *meet with* considerable opposition." *Meet with* (not *meet*) is used in the sense of "to suffer," "to undergo," and "to experience": "Betty *met with* a serious accident."

meet up with. This is a wordy, nonstandard expression. "I *met up with* some girls on the beach" is better expressed by "I *met* some girls on the beach" or "I *encountered* some. . . ."

meet with. *See* MEET.

melody. *See* HARMONY.

memo, memorandum. *Memorandum* is a word of Latin origin meaning "short note," "record of events," "brief message." *Memo* is an informal but widely used and acceptable abbreviation: "This executive begins each day with a *memorandum* (or *memo*) to all salesmen." The standard plural of *memorandum* is either *memorandums* or *memoranda;* the plural of *memo* is *memos:* "Please stop sending me so many *memorandums* (or *memoranda* or *memos*)."

meridian, meridiem. These words are so closely related in meaning that using one for the other is understandable and usually unnoticed. *Meridian* means "midday," just as *meridiem* does. Thus *postmeridian* (one word) and *post meridiem* (two words) mean "occurring after noon," "in the afternoon." When the abbreviations A.M. and P.M. are spelled out, the word should be *meridiem* (ante *meridiem,* post *meridiem*).

metaphor. *See* SIMILE.

meticulous, scrupulous. These words are often used interchangeably but should not be. *Meticulous* means "unusually careful about small details," "exact," "precise," "finicky": "She spends hours working with her hair because she is *meticulous* about her appearance." "A watchmaker has to be *meticulous* in his work." *Scrupulous* means "conscientious," "principled," "showing regard for what is considered right": "This person has a *scrupulous* regard for the dignity of others."

microbe. *See* GERM.

might, mighty. *Might* is the past tense of *may* (*see* CAN). Avoid such nonstandard expressions as "*might* of" and "*might* could" (for *might have* or *might*). In the senses of possibility and permission, *may* is more intense than *might*. "He *may* die" is stronger than "He *might* die," and "*May* I stay?" is more forceful than "*Might* I stay?" As a noun, *might* appears in such trite expressions as "with *might* and main" and "with all his *might*." *Mighty* is informal in the sense of "very" (*mighty* scared).

militate. *See* MITIGATE.

minimal, minimum. *Minimal* is an adjective meaning "smallest," "least possible": "He secured a loan at a *minimal* rate of interest." *Minimum* is primarily a noun meaning "the least quantity or amount possible" (Jack expended a *minimum* of time on studying), but is also used as an adjective with the same meaning as *minimal*: "This is a *minimum* risk." Neither *minimal* nor *minimum* means "just a little" or "not much"; both mean "the least possible." In adjectival use, careful speakers prefer *minimal* to *minimum*.

minimize. *See* DIMINISH.

minister. *See* PASTOR.

minority. *See* MAJORITY.

mishap. *See* ACCIDENT.

misplace. *See* DISPLACE.

misremember. *See* FORGET.

mitigate, militate. These "look-alikes" are easily confused. *Mitigate* means "to lessen," "to soften," "to moderate": "Because the culprit readily confessed his guilt, the judge *mitigated* the sentence." *Militate* means "to have effect or influence," "to operate against or for (usually against)": "The fact that he is an addict *militated* against him." "Everything *militated* in his favor because of *mitigating* circumstances in his background."

mobile, movable. What is *mobile* is *movable*, but what is *movable* is not always *mobile*. *Movable* means "capable of being moved" and "able to be rearranged": "This statue is heavy but *movable*." "Easter is a *movable* date." *Mobile* means "capable of moving," "responding to impulses and emotions": "Although the player was badly injured, he was still *mobile*." "She is a lively person with a *mobile* expression." A heavy sofa may or may not be *movable* but is never *mobile*. The antonym of *movable* is *immovable;* that of *mobile* is *immobile*.

mode. *See* FASHION.

moderate. *See* CONSERVATIVE.

modern, modernistic. These words can correctly be used synonymously, but in some situations their meaning differs. *Modern* should be applied as an adjective to anything that exists in the present age, exists now in contrast to existence in an earlier period: "Becky cannot adjust to *modern* city life." "Bob prides himself on his *modern* viewpoints." "That building is an excellent example of *modern* architecture." *Modernistic* can be used as *modern* is, but it is more often applied to items or ideas that have been, or may be, short-lived, exaggerated, or experimental: "I like up-to-date styles, but this furniture seems too *modernistic* to me." "His lifestyle is so *modernistic* as to seem unorthodox and even incredible."

modest, shy. A *modest* person is humble, someone who is free from egotism, vanity, and boastfulness. A *modest* individual is moderate in his behavior and speech. "Lincoln was a great but *modest* man." "Mrs. Morgan is a self-respecting, *modest* woman." A *shy* person is timid, easily frightened, and bashful. A *shy* girl wishes to escape notice and avoids close association with others: "Beth was once a *shy*, retiring girl who blushed easily." A *shy* person is diffident; a *modest* person is unassuming.

momentarily, momently. *Momentarily* means (1) "at any moment," (2) "from moment to moment," and (3) "for a moment": "The blast will be set off *momentarily.*" "Our chances are improving *momentarily.*" "Let's sit down and rest *momentarily.*" *Momently,* now rarely used, formerly meant only "at any moment": "He will get here *momently.*" In current speech and writing, *momently* may occasionally be used in any of the three meanings of *momentarily* but has largely disappeared from the language.

money, monies. *Money* is money, a collective noun or mass word that rarely appears in plural form. When a plural is needed, as in referring to the currencies of different countries, the preferred spelling is *moneys:* "The *moneys* of Great Britain, France, and Germany have a different base." In some financial reports and legal papers, the plural *monies* appears, but this form is not generally approved.

monologue, dialogue. From Greek terms meaning "one word" or "one person," *monologue* refers to a speech by one person. In drama, *monologue* applies to a form of entertainment by a single speaker or to an extended part of the text of a play uttered by an actor or actress. *Monologue* is sometimes used disparagingly to refer to the comments of someone who talks glibly and incessantly: "Several of the most moving passages in *Hamlet* are the *monologues* delivered by leading characters." "It's impossible to have a conversation with him because all he does is talk in *monologue.*" *Dialogue,* from Greek words meaning "two words" or "two speeches," refers to conversation between two or more persons. *Dialogue* is a currently popular term for an exchange of ideas on such issues as politics, human rights, economics, and religion: "The managers and workers in this plant should have a *dialogue* about their common problems."

moonlight, moonlit, moonlighted. Although *moonlight* is used most often as a noun ("the light of the moon"), it is also an adjective (a *moonlight* evening) and a verb ("to work at a spare-time job"). When used as a verb, *moonlight* forms its principal parts as does *light: moonlight, moonlighted* or *moonlit, moonlighted* or *moonlit*. Thus it is correct to say "He *moonlighted* for extra money"; "It was a *moonlighted* (or *moonlit*) night"; "The evening was *moonlighted* (or *moonlit*)." *Moonlit* is the preferred form of both adjective and past participle. *Moonlighted* is the preferred past tense of the verb. *See also* LIGHTED.

moot. This word when used as an adjective means (1) subject to debate, arguable, unresolved; and (2) of only slight importance or significance: "This is a *moot* question." "Whether the player is black or white is a *moot* consideration." That is, "a *moot* question" is debatable; "a *moot* point" is of no importance. In law schools, a *moot* court is a mock court in which contrived cases are tried as a method of training; in this situation, *moot* is used to mean both "arguable" and "hypothetical."

moral, morale. These words are distinct in pronunciation and meaning as well as in spelling. *Moral* (MOR·uhl or MAWR·uhl) is concerned with the goodness or badness of human action and character. *Morale* (mur·RAL or muh·RAHL) refers to the state of spirits of a person or group. "Most philosophers consider man a *moral* being." "A bonus plan was adopted in order to boost the *morale* of the sales force." No exact one-word synonyms exist for *morale*, but for *moral* you can use *ethical, upright, righteous, virtuous, noble,* and *scrupulous*.

morals. *See* ETHICS.

morbid, sordid. Although these words have a slight connection, they should be differentiated. A *morbid* person is in an unhealthy mental state, is excessively gloomy: "Dick has a *morbid* view of man's future." *Morbid* also means "gruesome," "horrible," "grim": "Motorists slowed down to observe the *morbid* sight of the recent accident." *Sordid* means "poor" or "run-down" (a *sordid* place to live) and "selfish" or "base" (the *sordid* methods of narcotics dealers). Approximate synonyms for *sordid* are *degraded, soiled, unclean, foul,* and *depraved*. Words related to *morbid* are *unhealthy, diseased, tainted, corrupted,* and *unwholesome*.

more preferable. *More* should be dropped from this wordy expression; *preferable* means "more desirable." Say "This apartment is *preferable* (not *more preferable*) to that one." (Notice that *to* is used in the preceding sentence; never say "prefer *than*.") The comparative degree of adjectives and adverbs expresses the idea of more (or less): *better* (not *more better*); *sicker* (not *more sicker*); *slower* (not *more slower*); *faster* (not *less,* or *more, faster*).

more than one. Although this phrase obviously expresses a plural idea, it is followed by a verb in the singular: "*More than one* story about this event *has* been printed." The verb is singular because of its relation (attraction) to *one*, not *more*. If the phrase is divided, however, the verb becomes plural: "More stories about this event than one *have* been printed." The same grammatical consideration applies to the phrase "all but one": "Sue says that all but one child *has* been fed." "All of the fifteen children but one *were* fed."

mornings. *See* AFTERNOONS.

moron, idiot, imbecile. Such experts in dealing with the human mind as psychologists and psychiatrists have never agreed on the exact meanings of these terms for mental deficiency. Each word is loosely used for individuals who seem silly, stupid, dull, half-witted, and foolish; each is often rejected in favor of *dunce, dolt,* and *numskull*. In the scale of mental ability, an *idiot* ranks below a *moron* or an *imbecile*. An *idiot* is one judged to be utterly senseless, foolish, and hopelessly deficient in developing beyond the mental age of three or four. An *imbecile* ranks above an *idiot* but lacks the capacity to develop beyond a mental age of seven or eight. A *moron* is someone with an intelligence quotient of 50 to 75 and a mental age of somewhere between eight and twelve years.

mortgager, mortgagee. A *mortgager* (the word is also correctly spelled *mortgagor*) is one who mortgages his property, that is, obligates or pledges material goods as security for repayment of money. (The word *mortgage* is derived from Latin terms meaning "death pledge.") A *mortgagee* is someone to whom property is mortgaged. *See also* LESSEE.

Moslem, Muslim. These terms refer to a believer in, or adherent of, Islam, a religion based on the teachings of the prophet Mohammed. *Moslem* is the spelling preferred in popular and newspaper usage, but students of religion normally use *Muslim*. This latter form is also employed by members of the Nation of Islam, an organization of American Negroes who call themselves Black Muslims.

most, mostly. Although *most* and *mostly* are adverbs meaning "almost entirely," "for the most part," they are not always interchangeable. When the desired sense is "extremely" or "to the greatest degree," *most* should be used: "Those *most* influenced are young children." In the sense of "in the main" or "on the whole," *mostly* is preferable: "The marchers were *mostly* weary." (If you mean the marchers were utterly exhausted, say "*most* weary.") *See also* ALMOST.

motion. *See* RESOLUTION.

motive, motif, incentive. A *motive* is a desire, need, or emotion that prompts or causes a person to act in a certain way; it is an inner urge that produces an act, but it also applies to the result of action: "Jeb's *motive* was to get even with those who had not helped him." "Fear was his *motive* in trying to escape." An *incentive* is something offered as a reward or prize, especially one proffered to spur competition: "Profit sharing is an *incentive* for every employee in this company." *Motif* comes from the same French word as *motive,* but it means (1) "a dominant idea or feature," (2) "a recurring subject or theme in an artistic work," and (3) "a distinctive form or shape in a design": "Isn't the profit *motif* the principal guide in every business?" "The *motif* of Verdi's *Rigoletto* differs from that of his *"Il trovatore."* "I like the *motif* of this wallpaper." Words allied in meaning to *motive* and *incentive* are *stimulus, spur, inducement, incitement, impulse, goad, prod,* and *encouragement.*

motto. *See* SLOGAN.

movable. *See* MOBILE.

Mr., Mrs., Ms. *Mr.* is the abbreviated form of the title *Mister* when used with a name. The plural is *Messrs.* (For comment on *Mrs.* and *Ms., see* MADAM.) Examples: *"Mr.* Seth Mieley and *Mrs.* Alix Greenway won the dance contest." *"Mmes.* (or *Mesdames*) Fogarty and Sloan and *Messrs.* Nieley and White attended the play." "Since I don't know and don't care whether Barbara is married or single, call her *Ms.* Barbara Kenneally."

muchly. This adverb has gradually gone out of use. Its departure from the language is no loss since *much* does all it ever did and with one less syllable: "What you have done pleases me *much.*" "I was *much* gratified by your reply."

mulatto, quadroon, octoroon. Each of these terms has a scientific basis, but each is considered offensive by many persons. Degrees of racial designation such as these terms and *half-caste* and *half-breed* do not always hide contempt or disdain. Although their use is not recommended, one should be accurate if he does need to employ them. A *mulatto* is someone with one white and one Negro parent, a person of mixed Negro and Caucasian ancestry. The term is loosely applied to individuals with light brown skin pigmentation. A *quadroon* is one-fourth Negro, one of the grandparents being Negro, the three others white. An *octoroon* is someone with one-eighth Negro ancestry.

multiform, multiple. *See* MANIFOLD.

murder. *See* HOMICIDE.

musical, musicale. *Musical* is an adjective referring in some way to music and its production: "The piano is a *musical* instrument." "We were invited to a *musical* entertainment." *Musicale,* a noun with its final syllable accented as "KAL," refers to a program of music forming all or part of a social occasion: "The *musicale* consisted of chamber music performed by six senior students."

Muslim. *See* MOSLEM.

must. In the sense of "something not to be missed" or a "requirement," *must* is tiresomely overused: "Paris is a *must* on any European trip." "A college degree is a *must* for this position." *Musta* is a clipped, unrecommended pronunciation of *must have.* Another nonstandard substitute for *must have* is *must of.*

mutual. For a discussion of the use of *mutual, see* COMMON, MUTUAL. An additional suggestion: avoid using *mutual* with words that imply working or being together. "*Mutual* cooperation" is a wordy phrase from which *mutual* should be deleted. How often is *mutual* needed with words such as *collaboration, concert, collusion, complicity, partnership, fraternity, fellowship, federation, tie-up, teamwork, unison, comradeship, combination,* and *concurrence?*

myself. This word is a reflexive pronoun, normally used in a sentence with *I* as the subject (I hurt *myself*). The use of *myself* for *me* as the object of verbs or prepositions is nonstandard; say "The supervisor spoke to Jane and *me* (not *myself*)." Also, do not use *myself* as the subject of a verb; say "The policeman and *I* saw the accident," not "The policeman and *myself* saw the accident." *See also* HIM.

mysterious, mythical, mystical. Each of these words refers to something that is not easily understood or explained. By being unknown or puzzling, that which is *mysterious* produces curiosity, awe, or amazement: "He is suffering from some *mysterious* illness that baffles the doctors." "She acted in a most *mysterious* way." That which is *mythical* involves a myth (a traditional or legendary story about superhuman beings) or is imaginary and without foundation: "His account of the trip was wholly *mythical.*" "This tale about dragons and unicorns is a delightfully *mythical* narrative." Anything that is *mystical* has a secret significance or meaning: "These rites are a *mystical* symbol of brotherhood." "Many of Edgar Allan Poe's best stories are *mystical.*" Related words include *occult, secret, esoteric, cryptic, obscure, inscrutable, enigmatic,* and *puzzling.*

myth, fable, legend. A *myth* is not only a legendary or traditional story, usually one concerning a superhuman being and dealing with events that have no natural explanation (*see* MYSTERIOUS), but also an unproved belief and an invented idea or story: "The story of Atlas holding up the world on his shoulders is a *myth.*" "It is a *myth* that all sharks are dangerous." "His excuses for his failure are only *myths.*" A *fable* is a simple story with animals as characters, one designed to teach a moral truth: "His favorite *fable* was the one about the fox and the grapes." *Fable* is also applied to stories about supernatural beings (resembling a *myth*), to accounts of extraordinary events, and to outright falsehoods: "Jim's account of flying with self-made wings is an outright *fable.*" A *legend* is a tradition or story handed down from earlier times and now popularly accepted as true, believable, or delightful: "A *legend* forms the basis of Irving's short story about a headless horseman in 'The Legend of Sleepy Hollow.' "

mythical. *See* MYSTERIOUS.

N

naïve. *See* INGENIOUS.

naked, nude. Each of these words means "without covering or clothing," "bare," "undressed," "undraped," "exposed." "The children ran *naked* on the lawn." "The fields lay *naked* under the winter moon." "Please tell me the *naked* truth." "This is a *nude* stretch of land laid bare by forest fires." "Some students make money by posing in the *nude* for art classes." Possibly *naked* seems "more bare" than *nude,* but the latter can hardly be termed a euphemism. *Nude* is reserved, however, for reference to an artist's painting of the human figure; Renoir painted *nudes,* not *naked* women.

nation, country. These words are used interchangeably, but careful writers distinguish between them. A *nation* is primarily a body of people who are associated with a particular territory. A *country* is a tract of land, a territory, that incidentally is the home of certain people. Emphasis upon either people or area is suggested in these sentences: "The United States is a *nation* of diverse peoples." "The United States is a *country* of vast dimensions."

natural. *See* NORMAL.

naught. *See* AUGHT.

nauseous, nauseated. *Nauseous* (NAW·zee·us) means "causing sickness"; *nauseated* means "feeling sickness," "being queasy." A gas, for instance, is *nauseous* and causes a person to become *nauseated*. (*Nauseous* is related in meaning to *noisome*, which means "foul," "filthy," or "dangerous," as in "a *noisome* odor.") "The audience was *nauseated* by the play." "Foul air *nauseated* the huge crowd." "Because the fumes were nauseous, the people became *nauseated*."

naval, navel. *Naval* has to do with ships: "What is the *naval* strength of that country?" "Tess is studying *naval* architecture." One's *navel* is a mark, or depression, in the surface of the abdomen marking the point of attachment of the umbilicus. A *navel* orange is so called because it has a formation shaped like a *navel* that contains a secondary fruit.

near, close. These words means "at or within a short distance or interval in time or space," but *close* is closer or nearer than *near*. That is, use *close* when you wish to stress immediate proximity: "A *close* shave," "a *close* call," "a *close* friend." *Near* more often conveys the idea of a narrow margin or approximation: "a *near* resemblance," "a *near* escape," "*near* neighbors." A photo finish is a *close* race, not a *near* one. Also, one does not set a *near*-record. Only a record is recorded, not a near-record.

near, nearly. *Near* is used as an adverb (come *near* me), as an adjective (the *near* side of the moon), as a preposition (*near* the house), and as a verb (the train *nears* the station). *Nearly* is an adverb only, with such meanings as "almost," "all but," "intimately," "with close agreement": "*nearly* sick with fear"; "a *nearly* perfect evening"; "*nearly* related persons." As an adverb, *nearly* is usually preferable to *near* except when place is involved: "I was *nearly* sick with a cold (not *near* sick)." "I was sitting *near* (not *nearly*) you." *See also* NEAR, CLOSE.

nearly, almost. Some linguists have tried to distinguish between these words by suggesting that *nearly* applies to time, space, or quantity (*nearly* midnight, *nearly* at his destination, *nearly* enough money) and *almost* to degree (*almost* nothing, *almost* dead). This distinction hardly seems worthwhile; in the illustrations given here, *almost* and *nearly* are interchangeable. If you wish to think of *nearly* as a positive word representing an approach and *almost* as a "minus" word subtracting from an idea, all right, but the difference seems too subtle for ordinary common sense. It is true, however, that in referring to one's state of mind or feeling, *almost* is preferable. One is *almost* afraid to do something, not *nearly* afraid. *See also* ALMOST.

necessaries. *See* NECESSITIES.

necessary, essential. These words are used interchangeably to mean "indispensable or requisite for the fulfillment or accomplishment of something." What is *necessary* or *essential* cannot be done without, cannot be dispensed with: "Water is *necessary* (or *essential*) to sustain life." "It is *essential* (or *necessary*) that you vote today." *Essential* is the stronger word: it means "pertaining to the very essence of being." If you tell someone that he must attend a meeting, that it is *necessary* for him to be there, you are expressing strong desire and are implying some compulsion. But if you tell him that it is *essential* for him to attend, the implication is that if he doesn't, the meeting will be canceled.

necessities, necessaries. These terms apply to items or matters considered essential, necessary, requisite, or at least important: "the *necessities* (or *necessaries*) of shelter and food." *Necessities* is the stronger and more generally used of the two, except perhaps in some sections of rural New England where *necessaries* has the meaning of "privies" or "chamber pots."

née. This French word (pronounced "nay") means "born" and is usually placed after the name of a married woman to indicate her maiden name: "May I introduce Mrs. Smythe, nee Brown." That is, Mrs. Smythe had the surname of Brown before she married a man named Smythe. It is incorrect to refer to a given name after *nee*. One is born with only a family name. Avoid saying "Mrs. James Smythe, nee Sally Brown." Omit the *Sally*.

need. *See* LACK.

negligent, negligible. Each of these words implies neglect and disregard. *Negligent* means "indifferent," "careless," "neglectful": "Some public officials are *negligent* in their duties." "Because she cared little about her appearance, Sis was *negligent* in her dress." *Negligible* refers to something or someone so trifling, unimportant, or small as to be neglected or disregarded: "The cut on my finger is *negligible*." "The added cost will be *negligible*."

Negro, black. A *Negro* is a member of the Negroid ethnic division of the human species. (*Negroid* is a term in anthropology applying to people who have black or brown pigmentation.) *Negro*, always spelled with a capital letter, is pluralized *Negroes*. *Negro* is a reputable term with scientific backing, but many people prefer the word *black*, perhaps for the same reason that *white* is usually preferred to *Caucasian*. In the United States, the term *Afro-American* is increasingly popular. Terms such as *Negress* (*see* ACTOR), *Nigra, nigger, darky,* and *spade* are offensive, contemptuous, evasive, and condescending words understandably resented by all *blacks*.

neither . . . nor. *See* EITHER . . . OR.

neophyte. *See* AMATEUR.

neurotic, neurasthenic. *See* PSYCHOTIC.

never, ever. *Never* means "at no time whatsoever," "not ever," "on no occasion," "in no way": "I will *never* learn to keep quiet." "*Never* mind, I'll help you." *Ever* has meanings exactly opposite those of *never: "Ever* since then, I have been careful." "He is *ever* alert to the needs of others." *Ever* should be used rather than *never* in negative statements: "Nobody *ever* (not *never*) said that to me before." (*See also* DOUBLE NEGATIVE.) *Ever* should also be used as an alternative to a negative: "I refused to help him, not then or *ever.*" *Never* is used as the alternative to an affirmative idea: "Seldom or *never* (not *ever*) have I seen anything like this." When *if* precedes, either *ever* or *never* may be used: "If *ever* I see you again!" "If I *never* see you again!"

nevertheless, nonetheless. These words mean "notwithstanding," "however," "in spite of that": "I don't like what you plan, but *nevertheless* (or *nonetheless*) I'll help." Since these are rather long words, why not occasionally use a shorter one such as *however, but, still,* or *yet?*

nexus. *See* FOCUS.

nice. This is a blanket word used and overused to describe persons, things, or events that more exactly may be *agreeable, pleasing, delightful, kind, choice, delicate, minute, accurate, respectable, dainty,* and *refined.* When *nice* can mean so many things, it is no wonder that it is rarely used *nicely* (that is, *suitably*).

nobody. *See* NO ONE.

no good, worthless. *No good* is colloquially used as both noun and adjective to mean "without worth," "of no use or value," "good-for-nothing," "useless": "This tramp is a *no good.*" "This steak is *no good.*" *Worthless* is more acceptable in the meanings cited above: "This counterfeit money is *worthless.*" *No good* is an acceptable term in a statement such as "Your help did me *no good,*" in which *good* is a noun, not an adjective.

nohow. This is a dialectal or illiterate term meaning "not at all," "in no manner." Never write or say a sentence such as "I couldn't go with you *nohow.*"

noisome, noxious, obnoxious. *Noisome* is not related to *noise* but, by derivation, is connected with *annoy*. It means "offensive," "destructive," "disgusting," and "harmful": "The odor of carbon monoxide is *noisome.*" "Catarrh is an especially *noisome* affliction." *Noxious* and *obnoxious* come from the same Latin root meaning "harmful," "hurtful," "injurious" and retain similar meanings: "The mists rising from the swamp are noxious." "The smells from the biology laboratory are *obnoxious* today." *Obnoxious* rather than *noxious* or *noisome* is preferred to refer to objectionable behavior or acts: "He was asked to leave the party because of his *obnoxious* manner." Related words include *detrimental, unwholesome, corruptive, deleterious, rotten,* and *odious*.

nom de plume, pseudonym, pen name. These terms mean "a name used by an author instead of his real name": The *nom de plume* (or *pseudonym* or *pen name*) of William Sidney Porter was O. Henry. *Pen name* is a literal translation of the French *nom de plume; pseudonym* is a Greek word for a fictitious name used to conceal identity. *Nom de plume* and *pen name* are usually restricted to the names of writers, whereas *pseudonym* can refer to a name assumed by anyone.

none. Since *none* is derived from *not one,* a long-standing rule provides that it should always be followed by a singular verb: "*None* of us *is* planning to go." Unfortunately for the sake of simplicity, this rule is neither grammatical nor logical; *none* can mean "not any" and "no amount" at least as often as it does "not one." A more sensible rule is this: think of *none* as a plural unless a good reason exists to regard it as singular. When *none* is followed by a singular noun, then the verb should be singular: "*None* of the money *was* paid to us." If you wish to stress the idea of a singular, then use a singular verb: "We were packed in the bus but *none was* hurt when we crashed." (Here *none* is emphasized as *not one,* but the sentence might better have employed *not one* or *no one* if the sense is to be "nobody at all.") And what about a statement such as this: "We have been holding discussions for weeks, but *none* has succeeded." It's not likely that "one discussion" is meant. Recommendation: always follow *none* with a verb in the singular when the clear and unmistakable meaning of *none* is "not one" or "no one." In all other situations, use a plural verb. Illustrations: "*None* (that is, *not one*) of us *has* any desire to read." "*None* of the clothing (singular noun) *is* clean." "*None are* more pitiable than the small children wounded by bombs." "*None* of my teachers *was* (or *were*) really interested in me." Remember that verbs and related pronouns should agree in number: "*None has his* hat on." "*None have their* hats on."

nonetheless. *See* NEVERTHELESS.

no one. Meaning "nobody," "no person," "not anyone," *no one* is always followed by a verb in the singular: "*No one* is here." Many careful users of the language feel that *no one* is somewhat more refined than *nobody,* but it is just as correct to say "*Nobody* answered" as "*No one* answered."

noplace. *See* ANYPLACE.

nor. *See* EITHER . . . OR.

normal, natural. *Normal* means "usual," "regular," "conforming to the standard type," "not abnormal": "Anyone with *normal* decency would have been horrified." "Resting when tired is *normal.*" Anything that is *natural* fits in with, and conforms to, its own nature: "Aging is a *natural* process." "When someone attacks us, it is *natural* to strike back in some way." Since *normal* people usually act in a *natural* way (in accord with their natures), the words are often interchangeable. *See also* COMMON, ORDINARY.

normalcy, normality. Each of these words is acceptable in the meaning of "the state of being normal," "adherence to an established level or pattern": After the strain of war, people long to return to a state of *normalcy* (or *normality*). In 1920, when Warren G. Harding was running for the office of President, he declared that what the United States needed was "not nostrums but *normalcy.*" Harding was criticized for using *normalcy* rather than *normality,* but he did not coin a word that had long been in use and that is now so much more common that one major dictionary does not list *normality* at all.

nostalgia, homesickness. *Nostalgia* comes from a Greek word meaning "return home," but its meaning has been extended to indicate a desire to return in thought or in fact to a former time in one's life. *Homesickness* (*home* plus *sick*) is illness, depression, or sadness caused by a longing for home; it is both more specific and more restricted in meaning than *nostalgia.* "Several young soldiers in this company are suffering from *homesickness.*" "Thoughts of his childhood home and happy youth caused a wave of *nostalgia* to sweep over the weary old man." The adjectives *nostalgic* and *homesick* convey the same primary meanings as the nouns from which they are formed: "This young traveler was often *homesick* and lonely." "That autobiography is a *nostalgic* account of the author's first thirty years."

notable, noted. *Notable* means "noteworthy," "worthy of notice or attention." *Noted* means "celebrated," "famous," "distinguished," "eminent," "renowned." Although these terms have related meanings and are often used interchangeably, *notable* is more often applied to events or inanimate objects than *noted* is, and *noted* is more frequently applied to persons. "This new model has had a *notable* success." "There has been a *notable* increase in company profits this year." "Dr. Popkin is a *noted* biologist." "This old lady was a *noted* beauty in her youth."

not hardly. As is pointed out in the entry HARDLY, *not hardly* is a substandard phrase that should not be used in speaking or writing. *See also* DOUBLE NEGATIVE.

notion. *See* IDEA.

not only . . . but also. This construction is common in the speech and writing of many persons who probably have no idea that they are using correlative conjunctions: "*Not only* Fred *but also* Lynn and Susie are planning to go." "She was *not only* cold *but also* hungry." Two problems arise in connection with this construction: (1) when to use it and (2) where to place the words. The phrase *not only* implies "partly," so that it is normally followed by *but also* (or some equivalent word or phrase like *as well, in addition, moreover, furthermore,* or *too*). It makes no sense to say "It was partly this, but that." It does make sense to say "It was partly this, but also that." However, some constructions do not require the use of *also*. *Also* should be dropped from a sentence such as "Diane is *not only* a dancer, *but also* an excellent dancer." Another point: the *not only . . . but also* construction is overused in many instances where *and* would do as well and save wordage. It is correct to write "*Not only* my hopes *but also* my definite plans centered on becoming a chemist." It also is correct (and less wordy) to say "My hopes and definite plans centered. . . ."

Correctly placing the words in this construction depends upon parallelism, which requires that the parts of speech or grammatical constructions following *not only* and *but also* be parallel (of the same kind). Revise a sentence such as "Kelly said that Marian *not only* knew Don *but also* Don's brother" to read "Kelly said that Marian knew *not only* Don *but also* Don's brother" (a noun to follow each part of the construction). If the construction following *not only* is an infinitive, that which follows *but also* should be an infinitive as well: a clause follows a clause, a phrase follows a phrase, and so forth.

notorious. *See* FAMED.

not scarcely. *See* DOUBLE NEGATIVE and HARDLY.

not too. In this often-used phrase, *too* means "very" or "much": "I am *not too* sure I want to do that." "I am *not too* inclined to pay the bill." *Not too* is an example of litotes, a term meaning "understatement," as in *not bad* for *good* and *far from certain* for *uncertain. Not too* is useful in suggesting modesty or an unwillingness to be dogmatic (I am *not too* sure of my position), and there is nothing incorrect about it. The use of a negative with its opposite is standard practice, but the device has become trite.

novice. *See* AMATEUR.

no way. This currently popular expression has already become hackneyed through overuse. As everyone knows, it means "not in any way," "without a chance," "not at all," and just about any other loose phrase indicating "No." There is *no way* in which its overuse can be justified.

nowhere near. This is a colloquial or dialectal expression meaning "not nearly" or "scarcely." Its use is not standard in a sentence such as "I am *nowhere near* ready to eat."

nowheres. *See* ANYWHERES.

noxious. *See* NOISOME.

nth degree. Although not mathematically accurate, *nth degree* is a popular expression for "the utmost extent" or "to a high degree or power": "Abigail believes in living life to the *nth degree.*" Aside from there being no sense of largeness or greatness in the expression, the only flaw in its use is triteness.

nude. *See* NAKED.

number. *See* AMOUNT and FIGURE.

nuptials. *See* MARRIAGE.

O

O, oh. Except as an infrequent variant of *oh, O* is used in direct address, is always capitalized, and is not followed by any mark of punctuation: "*O* Susan, please come here." "*O* dear!" "*O* God in Heaven." *Oh* is an interjection, may be followed by a comma or an exclamation point, and follows the usual rules of punctuation: "*Oh,* what a shame." "*Oh!* what is that?" "But, *oh* how we loved that woman!"

obese. *See* FAT.

objective. *See* TARGET.

oblige, obligate. In the sense of binding, constraining, and compelling, these words are synonymous: "The terms of my mortgage *oblige* me to make monthly payments." "I *obligated* myself to make the purchase." *Oblige* has the added meanings of "to make grateful or indebted," "to gratify the wishes of," "to do a service or render a favor": "We are *obliged* for your hospitality." "The charter plane *obliged* us by arriving early." *Oblige* and *obligate* are not interchangeable in the sense of gratitude or service, although a peron who has been *obliged* ("rendered a favor") may feel *obligated* to return that favor. "Much *obliged,*" a colloquial expression, is a kind of thanks; it acknowledges a favor or kindness but stops short of a direct "Thank you."

oblivious, forgetful. *Oblivious* means "unaware," "unmindful," "lacking memory of something." *Forgetful* implies a faulty memory or a tendency not to remember. *Oblivious* stresses unawareness, unresponsiveness, and inattentiveness. "Jackie was totally *oblivious* of her surroundings." "Because I was *forgetful,* I left the percolator plugged in all afternoon." *Oblivious* has been broadened in meaning to include unconsciousness: "In a deep coma, Betsy was *oblivious* to the world." *(Oblivious* may be followed by *to* or *of.)* In most instances, *forgetful* is preferable, because more readily understandable, to *oblivious* in the senses of "bemused," "abstracted," "unaware," and even "absentminded."

obnoxious. *See* NOISOME.

observance, observation. *Observance* means acting in accord with tradition, duty, law, or custom: "Drivers should be careful in their *observance* of traffic regulations." "Some religious people are strict in their *observance* of dietary laws." *Observance* also means "taking note of": "National holidays are set apart for the *observance* of some notable event." An *observation* is an instance or act of viewing, perceiving, or regarding: "Roving policemen make a careful *observation* of suspicious-looking persons." "Try to find a good *observation* point from which to watch the ceremonies in *observance* of Veterans Day."

obsolete, obsolescent. *Obsolete* means "no longer in general use," "discarded," "out of date": "In most sections of this country, the horse and buggy is an *obsolete* means of transportation." "'Gramercy' is an *obsolete* word for 'thanks.'" *Obsolescent* means "becoming outdated, outmoded, or out of use." Something *obsolete* has already been discarded; something *obsolescent* is in the process of being discarded: "The bow and arrow is an *obsolete* weapon in warfare; the battleship is *obsolescent.*"

obstacle, impediment. Each of these words refers to something that prevents, or interferes with, progress or action. An *obstacle* is anything that stands in the way of literal or figurative progress: "Lack of money was an *obstacle* to this medical student." "A roadblock was set up as an *obstacle* to the fleeing criminals." *Impediment* (from Latin words meaning "to snare" or "to weigh down" one's feet) is something that interferes with proper functioning or acting: "Stammering is a speech *impediment*." An *impediment* hinders or slows down rather than stops, obstructs, or prevents.

obtain. This word is usually replaced by GET. *Obtain,* from a Latin word meaning "take hold of," means "to acquire," "to come into possession of," "to procure" (*obtain* some information). Words related to *obtain* and *get* are *acquire, secure, earn, win, achieve, gain,* and *attain*. Careful users of the language employ *get* to mean "to come into possession of" in any manner; *obtain* is used to suggest the expenditure of effort: one *gets* a Christmas present; one *obtains* a salary increase.

Occident. *See* ORIENT.

occur. *See* HAPPEN.

octoroon. *See* MULATTO.

oculist, optician, ophthalmologist, optometrist. The distinction between and among these terms is important to those who are one or the other and to people who have eye trouble. *Oculists* and *ophthalmologists* are holders of the degree of doctor of medicine who specialize in diseases and disorders of the eye. An *optometrist* does not hold an M.D. degree and deals primarily with the range and power of vision. An *optician* is a person who makes and sells eyeglasses and other optical instruments.

odd. *See* QUEER.

odorous, malodorous. *Odorous* means "having, yielding, or diffusing an odor" (that property of something which affects the sense of smell). *Odorous* usually implies a fragrant or pleasant smell; the word *odor* normally refers to a bad or unpleasant smell or scent: "The air was *odorous* with the fragrance of lilies." "A rank *odor* drifted from the laboratory." Words related to *odorous* are *redolent, fragrant, aromatic, odoriferous,* and *perfumed. Malodorous* is formed from *odorous* and the Latin prefix *mal-*, meaning "ill" or "bad": "The *malodorous* skunk is not a welcome visitor." "The scent coming from this dank swamp is *malodorous.*"

of, off. Until a few centuries ago, *of* and *off* represented different pronunciations of the same word. Today, *of* has a basic meaning of "derived or coming from," whereas *off* means "at or to a distance from a nearer place," "no longer attached or supported." In constructions indicating possession, *of* may be followed by an uninflected noun (friend *of* my brother) or by a noun or pronoun in the possessive case (friend *of* my brother's, friend *of* his). One objection to the use of *of* is that it performs too many functions to be really useful. Another is that it is often used unnecessarily: one should omit *of* in expressions like "stay off *of*" and "alongside *of*." *Of* is also used illiterately as a substitute for *have* (must *of,* should *of*). Similarly, *off* should not be followed by *from* or *of:* "He walked *off* (not *off from* or *off of*) the stage." *Off* is illiterate when used to indicate a source; say "I got a meal *from* (not *off*) her." Avoid such clichés or slang terms as "*off* and on," "on and *off,*" *offbeat* ("unconventional"), "*off* the record," and *ofay* ("a white person").

of all. This phrase has respectable standing in an expression such as "*Of all* people, you . . . ," but it is a wordy, useless waster of time and space in expressions like "First *of all,*" "second *of all.*" *See also* FIRST.

off. *See* OF.

official, officious. *Official* pertains to holding an office or position of authority: "Mr. Rand is an *official* in the Treasury Department." "This is an *official* order from the commanding officer." *Officious* means "meddlesome," "offering unwanted or unnecessary advice": "The consul's manner toward all tourists was *officious.*" "Because he had no real authority, the clerk acted in an *officious* way."

of which. *See* WHO'S.

oh. *See* O.

O.K. This everyday term, which may be written with or without periods, is colloquial or business English for "all right," "correct," "approved." It is occasionally spelled *okay*, *okeh*. Of debatable origin, *O.K.* is acceptable in general speech. When used as an informal noun or verb, no one objects to it (get his *O.K.*, *O.K.* the arrangement). Avoid the use of *O.K.* as an adjective (Things are not *O.K.* with us) and as an adverb (The car was running *O.K.*). As noun, verb, adjective, and adverb, *O.K.* is overused.

old, older. The everyday word for someone advanced in age is *old*. *Old* is also applied to anything in existence of long standing or that originated in a prior age: "an *old* man," "an *old* church," "an *old* map," "an *old* poem," "an *old* model," "an *old* family." *Older* is the comparative of *old:* "This house is *older* than that one." *Old* is an overused word for which any one of several related words might be substituted: *aged, ancient, venerable, elderly, advanced, senile, veteran, senescent, antiquated, antique*. *Old* appears in many loose, trite, or slangy expressions such as "*old* hat," "*old* bean," "good *old* times," "*old* boy," "*old* chap," "*old* country," "*old* fellow," "*old* goat," "*Old* Nick" and "*Old* Scratch" (Satan), "*old* lady," "*old* man," "*old* school tie," "*old*-

timer," "*old* wives' tale," "*old* fogy," "*old*-world," "in days of *old*," and "*old* head on young shoulders."

older, oldest. *See* ELDER.

Olympic, Olympian. *Olympic* refers to games, *Olympian* to a mountain. *Olympic* can also mean "pertaining to Mount Olympus," but careful users restrict its application to Olympia, a plain in ancient Greece where the Olympic Games were held in honor of the god Zeus. *Olympian*, by referring to the home of the gods of classical Greece, has come to mean "majestic," "superior," "aloof." "This valley has true *Olympian* beauty." "He was *Olympian* in his attitude toward money." "The *Olympic* Games of 1972 were held in Sapporo, Japan, and Munich, Germany."

omission. *See* OVERSIGHT.

on. *See* ONTO.

on account of. This is a wordy phrase, especially when, as often happens, it is combined with *cause* or *due to:* "The *cause* of his absence was *on account of* his illness." Remove the deadwood: "The *cause* of his absence was illness." *See also* CAUSE.

on an average of. From this phrase one can usually drop *on*. "We sell *on an average of* one dozen every day" does not need *on*.

on balance. *See* BALANCE.

one another. *See* EACH OTHER.

one of the . . . if not the. These expressions often occur in comparisons but are frequently used ungrammatically: "It was *one of the* first, *if not the* first, attempts to bring together these warring nations." The plural *attempts* is correct after *one of the*, but how about "*if not the* first attempts"? To correct this flaw, add *of the:* "It was *one of the* first, *if not the* first, *of the* attempts. . . ." If this correction distorts meaning, and it may, then hold *if not the* for the end of the sentence: "It was *one of the* first attempts to bring together these warring nations, *if not the* first." Another comment: *one of the* is often a wordy, unnecessary expression: *"One of the* ideas I have" can be shortened without loss to "My idea" or "One idea I have."

one of those who. Should the verb following this expression be singular or plural, since *one* is singular and *those* is plural? Because *who* refers to *those,* use a plural verb: "Jack is *one of those who* were late." But if you were to say "Jack is the only *one of those who* was late," you would be correct in using a singular verb because only one person was late.

oneself, one's self. These expressions may be spelled and pronounced as *oneself* or *one's self* (wuhn·SELF, wunz·SELF). *Oneself* is generally preferred because it is shorter and easier to spell and pronounce: "On this firing range, it is easy to hurt *oneself.*" "It's impossible to become a great tennis player by *oneself.*" "In dangerous situations it is hard to be *oneself.*" *See also* HIM and MYSELF.

only. A frequent error in speech, a mistake made by nearly everyone, is misplacing a modifier such as *only.* When one says "Hank *only* wanted to borrow $5," he has said that the *only* thing Hank wanted was to borrow $5. What he probably had in mind was "Hank wanted to borrow *only* $5." Words like *only, scarcely, hardly, not, even, today,* and *tomorrow* are associated with the word or phrase immediately preceding or following. Modifiers should be placed in sentences so that they convey precisely the meaning intended. *Not only* requires as much care in placement as does *only.* "He *not only* saw Jack at the game but Jill, too" should read "He saw *not only*

Jack at the game but Jill, too." *See also* ALONE and NOT ONLY . . . BUT ALSO.

on the part of. This is a wordy way to say *by, for,* or *among*. Either *by* or *among*, for example, can replace *on the part of* in "There was no objection *on the part of* many of those present."

on the whole. *See* AS A WHOLE.

onto, on, on to. *Onto* and *on* are sometimes used interchangeably, but *onto* more strongly suggests movement toward something. "The dog jumped *on* the table" may mean that he was already on the table, jumping. "The dog jumped *onto* the table" clearly indicates that he leaped to the table from somewhere else. In constructions where *on* is an adverb and *to* a preposition, write and pronounce them as separate words: "We then moved *on to* the next building."

opaque, transparent. These words are antonyms but for some reason are not always readily distinguishable. *Opaque* means "not transparent," "not allowing light to pass through," "not bright," "dull," and "dark": "This thickly woven screen is *opaque.*" "Despite your help, the problem still seems *opaque* to me." *Transparent* has an exactly opposed meaning. A *transparent* substance permits light to pass through, can be seen through; *transparent* also means "frank," "open," and "obvious": "Clean water is *transparent.*" "His eagerness to accept the offer is *transparent.*" Words related to *transparent* are *clear, pellucid, crystalline, limpid,* and *translucent.*

operator, operative. An *operator* is someone who operates (works, handles) a machine, switchboard, or any kind of apparatus: "a switchboard *operator,*" "a telegraph *operator,*" "a Linotype *operator.*" As a noun, *operative* also means "a worker engaged, employed, or skilled in some particular task." What small distinction exists lies in the fact that *operative* is usually applied to someone engaged in a more skilled or subtle task than an *operator:* "He is an *operative* in the Treasury Department." "This spy spent years as an *operative* behind the Iron Curtain." As an adjective, *operative* means "effective," "workable": "Ordinances in this city are fully *operative.*"

ophthalmologist. *See* OCULIST.

opinionated, opinionative. These words are commonly used as synonyms, each meaning "obstinate," "dogmatic," "fixed in one's beliefs," "stubborn": "Don't call me *opinionated* (or *opinionative*) just because I am correct in my attitude." A distinction is sometimes made by careful writers: *opinionated* is used to convey the senses mentioned above; *opinionative* is employed to refer to matters of opinion, usually in the sense of "hypothetical" or "assumed": "You seem to have reached an entirely *opinionative* conclusion." In most instances, use *opinionated* and forget about *opinionative*.

optician. *See* OCULIST.

optimist, pessimist. Each of these words has a number of vague meanings, and each is loosely applied in everyday use. As commonly understood, an *optimist* has a tendency, or disposition, to look on the bright side of events, to anticipate favorable results, to believe that good triumphs over evil, that there is some good in all reality: "Because Bob is always cheerful and hopeful, he can only be called an *optimist.*" A *pessimist* takes an opposed point of view: he tends to expect the worst possible outcome of events, to feel that sorrow and evil are more prevalent than happiness and goodness, that all happenings will be disadvantageous. An *optimist* has been called "one who makes the best of it when he gets the worst of it"; a *pessimist* is "one who is not happy except when he is miserable," "a man who feels bad when he feels good for fear he'll feel worse when he feels better."

optimistic, sanguine. As is suggested in the entry OPTIMIST, *optimistic*, an adjective, means "inclined or disposed to take a favorable view of life." *Sanguine* has the somewhat related meanings of "cheerful," "confident," "hopeful": "He is a lively, *sanguine* person." (*Sanguine*, derived from a Latin term meaning "bloody," has acquired its present meaning because, in medieval physiology, ruddy-faced people were considered healthy, animated, spirited, and buoyant.) *Sanguine* is a more precise word than *optimistic*, which is overused. In a sentence such as "Tom is not *optimistic* about his chances for leaving early," either *sanguine* or *hopeful* might replace *optimistic*.

optometrist. *See* OCULIST.

or. *See* AND/OR.

oral, verbal, aural. *Oral* means "spoken rather than written" and "of or pertaining to the mouth." *Verbal* means "associated with words." *Verbal* can and does refer to what is written; *oral* does not. Be careful in using *oral* and *verbal* with words like *agreement, promise,* and *understanding*. If the agreement (promise, understanding) is not in writing, *oral* makes that sense clear. That is, *verbal* is less precise than *oral* in conveying the idea of "by mouth." When you can choose between a word that means two things *(verbal)* and one that can mean only one *(oral)*, try to be precise. Why not use *oral* and *written* for clear contrast? *Aural*, a rarely used word, applies only to the ear and the sense of hearing: "His *aural* sense is defective because of a damaged eardrum."

ordinance, ordnance. *Ordinance* means a regulation, rule, law, or a public injunction or decree: "It is a town *ordinance* to curb your dog." "The town council recently debated an *ordinance* concerning garbage disposal." *Ordnance,* a shortened form of *ordinance,* has come to mean (1) artillery, (2) military weapons of any kind, and

(3) that branch of a military force engaged in securing and storing supplies of varied kinds: "That recruit was placed in the *ordnance* department, where he was set to work stacking ammunition."

ordinary. *See* COMMON, ORDINARY.

Orient, Occident. *Orient,* a noun that is always capitalized, means "the East" and is normally used to refer to countries east and southeast of the Mediterranean Sea. *Orient* is commonly restricted to mean Asia, but it can mean the entire Eastern Hemisphere, which also includes Africa and Australia. Specifically, *Orient* is a term applying to what is known as the Far East, including China, Japan, Korea, and adjacent areas. *Orient* is derived from Latin terms meaning "the east" and "sunrise." *Occident* means "the West" and is usually restricted to the countries of Europe and the Americas. It, too, is an always-capitalized noun. Corresponding adjectives, *oriental* and *occidental,* have numerous meanings, most of which reflect the sense of east or west. "He has lived in the *Orient* for many years, principally in Korea." "Life in the *Occident* is not always easy for an *Oriental.*" "*Oriental* rugs are a prized possession in many *occidental* homes."

orient, orientate. Each of these verbs means "to familiarize with conditions," "to adjust to surroundings": "This training program will *orient* (or *orientate*) you in your new position." "These lectures are designed to *orient* (or *orientate*) all recruits." *Orient* is preferable to *orientate* and is much more commonly used. An *orientation* program is one that supposedly *orients* (or *orientates*) individuals.

ornate, ornamental. *Ornate* means elaborately or excessively adorned, dressed, or displayed. It means "showy," "pretentious," or "ostentatious": "This richly carved furniture is *ornate.*" *Ornamental* has a related meaning of "decorative," but it does not imply showiness, ostentation, or vulgarity: "The pot of ivy in that corner of the living room is *ornamental.*" "The light sweater that Anne wore across her shoulders was more *ornamental* than useful."

orthodox. *See* HETERODOX.

oscillate, osculate. *Oscillate* means "to swing to and fro," "to vibrate," "to fluctuate": "His mood *oscillated* between despair and fury." *Osculate* means "to come into close contact" and specifically "to kiss." It is possible that one who *osculates* a loved one will begin to *oscillate,* but even that person should know what each action entails.

other, otherwise. As an adjective, *other* means (1) "additional" or "further" (one *other* person); (2) "different" (coming from some *other* village); (3) "former" (some customs of *other* days); (4) "second" (every *other* week); (5) "recent" (the *other* night); and (6) "remaining of two or more" (on the *other* hand, the *other* clerks). As a noun, *other* means "the other one" (each loves the *other*). *Other* can also be used as an adverb: "He could not do *other* than speak out." In adverbial use, *otherwise* is preferable: "He could not do *otherwise* than speak out." *Otherwise* can also be used as an adjective: "Jack hoped that Mary's response would be *otherwise.*"

ought. *See* AUGHT.

out loud. *See* ALOUD, OUT LOUD.

out of, outside of. *See* INSIDE. As is pointed out in that entry, not all double prepositions are incorrect: one can walk *out of* a room, stroll *up to* a house, and go *over to* a nearby store. However, "looking *out of* a window," "walking *outside of* an office," and "falling *off of* a stairway" are wordy, nonstandard phrases.

outstanding. This is a badly overworked word (*outstanding* job, *outstanding* program, *outstanding* person). Word choice can be varied: *prominent, excellent, distinguished, salient, momentous, conspicuous, significant, consequential*.

overlay, overlie, underlay, underlie. Although *lie* (*see* LAY) is always an intransitive verb (that is, cannot take a direct object), it becomes transitive when preceded by *over-* or *under-*. When *lie* is combined with these prefixes, *underlie* and *overlie* in some instances are interchangeable with *underlay* and *overlay:* "The principle that *underlies* (or *overlies*) his actions is the so-called golden rule." The best rule to follow in choosing which of these four terms to use is to move *over* or *under* to the position of a preposition: "The principle that *lies* (not *lays*) *under* his actions. . . ." "The paint that *lay over* the surface of the wall. . . ." In geology, however, the form *lie* is preferred: "The clay that *underlies* the rocky surface. . . ."

overlook, oversee. *Overlook* means (1) "to fail to notice," (2) "to disregard or ignore," (3) "to rise above," (4) "to excuse": "He *overlooked* my mistake." "Robin is a girl who *overlooks* such minor matters." "My window *overlooks* a park." "The foreman will *overlook* your tardiness." *Oversee* means (1) "to observe secretly or unintentionally"; (2) "to direct, supervise, or manage": "Bert just happened to *oversee* the stolen kiss." "The superintendent is expected to *oversee* the performance of the entire staff."

oversight, omission. These words have a related meaning, but careful users distinguish between them. An *oversight* is (1) a failure to consider or notice and (2) an error due to carelessness: "Because of my *oversight* I never saw the landing." "Through *oversight,* I failed to date the check." *Omission* is a more general word implying something left out, not done, or neglected: "Lack of a signature is an *omission* on this check." An *oversight* is usually due to carelessness; an *omission* may be intentional or unintentional.

overt. *See* COVERT.

over with. From this phrase *with* can be omitted. "The pain will soon be *over*" means precisely what is conveyed by "The pain will soon be *over with*." Also, one can use *ended* or *finished*.

owing to. *Owing to* is an acceptable, idiomatically correct phrase meaning "because of" or "attributable to": "*Owing to* the lateness of the bus, we were unable to make connection with the train." As with *due to*, avoid adding *the fact that* to *owing to*. *See also* DUE TO.

P

pact, compact. These words have a shared meaning: "an agreement, contract, treaty, or deal": "Lynn and Suzanne made a *compact* (or *pact*) to stop eating candy." "The leading economists of Belgium and Sweden suggested an economic *pact* (or *compact*) between the two countries." *Compact* has numerous other meanings as is suggested by these sentences: "This is a *compact* trading center (arranged within small space)." "The congressman made a *compact* (brief) report." "This soil is *compact* (closely packed)." "His body is *compact* (solidly built)."

paid, payed. *Paid* is the past tense and past participle of the verb *pay:* "He *paid* all his bills promptly." *Payed* is used only in the sense of *paying* out a cable or line: "He *payed* out the anchor line slowly."

pair, pairs. As a noun, *pair* can be followed by a singular or a plural verb, but the singular is always used when *pair* emphasizes unity or oneness: "This *pair* of shoes *is* black." A plural verb may be used when the members of a pair are treated as individuals: "The *pair are* running rapidly now." After any numeral other than one, say *pairs,* not *pair:* "Sue bought three *pairs* of stockings." Do not say "a *pair* of twins" unless you are referring to four people.

paltry. *See* PETTY.

pamphlet. *See* BROCHURE.

pandemic. A *pandemic* disease is one prevalent throughout a country, a continent, or the entire world. *Pandemic* suggests "universal," "widespread," and "general": "Fear of atomic warfare is *pandemic*." *See also* EPIDEMIC.

pants, trousers. *Pants* is a term meaning "a pair of trousers." An abbreviation of *pantaloons, pants* refers to one garment but is treated as a plural in "*These* pants *are* dirty." To use the word with a singular verb, say "This pair of pants *is*. . . ." Some "experts" feel that *trousers* is a more genteel term than *pants,* but *pants* is a word calculated to stay in and, possibly, up.

pardner, partner. Constant watchers of western films and TV dramas may need reminding that there is no such word as *pardner* in standard use. It is a dialectal version of *partner,* a word meaning "associate," "friend," "colleague," "accomplice," or "sharer": "This is my business *partner.*"

pardon, pardon me. *See* APOLOGY.

parody. *See* BURLESQUE.

parricide. *See* PATRICIDE.

part, share, portion. *Part* is the usual word for "something less than the whole": "Here is *part* of the treasure." "For my *part,* I ask nothing." *Share* also means "part" but specifically refers to that which is allotted or designed for someone; it emphasizes the receiver: "I want my fair *share* of the money." "We divided the food into equal *shares.*" *Portion* means a "part that is given for a purpose": "My *portion* of the job is to entertain the visiting players." Related words include *piece, segment, section, sector, division, fragment,* and *component.*

part and parcel. This phrase is a trite expression meaning "an essential part": "Devotion to her work was *part and parcel* of her life." The phrase has some meaning in law, but it is a verbose expression in everyday use to which *and parcel* adds nothing but words.

partial, partially, partly. *Partial* is an adjective with two distinct meanings. The first meaning is "biased," "prejudiced," "showing favoritism," in such a phrase as "to be *partial* to." The other meaning of *partial* is "not complete or total"; in this meaning the adverb *partially* is a synonym of *partly*. Usually, you should prefer *partly* to *partially* unless the meaning is that of limited degree. "Jeb has always been *partial* to blue-eyed girls." "This is a *partial* payment of what I owe you." "The accident *partially* blinded him." "His *partial* knowledge of the subject was due *partly* to his youth."

partisan. *See* BIPARTISAN.

partner. *See* PARDNER.

party. *See* INDIVIDUAL.

passed, past, pass. *Passed* is the past tense of the verb *pass; past* is the past participle: "The car *passed* us at 60 miles an hour." "Your troubles are now *past.*" *Pass* is not only a verb; it is also a noun. It appears in hackneyed phrases that are idiomatically sound but informal or slangy: "make a *pass* at" ("make a sexually inviting gesture, action, or remark"); "*pass* out" ("lose consciousness," "faint"); "*pass* away" and "*pass* on" (euphemisms for "to die"); "*pass* the buck" ("refuse responsibility"); "*pass* off as" ("dispose of, or treat, deceptively"); "come to *pass*" ("happen," "occur"); "a pretty *pass*" ("ironic situation"); "*pass* up" ("reject," "refuse to take advantage of"); and "*pass* over" ("ignore").

pastor, minister, priest. Use of these terms differs between sects and denominations and even from one community to another. The general term for persons wholly engaged in religious work and set apart from nonprofessional and nonordained worshipers is *clergyman.* A clergyman may go by the titles of *pastor, minister, priest, preacher, parson, cleric,* and *reverend.* It is always safe to refer to such a person as a *cleric, clergyman,* or *man of the cloth* (unless the individual is a woman), but choice of other terms depends more upon custom than upon precise meanings of the words involved.

Pastor comes from a Latin word meaning "shepherd" and is specifically applied to one who has the spiritual care of persons entrusted to his charge. *Minister,* derived from a Latin word meaning "servant," is a somewhat general term that suggests the serving of spiritual needs by one dedicated to that service. *Priest,* a title largely confined to the Roman Catholic, Anglican, and Eastern Orthodox churches, refers to one whose office it is to perform religious rites of various kinds. The word *reverend* means "entitled to reverence and respect"; when capitalized it may be prefixed to the name of a clergyman but should always be followed by the title "Mr." or "Dr." or the first name of the individual specified: the "Reverend Mr. Parker" or the "Reverend Roland Parker," not "Reverend Parker."

patricide, parricide, matricide. The Latin element *-cide* means "killer" (as in *regicide,* the killing of a king; *genocide,* the planned annihilation of a cultural, political, or racial group; and *insecticide,* an agent used to kill insects). *Patricide* means "one who murders his father" or "the act of killing one's father." *Parricide* means "the act of murdering one's father, mother, or other relative" or "one who commits such an act." *Matricide* is "the act of murdering one's mother" or "one who murders his mother."

patron. *See* CLIENT.

payed. *See* PAID.

peak. *See* SUMMIT.

peculiar. *See* FUNNY.

pendant, pendent, pennant. A *pendant* is a hanging object, an ornament of some kind: "Priscilla fastened a gold *pendant* on her collar." *Pendent* is an adjective meaning "suspended," "hanging down," "dangling": "The tapestry *pendent* from the balcony was richly designed." A *pennant* is a small flag or emblem: "This *pennant* symbolizes the team's championship season."

pen name. *See* NOM DE PLUME.

people, persons. *People* and *persons* both refer to a number of individuals and are used interchangeably in most contexts. Neither can be used to refer to an individual: "one *people*" and "one *persons*" are absurd expressions. No safe rule exists for choosing between *people* and *persons* except possibly this: use *people* for large groups or an undetermined number of individuals and *persons* for a relatively small or exact number: "Thousands of *people* attended the fair. Fifty *persons* won prizes." *See also* INDIVIDUAL.

per. *See* A, PER.

percent, percentage. *Percent* (from Latin *per centum,* "by the hundred") may be spelled as one or two words; 10 *percent* means "10 out of 100" or "10 in 100." *Percent* is colloquial when used as a substitute for *percentage* (the noun). *Percentage* is colloquial when used in the meaning of "profit" or "advantage," as in "What's the *percentage* in hard work?"

performance. *See* RENDITION.

period of time. The word *period* conveys the idea of time; therefore *of time* is redundant in this expression. Also wordy is the phrase "lapse of time," since *lapse,* like *period,* connotes time. When a specific amount of time is mentioned (a lapse of ten hours), no wordiness is involved. *See also* POINT IN TIME.

permit. *See* ALLOW.

perpetrate, perpetuate. *Perpetrate* means "to commit or perform or carry out" and usually refers to a crime, misdemeanor, or hoax: "*perpetrate* a holdup," "*perpetrate* a practical joke." *Perpetuate* means "to preserve," "to make perpetual": "This father desires children who will *perpetuate* his name." "This foundation *perpetuates* the work that its founder began."

perplex. *See* PUZZLE, PERPLEX, BEWILDER.

persecute, prosecute. These "look-alikes" have related but different meanings. To *persecute* is to harass, to torment, to treat badly, to bother, to worry, to oppress, to trouble: "Some teen-agers feel that their parents *persecute* them." "Businessmen sometimes think that government agencies are set up solely to *persecute* them." *Prosecute,* primarily a legal term, means "to seek, force, or obtain by a legal process," "to start or conduct legal proceedings against." It also means "to carry forward some action already begun." "If you commit theft and are caught, you will be *prosecuted.*" "Now that war has begun, the government will *prosecute* it vigorously."

person. *See* INDIVIDUAL and PERSONAGE.

personage, person. *Personage* is a term reserved for an individual of importance or distinction and for a character in a play or novel: "Whether one liked him or not, no one could deny that the late Charles de Gaulle of France was a *personage.*" "Hamlet is a *personage* who shows both strength and weakness of purpose." *Person* refers to a human being, whether man, woman, or child: "Every *person* requires a certain amount of food." *See also* PERSONALITY.

personal, personnel. *Personnel* means "a group of persons." *Personal* involves a particular person, an individual. "This is a *personal* matter involving Judy and me." "The *personnel* in this office is very friendly." *Personal* is pronounced "PUHR·suhn·uhl"; *personnel* is pronounced "puhr·suh·NEL." The expression "*personal* friend" is usually wordy; it is possible to have as a business friend someone who is not necessarily a *personal* friend, but such instances are rare. How many friends can one have who are not *personal?* *See also* MATERIAL.

personality. This word has largely taken the place of *character* and is now used to refer to the qualities in an individual that impress others: "Gray is a boy with a pleasing *personality.*" It can also apply to atmosphere (a room with a warm *personality*) and, when used as a plural, can mean "heated remarks" or "quarreling": "The discussion began pleasantly but soon turned into a series of *personalities.*" *Personality* is also overused in the sense of PERSONAGE: "In his day W. C. Fields was a noted *personality.*"

personnel. *See* PERSONAL.

persons. *See* PEOPLE.

perspective, prospective. *Perspective* is primarily a noun referring to various techniques for representing three-dimensional objects and depth relationships. *Perspective* also refers to a picture or object using this technique: "an architect's *perspective* of a building." Often the word is employed to mean a mental prospect or point of view: "I need a better *perspective* on your proposal." *Prospective* is an adjective meaning "expected," "potential," "likely," or "in the future": "What are the *prospective* results of this campaign?" "She looked him over carefully as a *prospective* partner."

persuade. *See* CONVINCE.

pessimist. *See* OPTIMIST.

pessimistic. *See* GLOOMY.

petty, paltry, trivial. Each of these words refers to that which is so small or insignificant as to be unworthy of notice or regard. *Petty* conveys an idea of contempt or ridicule: "Your *petty* complaints are really childish." *Paltry* is an even stronger term, suggesting that what is beneath notice is actually to be despised: "Such a contribution from a wealthy person is *paltry*." That which is *trivial* is insignificant and even out of place in contrast to what is really important: "Your *trivial* comment on a great performance is silly." Related words include *negligible, slight, inconsequential, inconsiderable,* and *trifling*.

phenomenon, phenomena. A *phenomenon* is an observed or observable fact or circumstance, especially one that seems extraordinary or impressive: "The *phenomenon* of a man kissing his dog rather than his wife is not readily explainable." The plural is *phenomenons* or, preferably, *phenomena:* "This ecologist never tired of studying the *phenomena* of nature." It is nonstandard to say *phenomenas* and "This *phenomena* is."

physician, doctor. *Physician* is a general term for a *doctor* of medicine, someone legally qualified to practice medicine. The term is often employed to refer to anyone engaged in the general practice of medicine as distinguished from such specialists as surgeons, ophthalmologists, and pediatricians. All qualified *physicians* are *doctors* of medicine, but not all *doctors* practice medicine. *Doctor* refers to anyone who has been granted a *doctor's* degree. There are *doctors* of dentistry, veterinary science, philosophy, the arts, letters, literature, science, and many other disciplines.

piazza. *See* PORCH.

picture. As a noun or verb meaning "image," "representation," and "to represent," "to form an image," *picture* is a standard word. It is greatly overused, however, in such loose expressions as "Do you get the *picture?*" and "*Picture* that." "Pretty as a *picture*" and "*picture* of health" are especially trite phrases.

pitiable, piteous. *Pitiable* means "deserving of pity," "producing compassion," or "lamentable": "These hungry children are *pitiable.*" "The destitute family was living in a *pitiable* shack." *Piteous* refers to that which excites pity because it is suffering and miserable: "The *piteous* cries of the dying men echoed through the emergency room." A related word, *pitiful,* has the meanings of both *pitiable* and *piteous:* "a *pitiful* street beggar," "a *pitiful* exhibition."

plaintiff, defendant. Anyone who has difficulty remembering the distinction between these words should recall that *plaintiff* is related to *plaint* and *complaint* (meaning "grievance") and *complain* ("to protest"). A *plaintiff* is a complainant, one who brings a suit in a court of law: "Marcia was the *plaintiff* in this action." A *defendant,* as opposed to a *plaintiff,* is a defending party, a person sued or accused: "As *plaintiff,* you brought the action, and as *defendant,* I shall oppose you."

please. *See* KINDLY.

plentiful, plenteous. These adjectives, derived alike from a Latin word meaning "full," are interchangeable. Each refers to an overadequate quantity, an abundant amount: "The supply of food was *plentiful* (or *plenteous*)." *Plentiful* is usually preferable to *plenteous* because it is less "literary" and therefore more easily understood. Other words that could be used in this context include *copious, ample,* and *profuse*.

plump. *See* FAT.

plurality. *See* MAJORITY.

plus. This word is incorrectly and tritely used in the meaning of "something added or extra": "That's a *plus.*" *Plus* does not have the conjunctive force of *and;* say "Mike *and* his friends," not "Mike *plus* his friends." Since *plus* is a preposition rather than a conjunction, a following verb is singular or plural depending on the number of the subject: "Three *plus* three [a unit] *equals* six." Their purposes [plural] *plus* our general plan *are* excellent."

point in time. This currently popular expression has become a cliché because of its widespread use on television and radio programs. No excuse for it exists: it is both wordy and jargonish. "At this *point in time*" means "now" or "at this time." *See also* PERIOD OF TIME.

point of view, viewpoint, standpoint. Each of these terms means (1) "a specified manner of appraising or judging" and (2) "an opinion, judgment, or attitude": "From my *point of view* (or *viewpoint* or *standpoint*) your suggestion is unworkable." All three expressions are standard. *Viewpoint* is not recommended by some linguists because it is considered an awkward shortening of *point of view,* but this objection has been overruled by usage. A few purists have pointed out that *standpoint* is incorrect since one cannot stand on a point, a stupid comment since *point* here does not mean a physical point but a mental position. The only possible objection to any of these terms is that they are tiresomely overused and often are unnecessary. "From the moral *point of view*" says nothing that *morally* doesn't. "From where I stand" is mere wordage. Use any of the three terms sparingly and avoid meaninglessness.

polite, courteous. A *polite* person shows good manners toward others in his speech and actions; he is well bred and gracious. A *polite* individual avoids being rude as a result of training and because he is aware of the demands and requirements of civil manners. A *courteous* person is not only *polite;* he makes an active effort to be kindly, graceful, dignified, and poised. In most instances, the two words are interchangeable, but *courteous* is a stronger word than *polite* and suggests a fundamental attitude toward others, whereas *polite* relates to surface manners only: It is *polite* to say "Good morning" to someone; it is *courteous* to treat others with respect and kindness.

populace. *See* POPULATION.

popular, vulgar. These words are no longer synonymous, but for many centuries they were. *Popular* is derived from a Latin word meaning "people"; *vulgar* comes from a Latin term meaning "the general public." (The English word *mob* is a shortened form of Latin *mobile vulgus,* the changeable common people.) What is *popular* is regarded with favor by people in general (a *popular* public figure); *popular* also applies to attitudes or tastes prevailing among masses of people: "*popular* superstitions," "*popular* music." *Vulgar* can also mean *popular* in the sense of "common" or "current" (*vulgar* success, *vulgar* soap operas), but the term is now employed almost entirely in the senses of "indecent," "ignorant," "crude," "unrefined," or "lacking distinction": "*vulgar* language," "*vulgar* gestures," "*vulgar* display." Despite the related origins of the words and their occasionally shared meaning, no longer can one say that what is *popular* is *vulgar* or vice versa.

population, populace, populous. The *population* of a country is the total number of persons inhabiting it: "The estimated *population* of the United States in July 1972 was nearly 209 million." Although *populace* can be used to refer to all the inhabitants of a place (town, city, country), it is usually employed to designate the common people of a community or country as distinguished from the so-called higher classes. That is, the *populace* of a city bears some relationship to *mob* (*see* POPULAR). *Populace* implies contempt or condescension; *population* is an objective word without emotional implications. *Populous* is an adjective meaning "full of residents," "heavily populated": "California is the most *populous* state in the United States."

porch, piazza, veranda. Which of these terms one uses depends upon where he lives and the speech customs of his community. Each refers to an open space attached to the outside of a house or other building, usually roofed and partly enclosed. Although some architects distinguish among them, all three words are in widespread use throughout the United States. Perhaps *porch* and *veranda* have a wider geographic spread than *piazza*, a term in use largely in the South and New England.

port, harbor. A *port* is a place where ships load and unload; a *harbor* is a body of water providing protection for ships. Although the terms are somewhat loosely used interchangeably, *port* applies particularly to the town or city, including its commercial aspects, that provides a *harbor:* "New York is a great *port* city with an excellent *harbor.*" Both *port* and *harbor* have a meaning of "haven," a place of comfort, rest, and security: "any old *port* in a storm"; "a *harbor* for weary travelers."

portion. *See* PART.

position. *See* FUNCTION.

positively. *See* ABSOLUTELY.

possible. *See* FEASIBLE.

postpone. *See* DEFER.

postulate. *See* EXPOSTULATE.

potter, putter. Does one *potter* or *putter* about the house or in the garden? In the United States, one *putters;* in Great Britain, one *potters.* The words mean "to dawdle," "to move aimlessly," "to act with little energy or purpose": "Since this is not a workday, Nan plans to *putter* about the house and in her garden."

practical, practicable. A simple method of learning to distinguish the meanings of these words is to turn to the entry IMPRACTICAL and reverse the meanings of the terms involved. When applied to persons, *practical* means "realistic," "sensible," "efficient"; as relating to acts or processes, *practical* means "workable," "manageable." *Practicable* means "capable of being used," "feasible," "possible." "Jim is a man with *practical* views about business." "What we need is a *practical* way to solve this problem." "Your idea is clever but hardly *practicable.*" "There is no *practicable* method of keeping boys and girls away from each other." Basically, what is *practicable* can be done; what is *practical* can be done sensibly or usefully. An act can be both *practical* and *practicable:* It is *practical* to check the pressure in one's tires before starting on a trip (it's sensible to do so); it's also *practicable* to check the pressure (it's possible to do so).

practically, virtually. *Practically* means "effectively," "in a practical manner," "from a practical point of view": "It is *practically* useless to vote in this election." "Try to view your situation *practically.*" "*Practically* speaking, you are financially bankrupt." *Practically* is also used to mean "nearly," "almost": "The campers were *practically* out of food." *Virtually* means "for the most part," "just about," "almost entirely": "The loggers *virtually* completed the work in an hour." "Before he won the race he was *virtually* unknown." Recommendation: confine the use of *practically* to the meanings of practice and practical; use *nearly* and *almost* more often than *practically* and *virtually*, because in one limited sense, *practically* means *virtually* the same thing as *virtually*.

practice. *See* CUSTOM.

precede, proceed. *Precede* means "to come before," "to go in advance of." *Proceed* means "to go forward," "to carry on." "Senator Blunt *preceded* his staff into the room and *proceeded* to justify his vote on the measure."

precedence, precedent. These words have common origins in Latin terms meaning "to go before" and "to yield." *Precedence* refers to "the act or fact of going before," "priority in rank or order," "the right to go in front": "On highways, ambulances have *precedence* (or take *precedence*) over civilian cars." "The Secretary of State has *precedence* over other members of the President's Cabinet." *Precedent* means a preceding instance, case, or example; in law, it refers to a legal decision that acts as a guide in resolving later cases: "By living thriftily, some parents hope to set a *precedent* for their children." "The *Brown v. Board of Education of Topeka, Kansas,* decision of the Supreme Court in 1954 set a *precedent* for all cases involving public schooling in the United States."

precipitate, precipitous. With a common origin in Latin terms meaning "to cast down," these words have taken on dissimilar meanings. As an adjective, *precipitate* means "headlong," "moving rapidly and hastily," "rash": "Take your time; don't make a *precipitate* decision." "Braking too hard will cause a *precipitate* stop."

Precipitous means "steep," "abrupt," "perpendicular," "sheer" and is usually applied to mountains, cliffs, and all steep places: "Some of the streets of San Francisco seem almost *precipitous.*" "That *precipitous* cliff is nearly 1,000 feet high."

predicament, dilemma. *Predicament* means a difficult, perplexing, dangerous, or unpleasant situation or condition: "Having no room reservation put us into a *predicament.*" A *dilemma* resembles a *predicament* with emphasis upon the puzzling and perplexing elements present: "Julia's *dilemma* was how to get Jack out of the house before Tom arrived." "On the horns of a *dilemma*" is a trite expression, but it does accent the perplexity and puzzlement involved. Related words are *plight* and *quandary.*

premature. *See* IMMATURE.

première. This word is used as a noun, adjective, and verb to refer to the first presentation of a film, play, or other performance or to the leading lady of a theatrical or film company: "Tonight, the tourists will attend the *première* of a new film from Italy." "The *première* showing was attended by hundreds of notable people." The use of *première* as a verb (She will *première* in that production) is not yet acceptable.

prescribe, proscribe. *Prescribe* means "to direct," "to order." *Proscribe* means "to banish," "to outlaw." "What did the nurse *prescribe* for your cough?" "Playing the radio after midnight is *proscribed.*"

prescribed. *See* REQUIRED.

presentiment, presentment. A *presentiment* is a sense of something about to occur, a feeling, a foreboding: "Don had a *presentiment* that his good luck would soon run out." *Presentment* is a rarely used word meaning a "presentation," "the act of presenting, offering, or submitting": "This draft will be honored on *presentment* to the bank." "Many stores prefer cash to the *presentment* of a credit card."

presently, currently. A century ago, *presently* was used to mean "now," a meaning that some writers and speakers still attribute to it. *Presently* is more precisely used to mean "soon," "before long," "directly," and "in a short time": "I will be there *presently.*" Its use to mean "at this time" is debatable and inaccurate. *Currently* means "at the time now passing," "at this moment," "right now": "She is *currently* taking a bath." "I am *currently* far in debt." "Although I am *currently* not well, I hope *presently* to feel better."

presentment. *See* PRESENTIMENT.

presumably. *See* SUPPOSEDLY.

presume. *See* ASSUME.

presumptuous, presumptive. *Presumptuous* and *presumptive* come from Latin words meaning "to undertake beforehand," but they have different meanings in English. A *presumptuous* person is arrogant; he presumes too much; he takes too much for granted; he takes excessive liberties; he is bold: "It would be *presumptuous* of me to tell you how to handle your affairs." "To argue with an expert such as he is seems *presumptuous.*" *Presumptive,* chiefly a legal term, means "based on inference," "not fully established," "affording only a basis for a supposition": "This case cannot be tried on merely *presumptive* evidence." "Until the will is read, your role as heir to the estate is *presumptive.*"

pretty. This word is overused to mean many things: "attractive," "graceful," "pleasing," "delicate," "comely," "fair," and "lovely." It is also overused to mean "moderately," "somewhat," or "to a degree" (*pretty* tired, *pretty* lucky). Slangy or trite phrases to avoid include "sitting *pretty,*" "*pretty* up," "a *pretty* penny," and "*pretty* much."

prevent, hinder. These words are related, but *prevent* is a stronger word than *hinder.* When you *prevent* something, you stop it; when you *hinder* something, you slow or delay it. When something is *prevented,* it is effectively halted and rendered impossible: "Do not *prevent* us from going." "This treaty is designed to *prevent* war between our countries." To *hinder* is to delay progress: "Such interruptions will only *hinder* our reaching a solution." Related words are *obstruct, impede, thwart, obviate, forestall, hamper, retard, block,* and *balk.* Both *prevent* and *hinder* are often followed by a gerund: "*prevent* his going," "*hinder* his going." In such a construction, a noun or pronoun preceding the gerund is preferably in the possessive case; "*prevent* (or *hinder*) *him* going" is nonstandard, *his* is standard: "They tried to *prevent* *Jock's leaving* (not *Jock leaving*) the team."

preventative, preventive. These words mean "serving to hinder," "keeping from occurring." The form *preventive* is preferable and is so much more widely used that two standard dictionaries no longer record *preventative:* "The person arrested was placed in *preventive* detention." "What is your opinion of *preventive* medicine?"

priest. *See* PASTOR.

primeval, primitive. *Primeval,* a rarely used word, means "original," "belonging to the earliest age or ages." It is derived from a Latin word meaning "in the first period of life" and was thus used in Longfellow's *Evangeline:* "This is the forest *primeval.*" *Primitive,* from a Latin term meaning "first" or "in the first place," is more widely used than *primeval* and has several meanings: (1) "uncivilized" and "savage" (the *primitive* lusts of mankind), (2) "of the earliest period" (the *primitive* beginnings of this country), (3) "unaffected by civilization" (*primitive* tribal customs), (4) "crude and unpolished" (*primitive* living conditions). *Primitive* also has certain related meanings with special applications in biology, architecture, anthropology, and the fine arts. Related words are *primordial, prehistoric, primal, pristine, antediluvian, aboriginal,* and *original.*

principal, principle. These often-confused words have clearly defined and distinguishable meanings. As a noun, *principal* means "a sum of money" and "a chief person," "the head man." As an adjective, *principal* means "main" or "foremost." "The *principal* invested in that scheme amounted to $1,000." "The *principal* of this school is a woman of remarkable vigor." "His *principal* aim is to get well." *Principle,* a noun only, means "a governing rule or truth," "a doctrine," "a determined course of action": "The manager is a man of sound ethical *principle.*" "That statement expresses a *principle* of modern physics." "As a matter of *principle,* he refused to borrow money from anyone." "The *principal* of that academy is a person of *principle.*"

printing. *See* EDITION.

proceed. *See* PRECEDE.

profuse. *See* LAVISH.

prohibit. *See* INHIBIT.

proletariat. *See* BOURGEOIS.

prolix. *See* REDUNDANT.

prone. *See* PROSTRATE.

proof. *See* EVIDENCE.

prophecy, prophesy. *Prophecy* is a noun only, is pronounced "PROF·i·see," and means "a prediction," "foretelling," or "revelation of what is to come": "The official's *prophecy* was that the energy crisis would become even more acute." *Prophesy* is a verb only, is pronounced "PROF·i·sigh," and means "to predict," "to foretell," "to indicate what is to come": "The marriage counselor *prophesied* that the couple would be reunited." *Prophesy* is overused for such words as *predict* and *forecast*. Related words are *prognosticate, divine, project, foresee, prediction,* and *revelation*.

propose, purpose. In the meaning of "to intend," these words are interchangeable: "I *propose* (or *purpose*) to go to headquarters myself." *Propose,* much the more commonly used word, also means "to suggest" and "to nominate": "I *propose* that we send Jim." *Propose* is pronounced "pruh·POHZ"; as a noun *purpose* is pronounced "PUHR·puhs," but as a verb it may be pronounced "PUHR·puhs" or "puhr·POSE." One *purposes* for oneself; one *proposes* to others.

proposition. This word for *plan* or *scheme* is widely overused, especially in the sense of a matter requiring careful handling. The verb *proposition* is an informal term meaning "to propose," "to suggest," often with illegal or immoral intent. Approximate synonyms for the noun *proposition* are *suggestion, overture, design, recommendation,* and *proposal*.

propriety. *See* DECORUM.

proscribe. *See* PRESCRIBE.

prosecute. *See* PERSECUTE.

proselyte, proselytize. These words with different spellings have identical meanings as verbs: "to convert," "to cause someone to change from one religion, opinion, party, or belief to another": "His task was to *proselyte* (or *proselytize*) every disgruntled voter in the Democratic party." As a noun, *proselyte* refers to a person who has shifted from one belief, or sect, or whatever to another; such a person can be called a *convert* or a *proselyte*. Possibly because it is shorter and more easily pronounced, proselyte is the preferred spelling when the word is used as either noun or verb.

prospective. *See* PERSPECTIVE.

prostrate, prone, supine. These words are interchangeable in the sense of "lying flat," "level with the ground or other surface." They differ, however, in certain literal and figurative applications. *Prostrate* means "reduced to weakness," "helpless," "exhausted," "overcome": "The exhausted hikers sprawled *prostrate* by the stream." "That stretch of countryside was left *prostrate* by enemy shelling." *Prone* indicates a face-down position, not solely a horizontal one. A *supine* position is one in which a person lies face upward. *Prone* also has a common meaning of "inclined toward," "having a natural tendency or disposition": "This worker is accident-*prone*." *Supine* has the additional meanings of "passive," "indifferent," "inactive": "Jailed persons tend to become *supine* after a long stay in prison."

protagonist. *See* ANTAGONIST.

prototype. This Greek word has carried over into modern English its meaning of "original." It is now employed to refer to the model upon which something is based, to someone or something that illustrates the basic qualities of a model or example, and to anything similar to something of a different period: "This is a *prototype* of the first coffee grinder." "Mr. Shore is a *prototype* of the commuting businessman." "*Romeo and Juliet* is a *prototype* of the modern musical *West Side Story*." The phrase "*prototype* model" is wordy; use *prototype* or *model*, not both. Related words are *pattern*, *exemplar*, and *archetype*.

proved, proven. The past tense of *prove* is *proved;* the past participle is *proved* or *proven:* "The debater *proved* his point through the use of many illustrations." "This machine has *proved* (or *proven*) satisfactory." The preferred form of the past participle of *prove* is *proved* (David has *proved* his point). *Proven* is standard and preferred as an adjective used before a noun (a *proven* belief). Also, "not *proven*" is more commonly used than "not *proved*," although both phrases are standard.

proverb. *See* AXIOM.

provided, providing. Although originally participles, both *provided* and *providing* have long been accepted as conjunctions, and their use is both correct and interchangeable. Neither should be used as a general synonym for the word *if;* each implies a stipulation equivalent to "on the condition." "You may leave now *if* you wish." "You may leave *provided* (or *providing*) you have finished your work." Although both are standard words, *provided* is preferred and recommended.

prudent, prudential. These words are derived from a Latin term meaning "to look after," "to provide for." *Prudent* is employed to mean "wise," "cautious," "practical," "careful in providing for one's interests," "sensible about planning for the future": "It is always *prudent* to plan a trip carefully." "A *prudent* man will try to save money for family emergencies." *Prudential* is used to refer not to acts themselves or to persons performing acts but to considerations or motives leading to action. "A *prudent* person takes care of his health; *prudential* considerations often cause persons to watch out for their health." "A person is *prudent* if he has *prudential* motives."

pseudonym. *See* NOM DE PLUME.

psychiatrist, psychologist. A *psychiatrist* is a specially trained physician, the holder of a doctor of medicine degree, who practices *psychiatry,* the medical study, diagnosis, treatment, and prevention of mental illness. A *psychologist* is a person trained to do psychological analysis and research, that is, a study of mental processes and behavior. A *psychologist* may hold the degree of doctor of medicine or doctor of philosophy but not necessarily. Both a *psychiatrist* and a *psychologist* may engage in *psychotherapy,* the psychological treatment of mental, nervous, and emotional disorders, but it is generally accepted that this form of therapy, as well as *psychoanalysis,* is usually restricted to the practice of persons who have earned a medical degree. *See also* PHYSICIAN.

psychotic, neurotic, neurasthenic. These terms are loosely used interchangeably, and for good reason: it is difficult to separate and apply them exactly. A *psychotic* person suffers from a *psychosis,* any major, severe, and debilitating mental disease. A *psychotic* individual may or may not suffer the breakdown of some organ (or organs) of his body, but his intellectual powers are severely affected and he tends to withdraw from reality. A *neurotic* person experiences a *neurosis,* which is defined as any of several disorders of the mind or of the emotions, such as anxiety, nameless fears, and unwarranted dislikes for persons or objects. *Neurasthenic* applies to someone who is experiencing *neurasthenia,* a mental and physical condition marked by loss of energy, fatigue, feelings of inadequacy, and inability to remember details. A *neurasthenic* is one suffering what is vaguely known as a *nervous breakdown*. Only individuals with unusually severe mental illnesses should be referred to as *psychotic*. The exact term to be applied to others had best be left to psychologists and psychiatrists.

pupil, student, scholar. These words have related meanings, but *pupil* is usually applied to someone in elementary school, *student* to one in high school or college, and *scholar* to a mature person who is devoted to learning. "This little girl is a *pupil* in the second grade." "Del

Auray was a good *student* in high school and an even better one in college." "It is said that more than 1,000 serious *scholars* can be found in the British Museum at any one time."

purebred. *See* THOROUGHBRED.

purpose. *See* PROPOSE.

purposely, purposefully. *Purposely* means "deliberately," "by design," "with purpose": "She wore that dress *purposely* to create a sensation." "You *purposely* failed to speak to me on the street." *Purposefully* implies the same idea as *purposely* but suggests the presence of determination, of deliberation and infused purpose: "He *purposefully* did everything he could to get me fired." *Purposely* expresses the idea of "not unintentionally"; *purposefully,* a stronger word, means "intentionally."

putter. *See* POTTER.

puzzle. *See* RIDDLE.

puzzle, perplex, bewilder. Although these verbs have different origins, they mean about the same thing and can safely be interchanged. *Puzzle,* the most commonly used of the three terms, means "to put someone at a loss," "to mystify," "to baffle": "What you are trying to do *puzzles* me." *Perplex* means "to confuse mentally," "to make complicated," "to confound": "Just what action to take now *perplexes* the manager." *Bewilder,* the strongest of these words, means "to confuse utterly," "to daze," "to stagger": "Because you treat me differently every time we meet, I am utterly *bewildered.*" Related words are *nonplus, confound, mystify, vex, entangle,* and *frustrate.*

Q

quadroon. *See* MULATTO.

quaint. *See* QUEER.

qualitative, quantitative. These "look-alikes" are often confused but are easy to keep straight. *Qualitative* has to do only with quality (characteristics, properties, attributes): "*Qualitative* analysis enables a chemist to discover what elements are in a given substance." "On a *qualitative* basis, this skein of wool is superior to that one." *Quantitative* has to do only with quantity (amount, measure, size, volume): "*Quantitative* analysis enables a chemist to discover the amounts and proportions of constituents in a given substance." "On a *quantitative* basis, this skein of wool is superior to that one because it is 5 yards longer."

queer, quaint, odd. *Queer* means "unusually different," "differing from the normal or expected," "unconventional or eccentric": "His conception of loyalty to the company is indeed *queer.*" "You have a *queer* way of showing your appreciation." *Queer* is also a slang term meaning "fake" or "counterfeit" (*queer* money). *Quaint* means "old-fashioned," "interesting," "curiously pleasing," "out of date but endearing": "It was a *quaint* house with its cupola and gingerbread trimmings." "The druggist has a *quaint* way of peering at you over his glasses." *Odd* means "unusual," "unexpected," "differing from the ordinary," "freakish": "Wearing sneakers to a formal dance seemed *odd* behavior to the committee." "This woman has an *odd* habit of never speaking to anyone whom she passes on the street." Related words are *unconventional, strange, peculiar, singular, outlandish, eccentric, extraordinary, uncommon, rare, bizarre, anomalous,* and *abnormal.*

query, question, inquiry. A *query* is a *question,* not an *inquiry.* As a verb, *query* means "to question." An *inquiry* is a series of queries or questions, an extended investigation: "The *inquiry* by the coroner lasted for several hours." *Question* is a general term, whereas a *query* is usually confined to a specific, definite, and limited matter: "The clerk has a *query* about this particular charge." "After a lengthy sequence of *queries* (or *questions*), the judge ended his *inquiry* by releasing the accused man on bail."

question. *See* ASK A QUESTION.

queue. *See* CUE.

quick, quickly. *Quick* is a noun, an adjective, and an adverb. *Quickly* is an adverb only. Although such expressions as "Come *quick*" and "Move *quick*" are often heard, experts agree that *quickly* is preferable: "By acting *quickly* (not *quick*), they expect to make a big profit." It is better to use *quick* only as a noun ("cut to the *quick*" and "the *quick* and the dead" are trite expressions illustrating this use) and as an adjective (a *quick* mind.)

quid pro quo. This Latin term meaning "something for something" in English means "an equal exchange": "Helping me weed the garden is a *quid pro quo* for my washing your car." Pronounce the phrase "KWIDpro·KWOH," but use it sparingly because it has become a cliché.

quiet, quiescent. Both words mean "inactive," "motionless," "still," and are interchangeable in this sense: "My closest friend has a *quiet* (or *quiescent*) mind." *Quiet,* much more commonly used than *quiescent,* has several unshared meanings such as "free from noise," "restrained in speech and action," "not showy or ostentatious": "We live on a *quiet* street." "The coach has a *quiet* way of talking to his players." "The colors in this room are *quiet* and subdued."

quiet, quite, quite a. Careless speakers sometimes fail to distinguish between the sounds of *quite* and *quiet. Quiet* is pronounced "KWAI·uht"; *quite* sounds like "kwite." The meanings of *quite* are "positively" and "completely": "That is *quite* the reverse of what you intended." "You were *quite* wrong in everything you tried." In the senses of "really," "truly," and "to the greatest extent," *quite* is standard usage (*quite* ill, *quite* sorry, *quite* small), but it should not appear in such phrases as "*quite* similar" (the ideas are contradictory) and "*quite* complete" ("completely complete" makes little sense). "*Quite* all right" is logically indefensible, but the expression is widely used and idiomatically acceptable. The use of *quite* to mean "rather" (a *quite* handsome man) is colloquial but permissible. *Quite a* is often used in referring to an extraordinary quality or unusual personality (*quite a* joy, *quite a* comedian); in this sense, its use is informal but not incorrect. Its use to mean "extended" (*quite a* period of time) is colloquial.

quiz. As a verb, *quiz* means "to interrogate," "to question closely": "At the station house the desk officer will *quiz* you about the accident." As a noun, *quiz* means "an inquiry," "a questioning": "The professor gave the class a *quiz* that day." "The Senate *quiz* of oil dealers lasted for five weeks." The use of *quiz* is informal as both verb and noun; more importantly, the word has been overused beyond the point of mere triteness.

quote, unquote. As an abbreviation for the noun *quotation, quote* is an informal coinage (neologism) that should not appear in serious writing: "This is a *quotation* (not *quote*) from the Bible." As a verb, *quote* means "to copy or repeat the words of someone else," "to cite," "to refer to for illustration": "In my talk, I expect to *quote* from the Bible, the Koran, and other religious works." *Cite* is often a more appropriate word than *quote,* especially when no specific reference is intended. In the expression *"quote* and *unquote,"* reference is to *quotation* marks. The phrase is often used by a speaker to mark the beginning and ending of a quotation. This expression is acceptable in speech but not in writing.

R

rabbit, rarebit. The correct term for a certain kind of cheese dish is *Welsh rabbit,* but *rarebit* has been so widely substituted that both *Welsh rabbit* and *Welsh rarebit* are now acceptable in one's diction, although perhaps not always in one's stomach. As two words, *rare* and *bit* are standard: "That was a *rare bit* of acting." *Rabbit* appears in several overworked expressions: "*rabbit* punch" (an example of boxing shoptalk); "*rabbit* ears" ("sensitivity to jibes or insults," "television antenna"); "*rabbit's* foot" (a good-luck charm).

racket, racquet. *Racket* has a basic meaning of "din," "uproar," and "clamor": "The traffic at this intersection makes a frightful *racket.*" It is a slang term when applied to any business or job and trite when used to describe any dishonest or illegal practice (the latest get-rich-quick *racket*). *Racquet,* once the only word used to name a light bat employed in such games as tennis and badminton, is still so spelled in the game of squash racquets. Today, *racket* has superseded *racquet* to the extent that some modern dictionaries do not list *racquet* as a main entry.

radical. *See* CONSERVATIVE.

railroad, railway. These terms are used interchangeably by most speakers and writers. In exact usage, *railroad* is used to refer to the entire system involved: the tracks themselves, the stations, rolling stock, land, ticket offices, and other property used in transportation by rail. *Railway* refers specifically to a track providing a runway for wheeled equipment. "Amtrak is a system of *railroads* throughout the United States." "Every foot of the elevated *railway* in that city has been dismantled." As a verb, used informally, *railroad* means (1) "to rush or push through quickly" and (2) "to imprison on a false charge": "The legislature will *railroad* this bill today." "The attorney said, 'My client is innocent; don't try to *railroad* him into jail.'"

raise, rear, rise, raze. Once it was maintained that people *raised pigs* and corn and *reared* children. Careful speakers preserve this distinction, but the general public does not; therefore, you can *raise* or *rear* as many children as you can afford, with no purist in language to prevent you. The noun *raise* (a *raise* in pay) is also standard, although *rise* (a *rise* in pay) was once considered the only proper term in this construction. The expression "pay *raise*" is wordy. The verb *raise* is always transitive; the verb *rise* is always intransitive: One's arm *rises;* one *raises* his arm. *Raise* and *raze* are antonyms in the sense that *raise* means "to elevate," "to lift," whereas *raze* means "to tear down": "The workmen *raised* the scaffolding and then *razed* it." Try to avoid such clichés as "*raise* one's sights," "*raise* Cain," "*raise* hell," "*raise* money," "*raise* a siege," "*rise* to the occasion," "*rise* above the commonplace," "*rise* in the world," "*rise* to one's responsibilities," "*rise* from the dead," "*rise* on one's hind legs," "feel the yeast *rising,*" "*rear* guard," and "bring up the *rear.*" A horse *rears* (pronounced "reers") up on its hindlegs, not *rares* (rhymes with *dares*) up.

rare, scarce. Each of these words describes what is "in short supply," "infrequent," "hard to find," "uncommon": "Gasoline and butter were *rare* (or *scarce*) during the war." *Rare* is usually applied to items of quality and value, the worth of which is increased by permanent infrequency: "Diamonds are *rare* and precious forms of carbon." "Growing plants were *rare* in the dust bowl." *Scarce* is normally applied to everyday or ordinary items or occurrences: "Our milk supply is *scarce,* but we have enough to last until tomorrow." A *rare* book is valuable because of its age or importance or because only one or a few copies exist anywhere; a *scarce* book is one in short supply at a particular source (such as a library) but one of which numerous copies may be available elsewhere.

rarebit. *See* RABBIT.

rarely, rarely ever. *Rarely* means "seldom," "infrequently," "not often": "She *rarely* goes to the movies." The phrase "*rarely* ever" is wordy, unidiomatic, and illogical. Instead of saying "She *rarely ever* sings," say "She *rarely* sings" or "She *hardly ever* sings" or "She sings *rarely, if ever*" or "She sings *rarely or never.*"

rational, rationale. *Rational*, an adjective, means "of sound mind," "sane," "logical," "reasonable," "sensible": "Your explanation is entirely *rational.*" "This is a *rational* plan for lowering the sales tax in this state." *Rationale*, a noun, means "a logical basis," "fundamental reasons," "an exposition of principles": "I cannot understand the *rationale* for your action." "Does deliberate cruelty ever have a defensible *rationale?*"

raze. *See* RAISE.

re, in re. These terms are usually reserved for use by the legal profession, where they have the meaning of "in the matter of," "in the case of." (*Re* is the ablative case of Latin *res,* meaning "thing," "item," or "matter.") *In re* is a Latinism, the meaning of which is best expressed by *about, in regard to,* or *concerning*. Let the lawyers have *in re*.

reaction, response, reply. A *reaction* is "a *response* to a stimulus" and properly belongs in scientific work only. It is overused to mean "opinion," "attitude," "impression," "view," and "feeling." It is also overused to mean both *response* and *reply*. A *response* is an answer or the act of replying. A *reply* is a *response* by means of word or gesture. Recommendation: use *response* and *reply* interchangeably and don't use *reaction* at all unless a stimulus of some kind has been a cause. "The patient's *reaction* to the medicine was immediate." "My *response* to your proposal is negative." "My *reply* to your letter is in the mail."

reactionary. A dictionary definition of *reactionary* is "one who favors or inclines to reaction," an explanation that clarifies not at all. *Reactionary* is such an emotionally toned word that it is used to mean what the speaker or writer wishes it to mean and has little or no actual denotation. In the areas of morals, politics, religion, and related fields of concern, it is usually employed as an adjective to mean "backward," "behind the times," "overly conservative," "antiquated": "This legislator is a mossback, totally *reactionary* in his view of all new proposals." *See also* CONSERVATIVE.

readable, legible. In the sense of "capable of being read," *legible* and *readable* are interchangeable: "His handwriting was frail but *legible* (or *readable*)." *Readable* has additional meanings of "interesting," "pleasurable," "fascinating": "This is the most *readable* novel I have come across in weeks." "Although our son's letter from camp is *legible*, it is not especially *readable*." Corresponding nouns are *legibility* and *readability*. *See also* ILLEGIBLE.

real, really. Although *real* can be a noun (Is this for *real?*), it is regularly used as an adjective meaning "true," "actual," "genuine," and "sincere": "What is the *real* reason for your laughter?" "This is a story of *real* life." "That looks like a *real* ruby." "They formed a *real* friendship." *Really* is an adverb meaning "truly," "actually," "in reality," "genuinely," and "indeed": "This is how things *really* are." "She is a *really* lovely girl." "*Really*, is that your whole story?" *Really* should be used to modify verbs, adjectives, and other adverbs (*really* ill, *really* fast, *really* moving). *Real* should be used to modify only nouns and pronouns (*real* gems, the *real* him) and should not be used in expressions such as "*real* soon," "*real* pretty," and "*real* excited." "*Really* and truly" is grammatically correct but wordy and trite; use *really* or *truly* but not both in the same expression. *See also* ACTUAL.

realize, know. *Realize* means "to grasp clearly," "to understand fully." It is a stronger word than *know*, which also means "to perceive" or "to apprehend" but without the thoroughness and completeness suggested by *realize*. *Realize* also suggests the idea of warning or emphasizing. "I *know* that you are tired." "Do you *realize* that you might catch a cold in your weakened condition?" "You *know* that you are already late, but do you *realize* what the penalties for lateness may be?"

rear. *See* RAISE.

reason. *See* CAUSE. *Reason* appears in numerous trite expressions such as "It stands to *reason*," "theirs not to *reason* why," "within *reason*," "by *reason* of," "bring someone to *reason*," and "any *reasonable* person." Note that one word, *because*, can replace five words: "for the simple *reason* that." If one overuses *reason* by itself, he can try *understanding, intuition, judgment*, or *discernment*. In the sense of "cause" or "basis for action," occasionally substitute *purpose, motive, end, object*, or *objective*.

reason is because. *See* BECAUSE.

reason why. The word *why* is an adverb, conjunction, noun, and interjection and should not be used as a pronoun. Instead of saying "The reason *why* he left is unknown," say "The reason *that* he left is unknown."

When *why* is used as a conjunctive adverb (that is, part conjunction and part adverb), it properly appears in a remark such as "I never realized *why* he was upset."

rebound, redound. These "look-alikes" are easily confused. *Rebound* means "to spring back," "to cast back," "to recoil": "If you really want to, you can *rebound* from that bad luck." As a noun, *rebound* means "a bouncing back": "The center of that basketball team captured thirty *rebounds* during the game." *Redound* means "to have an effect or result," "to contribute," "to accrue," "to add to": "This generous act will *redound* to your credit." Although a few lexicographers include "recoil" as one meaning of *redound,* that meaning is better confined to *rebound*. Think of *rebounding* as "bounding" and of *redounding* as "deeds."

receipt, recipe. Only a few years ago, *receipt* had a basic meaning of "receiving" and was never used, except by uneducated persons, in the sense of *recipe* (a formula for preparing something, a set of directions for mixing measured ingredients). Today, *recipe* is still preferable to *receipt* in the sense of "formula," but widespread usage is gradually removing all restrictive labels from *receipt*. "Let us have your *recipe* (or *receipt*) for that cake." "He will give you a *receipt* for the money." "What were the *receipts* today from your business?"

reckon. *See* CALCULATE.

recondition, renovate. In the sense of improving by restoring or remodeling, *recondition* and *renovate* are interchangeable: "The new owner will *recondition* (or *renovate*) the house." *Recondition* is a somewhat stronger word than *renovate,* implying a more thorough overhauling or more extensive alterations. Having a hat cleaned and blocked results in a *renovation*. Having an automobile overhauled is a *reconditioning* process. *Renovate* has the added meaning of "to revive," "to impart new vigor to": "The physician claims that a long vacation will *renovate* you."

recrimination, accusation. This is a pair of "cause and effect" words. An *accusation* is a charge of wrongdoing, the act of asserting that someone is guilty: "The prosecuting attorney has decided upon an *accusation* of murder." A *recrimination* is a countercharge, an *accusation* in return: "If you libel this man, you can expect *recrimination.*"

recur, reoccur. These words are interchangeable in the meaning of "to occur again": "That was a dreadful experience which I hope will not *recur* (or *reoccur*)." *Recur,* more widely used than *reoccur,* implies the repetition more than once of an event or experience, sometimes according to a definite pattern: "The tide ebbs and flows in a *recurring* pattern." *Reoccur* suggests a one-time repetition: "After his appendix was removed, he knew that an attack of appendicitis could not *reoccur.*" Corresponding nouns are *recurrence* and *reoccurrence. Recurrence* is so much more widely used that several leading dictionaries no longer list *reoccurrence.*

recurring, frequent. *Recurring,* an adjective formed from *recur,* refers to something that happens repeatedly, occurs or shows up or comes up again and again: "His *recurring* attacks of asthma are becoming more and more severe." *Frequent* means the same thing, with one difference: it means happening again at short intervals: "He made *frequent* attacks on the refrigerator all evening." A growing boy may have *recurring* periods of depression, but he is certain to have *frequent* desires for food.

rebound. *See* REBOUND.

redundant, superfluous, prolix. These words have a common meaning of "too much," "more than is required or needed," "excessive": "The speaker's response to the question was *redundant* (or *superfluous* or *prolix*)." *Superfluous,* derived from Latin terms meaning "overflow," is applicable to anything that is excessive, but *redundant* and *prolix* are usually applied to speech and writing. Specifically, *redundant* refers to unnecessary repetition in expressing ideas, that is, wordiness: "His speaking style is slow and boring, largely because it is so *redundant.*" *Prolix,* from a Latin word meaning "long," applies to anything, especially speech and writing, that is not necessarily repetitious but is extended to great, tedious, and unnecessary length. Words related to *prolix* are *protracted, verbose,* and *prolonged.* Approximate synonyms for *redundant* are *repetitive, tautological,* and *pleonastic.* Instead of *superfluous,* occasionally say or write *excessive, extra, extravagant, immoderate,* and *disproportionate.*

refer, refer back. *Refer* has much the same meaning as ALLUDE. Specifically it means "to direct one's thoughts or attention" to something else: "Please *refer* to Chapter 10 for a further explanation of this topic." "The prisoner twice *referred* to his former employer during the hearing." *Refer* conveys the idea of *back* (it is derived from Latin words meaning "back" or "again" and "carry"). Omit *back* in *refer back* and avoid wordiness: "The speaker *referred* (not *referred back*) to his earlier comments." If the meaning is "to send back," then *refer back* is permissible but still wordy.

referee. *See* UMPIRE.

reflective, reflexive. These words are occasionally used as synonyms, but *reflective* conveys two meanings not contained in *reflexive. Reflective* refers to something that casts back light, heat, or sound (a *reflective* sheet of glass) and to someone who is thinking, pondering, or meditating (in a *reflective* mood). *Reflexive* is now used entirely in a grammatical sense, applying to a construction in which a verb has an identical subject and object (*I* dress *myself*). The *self* words such as *myself, himself,* and *themselves* are *reflexive* pronouns.

refutable, irrefutable. These words are antonyms. *Refutable* is an adjective applied to charges, statements, or beliefs that can be disputed, argued, and perhaps disproved. *Irrefutable* means "not refutable," "incontrovertible," "undeniable," "incontestable," "not questionable." Statements that can be challenged or confuted are *refutable;* those that cannot be denied, those the truth of which is clearly evident, are *irrefutable.*

refute, deny. Like *repudiate, refute* is a stronger, more powerful word than *deny.* To *deny* is to claim that an opinion, statement, allegation, or charge is simply not true. To *refute* is to "prove" that whatever is stated or believed is false, erroneous, and groundless. "Mrs. Cyrus will *deny* that she prepared a tasteless meal." "Here is my bank statement to *refute* your charge that I am penniless." "She *denies* that she left the dance early and has evidence to *refute* the rumor that she did." *See also* DENY.

regal. *See* KINGLY.

regard, regards. Both of these words suggest esteem, respect, admiration, and approbation: "I *regard* that minister highly." "Please accept my warm *regards.*" The singular form is used in prepositional phrases such as "in *regard* to," "with *regard* to," and "in *regard* of," although each of these expressions is wordy and usually can be replaced by *concerning* or *about.* The phrase "in *regards* to" is substandard and should never be used. "As *regards*" is standard but can usually be omitted without loss or can be replaced by *concerning.*

regret. *See* REPENT.

regretful, regrettable. *Regretful* means "sorrowful," "filled with sorrow or regret": "I am *regretful* that I cannot accept your invitation." *Regrettable* means "deserving sorrow or regret" and is applied to situations or events that elicit a sense of loss, distress, or longing: "Your failure to write an apology is *regrettable.*" In ordinary usage, a person is *regretful,* an event or condition is *regrettable:* "The culprit should be *regretful* for his *regrettable* act."

relation, relative. Both of these words are sanctioned by leading dictionaries as standard, interchangeable terms for a kinsman, a person who is related by blood or marriage: "I believe that this *relation* (or *relative*) of mine is a second cousin." Each word is more often used in plural than singular form, presumably because nearly everyone has numerous kinsmen: "My *relatives* (or *relations*) live in several different states." The idiom "no *relation* of," not "No *relation* to," should be used in a statement such as "Bob Moran is no relation *of* Hank Moran." However, *to* should be used in such sentences as "Bob Moran is not *related to* Hank Moran." Apparently more skilled writers use *relative* than *relation,* but the term to be selected is a matter of taste or local custom.

relatively, comparatively. These words mean about the same thing, and it makes no difference whether one says "It was a *relatively* minor accident" or "It was a *comparatively* minor accident." What does make a difference is the use of either term when there is actually nothing to be related or compared to. Neither word can be justified in a sentence such as "There was *relatively* (or *comparatively*) little discussion of this brand-new proposal." "Little discussion" *relatively* or *comparable* to what? Can any "little discussion" be typical? A "brand-new proposal" is unique and has not been discussed before, either at length or briefly. In short, *relatively* and *comparatively* are often meaningless words that add nothing.

remainder. *See* BALANCE.

rendition, performance. In recent years, *rendition* has become as popular as *performance* in the sense of providing musical, dramatic, or other forms of entertainment. Both words mean "the accomplishment or execution of acts, feats, or ceremonies": "The tenor's *rendition* (or *performance)* of classical songs was well received." *Rendition* is now something of a "vogue" word, perhaps because it stresses the unusual or distinctive qualities of a peformance or interpretation given by leading popular singers and public entertainers. Recommendation: use *performance* unless some spectacular or unique quality should be noted and stressed.

renovate. *See* RECONDITION.

reoccur. *See* RECUR.

repair. *See* MAINTAIN.

repeat again. *Again* means "another time" or "in return" and always suggests the idea of "in addition." Therefore, it is superfluous in such expressions as "repeat *again*" because the prefix *re-* has the meaning of *again*. Say "*Tell* your story *again*" or "*Retell* your story," not "*Retell* your story *again*"; "*Repeat* that, please," not "*Repeat* that *again*, please."

repel, repulse. Because each of these words can mean "to drive back," they are often misused in situations where their meanings should be distinct. One can *repel* or *repulse* someone who attempts to mug him, but only *repel* conveys the idea of disgust, aversion, and loathing: "His rude manner *repelled* everyone at the party." *Repulse* is commonly associated with *repulsive,* which does mean "disgusting" or "offensive," but *repulse* means only "to turn away," "to reject," or "to refuse":

"This girl *repulsed* every boy who wanted to dance with her because all of them *repelled* her."

repent, regret. These words are near-synonyms, but they do have slightly different applications. To *repent* is to feel sorrow and to engage in self-reproach, which is precisely the primary meaning of *regret*. But to *repent* is to go a step further: to feel so regretful as to try to make amends, to do something to atone for the acts or omissions that caused *regret*. That is, one may *regret* many things but *repent* of only some of them: "I *regret* not having written to you." "Because this rich man *repented* of his shady dealings, he decided to give away much of his money."

repertoire, repertory. These terms refer to a list of plays, operas, or other entertainments which a group or individual is prepared to perform: "The Old Vic Players have a *repertoire* (or *repertory*) of more than thirty Shakespearean plays." In this meaning, *repertoire* is the preferred term. *Repertory* is the correct word to designate a theatrical company that performs regularly: "To gain experience, she joined a touring *repertory* company."

replica, copy. *Copy* is a widely used term for a reproduction, imitation, or transcript of an original: "Please make a *copy* of this letter." *Replica,* a more learned word derived from a Latin term meaning "to repeat," is applied only to a *copy* or reproduction of an original that is produced by the maker of the original or prepared under his direct supervision. A *copy* of a painting, for example, is one reproduction among perhaps thousands produced by someone other than the artist himself. A duplicating mechanism, such as a Xerox machine (*see* XEROX), can make *copies* but not *replicas*. Words related to *replica* and *copy* are *facsimile, duplicate, imitation,* and *carbon.*

reply. *See* REACTION.

reported. *See* REPUTED.

reportedly. *See* ALLEGEDLY.

republic, democracy. These words are used interchangeably; the United States, for example, is referred to as a *democracy* as often as it is as a *republic*. The country was founded as a *republic,* a term meaning "a state in which the supreme power rests in citizens entitled to vote, which power is exercised by chosen representatives." "I pledge allegiance to the flag of the United States of America and to the *republic* for which it stands. . . ." A *democracy* is "a state in which supreme power rests in the people and is exercised by them." The distinction lies in "government by elected representatives" and "government by the people." In essence, the United States is both a *republic* and a *democracy,* but careful writers sometimes distinguish between the words. The words *Republican* and *Democratic* have no specific meaning except as the names of political parties. Depending upon their party, candidates have been known to say "Vote the Democratic ticket because this country is a *democracy*" and "Vote the Republican ticket because this country is a *republic.*" Recommendation: don't vote for either candidate; both are playing with words.

repudiate. *See* DENY and REFUTE.

repulse. *See* REPEL.

reputed, reported. *Reputed* means "held to be such," "supposed," "so considered": "He is *reputed* to be an excellent salesman." "She is the *reputed* owner of the stolen property." *Reported* means "communicated," "made known": "This theft was immediately *reported* to the police." "The *reputed* offender was *reported* to authorities."

reputedly. *See* ALLEGEDLY.

required, prescribed. That which is *required* is demanded, obligatory, necessary, and essential: "It is *required* that all applicants be citizens of this country." "A health certificate will be *required.*" That which is *prescribed* is recommended, suggested, or designated: "The physician *prescribed* bed rest for the patient." "This student's *prescribed* course of study contained several *required* subjects." A *requirement* is a demand; a *prescription* is a direction or recommendation.

research. The preferred pronunciation of this word as both noun and verb is "ri·SUHRCH." Also standard and often heard is "REE·suhrch." The word means "scholarly or scientific inquiry" and is used frequently when all that is involved is *study, examination, investigation, spot check, breakdown,* or *canvass.*

reside, live, dwell. *Live* is commonly, and properly, used to indicate occupying a house, home, or other place of habitation: "He *lived* there for ten years." *Reside* also means to exist permanently or for a time in a certain place, but the term is somewhat pretentious and should be reserved for the act of living in an important or historic setting: "The Governor now *resides* in a mansion furnished by the state." "When she is in residence in London, the Queen *resides* at Buckingham Palace." *Dwell* is somewhat old-fashioned (*dwell* in peace), but in noun formation *(dwelling)* is still popular and correct: "His *dwelling* is a costly cooperative apartment."

resolution, motion. Each of these words means "a formal expression of opinion," "a proposal," but *motion* always refers to a proposal requiring a vote or other action. A *resolution* is not necessarily formed or phrased in a legislative, judicial, or deliberative gathering; a *motion* always is: "Mr. Chairperson, I make a *motion* that this *resolution* be adopted."

respectfully, respectively, respectably. The first of these terms means "with respect": "He addressed the supervisor *respectfully.*" *Respectively* means "each in the order named": "Harry, Ned, and Steve were known as the Ace, the Banker, and the Nightcrawler *respectively.*" *Respectably* means "in a manner worthy of esteem": "That family lived *respectably* in this community for thirty years."

response. *See* REACTION.

restaurant, restaurateur. The former term, which derives from a French word meaning "to restore," is a somewhat more genteel word than *eating house, eatery, beanery,* and *hash house* (all slang) and *café, luncheonette, coffee shop, tavern, grill,* and *lunch counter*. It should be pronounced "RES·tuh·ruhnt" or "RES·tuh·rahnt." A *restaurateur* (pronounced "RES·tuh·ruh·tur") is the manager or owner of a restaurant.

restive, restless. These related words have a common Latin base, a term meaning "to remain standing." A *restive* person or animal is unable to remain at rest (that is, quiet) because he cannot bear restraint or control and becomes impatient with delay: "When tied to a hitching post, the horse became *restive.*" *Restless* is a commonly used word applied more to unquiet and unease of the mind or emotions than of the body and usually suggesting the absence of actual restraint: "This *restless* patient has grown *restive* under hospital regulations." *Restive,* unlike *restless,* also implies refusing to move, being balky or recalcitrant. A horse chafing under a bit and refusing to obey its rider's commands would be termed *restive,* not *restless*.

restrain. *See* CHECK, CURB, RESTRAIN, CONSTRAIN.

resume, continue. *Resume* means "to go on (or take up again) after an interruption." *Continue* has precisely the same meaning except that no interruption is involved. A group might *continue* to play bridge, but would *resume* playing after a stop for refreshments. "The rain *continued* for three hours, stopped for a few minutes, and then *resumed.*" Words related to *continue* are *persist, last, persevere, endure,* and *extend.* Phrases synonymous with *resume* are "begin again" and "start once more."

résumé, synopsis, summary. From a French word meaning "to sum up," *résumé* (pronounced with both *e*'s sounding like long *a*) is only a fancy word for *summary,* a brief but comprehensive presentation of facts or statements: "This *summary* is a terse statement of the main points made in your editorial." Both *résumé* and *summary* are usually applied to works of nonfiction such as history, biography, and magazine articles. *Synopsis* (from Greek words meaning "seeing with one's own eyes") also refers to a statement providing a brief, general review or condensation; it is most often used in connection with retelling the plot of a novel, story, or play. One may write a *résumé* or a *summary* of the Declaration of Independence and a *synopsis* of the plot of *Huckleberry Finn.* Related words include *digest, brief, abstract,* and *outline.*

reticent, taciturn. A *reticent* person is reserved, not inclined to speak freely or often, disposed to keep quiet. A *taciturn* person is also inclined to silence and reluctant to take part in conversation. However, a *taciturn* individual is usually considered surly, dour, sullen, and severe. That is, a *reticent* person is pleasantly shy, withdrawn, and silent; a *taciturn* individual is unpleasantly so. Related words are *silent, uncommunicative, reserved, still,* and *quiescent.*

return back. *Return* implies going or coming back to a former place, position, or condition. Omit *back* from this expression: "It is not easy to *return* (not *return back*) to one's childhood home."

revenge. *See* AVENGE.

reverend, reverent. *Reverend* means "deserving of respect, awe, love, or reverence"; *reverent* means showing these same feelings and emotions: "The Lincoln Memorial is a *reverend* symbol of this great American's contribution to his country. When they view it, most people look with *reverent* eyes and hearts." *Reverend* is primarily an adjective. For suggestions on using *reverend* as a title applying to the clergy, see PASTOR.

review, revue. As applied to theatrical entertainments, *review* and *revue* are synonymous, both coming from a French word meaning "to see again": "The most popular play of the season is a *review* (or *revue*) in which a dozen recent events, popular fads, and silly ideas are parodied and satirized." Professional theatrical personnel tend to use *revue;* others may take their choice.

reward. *See* AWARD.

rich, wealthy, affluent. These words mean "having an abundance of possessions," "amply supplied with funds, resources, or means," "of great value or worth": "This is a *rich* (or *wealthy* or *affluent*) country." Words related to these three are *opulent, moneyed,* and *well-to-do. Rich,* the most generally used of these terms, is more likely than the other two to suggest newly acquired possessions *(nouveau riche)* and is often used enviously or disparagingly: "That person is *rich* in worldly goods but poor in control of his own emotions." *Wealthy* implies a permanence or stability not suggested by *rich* and also is applicable to characteristics and personality traits: "He comes from an established family that is *wealthy* in material possessions and in concern for the needs of those less fortunate." *Affluent,* rarely used, applies to someone with a large income, usually an income spent freely: "She is an obviously *affluent* member of the international jet set."

riddle, puzzle, enigma. A *riddle* is a puzzling question or problem; a conundrum. The term is most often used in connection with problems expressed in words, obscure matters that can be clarified only by a guess: "Plutarch wrote that Homer died of worry and chagrin because he could not solve a certain *riddle.*" "Oedipus solved the *riddle* of the Sphinx by revealing that the person described was man, who 'walked' on four legs, then two, then three." A *puzzle* is a toy or other device designed to amuse by presenting a difficulty that can be solved through effort or ingenuity: "He works the crossword *puzzle* every morning that it appears in his newspaper." An *enigma* is a baffling problem or question that contains an air or atmosphere of mystery: "Zach concluded that his former wife would always be an *enigma* to him." In a radio broadcast early during World War II, Winston Churchill said: "I cannot forecast to you the action of Russia. It is a *riddle* wrapped in a mystery inside an *enigma.*"

right, rightly. *Right* can be a noun (you have a *right*), a verb (*right* this wrong), an adjective (my *right* foot), or an adverb (*right* after bedtime.) *Rightly* is an adverb only (*rightly* dressed). Both *right* and *rightly* can be used as adverbs to modify verbs (Spell it *right* or *rightly*), but only *rightly* is standard in the meaning of "properly": "The arrested man *rightly* refused to talk to the police." Both *right* and the plural *rights* have many additional meanings, but one can avoid overusing such already-hackneyed expressions as "be in one's *right* mind," "put things *right,*" "the *right* thing at the *right* time," "*right* of way," "*right* wing," "*right* about-face," "*right* away," "out in *right* field," "let the left hand know what the *right* hand is doing," "*right* to work," "in one's own *right,*" "in the *right,*" "by *rights,*" and "set to *rights.*" "*Right* along," "*right* soon," "*right* off," and "*right* smart" are informal and not-recommended phrases indicating the use of *right* as an adverb.

rise. *See* RAISE; *see also* GET UP.

robber, thief, burglar. These words all apply to a person who unlawfully takes property from another, but they have distinct meanings. A *robber* steals by the use of force or threat. A *thief* does his work in secret and by stealth. A *burglar* breaks and enters. Someone who takes your wallet while holding a knife in his hand is a *robber,* not a *thief* or a *burglar*. A person who lifts your wallet from the beach while you are swimming is a *thief*. An individual who forces open a window in your house and takes your wallet from the dresser is a *burglar*.

Roman Catholic. *See* CATHOLIC.

round. *See* ABOUT.

rout, route. *Rout* has several meanings, one of which indicates "a way," "a course," or "a road," the specific meanings of *route*. *Rout* is usually pronounced "rowt." "This is the pronunciation often given *route,* but the preferred pronunciation of *route* is "root." As a verb, *route* is pronounced both "root" and "rowt." "This serious defeat put the entire division to *rout.*" "We sailed for Europe by the North Atlantic *route*." "His job was to *route* deliveries to the proper departments."

royal. *See* KINGLY.

S

Sabbath, Sunday. The word *Sabbath* is derived from various words in Hebrew, Greek, and Latin, all of them meaning "to rest." *Sabbath* is the seventh day of the week (Saturday), named in the Ten Commandments of the Old Testament as a day of worship and rest and thus observed by Jews and some Christian sects. *Sabbath* is also a term for the first day of the week, *Sunday,* observed by most Christian churches as a day of rest. *Sunday* is derived from an Old English word meaning "day of the sun."

sacred, sacrosanct. *Sacred* means (1) "dedicated to the worship of a deity"; (2) "declared holy"; (3) "dedicated to a single purpose, person, or use"; (4) "worthy of respect": "He took a *sacred* oath never to bear arms against anyone." "This is a monument *sacred* to the memory of a great person." "Everyone's right to life is *sacred.*" "All great festival occasions of the church are *sacred* in their celebration." *Sacrosanct* means especially and particularly "sacred," "incorruptible and unassailable," "incapable of being violated": "The most *sacrosanct* part of the church is its sanctuary." "The constitutional rights of free speech, free press, and free assembly are considered *sacrosanct* by all American citizens."

saga. A *saga* (pronounced "SAH·guh") refers to any long narrative in verse or prose dealing with legendary or historic events. Like EPIC, *saga* is loosely used in place of such words as *story, tale, adventure, exploit,* and *event.* "The voyage of the British naval ship *Bounty* in 1789 was a *saga* of the sea." "This man's rise from poverty to wealth is a *story* (not *saga*) of real-life adventure."

said, same. As an adjective, *said* should not be used except in legal jargon (the *said* claimant). In general speech, this use of *said* is wordy because it is unneeded. If clarity demands some modifier, say *specified, aforementioned,* or *referred-to.* In a similar way, *same* is often used outside legal and commercial contexts in wordy, useless ways. Substitute *it* for *same* in a statement such as "I have your book and will return *it* (not *same*) tomorrow."

salon, saloon. A *salon* is a large room or hall for entertaining guests or exhibiting works of art. A *saloon* is a place where alcoholic drinks are sold and drunk. A *saloon* is a bar or tavern; a *salon* is a gallery or exhibition hall. The words should be distinguished, even though drinks may be consumed in a *salon* and artwork may be shown in a *saloon.*

same. *See* SAID.

sample. *See* EXAMPLE.

sanguine. *See* OPTIMISTIC.

sanitarium, sanatorium. Despite differences in spelling and pronunciation, these words are used interchangeably. *Sanitarium* is more often used, possibly because it refers to a general hospital. *Sanatorium* is sometimes restricted to the meaning of a health resort or rest home, but this distinction is not often made.

Both words are derived from a Latin term meaning "health."

sarcasm, satire. *See* IRONY.

saying. *See* AXIOM.

scandal. *See* LIBEL.

scarce. *See* RARE.

scarce, scarcely. Although *scarce* can be used as an adverb (*scarce* more than a bare living), its greatest use in contemporary speech and writing is that of an adjective meaning "infrequently found or seen," "insufficient," "not plentiful": "Pretty women are *scarce* in this town." *Scarcely* is an adverb meaning "barely," "by a small margin," "just": "He could *scarcely* breathe under the heavy covers." *Scarcely* has a negative sense and should not be used with another negative; avoid such expressions as "didn't *scarcely,*" "couldn't *scarcely,*" and "without *scarcely.*" *See also* DOUBLE NEGATIVE and HARDLY.

scent. *See* SMELL.

schmier, schmeer, smear. A currently popular slang expression meaning "everything" is "the whole *schmier* (or *schmeer* or *smear*)." It is not clear what spelling is intended or correct. The most common spelling is *smear,* a word defined as meaning "an oily substance" and "a smudge, spot, or stain." *Schmier* is a variant form adapted from the German word for smear cheese, or *Schmierkäse* (cottage cheese). *Schmeer* is a slang term for persons and things (possibly the meaning closest to the aforementioned phrase itself) and a colloquial word meaning "to bribe." However the expression is spelled, it is both slangy and trite and should be used rarely, if at all.

scholar. *See* PUPIL.

Scotch, Scot, Scotsman. *Scotch* is commonly used to refer to (1) the people of Scotland, but this application is correctly used only with a preceding *the* (*the Scotch, the Scotch* people); (2) whisky distilled in Scotland from malted barley; (3) any of several English dialects spoken in Scotland. *Scot, Scotsman,* and *Scotsmen* are the terms preferred in Scotland; *Scotchman* is considered incorrect and offensive there. *Scots* and *the Scotch* are widely used plural forms. *Scot* is not an adjective; *Scottish* and *Scots* are preferred adjectives, but *Scotch* is entrenched in such terms as "*Scotch* whisky" and "*Scotch* broth."

script, scrip. *Script* means (1) handwriting as distinguished from printing; (2) the text of a play or film; (3) in law, any original document. *Scrip* means (1) paper money issued for temporary use; (2) a small scrap of paper. "The letter I received is written in beautiful *script.*" "The soldiers were forced to take their pay in *scrip.*" "The *script* on this *scrip* is barely legible."

scrupulous. *See* METICULOUS.

sculp, sculpt. Once considered nonstandard, both words are accepted as shortened forms of "to sculpture." Both *sculp* and *sculpt* are derived from a Latin verb, *sculpere* ("to carve"). But doesn't *sculpture,* a perfectly good verb, sound better than *sculp* and *sculpt?* "The artist *sculptured* this model in two months of laborious effort."

seasonable, seasonal. *Seasonable* means "timely" or "appropriate to the season": "*Seasonable* rains resulted in an excellent wheat crop." "Cold weather is *seasonable* in February." *Seasonal* means "associated or connected with seasons," "what is controlled by, or depends on, seasons": "This decrease in employment is *seasonal.*"

secondly. *See* FIRST.

section, cross-section. *Section* means "a piece," "a portion": "This *section* of the farm lies in a valley." *Cross-section* means "a representative sample meant to be typical of the whole": "This recommendation is based on a *cross-section* of public opinion in this area."

seem to. *See* CAN'T SEEM TO.

segregation. *See* INTEGRATION.

semi-. This is an element from Latin meaning "half" and is prefixed to many words in English: *semiannual, semiautomatic, semicircle, semicolon, semifinal, semiformal, semiprofessional,* and so forth. *See also* BIANNUAL and BIMONTHLY.

sense, feel. As a verb, *sense* means "to become aware of," "to perceive," and informally means "to understand," "to detect": "I quickly *sensed* that I was in trouble." "Do you *sense* some problem coming up?" *Feel* has several meanings, two important ones being "to perceive through the sense of touch" and "to experience an emotion": "This velvet *feels* cool to my fingers." "I *feel* a great loss in his death." *Sense* and *feel* are loosely used for each other, although originally *sense* was restricted to matters or objects perceived through one of the five senses and *feel* to that which could be experienced through touch alone. *See also* BELIEVE.

sensual, sensuous. Several terms refer to satisfaction of the senses, among them *sensual, sensuous, epicurean, luxurious,* and *voluptuous*. *Sensual* applies to the physical senses only. *Sensuous* refers to what is experienced through all the senses, especially those involved in appreciation of art, music, literature, nature, and the like. One refers to *sensual* pleasures, such as eating and drinking, and to the *sensuous* sounds or delights of music, sculpture, etc.

sentinel, sentry. Each of these words refers to a guard, especially a soldier or other military person, posted at some spot to keep order and to prevent the entry of unauthorized persons: "The *sentry* (or *sentinel*) paced back and forth." *Sentry* is the more widely used term. *Sentinel* is employed frequently in literary or figurative senses: "The statue stood like a *sentinel* on the mountaintop."

separate, divide. To *separate* is "to set apart," "to keep apart," "to distinguish," "to differentiate between," "to detach": "Please *separate* the white shirts from the colored ones." "When did you and your partner *separate?*" "The candidate proposed that New York City *separate* from the State of New York." *Divide* has much the same meaning as *separate* but is correctly used to imply (1) splitting or breaking up according to a plan and (2) rearrangement in hostile or opposing groups: "The candy was *divided* equally among the children." "This issue will *divide* local and state representatives along party lines."

serve, service. As verbs, these words have similar meanings but are not always interchangeable. One could say "A good bus line *serves* the residents of that area," but *services* would be out of place in that sentence. Similarly, *service,* not *serve,* is appropriate in a statement such as "That company will install and *service* the elevators in your building." Because of the influence of advertising and the fact that apparently many people feel that *serve* suggests menial work, *service* is used in many writing situations where *serve* would "serve" as well. *See also* MAINTAIN.

set, sit. Predominantly a transitive verb, *set* means "to put," "to place": "*Set* the box on the floor, please." *Sit* is predominantly an intransitive verb with a basic meaning of "to place oneself": "When I *sit* down, you come and *sit* beside me." "*Set* used for *sit,* and *sit* for *set,* in the meanings indicated, are nonstandard. Do not say "*Set* yourself down" or "*Sit* it here."

Both *set* and *sit* have special meanings. The following are standard usage: "The sun *sets* behind that mountain every afternoon." "The house *sits* in a valley." "*Sit* the baby in the chair and then *set* her on her feet." The following expressions involving *set* and *sit* are hackneyed: "*set* one's face (or one's mind) against," "*set* one's heart on," "*set* by the ears," "*set* one's hand to the plow," "*set* the world on fire," "*set* one's teeth on edge," "*set* about," "*set* against," "*set* down," "*set* aside," "*set* forth," "*set* in," "*set* off," "*set* apart," "*set* upon," "all *set*," "get *set*," "*set* store by," "*sit* in on," "*sit* on," "*sit* out," "*sit* pretty," "*sit* tight," "*sit*-down strike," "*sit*-in," and "*sitting* duck."

settle. *See* LOCATE.

setup. In the sense of "an easy victory" or "an opponent easy to defeat," *setup* is slangy and informal: "This game will be a *setup* for our team." *Setup* is also widely used to refer to anything related to organization, circumstances, or conditions: "What's the new *setup* for the sales conference?" Although the term is a logical combination of *set* and *up*, it has become trite through overuse. Other words that might serve better: *plan, scheme, project, design, pattern, arrangement,* and *stratagem.*

sewage, sewerage. *Sewage* is the waste matter that passes through sewers. *Sewerage* means "a system of sewers," "the apparatus for removing waste water and refuse": "How much *sewage* will this *sewerage* system accommodate in an hour?"

sex. *See* GENDER.

shall, will. Distinctions in the use of *shall* and *will* have broken down, but some careful speakers still observe these principles: (1) Use *shall* in the first person and *will* in the second or third person to express future time: "I (we) *shall* leave soon." "You (he, they) *will* leave soon." (2) For expressing command or determination, use *will* in the first person and *shall* in the second and third: "I *will* speak, no matter who tries to stop me." "You *shall* speak (meaning 'You *must* speak')." (3) To express willingness, promise, or intention, use *will* (same verb, different meaning) with all personal pronouns: "I *will* help you now." "You *will* be a success." Even so accomplished a user of language as Winston Churchill disregarded the basic rules for using *shall* and *will* when he declared: "We shall fight on the beaches, we shall fight on the landing grounds, we shall fight in the fields and in the streets, we shall fight in the hills; we shall never surrender."

In general, use *should* and *would* according to recommendations for *shall* and *will*. Both *should* and *would* also have specialized meanings, *should* in the sense of obligation and *would* in the sense of habitual action: "You *should* go now." "He *would* take a walk every day."

share. *See* PART.

shibboleth. This is a term used to refer to a test or formula. *Shibboleth* was a word chosen by the Gileadites to distinguish fleeing Ephraimites who could not pronounce the *sh* sound. (The incident is recounted in the Old Testament, Judges 12.) *Shibboleth* has been extended in meaning (in Hebrew it meant "an ear of corn" and "a stream") beyond the concept of testing to refer to a peculiarity or oddity of speaking, acting, or dressing that distinguishes a particular class or set of persons: "The ability to make small talk is a *shibboleth* of that segment of café society."

ship. *See* BOAT.

shop, store. These words have numerous distinct uses separate from each other, but they share the meaning of an establishment where merchandise is sold, usually on a retail basis. *Store* is a more general term, *shop* being reserved for a small store or for a department in a large store selling a select or special type of goods. One refers to a department *store* or grocery *store* and to a *shop* that sells hats or gloves or china or other specialized wares. Again, one might mention a shoe *store* but would refer to a shoe repair *shop*.

short. *See* BRIEF.

should. *See* SHALL.

shut. *See* CLOSE, SHUT.

shy. *See* MODEST.

sick. *See* ILL.

sight, spectacle. Both *sight* and *spectacle* mean something seen or able to be seen: "We soon caught *sight* of land." "Palmetto trees on the beach were a lovely *spectacle.*" *Spectacle* is reserved for a *sight* that is unusual, such as a curiosity or marvel or some public performance or display. In this sense, it closely resembles the meaning of *sights:* "Lights on the Eiffel Tower are a *spectacle,* one of the marvelous *sights* of Paris." *Sight* is often used in a derisive or derogatory way (In that coat you are a *sight*). *Spectacle* can also be used in a disparaging sense (make a *spectacle* of oneself).

signature, autograph. Both *signature* and *autograph* mean the name of a person as written by himself (herself). Even the X or other mark that indicates identity may be called a *signature;* the word comes from a Latin term meaning "to mark with a sign." *Autograph* (from the Greek words meaning "written by oneself") is usually applied to the handwritten name of a person of distinction or notoriety. Those celebrities asked for an *autograph* may or may not write their actual names; many have a professional name different from their real name. If so, they give an *autograph* (assumed name) to those who ask but use a *signature* for checks or other transactions requiring genuine identification.

simile, metaphor. A *metaphor* is a figure of speech in which a term or phrase is applied to something to which it is not literally applicable. This is done in order to suggest a resemblance: "She is a perfect lamb." *Metaphor* and *simile* are allied in meaning; a *simile* expresses resemblance directly but does so by using *as, as if, like:* "She is as sweet *as* a flower." Unfortunately, most metaphors and some similes are either strained or trite. Many figures of speech are often mixed; standard advice is to sustain one figure and not suddenly shift to another: "We had the crankcase drained and thus nipped our trouble in the bud."

simple reason. Three good reasons exist for not using this tiresome expression: (1) The word *simple* implies a superior attitude toward the reader or listener (Why didn't you think of this yourself; you numskull?). (2) The *reason* may not be *simple* but quite complex. (3) The expression is uneconomical. Everything that "for the *simple reason* that" says can be expressed by one word, *because*.

simplistic, simplified. Each of these adjectives means "made less complex and complicated," "made easier or plainer": "This is a *simplified* (or *simplistic*) summary of the situation." *Simplistic* is currently a "vogue" word, overused because apparently it seems to many people to be more sophisticated and learned than *simplified*. Actually, *simplistic* has taken on the meaning of "overly *simplified*," "characterized by extreme or excessive *simplification*": "Your explanation of this serious problem is inadequate and *simplistic*."

simulate. *See* DISSIMULATE.

since, yet. Both of these words are adverbs expressing time but doing so in different ways and meanings. *Since* can mean (1) "at some past time," "before now" (She has long *since* forgotten me); (2) "between then and now" (He has *since* left town); (3) "from some time in the past up until now" (She came last week and has been making trouble ever *since*). The word *until* is usually superfluous in a *since* phrase: "He had not voted *since* 1972 *until* this fall" can better be expressed "He had not voted from 1972 *until* this fall." *Yet* means (1) "at this time" (Don't go *yet*); (2) "thus far" (The signal had not *yet* come); (3) "still" (Something is *yet* to be done); (4) "in addition" (*yet* another time); (5) "nevertheless" (poorer *yet* wiser). Because both *since* and *yet* cover time up to the present, an accompanying verb should be in the perfect, not past, tense: "There has been no agreement on the dispute that *has prevented* progress *since* the meeting began." "*Have* you *written* to her *yet?*" "Did you eat *yet?*" is nonstandard. "Have you eaten *yet?*" is standard. *See also* AGO.

sit. *See* SET.

slack, slake. As verbs, *slack* means "to shirk," "to leave undone," and *slake* means "to refresh," "to allay thirst": "He *slacked* his work for a minute while he *slaked* his thirst." Because both words can mean "to make less active and intense," they are often confused through misspelling or mispronunciation. In this latter meaning, *slack* is always followed by *up* or *off*. "He *slacked up* in his efforts." "Your indifference has *slaked* their enthusiasm."

slander. *See* LIBEL.

slogan, motto. Although *slogan* is derived from a Gaelic word meaning "army cry" and *motto* from a Latin word meaning "utterance," they are closely related in sense. Each suggests a saying or expression used as a guiding principle or rule of conduct. *Slogan* specifically means a "catchword" or "catch phrase" used by a political party, fraternity, or school group or in advertising and promotion: "The *slogan* of this company is 'When better beds are made, we'll make them.'" A *motto* is usually briefer than a *slogan* and more likely to express a moral aim or purpose: "The *motto* of the Boy Scouts of America is 'Be Prepared.'" Words related to *slogan* and *motto,* but with shadings of meaning, include *maxim, saying, saw, aphorism, catchword,* and *watchword.*

slow, slowly. Each of these words is an adverb, so that one can say "Drive *slow*" or "Drive *slowly.*" Careful speakers use *slowly* in such an expression. *Slow* is preferred in statements such as "This watch runs *slow.*"

sludge, slush. These words are closely related; each refers to mud, mire, or ooze. *Sludge* is often applied to matter that is heavier or bulkier than that referred to as *slush,* perhaps because of the sound of the two words. That is, the thick deposit of sediment in a steam boiler or the viscous oil waste in a garage is *sludge;* watery mire and partly melted snow are *slush.* Such a distinction, however, is more a matter of taste and feeling than of actual meaning.

smear. *See* SCHMIER.

smell, stink, scent. These nouns refer to the qualities and properties of objects and items that can be detected through the olfactory organs, or what is generally called the sense of smell. *Smell,* along with *odor,* is the most general, most commonly used, and most neutral of these words. A *smell* can be pleasant or unpleasant, but usually the word carries no particular connotation, favorable or unfavorable. *Stink* and its companion word *stench* always refer to disagreeable and unpleasant odors, especially those resulting from the decomposition of organic matter, such as the dead bodies of animals. *Scent* applies to a distinctive odor, usually delicate and usually connected directly with physical qualities of the item or object itself. Thus one would refer to the *smell* of wet grass, the *stink* of a dead body, and the *scent* of roses. As verbs, *scent* has principal parts of *scent, scented, scented; stink,* of *stink, stank, stunk; smell,* of *smell, smelled* (or *smelt*), *smelled* (or *smelt*). Words related to this trio of terms are *aroma, fragrance, stench, perfume, savor, bouquet, exhalation,* and *redolence.*

so. *So* is primarily an adverb meaning "thus" or "in the manner indicated": "He is ill and has long been *so.*" This overworked word can also be an adjective (What you say is not *so*), a pronoun (Be quiet and stay *so*), a conjunction (Drive slowly *so* you will not have an accident), and an interjection (*So!* I've caught you in the act). Two major objections to the use of *so* are (1) its overuse in statements where *therefore, thus,* and *consequently* would serve better and (2) its overuse as an intensive instead of *indeed* or *extremely:* "We couldn't go that day, *so* we sold our tickets" (use *therefore* or *consequently*). "After her departure, I felt *so* sad" (use *extremely* or some other intensive). *So* comes to mind "so" easily that everyone tends to overuse it.

so . . . as. *See* AS . . . AS.

so-called. Meaning "called by this term" or "so designated," *so-called* is usually employed to suggest incorrectness, sarcasm, or some degree of doubt: "This is a *so-called* improvement." "Those were his *so-called* friends." When *so-called* follows the noun to which it refers, the phrase may be written without a hyphen: "Those were our choices, *so called.*"

sociable, social. As nouns, these words have the shared meaning of "an informal gathering," "an occasion for conversation and pleasure": "The children are attending a church *social* (or *sociable*)." In this use, *social* is preferred. As adjectives, *social* and *sociable* have related meanings, but *social* is preferred for referring to community living and association in groups: "This is a highly *social* section of town." *Sociable* is more often applied to persons than is *social* in the sense of "friendly," "pleasant," "affable": "Our senator likes people and is a companionable, *sociable* person." "When you attend that *social*, try to be more *sociable* than you usually are."

solid, stolid. *Solid* has several meanings, *stolid* only one. A *stolid* person is impassive, one who has, or at least reveals, little emotion: "That farmer, immovable in his opinions, is *stolid* not from dullness but from feeling that he is right." *Solid* is correctly used in sentences such as these: "This is a *solid* block of ice (not hollowed out)." "That ring is *solid* gold (of the same substance throughout)." "There is a *solid* (continuous) block of cars." "We ate a *solid* (complete, substantial) meal." "You are a *solid* (upstanding, dependable) citizen." "Give me some *solid* (reliable, concrete) facts." A *solid* (trustworthy) individual may or may not be *stolid* (expressionless).

some, somewhat. *Some* is an adjective of indefinite number (*some* money, *some* fruit). Applied adverbially in the sense of *somewhat* ("rather," "to some degree"), *some* is nonstandard. Say "The patient is *somewhat* (not *some*) better today." *Some* is informal or slangy in the sense of "remarkable": "He is *some* swimmer."

somebody, someone. These terms are interchangeable, although *someone* is considered more "refined" and "cultured" than *somebody*. Both words are standard. Each requires a singular verb: "*Somebody* (or *someone*) *is* in the house." Proper forms of the possessive are *somebody else's* and *someone else's*, not *somebody's else* or *someone's else*. *See also* ELSE.

someplace. As is pointed out in the entry ANYPLACE, *someplace* is not a standard adverb. Write "I left my coat *somewhere* (not *someplace*)." When *some* is used as an adjective and *place* as a noun, no error is involved:

"There must be *some place* in this town where I can find a decent meal."

some time, sometime, sometimes. When *some* is used as an adjective and *time* as a noun, the expression is written as two words meaning "an indefinite time": "She and I met *some time* (not *sometime*) that year." As an adverb, *sometime* means "at a point in time": "I went to the store *sometime* last week." As an adjective meaning "occasional" or "being such now and then," *sometime* is informal and not recommended for serious writing; avoid such a sentence as "She was a *sometime* leading opera singer." *Sometimes* has the sense of a plural, "at times": "She visits me *sometimes.*" In the sense of "once" or "formerly," *sometimes* is obsolete.

someway, someways. *Someway* is an adverb meaning "in some way or another," "somehow": "She will get the dress *someway.*" The term can also be correctly split: "In *some way* she will get the dress." *Someways* is considered either informal or dialectal and should not be used. Most careful writers prefer the adverb *somehow* to *someway*.

somewhat. *See* SOME.

somewheres. *See* ANYWHERES.

soon. *See* EARLY.

sordid. *See* MORBID.

sort of, sort of a. When used to mean an approximation, *sort of* is informal but not incorrect; *sort of a* is considered both informal and wordy: "Dr. Billings is *sort of* an optimist" (but not *a sort of an*). In the sense of "rather" or "somewhat," *sort of* is dialectal and not recommended for writing or speaking; avoid a sentence such as

"I am *sort of* exhausted." *Sort of,* but not *sort of a,* may be correctly used to refer to a species or general subdivision: "What *sort of* snake is that?" Despite widespread usage to the contrary, one should neither say nor write "those *sort*" or "these *sort*": "Those *sorts* of tests are difficult." *See also* KIND.

special. *See* ESPECIAL.

specie, species. *Specie* means "coined money" or "coins." This word is a collective noun and has no plural: "The *specie* of France and that of Great Britain do not closely resemble each other." "The payment must be in *specie.*" *Species* has only one form for singular and plural in the meaning of a class with common characteristics: "What *species* of monkey is this?" One cannot refer to a category of organisms as *a specie:* "The *Anopheles punctipennis* is a *species* (not *specie*) of mosquito."

spectacle. *See* SIGHT.

spiritual, spirituous. The first of these words means "not material or physical," "relating to the spirit or soul": "Our pastor is a *spiritual* man." "His pain was more *spiritual* than physical." *Spirituous* means "having the nature of, or containing, alcohol produced by distillation": "Whiskey is a *spirituous* beverage."

splutter, sputter. *Splutter* is a combination of *splash* and *sputter*. *Splutter* and *sputter* mean much the same and can be used interchangeably in these senses: "to speak incoherently," "to say something hastily and confusedly," "to make a spitting sound": "The frightened boy *spluttered* (or *sputtered*) some kind of reply." "It is possible that to some ears *splutter* sounds more vigorous and picturesque than *sputter,* but choice between them is personal, not entirely logical.

spoiled, spoilt. The past tense and past participle of the verb *spoil* are *spoiled* or *spoilt*. Both forms are correct: "The food was *spoiled* (or *spoilt*)." "The mother *spoiled* (or *spoilt*) her children." "This stationery has been *spoiled* (or *spoilt*)." *Spoiled* is more generally used and therefore is recommended.

spoonful, spoonfuls. *See* -FUL. A recipe might read "Add three tablespoons full of broth and continue cooking." The *tablespoons* will be neither cooked nor edible; make the word *tablespoonfuls*.

sprain, strain. A *sprain* is a painful wrenching or tearing of the ligaments of a joint, such as an ankle or wrist. It may result from a *strain*, a more general term that implies misuse, overuse, or overexertion. That is, a *strain* is a stretching or forcing beyond proper limits: "Because he *strained* ligaments when he landed, he *sprained* his ankle."

sputter. *See* SPLUTTER.

square. This is slang for "a rigidly conventional person": "Get with it; don't be a *square*." Trite phrases and words to be wary of: "*square* peg in a round hole," "on the *square*," "*square* shooter," "*square* off" ("assume a fighting position"), "*square* up" ("to settle," "to pay"), "*square* the circle" ("to attempt the impossible"), "*square* with one's conscience," "*square* meal," and "*square* deal."

stalactite, stalagmite. Only geologists are likely to use these terms often, but others have difficulty in remembering which hangs down from the roof of a cave and which rises up from the floor. Both *stalactite* and *stalagmite* refer to deposits of calcium carbonate formed by the dripping of water. A *stalactite* is a column that hangs down; one that builds up from the floor is a *stalagmite*. Suggestion for remembering: associate *stalac-*

tite with *icicle*. If that doesn't help, think of *mite* and *mire*.

stamp. *See* STOMP.

standpoint. *See* POINT OF VIEW.

stanza. *See* VERSE.

stash. *See* CACHE.

stationary, stationery. *Stationary* is an adjective meaning "having a fixed or unmoving position," "not moving": "This huge rock is *stationary.*" "For a week, the stock market has been almost *stationary.*" *Stationery,* a noun, means "writing paper and envelopes." The word has been extended to include office supplies and retail shops that sell stationery and related supplies: "This stationer's supply of *stationery* is almost exhausted." How to remember which is which? *Stationary* means "standing" (note the *a*'s). *Stationery* is used for writing letters (note the *e*'s).

statue, stature, statute. A *statue* (STACH·oo) is "an image," *stature* (STACH·uhr) means "height" or "status," and a *statute* (STACH·oot) is a "law": "This is a *statue* of Senator Smith, who helped frame many *statutes* and who achieved great *stature* as an orator."

stay, stop. As a verb, *stay* has several synonyms: *remain, linger, tarry, sojourn, abide, wait,* etc. As a verb, *stop* is related to *arrest, check, halt,* and *terminate*. As these parallel words suggest, *stay* and *stop* do differ in meaning. For example, one *stays* rather than *stops* at a motel because *stay* means "to remain," "to abide," and *stop* means "to terminate." However logical this distinction, Americans pay little attention to it: one *stops* or *stays* at a hotel or motel as he pleases. *Stop* is a more popular word than *stay,* as note such phrases as "*stop* over," "*stop* by," "*stop* off," and "*stop* in," to which has been added the noun *stopover*.

stevedore. *See* LONGSHOREMAN.

still, still and all. *Still* is a proper adjective, conjunction, and adverb with numerous correct uses. Unfortunately, it is often dropped into a sentence as a filler with little or no meaning. Even more useless is *still and all*. *Still* has a legitimate function in speech or writing, but there is no excuse for *still and all*.

stimulant, stimulus. *Stimulant* refers to anything that temporarily arouses or speeds up mental or physical activity: "Alcohol, thought to be a *stimulant*, is actually a depressant." A *stimulus* is something that rouses to action, that incites activity, that produces a response: "Additional pay is a *stimulus* to harder work." The effect of a *stimulant* is short-lived; that of a *stimulus* does not necessarily involve time restrictions. The plural of *stimulant* is *stimulants;* that of *stimulus* is *stimuli*.

stink. *See* SMELL.

stolid. *See* SOLID.

stomach. *See* ABDOMEN.

stomp, stamp. *Stomp* means "to tread on," "to trample," "to step violently on or upon." As a verb, *stamp* has several meanings, including that of *stomp:* One can *stamp* (or *stomp*) a snake to death. One is more likely to refer to *stomping* horses or herds than to *stamping* horses or herds, but both adjectives are correct. In the sense of eliminating, getting rid of, and striking the ground with the human foot, *stamp* is preferred: "This action will *stamp* out slums." "In her anger, she *stamped* her foot on the floor."

stop. *See* STAY.

store. *See* SHOP.

stout. *See* FAT.

straight, strait. *Straight,* as an adjective, means "uncurved," "direct," "unswerving": "The road is *straight.*" "When you tell that story, try to keep a *straight* face." As an adverb, *straight* means "directly" and "honestly": "Please go *straight* home." "Don't lie, speak *straight.*" *Strait* means (1) "a narrow passage of water"; (2) "restricted," "confined"; (3) "a position of difficulty or distress" (usually in the plural): "This *strait* is just wide enough to accommodate the large ship." "*Strait* is the gate, and narrow is the way." "You must be in desperate *straits* for companionship."

strain. *See* SPRAIN and STRESS.

strange. *See* FUNNY.

strangely enough. *See* ENOUGH.

strategy, tactics. Essentially, *strategy* has to do with the planning of schemes or operations, *tactics* with putting these plans into effect. Military *strategy* is the art or science of command as applied to the overall conduct of large-scale operations. *Strategy* in nonmilitary application refers to the skill of employing stratagems in business, politics, domestic life, and so forth: "He has a definite *strategy* for investing money." "What is his *strategy* in dealing with his wife?" *Tactics* is the technique or science of obtaining or securing what *strategy* has planned. Although plural in form, *tactics* is used with a singular verb when it refers to the art, science, or general mode of procedure used in gaining success or advantage. When *tactics* refers to the maneuvers themselves, the verb is plural. *Tactic,* singular in form, is always used with a singular verb. "His *tactic is* to upset his opponents." "The *tactics* of military strategy *is* a complicated study." "The generals' *tactics* in that battle *were* masterly."

stratum, strata. A *stratum* is a horizontal layer of any material; in geology, the term refers to a layer of rock having the same composition throughout. *Strata* is the plural of *stratum*. "This is a *stratum* of volcanic rock." "This novel contains many *strata* of meaning." It is correct to say "One stratum *is*" and "All strata *are*." Neither *stratums* nor *stratas* is generally acceptable as a plural, although both occasionally appear in print.

stress, strain. *Stress* means "pressure," "the force exerted upon one object by another." For discussion of *strain, see* SPRAIN. Examples of use: "Under heavy *stress*, the cable broke." "It is a *strain* to work sixteen hours a day." The German expression *Sturm und Drang* literally means "storm and *stress*" but can equally well mean "*strain* and *stress*."

student. *See* PUPIL.

subconscious. *See* UNCONSCIOUS.

subsequent, consequent. These words are easily confused. *Subsequent* means "succeeding," "following in order or time": "*Subsequent* to his release from prison, he got back his old job." Each of the following constructions indicates "later": "*subsequent* events," "a talk held *subsequent* to the party," "a talk held *subsequently*." *Consequent* means "following as a natural result, effect, or conclusion": "Reckless driving was the charge, and *consequent* investigation caused him to lose his license." A *consequent* occurrence is always a *subsequent* happening, but a *subsequent* event is not necessarily *consequent*.

subsist. *See* EXIST.

substantially. *See* ESSENTIALLY.

successive. *See* CONSECUTIVE; *see also* CONTINUAL.

succinct, concise. These adjectives apply to the stating of much in few words. *Succinct,* from Latin words meaning "girded," "tucked up," emphasizes compactness and the omission of all elaboration: "This story is *succinct* because it contains no editorializing and very little description of setting." *Concise,* from a Latin term meaning "to cut," implies solidity and density achieved through the elimination of all unnecessary words: "Many of Hemingway's stories are *concise* because they contain few adjectives and adverbs and little direct characterization." Related words are *laconic, terse, epigrammatic, pithy, brief, curt,* and *condensed.*

succubus. *See* INCUBUS.

such. As a pronoun, *such* is informal, if not substandard, when used to mean "that" or "the same." Avoid saying "I could not bear *such*" when you mean "I could not bear *that* (or *the same*)." (*See* SAID.) *Such* should not be used to mean "the like," either. Avoid saying "At the circus we ate peanuts, popcorn, and *such.*" *Such* is colloquial and to be avoided as an intensive: "She is *such a* nice girl" could be better expressed by substituting *very* or *exceptionally* or *unusually* for *such a.* An overworked phrase meaning "undetermined" is "*such* and *such*" (at *such* and *such* a place).

sufficient. *See* ENOUGH.

suit, suite. These words have a common origin but are used in different ways. One speaks of "a *suit* of clothes," "a *suit* at law," "a *suit* of cards." *Suite* means "a company of followers," "a connected series of rooms," "a musical composition." *Suit* is pronounced "syoot";

suite is pronounced "sweet." In standard usage, only *suite* can be applied to "matched furniture pieces," but in this usage *suite* is often pronounced incorrectly like *suit*. Why not avoid difficulty and say "*set* of furniture"?

summary. *See* RÉSUMÉ.

summit, peak, top. Each of these words refers to the highest point of something, with *top* being the term in widest use (the *top* of the hill, the *top* of the house). *Peak* means a pointed extremity, the pointed *top* of a hill or mountain (*peak* of a roof, *peak* of a cap, *peak* of Mount Monadnock). *Summit* is close in meaning to *peak*, "the highest point of an elevation of any kind": "The *summit* of the hill was covered with wild flowers." Related words which also suggest the figurative meanings of *summit*, *peak*, and *top* include *apex*, *pinnacle*, *zenith*, *elevation*, *height*, *climax*, and *acme*. Thus one refers to a student at the *top* of his class as one who has reached the *summit* of his goals. When traffic is heaviest, it is at its *peak*. Diplomats conduct talks at the *summit*.

Sunday. *See* SABBATH.

sunlight, sunshine. Both *sunlight* and *sunshine* mean "the light of the sun," but *sunshine* additionally means (1) "happiness" or "cheerfulness," (2) the "source of happiness or cheerfulness," and (3) the "shining of the sun." "*Sunlight* lasted only a few hours today." "He basked in the *sunshine* of his friend's affection." "Your smile is all the *sunshine* I need." "She lies in the *sunshine* for an hour every sunny day."

superfluous. *See* REDUNDANT.

superior than, superior to. Only *superior to* is idiomatically acceptable: "She is *superior to* (not *than*) everyone else in the shop." *See also* DIFFERENT FROM and INFERIOR THAN.

supernatural, unnatural. *Supernatural* means "above or beyond what is natural," "miraculous," "abnormal," "not explainable by natural laws," "attributed to the exercise of divine power": "Ancient Greeks and Romans believed in *supernatural* beings whom they called gods." "The existence of this enormous crater must be traced to *supernatural* forces." "The guided missile seemed to accelerate at *supernatural* speed." *Unnatural* means "contrived," "artificial," "inhuman," "violating natural feelings," "inconsistent with prevailing customs": "This child's treatment of his parents is *unnatural.*" "It is *unnatural* for a physician to be a sadist." That which is *supernatural* is *unnatural,* but much that is *unnatural* is not *supernatural.* Related but relatively uncommon words are *supranatural,* a synonym of *supernatural,* and *preternatural,* meaning "exceptional," "unusual," and "abnormal."

supine. *See* PROSTRATE.

supplementary, complementary. *Supplementary,* an adjective, refers to something added in order to complete something else, to make up a deficiency, to extend or strengthen an object, item, or idea: "A food allowance was *supplementary* to his weekly pay." "He took vitamins as a *supplementary* part of his diet." *Complementary* is closely related to *supplementary* in meaning but emphasizes not so much addition as it does completion or an essential addition: "In winning basketball, offense and defense are *complementary.*" "In everyone's life, food and sleep are *complementary.*" "As a scholar, Professor Auray insists that reading plays a *complementary* role in his life."

suppose. *See* IMAGINE.

supposedly, presumably. *Supposedly* means "in a way assumed to be true or presumed as real or genuine." That is, what is *supposedly* a certain situation may not be a correct or accurate assumption: "He is *supposedly* in love with Helen, but this attachment seems to be only a rumor." *Presumably* means "probably," "reasonably," "capable of being taken for granted": "Since he is an expert, *presumably* he knows what he's talking about." What is *presumably* a truth is a probable or likely truth; what is *supposedly* a truth is a doubtful, questionable, suspicious, or undecided truth.

sure, surely. Correct usage calls for a strict division between *sure* (an adjective) and *surely* (an adverb). One says "That was a *sure* sign of his interest" and "That was *surely* a sign of his interest." In the first sentence, *sure* qualifies the noun *sign;* in the second, *surely* modifies the verb *was*. *Sure* can be employed informally as an adverb (*sure* enough), but this colloquial use is not recommended for careful writing. *See also* CERTAIN.

surprise. *See* AMAZE.

suspected. *See* ALLEGED.

sympathy. *See* EMPATHY.

synopsis. *See* RÉSUMÉ.

syntax. *See* GRAMMAR.

synthesis. *See* ANALYSIS.

systemize, systematize. Each of these words, both correct, means "to formulate," "to reduce to a system," "to arrange in a certain order": "Please *systemize* (or *systematize*) the filing cabinets in this office." "You can work more efficiently if you will *systematize* (or *systemize*) the contents of your kitchen." *Systematize* is the more commonly used term. Approximate synonyms are *organize, dispose, articulate,* and *order*.

T

tablespoonful. *See* -FUL and SPOONFUL.

taciturn. *See* RETICENT.

tactics. *See* STRATEGY.

tactile, tactual, textile. These "look-alikes" are often confused and with good reason, too, because *tactile* and *tactual* are close in meaning and use. *Tactile* and *tactual* refer to the sense of touch, with *tactual* being the somewhat more general and more generally used word. *Tactile* means "endowed with the sense of touch"; *tactual* means "arising from, or due to, touch," "communicating the sensation of contact": "The paws of a dog are extremely *tactile.*" "A kiss is usually an enjoyable *tactual* experience." *Textile* means cloth or fabric that is woven or knitted of fiber and yarn. As an adjective, *textile* applies to the manufacture of textiles. "Cotton is a popular *textile.*" "All these persons are employees of the local *textile* mill."

take. *See* BRING. *Take* occurs in numerous informal or incorrect expressions appearing in everyday conversation. "*Take* and" (I *took and* hit him on the nose) is an illiteracy. In the expression "*take,* for example," *take* is unnecessary and should be omitted. "*Take* in" is informal when used to mean "to attend" (We *took in* a show). "*Take* on" is informal in the sense of showing emotion (Don't *take on* so over the loss). "*Take* sick" is informal for "to become ill" (He *took sick* and nearly died). "*Take* it easy" and "*Take* care" are clichés. In fact, "*Take* it easy" and "Don't *take* any wooden nickels" are among the most tiresome of all hackneyed expressions.

take place. *See* HAPPEN.

talent. *See* GENIUS.

tall, lofty, high. Each of these terms means "having greater than ordinary height," "extending upward." Which of them to use depends upon what is being mentioned: one refers to a *tall* or *lofty* tree, a *high* or *lofty* mountain, a *high* wall, a *tall* woman, and a *lofty* elevation. *Tall* and *high*, the most general of these words, are most frequently used. *Tall* is used to refer to something that rises to a considerable extent and also applies particularly to people: "a *tall* building," "a *tall* boy." *High* applies to that which rises well above a base: "a *high* hill," "a shelf *high* on the wall." *Lofty* describes what is imposingly or majestically elevated: "This huge room has a *lofty* ceiling." Each of the terms is also used figuratively: "a man of *high* purpose"; "a *tall* tale"; "a *lofty* ambition"; "*high* ideals," "*lofty* pretensions," "*tall* talk."

tantalize, harass. *Tantalize* means "to torment," "to tease by arousing expectations," "to disappoint repeatedly." *Harass* implies persecution through demands, threats, or annoyances; it also suggests disturbing and troubling with repeated attacks. A girl *tantalizes* a boy when she seems to be responsive but refuses to go out with him. A telephone operator is *harassed* by the stream of silly requests that she receives. Related words are *pester*, *badger*, *hound*, *plague*, *bait, torment, disappoint, harry, vex, rack,* and *distress.*

target, objective. Literally, a *target* is something to be shot at, but its meaning has been extended to include any desired object and also anything that is to be acted upon with a view to altering it. An *objective* is something worked toward as a goal. *Target* has become a "fad" word in recent years and is often misused for *objective*. One can have a *target* or an *objective* in life, such as becoming a millionaire, but although one can raise or lower his *target,* it seems silly to speak of "achieving a *target.*" If one wishes to stop overusing *target* and desires to reduce his use of *objective,* he can try *purpose, goal, intent, intention, end, aim,* and *object.*

Tartar, Tatar. Standard dictionaries differ in their recommendation for the preferred use of this term. Both *Tatar* and *Tartar* refer to a member of one of the Mongolian tribes under Genghis Khan and his descendants which overran much of Asia and Eastern Europe in the thirteenth century. The term (either spelling) is also applied to descendants of such peoples who now live in Central Asia. By extension, both *Tatar* and *Tartar* mean "an unruly, intractable, or savage person." The expression "to catch a *tartar*" means "to deal with someone who is troublesome or powerful." Recommendation: use either *Tartar* or *Tatar* in ordinary writing; use *Tatar* if you are dealing with ethnic or cultural matters.

tasteful, tasty. *Tasteful* is standard in the sense of "having or displaying good taste." *Tasty* means only "having a pleasing flavor," "savory." One should usually refer to a *tasteful* affair or ceremony and to a *tasty* meal (which might also be served in a *tasteful* manner): "The diplomatic reception was a *tasteful* affair, and the food served at it was *tasty.*"

Tatar. *See* TARTAR.

teach. *See* LEARN.

teaspoonful. *See* -FUL.

teeth. For no particularly good reason, one has a *toothache*, not a *teethache*, even if more than one *tooth* is hurting. One also refers to a *toothbrush* and to *tooth* marks, although the brush works on more than one *tooth* and marks result from the bite of *teeth*. *Teeth,* the plural of *tooth,* outscores the singular form in the number of hackneyed expressions in which both appear: "long in the *tooth*" ("old," "elderly"), "*tooth* and nail" ("fiercely," "as hard as possible"), "a *toothsome* invitation," "by the skin of one's *teeth,*" "a kick in the *teeth,*" "put *teeth* in (or into)," "show one's *teeth,*" "put (or set) one's *teeth* on edge," "to the *teeth*" ("entirely," "fully"), "to throw into someone's *teeth*" ("to reproach"), and "cut one's *teeth* on" (referring to action during one's youth).

tell, inform. *Tell* is the commonly used word meaning "to narrate," "to communicate," "to recount," "to express with words": "*Tell* me a story." "*Tell* us what you did today." Mark Twain once wrote, "When in doubt, *tell* the truth." *Inform* conveys much the same meaning as *tell,* but it is a more formal word for disclosing or imparting information, often important or incriminating information: "Please *inform* the police of your accident." "Were you *informed* about the search warrant for your house?" *See also* DIVULGE.

temporal, temporary. These words refer to time, but in different ways. *Temporal* means "limited by time," "concerned with affairs of this world," "worldly, not spiritual"; "As a state official, he is occupied with *temporal* affairs that come up every day." "Many priests have little concern for *temporal* matters." *Temporary* means "impermanent," "transient," "for the time being": "These are *temporary* arrangements only." "She took a *temporary* job until she could find a permanent one."

temporize, extemporize. *Temporize* means "to compromise," "to act evasively so as to gain time or advantage," "to postpone action or a decision": "We need relief; don't *temporize* any longer." "Many a public official has found that he must *temporize* if he wishes to hold his office." *Extemporize* means to "speak with little preparation," "to say something without advance notice of having to speak": "A glib speaker, Senator Goff *extemporized* for nearly an hour." *Temporize* applies principally to actions, *extemporize* to words.

tend to. *See* ATTEND TO.

terminal, terminus. These words have a common origin in the Latin word *terminus*, meaning "boundary" or "limit." *Terminal* means (1) "either end of a transportation line" and (2) "concluding," "final": "Grand Central Station is a *terminal* for a major railroad serving the New England states." "Just before his discharge from service, the soldier was granted *terminal* leave." "In most instances, cancer is a *terminal* illness." *Terminus* also means "the end of something" and is used to refer to an objective or goal: "The campsite was the *terminus* of our hike that day." "The *terminus* of his ambition was election as governor of the state." The plural of *terminus* is *terminuses* or *termini*.

testimony. *See* EVIDENCE.

test out. This is a common expression, but a wordy one. *Out* is unnecessary: one *tests* (not *tests out*) a device or machine. *Out* is also not needed in phrases such as "prove *out*," "project *out*," and "process *out*."

textile. *See* TACTILE.

than, then. These words are often confused in writing and sometimes in pronunciation. *Than* is a conjunction in clauses of comparison: "He worked better today *than* he did yesterday." *Then* is an adverb of time: "We *then* went to a restaurant." Think of *than* only as a conjunction; it will *then* be easy to remember that a following pronoun should have the same case as its antecedent. Say "Everyone knows more about the situation *than he.*" Say "The supervisors counted on no one more *than him.*" "Someone *then* remarked: 'It is better to remain silent and have some people think me stupid *than* to say something and remove all possible doubt.'"

thanks. A standard but not especially polite word meaning "thank you," *thanks* is a weary cliché by itself and in such expressions as "*thanks* be to God," "*thanks* a million," "*thanks* a bunch," and numerous other phrases. "*Thanking* you in advance" is a hackneyed term in inferior business letters.

that, which, who. Of these relative pronouns, *that* is used to refer to persons, animals, or things; *which* to animals and things, not persons; and *who (whom)* to persons only. *That* is used in restrictive clauses (those that define and limit what precedes by providing information necessary to full understanding): "A man *that* pays his bills promptly is liked by everyone." *Which, who,* and *whom* are used largely in introducing nonrestrictive (not-defining, not-limiting) clauses: "This man, *who* pays his bills promptly, is liked by everyone." *That* is often used in illiterate or wordy expressions. For example, "*that* there" is both wordy and illiterate (*that there* child). "*That* is to say" is a wordy way to express "I mean" or "namely."

That and *which* (especially *which*) are often used in such a way as to create doubt about an antecedent. Avoid saying, for example, "They are coming if their daughter is well enough, *which* I doubt," because *which* has no definite antecedent. Say, instead, ". . . is well enough. However, I doubt that she will be." *See also* THIS.

theater, theatre. These are variant spellings of a word derived from a Greek term meaning "to watch," "to look at." *Theater* is much the more common spelling, although some writers and some persons in theatrical professions seem to feel that *theatre* has more appeal and dignity: "Let's go to the *theater* (*theatre*)." "Medical students spend much time in the operating *theater (theatre)*." "The *theater (theatre)* of war stretched across the entire eastern half of the country."

their, theirs. *Their* is the possessive form of the pronoun *they*. *Theirs* is a possessive pronoun, the absolute form of *their*. *Their* is used to qualify a noun that follows: "*their* dog," "*their* car." *Theirs* is used in other constructions: "a dog of *theirs,*" "all *theirs.*" *Their* means "belonging to them" and should be kept distinct from *there* and *they're*. *Their* is never written with an apostrophe (*theirs,* not *their's*). *See also* THEY.

their, there, they're, there's. These simple words cause considerable confusion but are not really hard to keep straight. *Their* is a possessive pronoun: "That is *their* daughter." *There* means "in or at that place": "I was *there* when she arrived." *They're* is a contraction of "they are": "We are disappointed because *they're* not going with us." *There's* is a shortened form of "there is": "*There's* money in the bank."

theism. *See* DEISM.

then. *See* THAN.

thence, hence. *Thence* is a somewhat old-fashioned and rarely used adverb meaning "from there," "from that place," "from that time," "therefrom": "She went first to the store and *thence* to the beauty parlor." "He declared bankruptcy and *thence* was rarely seen in town." "Our best salesman fell ill; *thence* came our decline in business." *Hence* means "from this time" and "for this reason": "The students will leave a week *hence*." "The dress was well made and *hence* expensive."

there. *See* THEIR.

therefore, therefor. *Therefore* is an adverb meaning "consequently," "as a result": "I've had enough rest, and *therefore* I'll go back to work." "The French philosopher Descartes once wrote 'I think, *therefore* I am.'" *Therefor* is an almost archaic adverb meaning "in exchange for"; "I am returning this suit and wish a refund *therefor*."

therein, wherein. These infrequently used adverbs mean, respectively, "in that circumstance or place" and "in what," "in what way": "I missed making a payment and *therein* lay my error." "This is the house *wherein* Thoreau once lived."

there's. *See* THEIR.

thesaurus. *See* DICTIONARY.

these kind, those kind, these sort, those sort. *Sort* and *kind* are singular nouns; *these* and *those* are plural modifiers. Say and write "this *kind*," "that *kind*," "these *kinds*," "this *sort*," "these *sorts*," and "those *sorts*." *See also* KIND.

they. This word, as well as *their, theirs,* and *them,* should have a definite antecedent (something to which it refers) or should not be used. "*They* have good weather in Hawaii" is a vague statement because no one can tell what or who is meant by *they*. "Hawaii has good weather" makes sense. "In my job, *they* have good training in office techniques" is much clearer if it is revised: "In my job, good training is provided in office techniques."

they're. *See* THEIR.

thief. *See* ROBBER.

thing. This is an all-purpose word used so loosely that it often has no real meaning. For instance, instead of "One *thing* I like about him . . ." why not say "one characteristic," "one trait," or "one distinctive feature"? Because *thing* means "whatever can be thought or believed to have an existence," a good rule to follow is this: one should never say *thing* unless he has some specific entity (object) in mind and then mentions the entity itself. This is a *thing* (rule, prescription, item of advice) none of us will ever achieve or do, but it's a *thing* (endeavor, activity, counsel of perfection) we should try to follow.

this, that. These constantly used words function as both pronouns and adjectives. Brief comments about them are as follows: (1) The plural of *this* is *these;* the plural of *that* is *those: "This* man," *"these* men," *"that* woman," *"those* women." (2) *This* and *that* can be used to mean "how much" and "how many": "I know *this* much." "I know *that* much." "I saw *that* many." "I knew *this* many." (3) *This, that,* and their plural forms *(these, those)* are demonstrative pronouns, which means that they refer to something that can be pointed out: *"This* is my hat." *"That* is yours." *"These* are my gloves." *"Those* are your books." "Is *this* you?" "Is *that* you in the dark?" (4) *This* and its plural can represent or sum up words that follow: "Let me tell you *this*. . . ." "The steps you should take are *these*. . . ." (5) *This* should be used to indicate a person, idea, event, or statement which is considered present, near, just mentioned, or supposed to be understood: *"This* situation now confronting us. . . ." *"This* idea you have expressed. . . ." "Give us *this* day our daily bread." *That* should be used to indicate a person, idea, event, or statement which has not been mentioned before or is not immediately present: "*That* is a lovely sight." "Where were you *that* day?"

thither. *See* HITHER.

thoroughbred, purebred. As noun and adjective, these words mean "of unmixed stock, race, or breed." It is correct to refer to a *thoroughbred* (or *purebred*) horse and to an animal as *thoroughbred* or *purebred*. Only *thoroughbred* is applied to people. When this is done, the implication is that the person referred to is "of good breeding," a phrase interpreted to mean "polite," "courteous," "refined," and "well trained." Although *purebred* may be applied to any domestic animal, the word *pedigreed* is being increasingly used to indicate not only that the animal is of unmixed stock but that a valid written statement exists to attest this fact.

those kind, those sort. *See* THESE KIND; *see also* KIND.

though. *See* ALTHOUGH.

thrash, thresh. These words have a shared meaning of flailing, especially of beating grains and cereals in order to remove the seeds or grain from their straw. That is, a farmer can *thrash* or *thresh* wheat. Commonly, *thrash* is used to mean "to whip," "to flog": "The headmaster *thrashed* the student soundly." *Thresh* is also used to mean "to discuss thoroughly," "to examine carefully": "We spent hours trying to *thresh* out the problem."

tidbit, titbit. A *tidbit* is a choice morsel of some sort, whether of food, scandal, gossip, or news: "We enjoyed delicious *tidbits* during the social hour that followed." "She whispered to me a delicious *tidbit* about the new couple in town." *Titbit* is also a correct spelling, one more often used in Great Britain than in the United States.

'til, till, until. Each of these words means "up until the time of," "near or at a specified time": "We shall wait for you *'til* (or *till* or *until*) sundown." "He did not arrive *until* (or *'til* or *till*) yesterday." *'Til* is a shortened, variant form of *until*. *'Til* seems needless, is obsolescent even in poetic diction, and should be used rarely, if at all. *Till* and *until* are interchangeable; each normally means "before," "up to," or "when." *Until* is usually preferred over *till* at the beginning of a statement because of its sound and to prevent confusion. *'Till* is nonstandard.

timber, timbre. These "look-alikes" have different origins and meanings. *Timber,* from Old English, means wood as a building material (lumber) and wooded land: "We collected enough *timber* to build a small shed." "That is a thriving stand of *timber.*" *Timbre,* from a Greek word meaning "drum," refers to the quality of a sound that distinguishes it from other sounds of identical pitch and volume: "This singer's voice has unusual range and *timbre.*"

tirade. *See* HARANGUE.

'tis, 'twas. These contractions of "it is" and "it was" are poetic and archaic. They should not be used in speech and writing unless some specific effect is intended.

titbit. *See* TIDBIT.

to. In addition to its primary meaning of "in the direction of," *to* is used before a verb to indicate an infinitive (*to* walk, *to* eat). In this usage, it may appear in place of the infinitive: "You may eat now if you want *to* (eat)." *To* is unnecessarily added to many verbs that mean "to assert": "admit *to,*" "certify *to,*" "swear *to.*" The addition of *to* in such instances results in weakening of the verb as well as in wordiness. *To* is nonstandard in the sense of "at": Say "Jack was *at* (not *to*) home." *To* should be omitted after *where*. Say "Where are you going?" not "Where are you going *to?*" *To-do* is slang for "a stir," "bustle," "a fuss." Among overworked expressions involving *to* are "*to* that end," "come *to*" ("return *to* consciousness"), "*to* the best of my knowledge," "turn *to* with a will," "*to* and fro," and "*to* a T" (here *T* stands for *tittle*, a small quantity, jot, particle; the expression means "down to the last small detail"). *See also* IN, INTO.

token. A tiresomely used phrase is "by the same *token*," in which *token* has a meaning of "sign," "mark," or "symbol." Either *moreover* or *furthermore* will express in one word what this trite phrase does in four. "In *token* of" is also hackneyed, as is "*token* of esteem." Possible substitutes for *token: sign, emblem, index, symbol, mark, stamp, image, evidence, proof, memento, augury*, and *indication*.

top. *See* SUMMIT.

tornado. *See* CYCLONE.

tortuous,torturous. *Tortuous* means "winding," "crooked." *Torturous* means "full of, or causing, torture (pain)." "The path of the stream is *tortuous.*" "The surgeon began a *torturous* examination of the patient's neck." Noting that *torturous* has two *r*'s will help one to associate it with *torture*.

toward, towards. These words for "in the direction of," "approaching," and "with regard to" are interchangeable. Take your pick. However, *toward* is one letter shorter and somewhat easier to pronounce. Always lean *toward* the shorter, simpler word.

town. *See* CITY.

trace, vestige. These words refer to something that has existed or gone before. *Trace*, the more widely used, is derived from Latin *tractus*, meaning "a dragging." It applies to any evidence, such as a footprint, a fragment, or a lingering odor that suggests the prior existence or presence of something: "There was a *trace* of perfume in the room." "There was no *trace* of their having spent the night here." *Vestige,* a more limited word, refers to some slight but actual indication (remains) of something that no longer exists: "In his weakened condition, he is a mere *vestige* of his former self." "Not a *vestige* of her once-great beauty remains." Related words include *track, trail, spoor, record, indication,* and *sign*.

trade up. In recent years, this phrase has been widely overused to mean "to substitute for something that one has something else that is more elaborate and expensive." People in *trade* (business, commerce, industry) may need this phrase. Everyone else can do without it.

tragedy. *See* DISASTER.

transitory, transient. These words mean "short-lived," "occurring or existing only briefly," "passing," "fleeting." *Transitory* is usually applied to events and situations; *transient* is applicable to people: "We are *transient* guests at this hotel, not permanent ones." "Going to parties is only a *transitory* pleasure." *Transient,* unlike *transitory,* can also be used as a noun. "A temporary guest is a *transient*." Related adjectives include *ephemeral, fugitive, fleeting, momentary, evanescent, provisional,* and *temporary*.

transparent. *See* OPAQUE.

transpire. *See* HAPPEN.

treachery, treason. Both *treachery* and *treason* imply a willful, deliberate betrayal of trust or confidence. *Treachery* could be applied to the act of being disloyal to a friend or to making unkind statements about someone behind his back. *Treason,* however, applies solely to betrayal of one's country, to disloyalty to one's citizenship, to violation of allegiance to one's chosen land: "Benedict Arnold committed an act of *treason.*" All *treasonable* acts are *treacherous,* but not all *treachery* is *treason.*

treble. *See* TRIPLE.

trigger. As a verb, *trigger* was originally applied to the pressing of the trigger of a gun but now is widely used to mean initiating or setting off something, such as a fight, a celebration, or an argument. *Trigger* is a respectable word as both verb and noun, but it is widely and tiresomely overused. Why not occasionally use *start, cause, produce,* or *signal?*

triple, treble. Although *triple* and *treble* share the meaning of "three-fold," "consisting of three parts," "thrice multiplied," *treble* is rarely used except for its special sense in music: "having the highest range or part" (young choir boys with *treble* voices). One might say "You can *triple* your income this year," although *treble* could be correctly substituted for *triple.* As a verb, adjective, and noun, *triple* is used in sentences such as these: "He *tripled* his planting of vegetables that spring." "This play has *triple* implications." "In the third inning, the player hit a *triple.*" "A rare occurrence in baseball is a *triple* play." Words or phrases of which *triple* forms a part include "*triple* time," "*triple* threat," "*Triple* Alliance," "*triple* measure," "*Triple* Entente," "*triple* rhyme," and "*triple*-decker."

triumphal, triumphant. These words are related, but *triumphal* is usually connected with a planned celebration (a *triumphal* reception). *Triumphant* means "exultant," "victorious" (the *triumphant* basketball team). *Triumphal* is not usually applied to persons but rather to events and activities: "The *triumphant* general led his troops in a *triumphal* victory march."

trivial. *See* PETTY.

trousers. *See* PANTS.

try and. *See* COME AND. Although *try and* is common in speech for *try to,* it should never be used except in highly informal conversation. Avoid such everyday expressions as "*Try and* make me," "*Try and* stop me," and "*Try and* come."

tubercular, tuberculous. Usage has established these adjectives as interchangeable in their meaning of "relating to, or having, tuberculosis." A person afflicted with this disease can be referred to as *tubercular* or *tuberculous*. Although *tubercular* is more often used than *tuberculous,* the latter is regularly used by medical personnel (*tuberculous* growth in the lungs, *tuberculous* cells).

tune. *See* HARMONY.

turgid, turbid. These "look-alikes" are frequently confused but have nothing in common except looks. *Turgid* means "swollen," "overblown," "inflated," "distended," and "pompous": "The candidate then delivered a long, *turgid* speech." "The stream is *turgid* because of spring floods." *Turbid* means "clouded," "not clear," "opaque," "muddy": "The *turgid* river is *turbid* (The swollen river is muddy)." "The solution in this test tube is *turbid,* but it will clear when sediment sinks to the bottom."

'twas. *See* 'TIS.

type. When accompanied by *of, type* is standard usage in expressions such as "that *type of* dress." When *of* is omitted, the expression is nonstandard: "that *type* dress." *Type* is a less general word than *kind* and *sort* (*see* KIND) and is preferably used when a clearly defined category is involved. In all other instances, prefer *kind* or *sort:* "He is the *kind* (or *sort*, not *type*) of man we can believe." Especially avoid such expressions as "high-*type* person" and "low-*type* store." "*Type* of a" is wordy; omit *a*.

typescript. *See* MANUSCRIPT.

typical. Overused by nearly everyone, *typical* should be restricted to the meanings of "distinctive," "characteristic," "representative," and "emblematic." "*Typical* of" is not a synonym for *like*. "Dr. Flack is *like* most pediatricians," not "Dr. Flack is *typical of* most pediatricians."

tyro. *See* AMATEUR.

U

uh-huh, huh-uh. The sound *uh-huh* (hardly a *word*) is an attempt through spelling to indicate a grunted *yes*. *Huh-uh* (or *hunh-uh*) somewhat resembles the sound of a grunted *no*. "*Uh-huh*, I think you're right." "*Huh-uh*, I don't want to go."

umpire, referee. Each of these terms is applied to a person to whom anything is referred for a decision or settlement (*referee* in bankruptcy). In sports, *referees* and *umpires* are officials charged with the regulation of a contest, ruling on plays, etc. Although the terms have the same general meaning, *referee* and *umpire* have different meanings in different sports; for example, we have a *referee* in boxing and basketball, an *umpire* in baseball, and both a *referee* and an *umpire* in football. If you are an athlete or a sportswriter, you know the difference. If you are neither, consult a sports authority; a dictionary will be of little help except as indicated here.

unable. *See* INCAPABLE.

unabridged, abridged, expurgated. *Unabridged* means "not reduced in compass or scope by condensing, omitting, etc."; that is, it means "full-length" or "not cut." *Abridged*, conversely, implies reduction. Thus we speak of an *unabridged* dictionary when we refer to one that is large and definitive, including virtually everything that it could reasonably be expected to contain. An *abridged* dictionary is one which is considerably shorter but which still retains all, or nearly all, information considered essential. An *expurgated* book is one from which passages thought obscene or otherwise objectionable have been removed. *Expurgated* has a sense of purging, of cleansing. *Abridged* and *unabridged* imply "shortened" and "full-length," without any connotation of moral, social, or ethical values.

unapt. *See* INAPT.

unaware, unawares. *Unaware* is an adjective meaning "not aware of," "unconscious of": "He was *unaware* of the danger that lay ahead." "*Unaware* as I was, I made a serious mistake." *Unawares* is an adverb meaning "unexpectedly," "by surprise": "They came upon the scene of the accident *unawares.*" "A sudden heavy snowstorm caught the campers *unawares.*"

uncomparable. *See* INCOMPARABLE.

unconscious, subconscious. *Unconscious* means "without awareness," "without conscious control," "involuntary." A *conscious* person has some control of his faculties, an *unconscious* person may be in a coma, suffering from shock, or asleep. As a noun, the *unconscious* is a term in psychoanalysis meaning that part of the mind containing the psychic material of which a conscious person is unaware. *Unconscious* has an additional meaning of "not intended," "not planned": "My failing to recognize you was an *unconscious* slight." Much less used, *subconscious* has many of the meanings listed here for *unconscious* but is specifically applied to unreportable mental activities, to one's mental processes of which he is not aware: "The *subconscious* thoughts and impulses of thousands of characters have been portrayed and plundered in modern novels and plays."

underlay, underlie. *See* OVERLAY.

undoubtedly, indubitably, doubtlessly. Each of these words means "certainly," "assuredly," "beyond question." They stem from a Latin word meaning "to waver" and hence convey the idea of steadiness, of something not subject to question: "She is *undoubtedly* (or *indubitably* or *doubtlessly*) the kindest person on this block." These words are interchangeable, although *indubitably* is less often used because it sounds somewhat more formal and pretentious than the others. The adjective forms of these adverbs *(undoubted, indubitable, doubtless)* are more often used and are also interchangeable.

uneatable, inedible. These words are synonyms, each meaning "unfit to be eaten," "not eatable": "The dinner was *inedible* (or *uneatable*)." *Inedible* is more often used and does not carry the label of "informal" which *uneatable* does. *Inedible* applies to something that could be eaten if it were properly prepared, cooked, or ripened, whereas *uneatable* is more likely to be applied to items never intended to be eaten, at least not by normal people or animals: wood, coal, iron, chalk, cloth, and the like.

unequivocal. *See* AMBIGUOUS.

unexceptional, unexceptionable. *See* EXCEPTIONABLE, EXCEPTIONAL, to which the meanings of *unexceptionable* and *unexceptional* are directly opposite. "Tom is an adequate worker but only that; his record is fair but *unexceptional.*" "Will has always worked hard; he has an *unexceptionable* record of accomplishment."

unfrequent, infrequent. These adjectives mean "not constant," "not regular," "not habitual," "occurring not often": "His visits to his parents were *infrequent* (or *unfrequent*)." *Infrequent* is much more often used and is preferred. In another adjectival form, however, *unfrequented* (meaning "not regularly visited," "usually empty") is correct, and *infrequented* is not: "This lovely campsite is far off the trail and therefore *unfrequented.*" "The park became littered with refuse and was *unfrequented* until it was cleaned up."

unhuman. *See* INHUMAN.

unilateral, bilateral. *Unilateral* means "involving, affecting, obligating, or recognizing one side only" of two or more parties, persons, or nations. *Bilateral* applies to two sides rather than one. For example, a *bilateral* agreement is binding on both parties, a *unilateral* agreement on only one. When two nations reach a *bilateral* decision, responsibility for it is shared. When a country acts independently, it does so in a *unilateral* way.

uninterested. *See* DISINTERESTED.

unique. This word means "having no like or equal" and expresses absoluteness, as do words such as *round* and *square*. Logically, therefore, the word *unique* cannot be compared; something cannot be "more *unique,*" "less *unique,*" "more *round,*" "less *round.*" If a qualifying word such as *nearly* is used, the illogicality is removed. "This is the *most unique* painting in the museum" is not standard, but "This is the *most nearly unique* painting in the museum" is. *Unique* is not only loosely used but overused; for it, certain words can be substituted on occasion such as *novel, exceptional, remarkable, rare, inimitable, peerless, incomparable, uncommon,* and *unusual. See also* INCOMPARABLE.

university, college. A *university* is an institution of higher learning that embraces two or more *colleges.* In the United States, a representative *university* would have teaching and research facilities comprising a graduate school and a number of other *colleges* (or so-called schools) devoted to arts and sciences and to professional training for law, medicine, and other pursuits. Normally, a *college* awards degrees for undergraduate work only; a *university* is equipped to offer master's and doctoral degrees: "Harvard *College* is a part of Harvard *University*." "After she was graduated from Dartmouth *College*, she studied law at the *University* of Virginia." In proper idiom, one goes *to* college and *to the* university.

unlawful. *See* ILLEGAL.

unless, unless and until. *Unless* means "except on the condition that." Its use as a synonym for *without* is nonstandard. Say "I will not go *unless* you go with me," not "I will not go *without* you go with me." *Unless and until* is a nonstandard phrase; the terms overlap. Do not say "I will not write *unless and until* you write me." Either word will convey the full meaning intended. *See also* IF AND WHEN.

unmoral. *See* AMORAL.

unnatural. *See* SUPERNATURAL.

unorganized, disorganized. *Unorganized* means "lacking system, order, or unity" and, in labor union circles, means "not unionized": "The files in this office are *unorganized.*" "These workers were urged to give up their *unorganized* status and form a union." *Disorganized* also suggests the absence of order and arrangement, but it implies having an existing system upset and overturned. That is, an office which has never been properly organized is *unorganized;* one whose pattern and arrangement have been disrupted or destroyed is *disorganized.*

unpractical. *See* IMPRACTICAL.

unqualified, disqualified. *Unqualified* means (1) "not having proper or required qualifications" (such as achievements, records, background) and (2) "not restricted, modified, or limited": "Until he passes the bar examination, he is *unqualified* to practice law in this state. When he does so, he will have my legal business and my *unqualified* confidence." *Disqualified* means "deprived of rights and privileges," "rendered unfit or declared ineligible": "After his conviction, he was *disqualified* from holding a public position."

unquote. *See* QUOTE.

unreadable. *See* ILLEGIBLE; *see also* READABLE.

unsanitary, insanitary. Each of these words, based on a Latin word for "health," means "unhealthy," "likely to cause disease." Although *unsanitary* is heard more often than *insanitary,* the latter is the preferred listing in five leading dictionaries. If conditions are so unclean, filthy, or contaminated as to be a threat to health, they may be called *unsanitary* or *insanitary,* as one chooses.

unsatisfied, dissatisfied. An *unsatisfied* person is one who is not content, who feels that something or someone has not met his expectations, who is not pleased with some condition or situation: "Your explanation leaves me *unsatisfied.*" "Although growing teen-agers eat a great deal, their hunger is often *unsatisfied.*" *Dissatisfied* means "displeased," "offended," "upset": "I am *dissatisfied* with the salary I am paid." "He had a sulky, *dissatisfied* expression on his face."

unsophisticated, artless. *Unsophisticated* is an adjective that applies to a person who is thought to lack worldly wisdom, who is not urbane, who is not experienced in, or knowledgeable about, prevailing customs and manners of living and thinking. *Artless* implies something of the meaning of *unsophisticated* but suggests a lack of guile or artificiality that results from unconcern about the reactions of other people. That is, an *unsophisticated* person lacks wisdom and experience in certain areas; an *artless* person has the same lacks but doesn't care because he is free from any desire to impress others. *See also* INGENIOUS.

unthinkable. *See* INCONCEIVABLE.

until. *See* 'TIL, TILL, UNTIL. Although the phrase "up *until* the time of" is used in explaining the meanings of these three words, it is doubtful that *up* is needed nearly so often as it is used. From a sentence such as "I'll wait for you *up until* noon" the *up* can be deleted without harm. *See also* UNLESS.

upward, upwards. As an adverb or adjective, *upward* means "toward a higher amount, degree, place, level, or position": "The stock market moved *upward.*" "Today, the market is having an *upward* turn." *Upwards* should not be used in either of these sentences. The phrases "*upward* of" and "*upwards* of" are standard, but only in their proper meaning of "more than," "in excess of a given quantity." Neither phrase should be used to mean "less than," "about," "almost," or "approximately." The statement "His accident cost him *upwards of* $500" means that it cost him more than that amount.

urban, urbane. Each of these words is derived from a Latin term referring to a city, but they have distinct meanings and pronunciations. *Urban* (UHR·bun) means "pertaining to a city," "characteristic of city life." *Urbane* (uhr·BAYN) has a meaning of "reflecting elegance or sophistication," "polished," "suave." "He came from the country and never adjusted to *urban* life." "This woman appears well dressed, poised, and *urbane.*"

us. *See* WE, US.

usage. *See* GRAMMAR.

use, used, used to. As a verb, *use* means "to put into service," "to make use of": "He will *use* my car today." The principal parts of *use* are *use, used, used:* "He *used* my car yesterday." "He has *used* my car for a week." When *did* is added to the verb phrase, however, the word should be *use:* "He did not *use to* borrow my car." When *used* is combined with any form of the verb *be,* it is followed by a verb form ending in *-ing:* "He was *used to* borrowing my car." When one wishes to express habitual action or everyday occurrence, *used* may correctly appear in a statement such as "He *used* to borrow only gasoline." Such expressions as "*used* to could" and "*used* to would" are dialectal and illiterate.

usual, customary, habitual. *Usual* applies to that which is considered normal, common, and expected: "He arrived at the *usual* hour." "You can expect the *usual* results from this medicine." *Customary* refers to whatever accords with the practices of an individual or group: "It was *customary* for us to have two coffee breaks every morning." "At that school it was *customary* for each girl to take her turn waiting on tables." *Habitual* suggests a fixed practice as the result of habit: "It is *habitual* for me to ignore my alarm clock." "He was a surly person with a *habitual* scowl on his face."

V

vacant. *See* EMPTY.

vacillate. *See* FLUCTUATE.

vainness. *See* VANITY.

valuable, valued. That which is *valuable* is of great merit or is worth money: "This is a *valuable* collection of paintings." "Time is *valuable* to him because he charges an hourly rate." What is *valuable* may also be *valued,* but the latter term has the additional meanings of "highly regarded," "esteemed," "appraised": "His services are highly *valued.*" "The estate was *valued* at more than $1 million." A childhood toy may be *valued,* but it is hardly *valuable.* Words related to *valuable* are *costly, expensive, dear, rare,* and *invaluable.* Related to *valued* are *highly thought of, cherished, esteemed,* and *respected.*

vanity, vainness. *Vanity* means "excessive pride," "lofty opinion of one's abilities, appearance, dress, and achievements": "His loss in the election was a blow to his *vanity.*" *Vanity* also has a meaning of "worthlessness," "something lacking in value": "He indulged in the *vanity* of a self-centered life." Related words include *ostentation, pride, egotism, vainglory, complacency, conceit, self-esteem,* and *self-admiration. Vainness,* as well as the adjectival form *vain,* is an uncommonly used synonym for *vanity,* particularly in the meanings of "valueless," "worthless," "baseness": "This pageantry is a show of pomp and *vainness.*" Words related to *vainness* and *vain* in their basic meaning are *trifling, trivial, futile, nugatory, profitless,* and *useless.*

vapid, insipid. These words mean "lacking flavor, life, or sharpness," "dull and tedious": "This cold drink is *vapid* (or *insipid*)." "The conversation we had was *insipid* (or *vapid*)." What distinction there is between the words is that *vapid* suggests stupidity or dullness and *insipid* implies tastelessness, flatness: "*vapid* talk at a cocktail party," "the *insipid* taste of the hors d'oeuvres served."

varied, various. *Varied* means "altered," "changed," "made different." *Various* means "distinct," "diverse," "of different kinds." "She traveled in *various* (not *varied*) parts of Europe." "He has a *varied* (not *various*) background."

venal, venial. These words look alike and sound somewhat alike, but *venal* (VEE·nuhl, VEE·n'l) has a connotation of corruption. *Venial* (VEE·ni·uhl), a term of mild reproach, means "excusable," "pardonable." It may help to keep them straight by remembering that *venal* comes from a Latin term meaning "for sale" (*venalis*) and *venial* from Latin *venia* ("forgiveness"). Associate *venal* with *penal* and *venial* with *genial.* "This corrupt administration has entered into many *venal* agreements." "Not sending them a wedding present was my *venial* offense against good manners."

veranda. *See* PORCH.

verbal. *See* ORAL.

vernacular, dialect. Each of these terms has several meanings, but both specifically refer to the word usage and patterns of language characteristic of a community, state, or country. *Vernacular* means (1) "native as opposed to literary" (the *vernacular* language of uneducated persons); (2) "using a native language" (a *vernacular* poet); (3) "plain," "ordinary," "everyday" (a *vernacular* man of the people); (4) "the native speech of a place" (Say that in *vernacular*, not literary, language). (*See* POPULAR.) *Dialect* has two primary meanings: (1) "a special variety of written or spoken language" (the *dialect* of mountain people in Appalachia) and (2) "a language considered as one of a group" (English is one of the Indo-European *dialects*).

verse, stanza. *Verse* is a term of several meanings, only one of which is fully accurate: "one line of a poem." The word *verse* comes from a Latin term meaning "a turning" and is correctly applied to the way in which one line of a poem "turns" into a new line. *Verse* is often confused with *stanza*, which is a succession of lines (*verses*) bound together by some scheme (usually a pattern of rhyme) and forming one of a series of similar groups that make up a poem. "The curfew tolls the knell of parting day" is the first *verse* of the first *stanza* of Gray's famous *Elegy Written in a Country Churchyard*. The poem contains 128 *verses* (lines) arranged in 32 *stanzas*.

very. Because *very* is primarily an adjective it should not be used to qualify a verb. Write "She was *very much* loved by her children," not "She was *very* loved . . ." However, when *very* is followed by a participle that has the effect of an adjective, informal use would allow *very* to appear without a qualifying word such as *much* or *greatly:* "She was *very* concerned." The only real objection to *very* is that it is uttered over and over in almost every conceivable instance calling for an intensive. One language expert once told his students never to say or write *very* unless they meant *damn* or *damned*, and then to delete the profanity. The message: use *very* "very" little or not at all.

vestige. *See* TRACE.

via. This overused Latin word meaning "by way of" should be pronounced "VAI·uh" or "VEE·uh." *Via* should not be used in the sense of "by means of," as in this faulty statement: "Aid was rendered the stricken country *via* food, clothing, and medicines."

viable, workable. These words refer to the ease with which, or likelihood that, something can be done. *Viable* means "capable of living," "physically fitted to live," but by extension has come to mean "able or likely to produce continued success or effectiveness" and is often used in a comparative sense: "Your plan is more *viable* than the one we have been using." *Workable* is applied to plans, suggestions, or ideas that will be successful if properly managed: "The foreman presented us with a *workable* production schedule." Words closely related to these near-synonyms are *feasible, practical,* and *possible.*

victim. *See* MARTYR.

video. Usage has made *video* (VID·ee·oh) a standard term. *Video* refers to the visual portion of a televised broadcast, as distinguished from the sound part, *audio* (AW·dee·oh). In general usage, *video* means "television": "She is a prominent performer on stage, screen, and *video.*"

viewpoint. *See* POINT OF VIEW.

village. *See* CITY.

virtual. *See* ACTUAL.

virtually. *See* PRACTICALLY.

virus. *See* GERM.

visit, visit with. To *visit* means "to pay a call upon," "to go to see": "He left me to *visit* another friend." Some linguists consider "*visit* with" a wordy expression, but actually the phrase means "to stay with for a time" and also "to communicate without physical presence": "She intended to pay a brief call on her grandmother but had such a pleasant time that she decided to *visit with* her the entire afternoon." "When you have some time, telephone me so that we can *visit with* each other in a long session." *See also* MEET.

vital. This word means "necessary for existence," "essential," "indispensable." *Vital* is both overused and misused because in few applications is it used to mean what it really means. It is absurd to say "Helen's presence at the dance is *vital*" unless it is undeniable that Helen's absence will cause the dance to be an unqualified failure. Generally related words with less exaggerated meanings than *vital* include *needed, wanted, beneficial, helpful, advantageous, desirable, useful, salutary,* and *serviceable,* and in the sense of "important," *effective, substantial, weighty, momentous, consequential, considerable, eminent, prominent, conspicuous,* and *significant.*

vocabulary. *See* DICTION.

vocation. *See* AVOCATION.

voluntary. *See* INVOLUNTARY.

vulgar. *See* POPULAR.

W

wager. *See* GAMBLE.

wait on, wait for. In the sense of "to serve," *wait on* is an acceptable expression: "Please *wait on* this customer." "If you have not been helped to make a selection, I'll be glad to *serve* (wait on) you." In the sense of "await," *wait on* is colloquial and dialectal: "You are late, and I don't want to *wait for* (not *wait on*) you."

wake, awake, awaken, waken. Our language has several verbs to express waking from sleep and waking someone from sleep. *Awake-awaked* and *awake-awoke* are correct, of course, but somewhat formal: "I *awoke* him." *Awaken-awakened-awakened* is even more formal than *awake:* "I *awakened* him." More commonly used than either is *wake-waked* or *woke:* "I *woke* him." *Waken-wakened-wakened* is less used than *wake-waked-waked:* "I *waked* him." Most commonly used of all are *wake up–waked up* or *woke up:* "I *waked up* (or *woke up*) at dawn." "She *waked up* (or *woke up*) her sister at dawn." Each of the verbs mentioned may be used transitively or intransitively, but *awake* is largely used intransitively (When did you *awake?*) and *waken* transitively (She *wakened* me early). *Wake* is the only one of these terms regularly used with *up: "Wake up,* you sleepyhead." The most commonly used past participle of *wake* is *waked* (not *woken* or *woke*); the preferred past participle of *wake* is *waked* (not *woken* or *woke*): the preferred past participle of *awake* is *awaked* (not *awoke*): "After I had *waked* him, I discovered my error." "I must have *awaked* several times that night."

wane. *See* WAX.

want. *See* LACK.

want, wish. These words share a meaning of "to long for," "to crave," "to desire": "Don't you *want (wish)* to go to the game?" "She *wishes (wants)* to sleep now." *Want* also expresses the idea of a lack or need: "He *wants* (desires) a job, but he *wants* (lacks) experience." *Wish* is the word to use when expressing an impulse or hope: "I *wish* you were my friend." *Want* (in the sense of need) rather than *wish* (in the sense of desire) should be used in a polite query such as "Do you *want* some more food?" "*Want* for" is a correct expression only when the idea to be expressed is "to have need": "We did not *want for* money on our trip." *Want* should not be accompanied by *for* when *wish* or *desire* is involved; "I *want* (not *want for*) you to stay." The constructions "*want* out" and "*want* in" are often heard but are informal. It is preferable to say "The dog *wants to get out* (or *wants to get in*)" rather than the elliptical "*wants out*" or "*wants in.*"

warp, woof. These words are much less commonly used than once they were, but the phrase "*warp* and *woof*" is often heard in the meaning of "the underlying structure upon which something is built," "the foundation or base": "The Constitution is the *warp* and *woof* of our system of government." Literally, *warp* refers to the threads that run lengthwise in fabric, crossed at right angles by the *woof*, the threads that run crosswise: "The *warp* and *woof* of this piece of cloth provide a clear impression of its texture."

warranty. This is chiefly a legal term meaning (1) "a convenant in which the seller vouches for the security of the title to what is being sold," (2) "a guarantee that the goods sold are as represented," (3) "a guaranty that the facts as stated are correct." *See also* GUARANTEE.

was, were. Do you say "I wish I *was* there" or "I wish I *were* there"? Do you say "If I *was* you" or "If I *were* you"? Whether you say *was* or *were* in such constructions, you have company. Actually, you should say *were* in both quoted sentences, even though *was* and *were* are alike in that they form the past tense of the verb *be.* It's a question of mood, the state of mind or the manner in which a statement is made: a fact (*indicative* mood), a request or command (*imperative* mood), a condition or probability (*subjunctive* mood).

The subjunctive mood (here the form *were*) is generally used to express (1) a condition contrary to fact, (2) a supposition, (3) an improbable condition, (4) uncertainty or doubt, (5) necessity, (6) parliamentary motions, and (7) a desire. In "I wish I *were* there" the subjunctive *were* is standard because "I" is not there (a condition contrary to fact) and also because the speaker is expressing a desire. One of the same conditions applies to the second quoted sentence. Use *were* (the subjunctive), not *was* (the indicative), in such sentences as these: "Suppose he *were* to arrive now" (supposition). "He drank ale as if it *were* going to be prohibited forever" (an improbable condition). "Roberta wishes that she *were* going to be invited" (desire). Now that these distinctions have been made, you can relax in the sure knowledge that *was* is heard at least as often as *were* in statements such as those cited.

wax, wane. Perhaps because these once-popular words are now used infrequently, they are often misunderstood or confused. *Wax* means "to grow gradually larger," "to increase in strength or size." *Wane* means the exact opposite: "to decrease," "to decline." Both terms are most often used to refer to the comparative fullness of the moon, but they can and do appear in statements such as these: "His anger *waxed* strong and then subsided."

"My enthusiasm for your plan is beginning to *wane.*" Words related to *wax* are *grow, extend, enlarge, dilate,* and *lengthen.* Near-synonyms of *wane* include *fail, diminish,* and *sink.*

way, ways, weigh. *Way* is colloquial when used to mean "away": "The mine is *away* (not *way*) across the mountain. Equally colloquial and to be avoided in formal writing are "in a bad *way,*" "to come my *way,*" ("to achieve success"), and "act the *way* he does." In an expression such as "a long *ways* to town," *ways* is a dialectal, substandard substitute for *way.* In nautical terms, the expression should be "under *way,*" not "under *weigh.*" That is, a vessel must *weigh* (lift) its anchor before it can get "under *way.*" "*Ways,* the plural of the noun *way,* is correct in sentences like this: "Many *ways* were open to him." "The newly christened ship slid down the *ways* into welcoming water." Except as the name of a committee, "*ways* and means" is a wordy phrase: *ways* and *means* are interchangeable in meaning. The overused expression "in any *way,* shape, or form" is redundant because these terms are synonymous: reduce six words to three.

we (editorial). The plural pronoun *we* is occasionally used by writers (especially newspaper writers) as a substitute for a repetitive *I.* It is a device, not a gesture toward modesty, so that when a columnist writes "*We* think," he means "*I* think." The first-person personal pronoun can be overused and often is, but many writers and readers consider this conventional use of *we* both artificial and pretentious.

we, us. These are first-person plural personal pronouns. *We* is in the nominative (or subjective) case; *us* is in the objective (accusative) case. Choice between them depends upon the function each fulfills in a statement: "*We* taxpayers are entitled to a referendum." "For *us* taxpayers the outlook is dubious." After *as* or *than* in a comparison in which the first term is in the objective case, use *us:* "The waiter gave them more food than *us.*" Conversely, write "Those men are taller than *we*" because *we* is understood as the subject of the omitted verb *are,* exactly as *us* in the immediately preceding sentence is the object of the omitted verb *gave.* In addition to *us* and *we,* there are five other regularly used personal pronouns with nominative and objective cases: *I* and *me, he* and *him, she* and *her, they* and *them, who* and *whom.* These pronouns should always be used in their nominative (subjective) forms except when they are (1) the object of a verb, (2) the object of a preposition, or (3) an indirect object: "*I* love *her.*" "*She* loves *me.*" "*He* hates *him.*" "*They* have come." "I saw *them.*" "*Who* is that?" "*Whom* did you see?" "I talked to *her.*" "I gave *him* a hug."

wealthy. *See* RICH.

wedding. *See* MARRIAGE.

weigh. *See* WAY.

well. *See* GOOD.

were. *See* WAS.

what all. In a question such as "*What all* does he expect of me?" *what all* is considered narrowly dialectal or illiterate. *All* is apparently added for intensifying effect, but its addition is not recommended in either *what all* or *who all* (*Who all's* there?).

whatever. As an adjective, *whatever* means "any . . . that." It should not be followed by *that* in a sentence such as "I won't pay any attention to *whatever* objection *that* you may have." *Whatever* is a pronoun in "*Whatever* did you mean?" *What* is a pronoun, and *ever* is an adverb in "*What* did you *ever* mean?" In formal usage, *whatever* should not be divided.

what for. This phrase appears in two nonstandard uses. When it means "punishment" or "reproof" (The boss gave George *what for* because he was late), it constitutes an illiteracy. When *what for* is substituted for *why* (*What* did you do that *for?*), the expression may be considered illiterate or wordy.

when, as, and if. This expression appears often in conversation, especially business talk: "I'll buy your product *when, as, and if* you increase the discount." Either *when* or *if* will convey the idea. *See also* IF AND WHEN.

when, where. *See* IS WHEN. The objection to *is when* and *is where* may or may not be based on grammatical grounds, but unquestionably both phrases are childish, immature, and overused. A further objection is that *when* and *where* are often used in situations where their meanings are not applicable. For example, *when* has a meaning of time and is illogical in a sentence such as "This plan *is when* they refuse to let anyone under sixteen enter the theater."

whence, whither. These somewhat old-fashioned words contain the idea of "from" or "to." *Whence* means "from which place" or "from which position." *Whither* means "to what place, condition, or position." Few occasions arise for the use of either *whence* or *whither,* but when one or the other is needed, omit *from* or *to:* "*Whence* have you come?" "*Whither* are you going?" *See also* FROM WHENCE.

where. *See* WHEN and IS WHEN. *Where* is nonstandard as a conjunction equivalent to *that.* Use *that* instead of *where* in such statements as "I see *where* the Senate is going to recess" and "Jim read *where* his favorite team had lost two straight games." *Where at* (*Where at* is the house?) is a wordy, illiterate phrase. Omit *at.*

whereabouts. This word can be an adverb (*Whereabouts* did you go?) and a noun. As a noun, it is formed from an adverb *(where)* and a preposition *(about)* with an *s* tied to the end. As a noun, *whereabouts* is singular and requires a singular verb unless it is made clear that more than one *whereabouts* is involved: "The neighbors are away, but I do not know what their *whereabouts is.*" "The parents went one direction and the children another; I don't know what their various *whereabouts are.*"

wherein. *See* THEREIN.

whether. *See* IF.

whether or not. In most sentences, the *or not* in this phrase is unnecessary. *Or not* is a mere filler in a sentence such as "*Whether* the remark was accurate *or not* is not certain." However, in certain constructions equal force or stress should be given to alternatives: *or not* is required in a statement such as "We shall go whether it rains *or not.*" To decide whether *or not* is needed, substitute *if* for *whether.* If the *if* results in a different meaning, then *or not* is needed. The sentence quoted would make quite different sense if it read "We shall go *if* it rains . . . ."

which. *See* THAT.

whiskey, whisky. These are variant spellings of a word derived from *usquebaugh,* a Gaelic name for a strong alcoholic liquor distilled from the fermented mash of such grains as barley, rye, corn, and wheat. The preferred spelling in the United States and Ireland is *whiskey;* in Great Britain and Canada, *whisky. See also* LIQUEUR.

whither. *See* WHENCE.

who, whom. No situation in English speech and writing causes more difficulty for more persons than choosing between *who* and *whom* (and *whoever, whomever* when they are used). Current usage studies indicate that the distinction between these forms is breaking down, partly because keeping them straight is difficult and partly because many speakers begin a sentence or clause with *who,* not knowing how they are going to end the statement. Because most people consider *whom* less natural than *who,* they sometimes disregard grammatical requirements and use *who* even when *whom* is clearly indicated.

The grammatical rule is simple: use *who* (or *whoever*) as the subject of a verb or as a predicate pronoun. Use *whom (whomever)* as the object of a verb or preposition. Here are some correct illustrations.

1. The question of *who* can go is unimportant. (Here, *who* is the subject of *can go*. The entire clause, *who can go,* is the object of the preposition *of*.)

2. This is the fireman *whom* we saw on top of the building. (Here, *whom* is the object of *saw*.)

3. He asked me *who* I thought would be elected. (The case of a pronoun depends upon its use and should not be influenced by words that come between it and its antecedent. Check this sentence by omitting *I thought. Who* is then seen to be the subject of *would be elected.*)

4. I danced with the girl *whom* everyone suspected the committee had chosen Beauty Queen. (Here, check by omitting *everyone suspected.*)

When doubtful, substitute *he* or *him* for *who* or *whom* to arrive at a decision:

1. *Who/whom* are you voting for? (For *who/whom* are you voting?) *He/him* are you voting for? (For *he/him* are you voting?)

2. This is the kind of public servant *who/whom* we need. (. . . we need *who/whom;* . . . we need *he/him.*)

One final word: unless you are reasonably certain that *whom* is required, use *who.* You'll be right much more than half of the time. *See also* THAT.

who all. *See* WHAT ALL.

whoever, whomever. *Whoever* is an interrogative pronoun in the nominative case; *whomever* is the objective form of the same pronoun. They follow precisely the same rules as those for *who* and *whom* (*see* WHO).

who's, whose. *Who's* is a shortened form of "who is": "*Who's* ahead in the office pool?" *Whose* is the possessive case of the pronoun *who: "Whose* shoes are these?" Some grammarians formerly insisted that *whose* should be applied only to persons: "The car the body *of which* needed paint" rather than "The car *whose* body needed paint." Both common sense and the fact that *which* has no possessive form of its own have succeeded in discarding this "rule." Therefore, continue to sing about the flag "*Whose* broad stripes and bright stars, through the perilous fight,/ O'er the ramparts we watched were so gallantly streaming."

wide. *See* BROAD.

widow, widower. The primary meaning of *widow* is that of a woman whose husband has died and who has not remarried. *Widower* is the male counterpart of *widow.* A "grass *widow*" is separated or divorced or lives apart from her husband. (The expression comes from the meaning of "at grass," that is, "roaming loose.") A "golf *widow*" ("tennis *widow,*" "fishing *widow*") is a woman whose husband leaves her while he goes to play his favorite game. "*Widow* woman" is an illiteracy.

will. *See* SHALL.

wire. Once considered informal when used to mean "a telegram" or "to telegraph," *wire* is now standard usage in these senses. These are hackneyed expressions involving *wire;* "under the *wire*" ("within limits," "by a deadline"), "pull *wires*" ("to use connections or associations to advantage"), "on the *wire*" ("on the telephone"), and "lay *wires* for" ("to make preparations").

-wise. The practice of attaching this suffix to nouns with the meaning of "with reference to" and "concerning" is widespread and indiscriminate. No one objects to such a sensible word as *clockwise,* but how about *jobwise, attendance-wise, flavorwise, saleswise, economy-wise, politics-wise* and a dozen other terms that you can readily recall (or manufacture)? Surely some clearer, less jargonish means can be found to say what is conveyed by "*Taxwise,* your plan is sensible."

Among informal, trite, or slangy words and expressions to avoid are "*wise* up," "a *wise* move," "get *wise,*" "*wisecrack,* "*wise guy,*" *wisenheimer* ("an offensive, arrogant person"), *wiseacre* ("an overly self-confident person"), and "put someone *wise.*"

wish. *See* WANT, WISH.

wit. *See* HUMOR.

without. This adverb and preposition is nonstandard when used as a conjunction meaning "unless." It is correct to say "We can't live *without* money" (*without* is a preposition here), but it is incorrect to say "We can't live *without* we have money." Hackneyed expressions using *without* include "*without* let or hindrance," "*without* a doubt," "*without* rhyme or reason," "make do *without,*" "*without* the law," and "*without* a prayer." *See also* UNLESS.

woman. *See* GENTLEMAN.

wont, won't. *Wont* is an adjective and noun meaning "accustomed," "used to" and "habit" or "practice": "He was *wont* to take a daily walk." "It was her *wont* to take a cold bath every morning." *Won't* is a contraction of "will not": "She *won't* do what I want her to." "No, I *won't.*"

woof. *See* WARP.

work. *See* FUNCTION.

workable. *See* VIABLE.

worse, worst. *Worse* is the comparative of *bad; worst* is the superlative. The phrase "if *worst* comes to *worst*" is illogical, but that's the way it should be said, provided one wishes to use such a hackneyed expression at all. Informal, slangy, or trite expressions to avoid include "*worse* and *worse*," "in the *worst* way," "get the *worst* of it," and "at the *worst*." In the sense of "more," *worse* is not fully accepted; nor is *worst* in the sense of "most." Avoid such statements as "I dislike insects *worse* than I do snakes." "*Worst* kind" and "in the *worst* way" are slang for "much" and "very much." "She would like to aid you in the *worst* way" is ambiguous. If you revise the statement to "She would like the *worst* way to aid you," you may have added suspicion of immorality to plain confusion.

worthless. *See* NO GOOD.

would. *See* SHALL.

would of. Because of careless or hurried pronunciation, *would have* often sounds like *would of* or *would've.* A verb *(have)* is needed with *would,* not a preposition *(of)*: "Yes, I *would have (would've)* noticed that."

would rather. *See* HAD BETTER.

write-up. This fabricated word has become a standard noun and verb, but the same usage that has elevated it to respectability has reduced it to triteness. Possible substitutes: *report, account, notice, article, review, description, analysis.* "This is an excellent *report* of the meeting."

wrong, wrongly. *Wrong* is both an adjective and an adverb. It is correct to say "That's the *wrong* attitude to take" and "Everything went *wrong* that day." *Wrongly,* an adverb only, should be used before a verb: "The word was *wrongly* pronounced." *Wrong* in its adverbial function is preferred over *wrongly* in a statement such as "I was quoted *wrong,*" but *wrongly* is not incorrect in such constructions. *Wrong* appears in numerous everyday expressions that have become trite: "*wrong* tack," "get in *wrong,*" "*wrong* side of the tracks," "in the *wrong,*" and "go *wrong.*" Possible substitutes for overworked *wrong* include *wicked, sinful, unjust, reprehensible, evil, bad, crooked, iniquitous,* and *immoral.*

X

Xerox. This term is a trademark for a process that copies printed, written, or graphic material by xerography. (Xerography, like *Xerox* based on a Greek word meaning "dry," involves transferring an image, the original material, by the action of light to an electrically charged surface to which the image attracts dry ink particles. These particles are then fused on the copy paper, thus reproducing the original.) The corporation that makes and sells Xerox machines insists that one cannot "Xerox" something but rather "makes a Xerox copy." In common usage, *xerox* is often employed as a verb to mean making a copy of something by xerography or by any other copying process.

Xmas. This is an informal abbreviation of *Christmas*. In this word, *X* represents the figure of Jesus Christ and also the cross upon which He was crucified; *X* also suggests the Greek letter X, transliterated as *Kh* (the Greek *chi*, the letter with which *Christos*, the Greek word for Christ, begins). *Xmas* has been used for centuries in writing and is pronounced "exmas" in speech, but the term is considered inappropriate in formal writing, if not disrespectful and sacrilegious.

Xray, x-ray. This term, also correctly spelled *x ray* and *X-ray,* was so named because its exact nature was unknown. *X ray* (in any of its various spellings) is now standard in its roles as noun *(X ray, X rays),* as verb (to *X ray* a fracture), and as adjective (an *X ray* machine).

Y

yet. *See* SINCE. Both *yet* and ALREADY are adverbs expressing time. They are not interchangeable and should not be used together. "He's a rich man *already yet*" is a nonstandard construction.

you. When speaking directly to a person or group of persons, say *you.* If you wish to refer to a number of people in general and to no one in particular, use pronouns like *one* or *anyone* and general nouns such as *people, persons,* and *citizens.* It may not be rude, but it certainly is informal to say to no one specifically "*You* can see the importance of good health" and "When *you* become a Girl Scout, *you* learn much useful information." (This indefinite use of *you* occurs more often in writing than in speaking because one's readers, unlike one's hearers, are rarely present.) Also, try to use less frequently those tired conversation fillers "*You* see what I mean?" and "*You* know what?"

you all. This is an informal expression sometimes meaning only one person, sometimes meaning "all of you." In the latter sense *you all* is unobjectionable, but since the phrase is not fully standard in every meaning, perhaps *all of you* should forget it.

you know. In recent years, *you know* has become an even more ubiquitous phrase than "You see what I mean?"

and "You know what?" When followed by an object (*You know* that . . .), the phrase is standard, but it usually appears in conversation with no more meaning or purpose than *uh* or any other pause that is merely a time-waster.

young, youthful. As adjectives, both *young* and *youthful* refer to being in an early period of life or growth (a *young* person, a *youthful* person). In this sense, *young* more often than *youthful* is applied to nonhuman objects: "a *young* tree" rather than "a *youthful* tree." Somewhat more effectively than *young, youthful* suggests favorable aspects of youth such as vigor, strength, liveliness, and hopefulness: "She has a healthy, *youthful* attitude toward life." "She is not *young* in years, but somehow she has kept her *youthful* figure." A wise person has said that although no one can remain *young* always, everyone wishes to stay *youthful.*

youngster. *See* KID.

your, yours. *Your* is grammatically defined as a possessive pronominal adjective; it means "belonging to," "done by you": "That is *your* opinion." "You must have lost *your* mind." *Your* should not be confused with the contraction *you're,* meaning "you are": "This is *your* decision and *you're* going to have to live with it." The form *yours* is used in any construction where *your* will not fit: "This is a letter of *yours.*" "The complimentary close of the letter was '*Yours* truly.'" "This is *yours* and *your* sister's affair." *Yours* is never written with an apostrophe: if there were such a term as *your's,* which there isn't, it would have to mean "your is," an obvious illiteracy.

yourself, yourselves. These are reflexive or intensive pronouns (give *yourself* a chance). They are not always interchangeable with *you.* Don't say "My wife plans to write to Mary and *yourself"*; substitute *you* for *yourself.* In "I'm hoping that the Smiths and *yourselves* will vote today," substitute *you* for *yourselves.* Say *"You* (not *yourself*) and your friends are welcome."

youthful. *See* YOUNG.

Z

zealous. *See* JEALOUS.

zero hour. This word meaning "the time set for an attack" has become a cliché meaning "any critical moment": "The *zero hour* for my physical exam is set for tomorrow." In this age of rockets and missiles, *H-hour* is likely to replace *zero hour* and itself become trite.

zoom. As a term in aeronautics, *zoom* applies only to upward movement. Through usage, it now refers also to movement over a level course (The motorcycle *zoomed* along the highway), but it is nonstandard when applied to downward movement. Use *swooped* in a sentence such as "The kingfisher *zoomed* down on its prey."

zzz. No entry can follow this one alphabetically, except one with more *z*'s. *ZZZ* represents the sound of someone snoring. If when one writes, he solves the problems dealing with words and expressions, his readers will stay awake and pay attention. And when he speaks, his listeners will not go *zzz*.